THE SOCIAL ECONOMICS OF HEALTH CARE

With a social economic approach, this collection investigates the role for such principles as equity, fairness, justice, dignity, and community in health care economics and health care systems.

The authors challenge the traditional efficiency and market-based approaches of standard economics regarding how resources should be delivered and distributed in health care. They demonstrate the importance and complexity of ethical questions and social values and show how we may begin to incorporate a range of normative principles in thinking about health care decision making. Critically examined topics include:

- Contemporary health economics and alternatives to its market-based view of health care.
- Changes in the health care systems of the UK and Canada, where health care based on principles of social insurance has been challenged in recent years by the introduction of market concepts.
- The US Medicare system.
- The issues of aging populations and increased longevity and the impact of technological change in health care in connection with genetic testing are explored from the perspective of our social values regarding personal dignity and individual rights.

This important contribution will be of interest to all students and researchers in health economics. It will particularly appeal to those concerned with the institutional foundations of health care systems and professionals involved in public policy deliberations regarding health care systems.

John B. Davis is Professor of Economics at Marquette University. He is the editor of the *Review of Social Economy* and past President of the History of Economics Society.

ADVANCES IN SOCIAL ECONOMICS

Edited by John B. Davis

Marquette University

This series presents new advances and developments in social economics thinking on a variety of subjects that concern the link between social values and economics. Need, justice and equity, gender, cooperation, work poverty, the environment, class, institutions, public policy, and methodology are some of the most important themes. Among the orientations of the authors are social economist, institutionalist, humanist, solidarist, cooperatist, radical and Marxist, feminist, post-Keynesian, behavioralist, and environmentalist. The series offers new contributions from today's foremost thinkers on the social character of the economy.

Published in conjunction with the Association of Social Economics

SOCIAL ECONOMICS
Premises, findings and policies
Edited by Edward J. O'Boyle

THE ENVIRONMENTAL CONSEQUENCES OF GROWTH
Steady-state economics as an alternative to ecological decline
Douglas Booth

THE HUMAN FIRM
A socio-economic analysis of its behaviour and potential in a new economic age
John Tomer

ECONOMICS FOR THE COMMON GOOD
Two centuries of economic thought in the humanist tradition
Mark A. Lutz

WORKING TIME
International trends, theory and policy perspectives
Edited by Lonnie Golden and Deborah M. Figart

RECLAIMING EVOLUTION
A Marxist institutionalist dialogue on social change
William M. Dugger and Howard J. Sherman

THE SOCIAL ECONOMICS OF HEALTH CARE
Edited by John B. Davis

THE SOCIAL ECONOMICS OF HEALTH CARE

Edited by John B. Davis

LONDON AND NEW YORK

Published 2001
by Routledge
2 Park Square, Milton Park, Abingdon, Oxon, OX14 4RN

Simultaneously published in the USA and Canada
by Routledge
711 Third Avenue, New York, NY 10017, USA

Routledge is an imprint of the Taylor & Francis Group, an informa business

Typeset in Garamond by
The Running Head Limited, Cambridge

British Library Cataloguing in Publication Data

A catalogue record for this book is available from the British Library

Library of Congress Cataloging in Publication Data

Davis, John Bryan.
The social economics of health care / John B. Davis.
p. cm. – (Advances in social economics)
Includes bibliographical references and index.
1. Medical economics. 2. Medical care–Moral and ethical aspects. 3. Medical care–Social aspects. 4. Medical policy–Social aspects. I. Title. II. Series

RA410.5.D38 2000
338.4'73621–dc21 00-51778

ISBN 13: 978-0-415-25162-4 (pbk)

CONTENTS

TABLES

FIGURES

CONTRIBUTORS

Paul Anand works on foundations and applications of decision theory and social choice. His main work, *Foundations of Rational Choice under Risk* (Oxford University Press, 1993 and 1995) indicates why even rational agents may violate the axioms of expected utility. He is director of research in economics at The Open University and an editor of *Risk Decision and Policy*, published by Cambridge University Press.

Joshua Cohen is a Senior Research Fellow with the Tufts Center for the Study of Drug Development. He received a PhD in economics from the University of Amsterdam in 1997. His current research interests focus on public health policy, pharmacy benefit management, and managed care. He has authored articles in both medical and economics research journals.

Diane M. Dewar is an Assistant Professor of Health Economics in the Department of Health Policy, Management and Behavior, and in the Department of Economics at the State University of New York at Albany. Her research interests encompass: the assessment of the impact of health system reforms on access and utilization of health services; analyses of the technological trends in the US and Canadian health economies, and economic evaluations of health services used by older or vulnerable populations. She has presented her work at a variety of national and international economics and health policy conferences. Her work has also been published in medical, economics and policy journals including: *Critical Care Medicine*, *CHEST*, *Review of Social Economy*, *Economics of Education Review*, and the *International Journal of Technology Assessment in Health Care.*

William A. Jackson is Lecturer in Economics at the University of York, UK. His main teaching and research interests are in population economics, the economics of social policy, economic methodology, and non-neoclassical economic theory. He is the author of *The Political Economy of Population Ageing* (Edward Elgar, 1998).

Michael Keaney is a Lecturer in Economics at Glasgow Caledonian University. He has published articles and reviews in the *Journal of Economic Issues*,

Review of Radical Political Economics, *International Journal of Social Economics*, *History of the Human Sciences*, *Health Care Analysis*, *International Journal of Health Care Quality Assurance*, *Millennium: Journal of International Studies*, *Cultural Dynamics*, and the *Scottish Journal of Political Economy*. He also contributed an introductory essay to the reissue of Douglas F. Dowd's *Thorstein Veblen* (Transaction Publishers, 2000), and is the editor of *Economist with a Public Purpose: Essays in Honour of John Kenneth Galbraith* (Routledge, 2000).

Robert McMaster is a Lecturer in Economics at the University of Aberdeen. He has research interests in institutional economics, and the contractualization of welfare state activities. Recent publications have appeared in the *Review of Social Economy*, and the *Scottish Journal of Political Economy*.

Gavin Mooney is Foundation Professor of Health Economics and Director of the Social and Public Health Economics Research Group (SPHERe) at the University of Sydney. He has published widely in health economics, particularly on issues related to equity and ethics. His current research interests lie mainly in Aboriginal health. He is also Director of the web-based international Graduate Diploma Course in Health Economics from the University of Sydney.

Cameron Mustard has recently been appointed Associate Professor in the Department of Public Health Sciences, Faculty of Medicine, University of Toronto, and Scientific Director, Institute for Work and Health. Previously he was a member of the Manitoba Centre for Health Policy and Evaluation, Department of Community Health Services, University of Manitoba. He is Associate Director and Fellow of the Population Health Program of the Canadian Institute for Advanced Research, a recipient of an MRC Scientist Award (1997–2002). In the period of 1997–8, he served as a member of the federal Advisory Committee on Health Information Structure. He is a member of the Board of Directors of the Canadian Institute for Health Information, Chair of the Canadian Population Health Initiative Council, and currently serves as Chair of the Population Health Review Panel of the Medical Research Council. During the period February 1999 to April 2000, he was a member of the Interim Governing Council of the Canadian Institutes for Research Health. Dr. Mustard has active research interests in the areas of work environments, labor market experiences and health, the distributional equity of publicly funded health and health care programs in Canada, and the epidemiology of socio-economic health inequalities across the human life course.

Thomas Rice is Professor of Health Services at the UCLA School of Public Health. He is a health economist, having received his doctorate in the Department of Economics at the University of California at Berkeley in 1982. Before joining the faculty at UCLA in 1991, Dr. Rice taught at the

University of North Carolina School of Public Health. His areas of interest include physicians' economic behavior, Medicare, health insurance, and competition. His book, *The Economics of Health Reconsidered*, was published in 1998. He is currently the editor of the journal, *Medical Care Research and Review*.

Robert F. Rizzo received a PhD in Religious Studies from The Catholic University of America, Washington DC, in 1971. Since 1969 he has taught major courses in social ethics and bio-ethics in the Department of Religious Studies at Canisius College (now full professor). In the 1970s, he initiated the development of interdisciplinary courses, involving several departments: he has taught the course in bio-ethics with a biologist since 1976. He has published articles on such subjects as clinical death, euthanasia, hospices, living wills, the nuclear arms race, health care reform, and genetic testing and therapy. His teaching, research and writing focus on the moral, legal, social, economic and political dimensions of problems and their interrelation.

Rose M. Rubin is Professor of Economics in the Fogelman College of Business and Economics at the University of Memphis. She is co-author of *Expenditures of Older Americans* (Praeger Publishers, 1997) and *Working Wives and Dual-Earner Families* (Praeger Publishers, 1994) and author or co-author of over thirty research articles in economics, gerontology, health policy, and social science journals. She has published research findings on aging issues in *The Journals of Gerontology: Social Sciences*, *The Gerontologist*, the *Journal of Applied Gerontology*, *Medical Care*, *Social Science Quarterly*, the *Monthly Labor Review*, and other economics journals. She has received research grants from the National Science Foundation, the AARP Andrus Foundation, the Robert Wood Johnson Foundation, the National Endowment for the Humanities, the Texas Advanced Research Program, and Blue Cross–Blue Shield of Texas, as well as numerous Faculty Research Grants from the University of North Texas and the University of Memphis.

Terrence Sullivan is President of the Institute for Work and Health, a university affiliated, non-profit organization which conducts innovative population-based health studies investigating the determinants of modern workplace health and the effective treatment and management of musculoskeletal injury. He previously played senior public policy roles for the Ontario Government to the rank of deputy minister. These included work in the Ministries of Health, Constitutional, and Intergovernmental Affairs. A medical sociologist with an interest in Human Development and Workplace Health, his recently published work includes: *Health Reform: Public Success, Private Failure* (with Daniel Drache, Routledge, 1999), *Injury and the New World of Work* (University of British Columbia Press, 1999) and the double millennial issue of the *International Journal of Law* *and Psychiatry (Work Stress & Disability)* with chief judge Steve Adler of the Israeli labor court. He holds an appointment in the Faculty of Medicine at the University of Toronto (Health Administration) and the Faculty of Graduate Studies at York University. He is the leader of the Workplace Laboratory in the McMaster-led Network of Centers of Excellence in Health Research (HealNet). He also sits on the advisory committee for the population health program of the Canadian Institute for Advanced Research (CIAR), the Board of the Robarts Centre for Canadian Studies at York University and the Board of trustees of the University Health Network.

Peter Ubel is Professor of Medicine at the University of Pennsylvania. He received a BA in Philosophy from Carleton College and an MD from the University of Minnesota. His research interests focus on the allocation of scarce health care resources and on the psychology of moral decision making. He has published extensively in both medical and social science research journals.

Shelley White-Means is Professor of Economics in the Fogelman College of Business and Economics at the University of Memphis and was named the University's Eminent Scholar in 1996. She has published extensively on the health and health services utilization patterns of underserved populations, including ethnic minorities, women and elderly persons, and on the economic choices of caregivers of elderly persons. Dr. White-Means' research has been funded by grants from the Milbank Memorial Fund, the Retirement Research Foundation, the R. Smithers Brinkley Fund, and the Department of Agriculture. Findings from her recent Retirement Research Foundation funded study of the opportunity cost of caregivers were published in *The Journals of Gerontology: Social Sciences*. Her research also appears in *The Gerontologist*, the *Journal of Applied Gerontology*, *The American Economic Review*, *The Milbank Quarterly*, *Social Science Quarterly*, and other economics and family economics journals.

INTRODUCTION

John B. Davis

A Social Economics of Health Care begins with recognition of the central role that a diverse array of social values play in determining the delivery and distribution of health care resources in contempory economies. Current health care economics, in contrast, generally restricts its attention to the values of efficiency and individual preference satisfaction, and moreover assumes that the market and an exchange-based organization of health care will resolve complex social issues regarding who shall have what health care. Since Amartya Sen's critique of the dominant approach in economics as 'welfarist,' however, economists have begun to question the narrowness of their normative framework. These doubts are particularly unsettling for health economics, since the subject of health concerns individuals' well-being in an especially personal and fundamental manner. Thus, unlike many other subjects economists investigate, the subject of delivery and distribution of health care immediately raises questions regarding equity, fairness, need, rights, trust, caring, and dignity alongside economists' usual concerns with welfare and good consequences. To complicate matters further, these additional social values concerns are not easily explained within the framework of the market as an impersonal exchange between atomistic individuals. Indeed, relationships between health care providers and patients can be highly personalized, and the institutions that modern societies have created to provide health care often depend upon people sharing a very real sense of community with one another.

Thus emphasis on social values in a Social Economics of Health Care implies fundamental changes in the way health economics is pursued. The eleven chapters in this volume make valuable contributions to this alternative orientation. In different ways, they each exhibit the complexities involved in providing economic understanding of subjects that contain significant social and ethical components. The volume as a whole is divided into four parts. The chapers in the first part, 'Alternatives to the market view of health care and health economics,' examine contemporary health economics and its market-based view of health care. The chapters in the second part, 'Resistance to market-based reform of health care systems,' examine the health care systems of the United Kingdom and Canada, where in recent years delivery and distribution of health care based on principles of social insurance have been challenged by the introduction of market concepts. The chapters in the third part, 'Issues surrounding health care and aging,' address one of the most important social structural changes in developed economies: aging populations and increased longevity. Finally, the single chapter making up the last part of the volume examines social issues associated with one of the most important technological changes in the domain of health care.

Alternatives to the market view of health care and health economics

Thomas Rice, in 'Should consumer choice be encouraged in health care?' argues that three central ideas permeate most applications of economic theory to the health care field: the focus on the individual, the emphasis on efficiency over equity, and the superiority of relying on consumer choice to allocate goods and services in health care. This chapter examines the standard case for the last of these ideas, then turns to a number of instances in which consumer choice may be disadvantageous both to individual consumers and to society at large, applies all this to health care, and finally uses this analysis to consider implications for health care policymaking across countries according to differences in the degree of choice given to consumers. Although a number of countries have experimented with 'internal markets' in health care, none have gone as far as the United States in relying upon markets and consumer choice for the delivery and distribution of health care. Limitations on consumer choice, however, may enhance not only equity but efficiency as well, and Rice recommends that health care economists give more attention to different conceptions of choice.

Gavin Mooney, in 'Communitarianism in health economics,' takes as his starting point Rice's critique of the market in health care, and calls for rethinking the role of the market and the value base it represents to produce a new paradigm for health care economics alternative to the neoclassical one. He notes that there are a number of ways in which this work has already been begun, including applying Sen's ideas on functionings and capabilities, A.J. Culyer's work on extra-welfarism, and the idea of health care systems possessing constitutional frameworks. This paper adds to these points of entry the idea of there being defensible communitarian claims regarding allocating society's scarce health care resources, where these claims imply duties which communities owe to their members—duties, moreover, which are good in themselves. Mooney combines these ideas with Elizabeth Anderson's expressive theory of action, elements from constitutional economics, and reflections upon individualism and community. Addressing Rice's concerns about the nature of individual preference, Mooney emphasizes the role a constitutional paradigm plays in establishing community and individual preferences.

Paul Anand, in 'Social choice as the synthesis of incommensurable claims: the case of health care rationing,' looks at health care rationing within an expanded social choice framework with the intention of providing a practical application of Amartya Sen's critique of welfare economics. Sen's rights-based critique is argued to be relevant to the main social choice problem in health care rationing, but that may also be usefully developed by being viewed in terms of the integration of competing claim types in contrast to the standard approach in the social choice literature of aggregating conflicting preferences. In health, these claim types are consequences, agent relativities (rights and duties), social contracts, and process norms. Distinguishing between the QALY as a measure and as a decision rule, Anand suggests that the former can be used to indicate when some of these claims have not been met. The chapter develops a non-linear programming model to show that non-consequential claims can be incorporated in the setting of health care priorities, and provides survey evidence that UK voters have preferences consistent with the social choice as integration model proposed.

Joshua Cohen and Peter Ubel, in 'Accounting for fairness and efficiency in health economics,' begin by noting that as economics has become increasingly quantitative so has health economics. But this development appears harmful for health economics, since it makes it more difficult for health economists to focus attention on less quantifiable ethical values such as fairness, and easier to give great weight to more quantifiable ethical values such as efficiency. One implication of this is that the economics tradeoff between fairness and efficiency may be misunderstood. Cohen and Ubel consequently recommend that health economics distinguishes rights and dollar domains in society, and argue that policymakers face two types of tradeoffs: within the dollar domain and between the dollar and rights domains. They then use their revised view of the fairness–efficiency tradeoff to evaluate a case of explicit health care rationing in the 1991 Oregon health care initiative. They find that the Oregon initiative sets both rights and dollars targets, and does not require that fairness and efficiency simply be traded off against one another.

Resistance to market-based reform of health care systems

Robert McMaster, in 'The National Health Service, the "internal market" and trust,' focuses on trust as a socially embedded quality that manifests itself in expectations of others' behavior, their competences, and their motivations. Trust is influenced by shared values and loyalty, and organizations, institutions, and societies demonstrate considerable variation in entrustment patterns. This chapter examines the importance of trust and the impact of institutional change on trust in connection with changes in the UK National Health Service (NHS): the 1990 'internal market' reform and 1997 reform amending previous legislation. It argues that the 1997 reform was not a return to status quo ante, and that key aspects of the 1990 legislation were retained. These organizational changes superimposed market-oriented reforms on previously existing routines, and may have corroded some forms of trust within the NHS. The 1990 reforms may thus have introduced rather than resolved agency problems, thereby leading to continued institutional rigidities in service provision. McMaster sees little evidence of any awareness of the need to address trust corrosion in the NHS.

Michael Keaney, in 'Proletarianizing the professionals: the populist assault on discretionary autonomy,' focuses on that part of the reform process in the NHS that has sought to implement a new regime of 'clinical governance.' Ostensibly meant to assure best practice and regulate the decision making behavior of health professionals in response to fiscal pressures, it involves the circumscription of clinical judgment by rules based on statistical inference and the elevation of 'business values' of efficiency and effectiveness. The climate of opinion in which clinical governance has been instituted is one of increasing public distrust of medical professionals. However, the promotion of an alternative consumerist model of health care does not enhance patient participation in health care decision making any more than did the traditionally authoritarian status enjoyed by consultant doctors. Using John Dewey's emphasis on a symbiosis of means and ends, Keaney argues that what is needed is a partnership model promoting transparency and trust via patients' active participation in and common ownership of the process of health care.

Terry Sullivan and Cameron Mustard, in 'Canada: more state, more market?' provide a short history of health insurance in Canada, and then explore how current institutional arrangements meet the policy objectives of providing a comprehensive range of insured services for citizens, providing an efficient delivery system, and generating social arrangements which produce health. This facilitates a review of such current issues as rapid evolution of regional authorities in Canada, passive cost shifting of pharmaceutical and home care spending onto families, waiting list management, legal challenges to public administration provisions of the Canada Health Act, and the distributive consequences of health care spending in Canada. The last topic draws on recent Canadian work highlighting considerable differences in how social arrangements influence health in Canada compared to the United States. Canada is the international outlier in administratively inhibiting private insurance to 'jump the line' in health care. Canada has also taken to heart (albeit rhetorically) research on the social determinants of health. The chapter concludes by considering how market forces will compete with the policy aspirations regarding the social determinants of health.

Issues surrounding health care and aging

William A. Jackson, in 'Age, health and medical expenditure,' provides a comprehensive discussion of the relationships between age and medical expenditure to introduce a subject of increasing importance for health care and health care economics. Population aging is a trend common to most developed societies, yet is only beginning to be addressed. Moreover, difficult ethical issues arise in connection with the topic of age discrimination. The basic argument of the chapter is that the age–medical expenditure link should not be seen as being simple, mechanical, and biologically based, but rather as being complex, variable, and contingent on numerous social and ethical factors. This means that public policy regarding health care and aging does not merely respond to an exogenous, biologically-driven aging process, but also helps mould social perceptions of aging, and thus acts as a causal influence on aging. Topics in the chapter include the nature of the age–medical expenditure relation, the biological, social, and ethical factors that influence this relation, and policy implications of an aging population for health care and medical expenditure.

Diane Dewar, in 'The societal costs and implications of using high cost critical care resources for the elderly,' focuses on critical care services for the elderly that utilize nearly a third of hospital resources in the US. In light of the intensity of resources used for mechanical ventilation in critical care units, a social economic evaluation of managed care and other payers who have mechanical ventilation and tracheostomy is used to illustrate the problem of allocating resources for the elderly in health care. Predicted payments per survivor are compared to the value of extending life, with and without age and quality of life adjustments, to determine when net benefits are maximized. This example illustrates that improved efficiency for high-risk critical care services may be gained by combining clinical excellence and fiscal consciousness. Quality of life measures need to be incorporated to determine the appropriateness of lower cost venues of care or the withdrawal of aggressive treatment for the chronically ill or very old. The chapter also examines the concepts of medical futility and mortality in health care not as 'bad outcomes,' but as outcomes in which patient, family, and provider participate in end-of-life decisions.

Rose Rubin and Shelley White-Means turn to US reform strategies for health care for the elderly, in 'Medicare HMOs: the promise and the reality.' Medicare, the US health care system for the elderly, is now bigger than General Motors and is the largest US business-type organization. Spending over $5,000 per beneficiary, Medicare accounts for 2.5 percent of total US production. Medicare is now testing new formats that may lead to broader structural change from almost exclusive reliance on traditional and fee-for-service providers to a broader array of beneficiary choices. One of the most widely recognized and much debated actions for breaking the continuing

Medicare cost spiral is a more widespread utilization of managed care. This chapter presents an overview and evaluation of this evolutionary shift occurring in Medicare. Rubin and White-Means find that much of the promise of Medicare managed care has yet to be realized, though the foundations of enrollment growth and beneficiary acceptance are well under way. Expanded use of managed care for Medicare beneficiaries is expected to enhance both equity and efficiency.

The challenge of technology

Robert Rizzo addresses one of the most difficult issues facing a social economics of health care created by the advance in medical technologies, in 'Safeguarding genetic information: privacy, confidentiality and security?' Though genetic testing and therapy have the potential to create significant advances in health care, they also raise serious issues for a health care system rooted in the marketplace and fueled by the profit motive. In the context of health care development in the US, genetic advances marketed as commodities might mostly stress economical health care, and fail to meet ethical and legal standards that protect autonomy, privacy, confidentiality, and equity. Many individuals might find themselves excluded from the benefits of genetic testing and therapy. Individuals might be vulnerable to employment and insurance discrimination. This chapter surveys the range of issues associated with genetic testing and information, and provides a detailed account of the developing legal frameworks in the US surrounding the use of genetic information. It closes with a commentary on the dilemmas that will need to be faced to balance the needs of individuals and the demands of the marketplace.

Part I

ALTERNATIVES TO THE MARKET VIEW OF HEALTH CARE AND HEALTH ECONOMICS

1

SHOULD CONSUMER CHOICE BE ENCOURAGED IN HEALTH CARE?

Thomas Rice

Introduction

There are, in my view, three central ideas that permeate most applications of economic theory to the health care field. The first is the focus on the individual. Although economic theory does recognize the concept of 'social welfare,' it is generally conceived to be based solely on some aggregation of individual utilities. Kenneth Arrow (1984), for example, has written that, 'Society, after all, is just a convenient label for the totality of individuals . . .' (80). This conception, although dominant, does not enjoy universal acceptance. Amartya Sen has coined this philosophy as 'welfarism,' which 'is the view that the only things of intrinsic value for ethical calculation and evaluation of states of affairs are individual utilities' (Sen 1987: 40). He makes a number of counter arguments.[1]

Related ideas have been applied to health care by Gavin Mooney (1998) and others under the heading of 'communitarianism.'

The second key focus of economic theory is the emphasis of efficiency over equity. Although individual economists are often concerned about equity, the traditional economic model does not examine how people come into possession of their wealth so much as how they allocate resources over which they have already been assigned property rights (Young 1994). Typically, it is argued that any remaining inequities can be remedied by taxing some and subsidizing others with the tax revenue. The focus on efficiency has blinded the field to the importance of considerations of fairness and social justice. As John Rawls (1971) has argued, if one considers social justice in configuring an economic system, the resulting distribution of resources would be markedly different than one in which utilitarianism comprises the dominant economic ethic.

The third overarching theme of economic theory—and the focus of this chapter—is the superiority of relying on consumer choice for the allocation of goods and services. The second section examines the advantages of consumer choice in more detail, while section three provides a number of instances in which consumer choice may be disadvantageous both to individual consumers as well as to society at large. Section IV, the main section of the paper, applies the issues raised in the previous two sections to health care. Section V uses this analysis to consider the role of choice in health care policy internationally.

The emphasis throughout the paper is on problems inherent in providing more choice in health care. The reason for taking this tack is because the prevalent viewpoint is that more choice is nearly always better. This paper is designed to provide a warning that this is not necessarily the case. If one heeds these warnings, then some entity other than individual consumers—possibly government—should perhaps be making more choices. Government, however, may very well have its own problems in making good choices for consumers, or in limiting the array of choices available. This paper does not go the next step and carry out a parallel analysis of problems inherent in government decision making, although a number of such problems are raised throughout the discussion.

The advantages of consumer choice

There are three main reasons to believe that relying on consumers' own choices will result in higher social welfare. The first stems from the theory of *revealed preference*—basically, that people's own choices, by definition, are the things that make them best off. As developed by Paul Samuelson (1938), people are assumed to prefer whatever bundle of goods they choose to purchase. If they choose one bundle over any other, they have 'revealed themselves' to prefer the former. This theory is quite powerful because it does not require one to understand any underlying motivations. As Robert Sugden (1993) has written,

> [The] most significant property of the revealed preference approach . . . is that we do not need to enquire into the reasons why one thing is chosen rather than another. We do not look into the factors that go into the deliberation which leads to a choice; we look only at the results of that process. (1949)

What the theory of revealed preferences allows us to do is to rely on the individual to make his or her own utility-maximizing choices. If one goes one other step by assuming that social welfare is simply the sum of all individuals' welfare (which, as argued above, is one of the key tenets of economic theory), then one can conclude that allowing consumers to make their own choices will lead to the highest level of social welfare. This, of course, is the argument made by proponents of competition, in health care and throughout the economy: markets allow people to choose, and this results in the best possible outcome for society.[2]

The second reason for believing that consumer choice will improve social welfare is more psychological in nature. It is simply this: individuals may very well enjoy the goods and services they consume more if they get to choose them. Although I am unaware of empirical tests of this concept, it does seem plausible that a person would tend to prefer a particular good he or she picked out of a set of alternatives rather than having had it assigned by an outside agent.[3] Consider a simple thought experiment. An outside agent such as your employer knows you need a new car to get to work, knows you have a certain amount to spend, and assigns you a particular make, model, and color, withholding its cost from your paycheck. Compare that to a situation where you go and pick your own car. Even if the same choice is made, the latter situation would likely make more people happier because they know it was *their* choice. When the make and model is assigned to a person, there will often be a nagging suspicion that he or she would have chosen differently if given the choice. As a result, the person might not enjoy the same satisfaction from the purchase of the car.

The third key reason for encouraging choice is that the use of markets can lead to better value. Choice, of course, is a characteristic of a competitive market. Having a choice leads to a situation where firms strive to operate efficiently to keep prices low. And to the extent that the goods sold are not homogenous, competition may also take place on the basis of quality.[4] One should not underestimate the significance of this argument in favor of choice, as better value through lower prices and better quality has the potential to provide overwhelming advantages to consumers.

Problems with consumer choice

As convincing as these arguments are, there are several reasons to believe that providing more choice could harm social welfare. They can be divided into two categories: those affecting the individual directly, and those affecting society as a whole.

Problems with choice for individual consumers

There are at least three instances in which providing choice can make an individual worse off:

- When individuals do not know (as well as some other entity does) which choices will make them best off.
- When individuals cannot obtain and/or process the necessary information about alternative choices.
- When the provision of choice, per se, reduces utility.

Individuals do not know which choices will make them best off

Odd as it may seem, there are many instances in which individuals do not know what choices will make them best off. An obvious one is drug abuse.[5] But the problem may be much more widespread, transcending addictions to everyday life.

Robert Frank (1985, 1999) argues that people are overly concerned with their status and will make self-destructive decisions to enhance this status. He further argues that spending their time and income on other things would make them much better off. Frank laments how Americans have not used their rising standards of living to increase leisure time, but rather have spent it on consumables that bring almost no extra utility when everyone else ends up making the same purchases. But he also argues that this vanity is mutable. Frank (1999) suggests imposing large, progressive consumption taxes designed to make everyone think twice before earning an extra dollar to be spent on more and more goods that do less and less to make their lives better.

Another, less introspective reason to doubt that consumers can always make the best choices for themselves is that they simply are not expert in a particular area. In such a case, someone other than the individual could perhaps make better choices, although to do so it would be necessary for such an agent to have the consumer's interest at hand. Tibor Scitovsky (1976) illustrates this nicely:

> The economist's traditional picture of the economy resembles nothing so much as a Chinese restaurant with its long menu. Customers choose from what is on the menu and are assumed always to have chosen what most pleases them. That assumption is unrealistic, not only of the economy, but of Chinese restaurants. Most of us are unfamiliar with nine-tenths of the entrees listed; we seem invariably to order either the wrong dishes or the same old ones. Only on occasions when an expert does the ordering do we realize how badly we do on our own and what good things we miss. (149–150)

Individuals cannot obtain and/or process the necessary information

Sometimes people know what they want but they lack the resources—either external information or the internal wherewithal—to make the right choices. The problem could either be that sufficient information is not available to make utility maximizing choices, or alternatively, there is information available but the person is not, for whatever reason, able to properly use the information that is available. Either way, poor choices may result. Because this should be clear enough, further discussion will be postponed until Section IV, where these problems are examined in the context of health care.

Provision of choice reduces utility

Strangely enough, sometimes people don't want to have a choice. Richard Thaler (1991) suggests two related ways in which the provision of choice, per se, can reduce utility: (a) when a person has problems of self-control; and (b) when having to make a choice is likely to induce subsequent regret.

Thaler introduces the self-control issue by suggesting that a person may exhibit two competing personality traits: at the same time, he or she is both a 'planner' and a 'doer.'[6] The planner has a long-run view but the doer is more myopic, focusing just on the short run. If this is true, then the planner side of the brain might wish to reduce the number of choices available down the road so that the doer does not make a rash one. Although this might seem abstract, there are countless examples supporting it: putting money into a 'Christmas fund' at a bank to avoid spending it in the meantime; over-withholding on income taxes so there is an 'unspent' refund at the end of the year; keeping cookies out of the cupboards to avoid binging; cutting up one's credit cards so as to avoid their overuse; etc. All of these are designed to increase utility by restricting one's own choices.

The argument that a person will want to limit choice if having to choose will lead to regret may be less familiar. Thaler (1991) writes, 'Whenever choice can induce regret consumers have an incentive to eliminate the choice. They will do so whenever the expected increase in utility (pleasure) derived from making their own choices is less than the expected psychic costs which the choices will induce' (16). One set of illustrations involves the entertainment industry: theme parks charge a set entry fee but do not charge for rides once inside the park. Consumers probably prefer this method because having to pay separately for each ride would induce regret at each marginal expenditure, which would make the entire experience less satisfying. Section IV illustrates this in the health care area.

There is a third, less complex, and perhaps more compelling reason why more choice can reduce utility: consumers do not have the cognitive ability and/or the interest to face and make such a large array of choices. What American has not faced the numerous choices available concerning, say, selecting a long-distance telephone carrier and not come away with the uneasy feeling that the choice they have made is not the best one? Every year we are faced with more of these choices (e.g. utilities, cable services, internet travel sites—the list goes on and on) and the sheer number of options, let alone the time it takes to wade oneself through them, very often reduces utility.[7]

Problems with choice for society at large

There are also at least three instances in which providing choice can make a society at large worse off:

- When allowing some people to have certain choices reduces the utility of others who do not have such a luxury.
- When spillovers from the choices one group makes negatively affects others.
- When allowing choice results in societal costs that exceed benefits.

Each of these is elaborated upon, below.

Allowing some people to have choice reduces the welfare of others

If people cared only about what goods and services they possessed, and not about how this compared to those possessed by others, then allowing unfettered choice would tend to be in a society's best interest. As much as one might wish this were the case, however, it is not. People care deeply about how their bundle of possessions compares to others.[8] If, for example, you buy a fancy car, it may raise your utility, but it can lower mine because my car—and by analogy, *I*—no longer seem so special.

Traditional economic theory does not operate very well in the presence of so-called 'negative consumption externalities.' This is illustrated by a statement of Lord (Lionel) Robbins (1984):

> If the remaining groups regard their position relatively, they may well argue that the spectacle of such improvement elsewhere is a detriment to their satisfaction. This is not a niggling point: a relative improvement in the position of certain groups *pari passu* with an absolute improvement in the position of the rest of the community has often been a feature of economic history; and we know that has not been regarded by all as either ethically or politically desirable. (xxii–xxiii)

Suppose that one accepts the notion that people care about how they compare with others. It could still be argued that even if concern about relative position does exist, it is an irrational and/or flawed character trait that should not be respected by the analyst or policymaker (i.e. even if people are envious of one another, public policy should ignore this fact). But there are two problems with this argument. First, economic theory does not view any individually-held preferences pejoratively—and that would include the likes of envy, rank, or status. Second, it is not at all obvious that concern about one's status compared to others is an irrational or even undesirable character trait. Tibor Scitovsky (1976) makes a strong argument to the contrary:

> The desire to 'live up to the Joneses' is often criticized and its rationality called into question. This is absurd and unfortunate. Status seeking, the wish to belong, the asserting and cementing of

> one's membership in the group is a deep-seated and very natural drive whose origin and universality go beyond man and are explained by that most basic of drives, the desire to survive. (115)

Spillovers from one group's choices negatively affects others

This is a different type of negative externality. It is possible that allowing one group certain choices will negatively affect the choices available to other groups. This will not be discussed further here because some of the main applications are in health care. One concerns selection bias. If sufficiently sensitive risk-adjustment procedures are not undertaken, and if healthier people choose one type of health plan, this will drive up the premiums for less healthy people, resulting, among other things, in more people going uninsured.

Choice results in social costs exceeding benefits

Finally, allowing more choice can result in large social costs. As in the previous case, some of the best examples are in the health care sector—e.g. higher administrative costs associated with allowing a choice of health plans—so this will also be discussed in detail in the next section.

Choice in health care

After listing the different choices that can be made available to consumers in health care, this section applies the material presented earlier to these different types of health care choices, to draw inferences about where choice would seem to be both advantageous and problematic in health care.

Possible choices available to consumers in health care

There are numerous possible choices that we can put into the hands of consumers concerning their health care. Even if one listed them all, it would be overly simplistic because choices made upstream will affect the kinds of choices (if any) available downstream (McLaughlin 1999). If, for example, a person has a choice of health plan and chooses an HMO (health maintenance organization), that reduces his or her choice of physician and hospital when seeking care.

Here, I list six key choices that a society can give to its potential consumers of health care. They are:

1 whether to have health insurance
2 particular benefits provided by health insurance
3 particular health plan or insurer

4 particular physician
5 particular hospital
6 specific medical intervention.

Advantages and disadvantages of offering choice

Whether to have health insurance

The first choice that a society may wish to offer its members is whether or not to have health insurance. Although universal coverage (an example of no choice) is standard in most developed countries, this is not the case in the United States. Individuals can choose to purchase or not to purchase coverage; employers can choose to provide or not to provide it through the workplace; and, with the notable exceptions of people with Medicare and Medicaid coverage, government does not grant health insurance entitlements.

There are two related advantages to providing such a choice. First, some people would simply prefer to spend their resources on something other than health insurance, perhaps because they legitimately recognize that their risk of illness or accident is low. Alternatively, they may not believe in formal medical care or may have higher budgeting priorities. In addition, insurance (unless given away rather than paid for) conveys relatively little benefit to those with very high or very low incomes, or those who are risk takers rather than risk averse (Feldstein 1988).[9]

Second, health insurance may be a poor value to some people because of moral hazard considerations. In his famous essay commenting on Kenneth Arrow's (1963) seminal article, Mark Pauly (1968) argues that compulsory comprehensive universal health insurance is not necessarily in a country's best interest. This is because when people are fully insured, they may demand services from which they derive very little benefit—but which are still costly for society to produce, resulting in a social 'welfare loss.'[10] Thus, the total cost of providing such coverage (say, through taxes) can exceed the total benefits derived.

There are, nevertheless, several reasons why offering a person the choice of whether to purchase coverage can make the individual and society as a whole worse off. Some people may believe wrongfully that having medical coverage is unnecessary—because they have not considered the fact that they might need care in the future. Although paternalistic in nature, it may be that others do have a better understanding of their well-being than they themselves have. But why would people have such a poor conception of their own welfare? One possibility is that they are engaging in 'cognitive dissonance.'[11] George Akerlof and William Dickens (1992) have used this theory to predict various economic behaviors, including social (old age) insurance, stating that:

> If there are some persons who would simply prefer not to contemplate a time when their earning power is diminished, and if the very fact of saving for old age forces persons into such contemplations, there is an argument for compulsory old age insurance . . . [They] may find it uncomfortable to contemplate their old age. For that reason they may make the wrong tradeoff, given their own preferences, between current consumption and savings for retirement. (317)

A similar argument can be made concerning some people's unwillingness to consider that they might become seriously ill.

Another reason that offering a choice of whether to buy health insurance may not be in an individual's best interest is that, for some people, the choices are simply not affordable. Uwe Reinhardt (1996) puts it this way: '[T]o tell an uninsured single mother of several possibly sickly children that she is henceforth empowered to exercise free choice in health care with her meager budget is not necessarily a form of liberation, nor is it efficient in any meaningful sense of that term. It is rationing by income class' (1804).

When some people can afford insurance and others cannot, it puts a wedge in society between the 'haves' and 'have nots.' Research evidence is clear that people with health insurance are more likely to get state-of-the-art medical treatment. What has received less attention is how this disparity has affected society as a whole. I would argue that social strife would be minimized and harmony enhanced when there is a societal ethic that results in everyone having health insurance.

A final problem with making health insurance voluntary concerns a different sort of societal cost—the need to provide a 'safety net' for those who remain uninsured. This includes both the costs of putting together a patchwork system of coverage for some as well as providing the medical services—which are often provided in costly, inappropriate settings such as emergency rooms—to those who remain uncovered.

In summary, although there will be some gain to a limited number of individuals if they are allowed to forgo insurance coverage, I would conclude that far more people—and society as a whole—would gain if everyone were covered through a universal health insurance program.

Particular benefits provided by health insurance

The next issue to be considered is whether people should be able to choose any set of health insurance benefits that they wish, or alternatively, if there should be limits (perhaps severe ones) put on this. The advantages of providing choice are rather straightforward and need little elaboration: different people have different needs and tastes for different kinds of medical care. For example, one person might want coverage for so-called 'alternative medicine';

another might want paediatric well-care visits covered; still another might want health insurance with a liberal policy regarding experimental procedures. If all are required elements of health insurance, that insurance will, in most cases, be more expensive;[12] if so, either fewer people will purchase it, or, if there is universal coverage, its costs will be higher.

There are, nevertheless, some resulting problems. One will be addressed in the next section when choice of health plans is discussed: the possibility that two tiers of coverage will result based on incomes. Two others will be addressed here: problems in understanding the choices available, and the issue of adverse and favorable selection.

Beginning with consumer information, offering a choice is not necessarily good for individuals if they do not understand the alternatives from which to choose. Health insurance benefits are hardly transparent; in fact, it often takes a great deal of effort to even find out what benefits are offered by health insurers. Even with this information, making cost-effective choices is extremely difficult when each insurer offers a different set of benefits. This is why many proponents of managed competition, including Alain Enthoven, have tended to favor the standardization of benefits (Enthoven 1988, 1989).

An example of how complicated benefits can be is evident in the market for Medicare HMOs. In an analysis of benefits among just three of the dozen or so Medicare HMO plans in Los Angeles County, Fox et al. (1999), found that:

> PacifiCare's prescription drug benefits are unlimited; Kaiser has an annual limit of $2,000; and CareAmerica has no limit on generics but imposes a limit on brand-name drugs of $900 per quarter . . . Copayments also may vary depending on whether a drug is brand-name or generic, if it is obtained through mail order, and what the maximum supply is that can be prescribed without requiring a new copayment . . . PacifiCare charges $20 for in-area emergency services, Kaiser charges $3, and CareAmerica charges the lesser of $25 or 20 percent of charges. PacifiCare and CareAmerica waive the copayment if the beneficiary is admitted to the hospital; Kaiser apparently does not do so. (45)

Benefits available from health plans that are marketed to the working age population are often equally complicated and also tend to lack uniformity.

The other problem is that of selection bias. When people have a choice of benefits, they are likely to choose those that they plan to use. This results in higher costs for those people who would like the protection, but who will not necessarily use the services, and might make such a choice prohibitively expensive. If, alternatively, everyone has the same benefits, then the costs of providing the benefit are averaged over everyone and thus become more affordable.

Thus, there are advantages and disadvantages to allowing choice of benefits. A reasonable compromise might be to have a standardized set of benefits as part of a universal health care program, but with individuals given the opportunity to purchase additional benefits with their own resources. This is consistent with the practices used in most other developed countries.

Particular health plan or insurer

Giving consumers a choice of health plans is one of the key components of proposals to revamp health care systems through 'managed competition.' Although no country has adapted all of its tenets, the US health care system has evolved in a way consistent with a number of facets of managed competition. Rather than examining in isolation the advantages and disadvantages of allowing a choice of health plans, it is more useful to consider choice as part of this sort of broader reform. The final part of the section will consider one other aspect of health plan choice: whether employers can be trusted to act as good agents for their employees.

THE THEORY OF MANAGED COMPETITION

Proponents of managed competition contend that it could dramatically improve performance in the health care sector by controlling expenditures, ensuring quality, and enhancing access to care. This is best described in many of Alain Enthoven's writings (e.g. Enthoven 1978; Enthoven and Kronick 1989). Under managed competition, consumers choose a health plan based on both the quality of the care provided and its cost. By having a sponsor disseminate information on both costs and quality indicators, consumers would have sufficient knowledge of the market to make an informed, intelligent choice. Furthermore, because everyone would have a choice of health plans—none of which would receive a greater subsidy than others from either employers or the tax system—those plans that provided the best product per premium dollar would attract the greatest number of enrollees. In contrast, plans that were relatively expensive but offered little tangible in return, and those that did not deliver a quality product, would eventually go out of business.

These pressures on health plans to provide an efficiently priced benefit package would be transferred to providers. In order to compete, plans would look for providers who would not squander resources. Hospitals, physicians, and other providers that could not demonstrate their ability to provide cost-effective care would have difficulty finding health plans willing to purchase their services. Enthoven believed that group and staff model HMOs, which were capitated and which had in place an integrated network of care, would operate well in such an environment.

Managed competition would help control costs for a number of reasons. Consumers would be given a choice of health plans in their area, all of which would provide a minimum specified set of benefits. Alternatively, under some proposals, benefits would be standardized across all plans. Either way, consumers should find it easier to compare the costs and benefits of alternative plans. In addition, there would no longer be a tax subsidy given toward the purchase of more expensive health plans (although actually enacting such a proposal would face a great deal of political opposition).

Because plans would compete—partly on the basis of price—to attract enrollees, they would have to find ways to control the amount of premiums they charge. Since choosing a healthier mix of enrollees would be prohibited, the best way to keep premiums down would be to operate more efficiently. They would therefore have a strong incentive to do any of the following things: (a) pick a provider panel that did not waste resources; (b) pay providers in a way that gives them an incentive to conserve resources; and (c) implement programs that control the use of unnecessary and costly services.

To ensure high quality, managed competition seeks to force plans to compete on the basis of quality as well as price. For this to occur, it is necessary for consumers to have available to them information on the quality of competing plans. Most managed competition proposals contain a mechanism for requiring each plan to provide such information to sponsors, who in turn would disseminate it to prospective and current enrollees. By comparing not only costs but also quality differences of the many plans in an area, consumers can seek coverage from the plan that provides the most 'bang for the buck.'

Managed competition could enhance access to care for several reasons. First, all such proposals call for the poor and near-poor to receive subsidies toward purchasing coverage. Second, plans are not able to discriminate against particular people (e.g. the poor and sick) or groups (e.g. small employers that currently find it difficult to purchase affordable coverage) by charging them more than they charge others, nor are they allowed to deny coverage or impose stringent preexisting condition limitations on coverage. Third, more people than is currently the case would be given a choice of health plans. Finally, unlike the current situation where poor people are either given Medicaid coverage, pay out-of-pocket, or seek free care, under managed competition they would be given a choice of plans that are available to the non-poor.

CONCERNS ABOUT OFFERING CHOICE THROUGH MANAGED COMPETITION

There are numerous concerns about offering choice through managed competition. To organize the discussion, it will be divided into subsections based on several of the 'problems of consumer choice' presented earlier.

Individuals do not know best choice or cannot obtain/process information I have combined the first two problems of choice because in this case it is hard to distinguish whether consumers simply do not know what health choices will make them best off, or alternatively, if the problem is one of obtaining and processing the necessary information.

There would seem to be several problems involved in giving individuals a choice of health plans. One is that consumers do not understand what such a choice means. Suppose, as is the case in many areas of the US, health plans have overlapping provider panels (e.g. your doctor is in several different plans), and furthermore, that the benefits offered appear to be about the same (e.g. preventive services, outpatient mental health care, prescription drugs are covered). In such a case, it is not surprising that consumers have shown themselves to be extremely sensitive to premiums (Buchmueller and Feldstein 1997). This, of course, is exactly what would be predicted by economic theory when a product is homogenous.

But in this instance, is the product really homogenous? Can consumers understand what they are buying into based on a listing of benefits, premiums, and eligible providers? This is doubtful. Although it appears that many health plans essentially are the same, they can and do differ on a number of levels. A few examples:

- Some plans are more liberal than others in defining covered treatments and have a broader drug formulary list.
- Some plans are more likely to approve state of the art procedures, while others leave them uncovered because they are 'experimental.'
- Plans vary in how stringently they apply utilization review techniques.
- Different plans have different ways of paying medical groups and providers, which in turn is likely to affect such things as how much time physicians spend with patients as well as their willingness to provide referrals to specialists and hospitals.

Most disconcerting in this regard is that consumers usually believe that the health plan they choose is not an important determinant of the quality of care they will receive (Hibbard, Sofaer, and Jewett 1996; Jewett and Hibbard 1996). Such a belief indicates a lack of awareness of the many levers health plans have available to them to affect the types, quantity, and quality of services provided to plan members.

An even larger problem than this, however, is that consumers, at least thus far, have shown themselves surprisingly ignorant of the things they need to know to make the right plan choices for themselves. Perhaps the most basic requirement—understanding the rudiments of managed care and the basic health plan types (e.g. fee-for-service, HMO)—is not met (Isaacs 1996). Much emphasis is now being put on Medicare beneficiaries choosing between fee-for-service benefits and HMOs, but researchers Judith Hibbard and colleagues have found that only 11 percent have sufficient understanding to make an informed choice (Hibbard et al. 1998).

There is also much interest in giving consumers information on health plan quality so that they can make good choices. One important, relatively new area in which consumers will need to be skilled at using information, is for health care 'report cards.' People may obtain these report cards from their employer, and then are supposed to choose a health plan by weighing such factors as quality, convenience, flexibility, and costs.

There is not any one standard report card format, and in fact, some health plans are no longer providing the information necessary for formulating a report card on their performance. Passage of comprehensive health care reform in the US during the early 1990s would have spurred the development of consistent information of this type. It is not clear, however, that the market will quickly come up with a standard report card. Some of the data items on early iterations of these report cards, such as satisfaction levels, are more easily understood by consumers, but they are not necessarily good barometers of overall quality. Other elements may be even more problematic. Consumers may not be able to know how to effectively use information on utilization rates for alternative services, or understand the relative importance of survival rates from high vs. low incidence procedures. But when plan sponsors summarize this information and rate plans in very aggregate terms such as 'above vs. below the average level of quality,' a great deal of information is lost.

Most of the current quality measures on report cards are based on the Health Plan Employer Data and Information Set (HEDIS), sponsored by the National Committee on Quality Assurance. HEDIS includes various measures of health plan performance in such areas as provision of preventive care to members, the appropriateness of care for particular problems, as well as patient satisfaction. When asked what they would expect to learn from different HEDIS measures, consumers typically ignore the data elements that they do not understand—which tend to be the 'objective' measures of quality such as various utilization rates. Similarly, they over-interpret what can be learned from simple satisfaction data, the one element that they do tend to understand. Hibbard and Jewett (1997) report that

> consumers perceive that patient ratings of overall quality give more information about the monitoring and follow-up of a condition than do the HEDIS indicators designed specifically for this purpose (such as rates of eye examinations among diabetic members, asthma hospitals, and low-birthweight infants) . . . These findings suggest that consumers are unsure of what many indicators are intended to tell them. (224–225)

A final issue in this regard is whether HEDIS and related data, which are based on plan self-reports, are really objective. If consumers begin placing more emphasis on quality indicators when choosing health plans, the latter will have an enormous incentive to provide HEDIS data that make them look good. In this regard, James Lubalin and Lauren Harris-Kojetin (1999) write, 'Numerous studies have found that consumers want to know that the plan comparative information reported to them was collected and analyzed by an independent, unbiased, trustworthy third party with expertise in health care quality—which, in operational terms, means that the data are not being collected and reported by the health plans themselves' (74).

It is therefore not surprising that in a study of managed care in 15 representative communities during 1995, it was concluded that although there is much competition on the basis of quality, '[i]n general, there was almost no competition on the basis of measured and reported technical quality process or outcome measures' (Miller 1996: 116). Similarly, multivariate findings on how quality ratings affect plan choices show little systematic relationship between the two (Chernew and Scanlon 1998).[13]

Allowing some to choose reduces the utility of those who cannot A much different problem concerns the negative externalities that can result when some people are given choices that others cannot afford. The concern, of course, is that allowing choice of health plans will result in a situation where well-to-do consumers will be able to afford better choices: e.g. plans with better providers, more liberal benefits and fewer restrictions, easier access to both providers and medical technologies, etc. (Rice, Brown, and Wyn 1993).

Allowing different 'qualities' of goods and services according to income class is certainly the norm, especially in the US. There is, nevertheless, a potentially important problem when we allow large variations in the quality of health plans. In this regard, Uwe Reinhardt (1992) writes:

> Suppose [that a] new, high-tech medical intervention [is available] and that more of it could be produced without causing reductions in the output of any other commodity. Suppose next, however, that the associated rearrangement of the economy has been such that only well-to-do patients will have access to the new medical procedure. On these assumptions, can we be sure that [this] would enhance overall *social welfare*? Would we not have to assume the absence of *social envy* among the poor and of guilt among the well-to-do? Are these reasonable assumptions? Or should civilized policy analysts refuse to pay heed to base human motives such as envy, prevalent though it may be in any normal society? (311)

Reinhardt's implicit conclusion is that society is made worse off when there are gross disparities in the availability of medical resources to different socio-economic groups.

Spillovers from choices of one group negatively affect others Another type of negative externality concerns how health plan choices of one group can affect the quality of the choices available to another. The prime example of this is selection bias. If healthier people tend to choose one type of health plan, it raises the premiums of sicker people who prefer another type. This will either mean that they will pay more, or will have to forgo this preferred choice. The vast majority of evidence accumulated from the US—both among the working age and Medicare populations—indicates favorable selection into HMOs and unfavorable selection into fee-for-service plans (Hellinger 1995). The group of greatest concern are those with expensive chronic illnesses. These individuals are more likely to have ties to providers and therefore are less interested in joining health plans with restrictive provider networks.[14] Unless sufficiently sensitive risk-adjustment procedures are developed and implemented to correct for this problem—something about which there is still much doubt—these individuals will increasingly find themselves facing higher and higher premiums. The alternative to all of this—not providing a choice of plans—averts this problem since premiums or costs would be computed based on the entire population rather than a selective, non-random component.

Choice results in social costs exceeding benefits As discussed earlier, one of the key advantages of consumer choice is that it can provide for competition that lowers societal costs. There are examples, however, where these savings may be exceeded by so called 'costs of competition.'

In other papers (Rice 1999a, 1999b) I distinguish between two kinds of regulation: 'micro' and 'macro.' Micro-regulation is what we normally think of when we hear of regulation: direct control. Macro-regulation, on the other hand, is more indirect: the setting of ground rules to meet particular goals.

Other developed countries, much more so than the US, rely on macro-regulation. The classic example is the use of regional global budgets, under which health care providers generally are free to practice as they wish. There is little direct oversight of the provision of care, but there are strict controls on unit prices paid out. Another example is tight control over the diffusion of medical technologies.

What we are seeing increasingly in the US is more micro-regulation. This, perhaps surprisingly, is the inevitable result of more competition among health plans. Now that health plans compete largely on the basis of price, they need to find ways to control their costs. One way they do this is to closely monitor the services rendered by their providers panels, which involves a great deal of oversight into the doctor–patient interaction. Another is through financial incentives to providers, particularly the use of capitation payment. In order to assure that quality is not compromised, government oversight is necessary.

What we are left with is a situation in which both health care firms and government are forced to engage in expensive and intrusive micro-regulation: firms, to ensure that they can keep their costs down, and government, to ensure that quality is not compromised in the process. This is the odd result that comes from relying more heavily on market involvement in health care. The key point is that just as competition based on consumer choice of health plan has efficiencies associated with it, there are also these additional costs to society that need to be considered.

CAN EMPLOYERS BE TRUSTED TO ACT AS GOOD AGENTS?

One final issue concerning health plan choice—largely unrelated to managed competition—concerns the role of the employer. In the US, most health plan decisions are made by employers rather than employees. The first decision is whether or not to offer a choice of health plans. Among employers offering health coverage, about 80 percent of employees who work for firms with a staff of 200 or more are offered a choice of plans. This is true, however, of only 10 percent in firms with 3–9 employees, 15 percent in firms with 10–24 employees, and 28 percent in firms with 25–199 employees (Rice et al. 1998). When firms offer a choice of plans, they screen available offerings and give their employees a fairly limited menu, with only the largest firms offering more than two or three.

This screening process can be viewed in two alternative ways. On the one hand, employee benefits managers often are more skilled and experienced than employees in discerning whether alternative health plan choices provide good value. On the other hand, there are concerns about whether employers can be trusted to be good agents for their employees. In this regard, Ezekiel Emanuel (1999) writes:

> [T]he fundamental problem with the imagined ideal of the employer as the representative of the consumer, member, or patient is the conflict of interest generated by cost concerns. The dominant theory of business ethics, and the practice of most employers, is based on the need to maximize shareholder value. This objective of employers requires that their primary concern in health care decisions is to minimize costs in order to maximize profit margins, dividends, stock prices, and so on. In direct contrast with physicians, this business ethic mandates that health care of employees be a secondary interest, secondary to stockholder returns. Thus, inherent in the business ethic of employers is to maximize cost savings from health care coverage. (134)

That being said, it is also true that employers need to attract and retain good employees, and to do so they often must provide good health benefits.

How effective an agent the employer is, then, may depend in large measure on the tightness of the particular labor market in which it is competing, and the skill level (substitutability) of employees.

In summary, although there are likely to be certain efficiencies associated with allowing competition in health insurance markets, there are costs as well. The key issue that needs to be considered among those responsible for future health policy in the United States is whether consumers really gain very much by being given a choice of health plans, or alternatively, if they prefer that their choices be focused in other areas, such as who will serve as their primary care physicians.

Particular physician

A hallmark of health policy worldwide is allowing individuals to choose their physicians. Such a choice is considered fundamental—at least for primary care—since the physician acts as a person's most important personal agent, using his or her expertise to help choose the health care services to be consumed. Although sometimes individuals are more limited in their choice of any physician such as in a closed panel HMO, there is usually still a fairly large choice available. Consumers have repeatedly shown that being given a wide choice of providers is a key attractive trait of any health plan choice.

There would seem to be little gained from restricting choice of primary care physician. None of the six concerns about choice listed in the third section would seem to apply, with the possible exception of individuals not knowing how to obtain or process the necessary information—in this case, about quality. I believe that this is better dealt with not by taking away an individual's right to choose his or her own personal physician, but rather by setting standards that must be met in order for a physician to enter and continue practicing medicine. Society, of course, may wish to set these standards at a higher or lower level than is currently the case.

The situation for specialists may be somewhat different, however. Because individuals often have less experience in and understanding of the procedures that specialists perform, they often are not in as good a position to make these choices. In addition, there is evidence to indicate that the specialists chosen often do not provide the best outcomes. Research by Hannan et al. (1991) found that when coronary artery bypass operations are done by high-volume surgeons in high-volume hospitals, mortality rates are 38 percent lower. This hardly means that one should go so far as to say choice of specialist should be curtailed. Rather, it may be that in certain circumstances others besides the consumer (e.g. credentialing boards) could be helpful in narrowing these choices down, perhaps by requiring a certain amount of training, continuing education training, experience, or minimum case load for particular procedures.

Particular hospital

Perhaps an even more intriguing question is whether there should be free choice of hospital. Such a free choice of hospital is characteristic of the fee-for-service system in the US, but is less true elsewhere. It may be the case, however, that there has never been truly free choice of hospital in the US. Some years ago Paul Ellwood stated, 'Hospitals don't have patients; doctors have patients and hospitals have doctors' (Fuchs 1983: 58). Indeed, it has been found that US doctors treat, on average, 90 percent of their patients in a single hospital (Miller, Welch, and Englert 1995).

There are two primary advantages to offering consumers a choice of hospital. First, an individual is usually in the best position to weigh the tradeoffs between convenience, costs, and *perceived* quality. Second, if the consumer does sufficient research on quality, he or she can insist on going to a hospital with excellent medical outcomes.

There are, on the other hand, two reasons that providing free choice of hospital would not be best for individuals and for society as a whole. First, there is considerable research evidence to indicate that medical outcomes are positively correlated with hospital volume. One of the earliest studies of this type found that hospitals that performed over 200 operations per year of a particular type had mortality rates 25 to 41 percent lower than lower-volume hospitals, after controlling for case-mix differences (Luft, Bunker, and Enthoven 1979), a finding that has been largely confirmed with more recent data (e.g. Hannan et al. 1991). Unfortunately, many people unknowingly go to hospitals with a track record of poor outcomes. A study from Maryland for one general high-risk procedure showed that almost half of patients received care from low-volume hospitals with relative mortality risks that were 4.0 to 8.7 times higher than the high-volume regional provider (Gordon et al. 1995).

If this is the case, wouldn't it be better just to give this information to consumers and let them decide? The problem is that evidence to date indicates that consumers do not do a good job in using data on quality to choose hospitals. One study examined how consumers responded to information provided each year by HCFA on hospital mortality rates (Mennemeyer, Morrisey, and Howard 1997). Between 1986 and 1992, for each acute care hospital in the US, HCFA provided information on actual and predicted mortality rates for Medicare beneficiaries. Predicted rates were based on age, sex, comorbidities of cancer, cardiovascular disease, liver disease, or renal disease; and previous hospitalizations. The results show that quality ratings had very little impact on consumer choice of hospitals. A hospital that had twice the expected death rate had less than one fewer discharge per week in the first year, and only 116 fewer discharges over nine years. In contrast, if there is a press report of a single, unexpected death, there is a 9 percent reduction in admissions for the next year.

These results are similar to those of another study that examined how cardiac surgery performance reports affected referral practices (Schneider and Epstein 1996). What is significant about the latter study is that it considers the role of physician as the patient's agent in distilling information on quality. Pennsylvania publishes a consumer guide that provides annual risk-adjusted mortality rates for all hospitals and surgeons in the state. The guide

> lists, by surgeon and by hospital, the number of coronary-artery bypass graft (CABG) surgeries performed in a calendar year; the actual in-hospital mortality rate among patients treated by each surgeon and hospital; and the expected range in in-hospital mortality rates, derived from statistical models that take into account the severity of the patient's illness and coexisting conditions. Each surgeon and hospital receives a grade indicating whether the actual in-hospital mortality rate is significantly lower than the expected range. The Pennsylvania report and a similar report in New York State represent the most sophisticated and widely publicized risk-adjusted data on the performance of hospitals and surgeons. (251–252)

In a survey of cardiologists and cardiac surgeons in the state, it was found that very few discussed this information with their patients. Just 10 percent found the information to be 'very important,' and fewer than 10 percent discussed the guide with more than 10 percent of their patients who were considering a CABG operation (Schneider and Epstein 1996).

In contrast, another recent study, by Mukamel and Mushlin (1998), found that publication of risk-adjusted mortality rates for coronary artery bypass surgery in New York State did affect future volumes of patients for both hospitals and surgeons. They attribute these findings to greater credibility of the New York information to both physicians and patients, and to wider media attention. In an accompanying commentary, however, Chernew and Escarce (1998) note that confounding factors could in part explain the results.[15]

The alternative to giving consumers such a choice is to regionalize hospitals such that each provides a high volume of particular services. In addition to the argument that such regionalization would enhance quality, there are two other reasons to believe that it could reduce societal costs. First, there are major economies of scale associated with concentrating volumes of particular services in a single hospital (Finkler 1979). Second, if a particular service is concentrated in a single hospital, hospitals do not have to spend resources competing for patients and physicians. This has to be weighed against higher costs that may accrue from giving hospitals more monopoly power.

In summary, then, although it would seem desirable to let people choose their own hospitals, it is not clear that—at least up till now—that consumers do indeed make the best choices. They often choose low-volume hospitals with poor risk-adjusted outcomes, and most evidence indicates that they do not use information on hospital quality that is available to them. Restricting choices to higher-volume, regionalized hospitals—a policy in place in most other developed countries—could result in both lower societal costs and better patient outcomes.

Specific medical intervention

The final choice to be considered is whether the consumer should be able to choose the specific medical intervention that they receive. Obviously there are limits on this—services such as surgery, the decision to be admitted to a hospital, the writing of a prescription are determined not by the patient but by the doctor. Within these confines, however, consumers can exercise various degrees of control over the choices of particular medical interventions.

On the surface, it would seem that providing consumers with such flexibility would be unambiguously advantageous. Not only is it his or her life and limbs at stake, but the patient is likely to be in the best position to trade off such things as risk vs. disability vs. pain. Indeed, almost all countries worldwide allow a large degree of patient choice.

Under what conditions, then, are there disadvantages to providing more choice? One of the individual concerns about choice is relevant here. It involves situations in which the provision of choice, in and of itself, reduces a person's utility. Richard Thaler (1991) discusses why a society might prefer to give individuals comprehensive insurance with little cost sharing, instead of having high cost sharing which essentially requires patients to make difficult consumption decisions on a treatment-by-treatment basis. Thaler writes,

> Why do consumers want the first dollar coverage? I believe the reasons involve regret. Most consumers find decisions involving tradeoffs between health care and money very distasteful. This is especially true when the decision is made for someone else, like a child. A high deductible policy would force individuals to make many such decisions, at considerable psychic costs. The costs can occur no matter which way the decision is made. Consider a couple who must decide whether to spend $X for a diagnostic test for their child. There is some small probability *p* that the child has a serious disease. If the disease can be fatal, then the regret may loom so large that the test will be administered even for very large values of X or very small values of *p*. Yet once the test is ordered and the likely negative result is obtained, the couple may regret the expenditure, especially if it is large relative to their income. Obviously, these costs are avoided if all health care is prepaid, via either first dollar coverage or a prepaid health organization. (16–17)

This issue has implications for Medical Savings Accounts (MSAs). Under most MSA proposals, individuals (usually employees) would be able to choose a health plan with a very large annual deductible (often several thousand dollars), but which covers medical expenses above that amount in full. The savings in premiums could be used to make payments toward the deductible or, alternatively, to spend (or save) on anything that the consumer desires. Thaler's point relates to this: consumers who are put in this sort of position might experience regret in the process of weighing the costs and benefits of seeking additional medical care. Although researchers disagree as to why MSAs have not caught on given their tax advantages, I would posit that this is one of the primary reasons: consumers dislike large deductibles in medical care because it makes them face choices that they would rather not contend with.

The alternative to relying on consumer demand (and its associated level of out-of-pocket costs) is to rely instead on supply-side levers to allocate scarce medical resources, an issue discussed more fully in the concluding section.

The role of choice in health care policy internationally

Different countries have very different health care systems. These differences can be illustrated in various ways, one being the concept of choice. The US allows consumers a large number of key choices with regard to health care. In fact, of the six key choices that were listed earlier, the US allows an unusual degree of choice.

Individuals in the US have a choice of whether to purchase health insurance, although, as argued earlier, for some people who cannot afford it this is not a real choice. There is also a choice of health benefits and health plans, though again, choice is somewhat limited since the employer makes many of these decisions. There is also free choice not only of physician but of hospital; HMOs often limit this choice, but usually there are still a number of options. And there tends to be a large amount of choice concerning specific medical interventions.

Although it is difficult to generalize about the health care systems in other developed countries, none offers consumers choice in so many realms as does the US. Beginning with the coverage, in most countries there is little or no choice: health insurance is universal and typically is paid for through mandatory payroll assessment or through taxes. Nor is there a choice of health insurance benefits: benefits tend to be standardized in a particular geographic area, although in many countries it is possible to purchase some form of supplemental coverage and in almost all one can purchase services privately rather than go through the national health care system.

One of the key differences between the US and other countries concerns choice of health plan or health insurance. The US is unique in giving so many people a choice of health plan. In other countries there tends to be only one choice in a particular region, or if there are more, people are assigned to one based on factors such as occupation.[16]

All countries allow a choice of physician but not of hospital. More common is a system of regionalization, where only one hospital in an area provides a particular procedure, and/or separate hospital-based and office-based physicians so that the latter do not have the privilege of treating inpatients. Finally, all developed countries do allow a large degree of consumer choice with respect to specific medical interventions. Choice is limited outside of the US in certain ways, however. Although rarely done explicitly, services are sometimes rationed through such things as long queues that result from restrictions on the supply of providers or medical technologies.

What can we make of these substantial differences across countries in the degree of choice given to consumers? I would contend that they are emblematic of the two major differences between the US health care system and that of most other countries:

- There is much more concern about equity in health care services in other countries than in the US.
- More so than in other countries, the US seeks efficiency in health care services through markets (although many would argue that it doesn't succeed in this regard).

Equity

The relative lack of choices in other countries, as compared to the US, strongly reflects their concerns about equity. Universal coverage implies a lack of individual choice about whether to have coverage (and whether to pay for it through higher taxes), but makes health care services affordable to the entire population. Similarly, for most basic health care services, copayments are low, another way of transferring incomes from the healthy to the sick. The fact that there tend to be uniform health insurance benefits is also symptomatic of less choice, but it results in most of the population having comparable coverage. Finally, the lack of hospital competition in most countries, coupled with strong limits on the diffusion of medical technology, also reduces choice, but in doing so, puts most citizens on a relatively level playing field when seeking health services.

Choice is a hallmark of the US system but it has resulted in larger inequities than in other countries. About 18 percent of the population under age 65 is uninsured, and, adjusting for health status, use far fewer services. Furthermore, those without insurance and others who are disadvantaged have less access to state-of-the-art medical care services (Wenneker, Weismann, and Epstein 1990; Braveman et al. 1991).

These differences among choice offerings, and the resulting impact on equity, can be illustrated in a number of ways. Research on views about equity in several developed countries, conducted by Eddy van Doorslaer, Adam Wagstaff, and their colleagues, shows the importance of equity in the health care systems of many developed countries (van Doorslaer, Wagstaff, and Rutten 1993). They conclude that,

> There appears to be broad agreement . . . among policy-makers in at least eight of the nine European countries [studied] that payment towards health care should be related to ability to pay rather than to use of medical facilities. Policymakers in all nine European countries also appear to be committed to the notion that all citizens should have access to health care. In many countries this is taken further, it being made clear that access to and receipt of health care should depend on need, rather than ability to pay.
>
> (Wagstaff and van Doorslaer 1992: 363)

Further differences between the US and other countries in this regard are illustrated through survey results reported on by Robert Blendon and his colleagues. The study found that only 23 percent of Americans agreed with the statement, 'It is the responsibility of the government to take care of the very poor people who can't take care of themselves.' The numbers for other countries were considerably higher: 50 percent of Germans agreed with the statement, as did 56 percent of Poles, 62 percent of British and French, 66 percent of Italians, and 71 percent of Spaniards (Blendon et al. 1995).

Although it is always risky to make generalizations across countries, these numbers (and others that could have been cited) graphically illustrate the very different social ethics that exist in the US vs. elsewhere. In a country like the US in which communitarian values are weak and markets are relied upon to distribute so-called 'merit goods' like health care, enacting reform like universal coverage is extraordinarily difficult. To do so it probably will be necessary for there to be a change in the prevailing social ethic, or—and this is perhaps the more likely route—to elect officials with this ethic who have the ability to pull the populace along with them.

Markets

Although a number of countries are experimenting with so called 'internal markets' in health care, no developed country has gone as far as the US in relying on markets to bring about economic efficiency in the delivery of health care services. Again, these differences stem, in large part, from the amount of choice offered consumers in different countries. It is also indicative perhaps of a larger degree of paternalism—and the greater sense of social justice—in health care outside of the US.

Markets encourage efficiency by relying on consumers to make informed choices. The use of markets goes hand-in-hand with a reliance on so-called 'demand-side' policies. In the US, demand side policies that rely on consumers making such choices are more common than in other countries. In particular, the choice of health plan is designed to provide strong incentives for plans to keep costs down and quality up; the choice of hospital (which is often limited by the health plan) is also designed to encourage them to act efficiently. Equally important is the reliance on patient cost-sharing in the US, which allows consumers to choose whether or not a particular service is worth the price.

Most other developed countries have, in contrast, relied on 'supply-side' policies in their health care systems. (This is not to say that the US has eschewed these policies; rather, both demand- and supply-side policies are used simultaneously.) One can only go so far in generalizing about different countries because there are substantial differences among them, but there are some common threads.

One commonality is the use of global budgets, which 'tend to be prospectively set caps on spending for some portion of the health care industry' (Wolfe and Moran 1993: 55). The exact meaning, however, varies country to country. In some countries, such as Canada, hospitals receive an annual global budget to cover their entire operating budget. In Germany, there are regional budgets for different types of physician services. Regardless, global budgets imply a reliance on decisions made by officials other than the ultimate consumer of health care services.

Global budgeting has not been used in isolation, however. Most countries employ other supply-side policies. One of the most common is the control of the diffusion of medical technologies, which has limited their availability. This again reduces consumer choice, either directly or indirectly if it results in long queues to receive services.

More generally, many countries rely on their monopsony[17] power over provider payments and other aspects of the system such as technology diffusion (Evans 1983, 1990). This holds true not only in Canada, but in Europe as well, where Brian Abel-Smith (1992) concluded his analysis of European systems by stating:

> The main message from the experience of the European Community is that it is technically possible to control health care costs by government regulation of supply rather than demand, particularly by applying budgets to hospitals . . . The key to Europe's success is the use of monopsony power whereby one purchaser dominates the market, and not just the hospital market. Where there are many purchasers, as in Germany, they are forced to act together. Because the insurers are not allowed more revenue, either from tax or contributions, and because what they can charge the insured in copayments is centrally determined, they are forced either to confront providers or to ration their allowable resources. In most countries this does not lead to lines of patients waiting for treatment. (414)

As in the other instances, the use of monopsony indicates that someone other than the consumer is making key choices in health care—although almost never in the choice of primary care provider.

Summary

Consumers are granted a greater range of choices in the United States than in other countries, although some of their choices—e.g. choosing to be in a closed-panel HMO—may limit subsequent choices such as the hospital to which they go. Generally speaking, individuals in the US can choose whether or not to have health insurance, and often can choose the benefits provided by health insurance and the particular health plan—choices that generally are not offered in other countries. In addition, the US also tends to give more choice of hospital. Other countries have chosen to limit these choices; such a limitation on choice might not only enhance equity but increase efficiency as well.

Although most of this paper has focused on problems inherent in allowing consumer choice in health care, one cannot conclude from it that the current level of choice, or even more choice, is undesirable. I have not provided a parallel analysis of the problems inherent in the alternative: that is, allowing another entity, such as government, to make the choices. The reason for my focus is the general belief that choice is nearly always good; I have tried to show that in health care, this is not necessarily the case. It is my hope that a better understanding of where choice in health care is advantageous and where it may not be, as well as how different countries' health care systems are built around these different conceptions of choice, will help stimulate more thinking on the advisability of alternative ways of reforming health care systems, both in the US and abroad.

Acknowledgment

Versions of this paper were presented at the session, 'The value base in health economics,' at the International Health Economic Association Meetings, Rotterdam, Netherlands, June 1999, and at a seminar in the Department of Health Services, UCLA School of Public Health, Los Angeles, California, USA, February 2000. I am grateful to Robert Valdez for providing extensive comments on a draft.

Notes

1 One is that a welfarist approach does not allow us to distinguish between different qualities of utility. If an individual derives utility from something, even if it is as base as the unhappiness of others, that counts as much as more lofty desires. Sen also criticizes this conception as overly materialistic, being

based on the goods and services one uses rather than any factors that are perhaps more important in making people's lives seem worthwhile.

2 This conclusion, of course, relies on many assumptions, some of which are discussed in the next section. For an analysis of a full list of such assumptions and their application to health care, see Rice (1998).

3 Curiously, as plausible as this may seem in many circumstances, it is contrary to the conventional economic theory. Under the theory, it is the goods themselves, rather than how they were obtained, that is the sole determinant of individual welfare (Hahnel and Albert 1990).

4 In this regard, two of the key criticisms of monopolies are they charge more than would be charged in a competitive marketplace, and they have less incentive to be innovative. When firms have competitors they do not have these luxuries.

5 Not all economists agree with this; some, for example, have tried to show that many seemingly self-destructive human behaviors, such as drug addiction and even suicide, are the result of utility maximizing decisions. Using what they call 'rational addiction' theory, Becker and Murphy (1988) state that 'addictions, even strong ones, are usually rational in the sense of involving forward-looking maximization with stable preferences' (675), and that even though unhappy people often become addicted, 'they would be even more unhappy if they were prevented from consuming the addictive goods' (691).

6 Thaler also suggests that this is consistent with current theories of brain functioning: 'The prefrontal cortex has been called the "executive of the brain" and has been identified as the location of rational thought and planning. The planner in our model represents the prefrontal cortex. The prefrontal cortex continually interfaces with the limbic system, which is responsible for the generation of emotions. The doer in our model represents the limbic system. It is well known that self-control phenomena center on the interaction between the prefrontal cortex and the limbic system' (93).

7 Thanks to Robert Valdez for suggesting this point.

8 See Rice (1998) for a review of evidence on this.

9 Nyman (1999) points out another important advantage of health insurance: it allows individuals to afford purchasing expensive care that otherwise would be out of reach financially.

10 For a critique of this conception of welfare loss, see Rice (1998: 81–93).

11 As explained by Elliot Aronson (1972), 'cognitive dissonance is a state of tension that occurs when an individual simultaneously holds two cognitions (ideas, attitudes, beliefs, opinions) that are psychologically inconsistent . . . Because [its] occurrence . . . is unpleasant, people are motivated to reduce it' (92–93).

12 There are instances in which additional benefits will not increase overall costs. This can occur when, say, a new insured benefit substitutes for another covered service, or when the use of the new benefit reduces treatment costs in the future.

13 Chernew and Scanlon (1998) write, 'the experience in one large company indicates that employees do not appear to respond strongly to plan performance measures, even when the labeling and dissemination were intended to facilitate their use' (19).

14 In addition, there is some evidence to indicate that individuals with chronic conditions fare worse in managed care than in fee-for-service medicine (Ware et al. 1996).

15 They write, 'using data prior to the release of the report cards, Yip found that the market for CABG surgery in New York State tended to become increasingly concentrated over time (i.e. surgeons with high market shares experienced disproportionate growth in market share). Because CABG surgery volume is likely

to be inversely correlated with mortality, baseline market share is a potential confounding factor in Mukamel and Mushlin's analysis' (943).

16 Even countries that have embarked on reform using some of the tools of managed competition (e.g. Switzerland and the Netherlands) do not allow individuals to choose among alternative insurers.

17 A monopsony occurs when there is only one buyer of a particular product (here, health care).

References

Abel-Smith, B. (1992) Cost containment and new priorities in the European Community, *Milbank Quarterly* 70: 393–422.

Akerlof, G.A. and Dickens, W.T. (1992) The economic consequences of cognitive dissonance, *American Economic Review* 72: 307–319.

Aronson, E. (1972) *The Social Animal*, San Francisco: W.H. Freeman & Co.

Arrow, K.A. (1963) Uncertainty and the welfare economics of medical care, *American Economic Review* 53: 940–973.

—— (1984) *The Economics of Information*, Cambridge MA: The Belknap Press of Harvard University.

Becker, G.S. and Murphy, K.M. (1988) A theory of rational addiction, *Journal of Political Economy* 96(4): 675–700.

Blendon, R.J., Benson, J., Donelan, K., Leitman, R., Taylor, H., Koeck, C., and Gitterman, D. (1995) Who has the best health care system: a second look, *Health Affairs* 14(4): 220–230.

Braveman, P.A., Egerler, S., Bennett, T., and Showstack, J. (1991) Differences in hospital resource allocation among sick newborns according to insurance coverage, *Journal of the American Medical Association* 266: 3300–3308.

Buchmueller, T.C. and Feldstein, P.J. (1997) The effect of price on switching among health plans, *Journal of Health Economics* 16: 231–247.

Chernew, M. and Escarce, J.J. (1998) Consumer response to quality information, *Medical Care* 36: 943–944.

Chernew, M. and Scanlon, D.P. (1998) Health plan report cards and insurance choice, *Inquiry* 35: 9–22.

Emanuel, E.J. (1999) Choice and representation in health care, *Medical Care Research and Review* 56 (supplement 1): 113–140.

Enthoven, A. (1978) Consumer choice health plan, *New England Journal of Medicine* 298: 650–658, 709–720.

—— (1988) *Theory and Practice of Managed Competition in Health Care Finance*, Amsterdam: North-Holland.

—— (1989) Effective management of competition in the FEHBP, *Health Affairs* 8 (Fall): 33–50.

Enthoven, A. and Kronick, R. (1989) A consumer-choice health plan for the 1990s, *New England Journal of Medicine* 320: 29–37, 94–101.

Evans, R.G. (1983) Health care in Canada: patterns of funding and regulation, *Journal of Health Politics, Policy, and Law* 8: 1–43.

—— (1990) Tension, compression, and shear: directions, stresses, and outcomes of health care cost control, *Journal of Health Politics, Policy, and Law* 15: 101–128.

Feldstein, P.J. (1988) *Health Care Economics*, New York: Wiley.

Finkler, S.A. (1979) Cost-effectiveness of regionalization: the heart surgery example, *Inquiry* 16(3): 264–270.

Fox, P.D., Snyder, R., Dallek, G., and Rice, T. (1999) Should Medicare HMO benefits be standardized? *Health Affairs* 18(4): 40–52.

Frank, R.H. (1985) *Choosing the Right Pond: Human Behavior and the Quest for Status*, New York: Oxford University Press.

—— (1999) *Luxury Fever: Why Money Fails to Satisfy in an Era of Excess*, New York: The Free Press.

Fuchs, V.R. (1983) *Who Shall Live?* New York: Basic Books.

Gordon, T.A., Burleyson, G.P., Tielsch, J., and Cameron, J.L. (1995) The effects of regionalization on cost and outcome for one general high-risk surgical procedure, *Annals of Surgery* 221: 43–49.

Hahnel, R. and Albert, M. (1990) *Quiet Revolution in Welfare Economics*, Princeton NJ: Princeton University Press.

Hannan, E.L., Kilburn, H., Bernard, H., O'Donnell, J.F., Lukacik, G., and Shields, E.P. (1991) Coronary artery bypass surgery: the relationship between inhospital mortality rate and surgical volume after controlling for clinical risk factors, *Medical Care* 29(11): 1094–1107.

Hellinger, F.J. (1995) Selection bias in HMOs and PPOs: a review of the evidence, *Inquiry* 32: 135–142.

Hibbard, J.H. and Jewett, J.J. (1997) Will quality report cards help consumers? *Health Affairs* 16(5): 218–228.

Hibbard, J.H., Sofaer, S., and Jewett, J.J. (1996) Condition-specific performance information: assessing salience, comprehension, and approaches for communicating quality, *Health Care Financing Review* 18: 95–109.

Hibbard, J.H., Jewett, J.J., Engelmann, S., and Tusler, M. (1998) Can Medicare beneficiaries make informed choices? *Health Affairs* 17(6): 181–193.

Isaacs, S.L. (1996) Consumers' information needs: results of a national survey, *Health Affairs* 15(4): 31–41.

Jewett, J.J. and Hibbard, J.H. (1996) Comprehension of quality indicators: differences among privately insured, publicly insured, and uninsured, *Health Care Financing Review* 18: 75–94.

Lubalin, J.S. and Harris-Kojetin, L. (1999) What do consumers want and need to know in making health care choices? *Medical Care Research and Review* 56 (supplement 1): 67–102.

Luft, H.S., Bunker, J.P., and Enthoven, A.C. (1979) Should operations be regionalized: the empirical relation between surgical volume and mortality, *New England Journal of Medicine* 301: 1364–1369.

McLaughlin, C.G. (1999) Health care consumers: choices and constraints, *Medical Care Research and Review* 56 (supplement 1): 24–59.

Mennemeyer, S.T., Morrisey, M.A., and Howard, L.Z. (1997) Death and reputation: how consumers acted upon HCFA mortality information, *Inquiry* 34: 117–128.

Miller, M.E., Welch, W.P., and Englert, E. (1995) Physicians practicing in hospitals: implications for a medical staff policy, *Inquiry* 32: 204–210.

Miller, R.H. (1996) Competition in the health system: good news and bad news, *Health Affairs* 15(2): 107–120.

Mooney, G. (1998) Communitarian claims: as an ethical basis for allocating health care resources, *Social Science and Medicine* 47: 1171–1180.

Mukamel, D.B. and Mushlin, A.I. (1998) Quality of care information makes a difference, *Medical Care* 36: 945–954.

Nyman, J.A. (1999) The value of health insurance: the access motive, *Journal of Health Economics* 18: 141–152.

Pauly, M.V. (1968) The economics of moral hazard: comment, *American Economic Review* 58: 531–537.

Rawls, J. (1971) *A Theory of Justice*, Cambridge MA: The Belknap Press of Harvard University.

Reinhardt, U.E. (1992) Reflections on the meaning of efficiency: can efficiency be separated from equity? *Yale Law & Policy Review* 10: 302–315.

—— (1996) Comment on Mark Pauly, in *Looking Back, Looking Forward: 'Staying Power' in Issues in Health Care Reform*, Washington DC: Institute of Medicine.

Rice, T. (1998) *The Economics of Health Reconsidered*, Chicago: Health Administration Press.

—— (1999a) Macro versus micro regulation, in S.H. Altman, U.E. Reinhardt, and D. Shactman (eds) *Regulating Managed Care: Theory, Practice, and Future Options*, San Francisco: Jossey Bass.

—— (1999b) The microregulation of the health care marketplace, *Journal of Health Politics, Policy, and Law* 24: 967–972.

Rice, T., Brown, E.R., and Wyn, R. (1993) Holes in the Jackson Hole approach to health care reform, *Journal of the American Medical Association* 270: 1357–1362.

Rice, T., Pourat, N., Levan, R., Silbert, L.J., and Brown, E.R. (1998) *Trends in Job-Based Health Insurance Coverage*, Los Angeles: UCLA Center for Health Policy Research.

Robbins, Lord (Lionel) (1984) Politics and political economy, in *An Essay on the Nature and Significance of Economic Science*, 3rd edn, London: Macmillan.

Samuelson, P.A. (1938) A note on the pure theory of consumer behaviour, *Economica* 5: 61–71.

Schneider, E.C. and Epstein, A.M. (1996) Influence of cardiac surgery performance reports on referral practices and access to care, *New England Journal of Medicine* 335: 251–256.

Scitovsky, T. (1976) *The Joyless Economy*, New York: Oxford University Press.

Sen, A. (1987) *On Ethics and Economics*, Oxford: Blackwell.

Sugden, R. (1993) Welfare, resources, and capabilities: a review of inequality reexamined by Amartya Sen, *Journal of Economic Literature* 31: 1947–1962.

Thaler, R.H. (1991) *Quasi-Rational Economics*, New York: Russell Sage Foundation.

van Doorslaer, E., Wagstaff, A., and Rutten, F. (eds) (1993) *Equity in the Finance and Delivery of Health Care: An International Perspective*, Oxford: Oxford Medical Publications.

Wagstaff, A. and van Doorslaer, E. (1992) Equity in the finance of health care: some international comparisons, *Journal of Health Economics* 11: 361–387.

Ware, J.E., Jr, Bayliss, M.S., Rogers, W.H., Kosinski, M., and Tarlov, A.R. (1996) Differences in 4-year health outcomes for elderly and poor, chronically ill patients treated in HMO and fee-for-service systems: results from the Medical Outcomes Study, *Journal of the American Medical Association* 276: 1039–1047.

Wenneker, M.B., Weismann, J.S., and Epstein, A.M. (1990) The association of payer with utilization of cardiac procedures, *Journal of the American Medical Association* 254: 1255–1260.

Wolfe, P.R. and Moran, D.W. (1993) Global budgeting in the OECD countries, *Health Care Financing Review* 14(3): 55–76.

Young, H.P. (1994) *Equity in Theory and Practice*, Princeton NJ: Princeton University Press.

2

COMMUNITARIANISM AND HEALTH ECONOMICS

Gavin Mooney

Victorious in the battles he has fought, man looks on a world depopulated of protective powers, and is astonished at his victory . . . No voice of those that are no more is prolonged into the life of those still living, and the voice of the living must soon be engulfed by the same eternal silence. What shall man do, without memory, without hope, between the past which abandons him and the future which is closed before him?

Benjamin Constant

Plant a stake crowned with flowers in the middle of a square; gather the people together there, and you will have a festival. Do better yet; let the spectators become an entertainment to themselves; do it so that each sees and loves himself in the others so that all will be better united.

Jean-Jacques Rousseau

Introduction

This chapter first mounts a partial critique of certain value aspects of current health economics. Thereafter it proposes some possible routes for developing the value base of health economics with the intention of reassessing the project of health economists, especially in the context of health care services (rather than health more widely).

In so far as questions of values, the choosing of values and the eliciting of values underlie much of the emphasis of the paper, it echoes some of the sentiments expressed by Fuchs (1996) in a recent address to the American Economic Association Conference when he reviewed the state of the art of health economics. He suggested that as health economists 'we must pay more attention to values than we have in the past. Through skilful analysis of the interactions between values and the conclusions of positive research, we will be able to contribute more effectively to public policy debates.' The point is endorsed by Reinhardt (1992). He writes that 'to begin an exploration of alternative proposals for the reform of our [US] health system without first setting forth explicitly, and very clearly, the social values to which the reformed system is likely to adhere strikes at least this author as patently inefficient; it is a waste of time'. Reinhardt continues: 'Would it not be more efficient to explore the relative efficiency of alternative proposals that do conform to widely shared social values?'

There is a recognition by other health economists that there are important unresolved value questions underlying the sub-discipline of health economics as it currently is that are not being aired or investigated adequately. Tom Rice's book, *The Economics of Health Care Reconsidered* (1998), provides an excellent critique of neoclassical health economics. In a review of that for *Health Economics*, I wrote that there was now a need to put something reasonably comprehensive in its place. It is not that there is no alternative available but there is a need for something more cohesive and comprehensive. I suggested that, as Rice had done the critique, it was for others to pitch in and help to undertake the rebuilding. It then struck me that I should at least try to make a contribution. Further, working with my SPHERe (Social and Public Health Economics Research Group) colleagues, Steve Jan and Virginia Wiseman, in Aboriginal health in particular but also in health service priority setting and the eliciting of community values, has made me appreciate better the deficiencies in some of the techniques we as health economists are currently using. It has also allowed me to get some inklings into ways, if not of overcoming, at least perhaps of addressing, some of these deficiencies.

Ethics, values and a constitution

There is a growing recognition within economics that we cannot continue to ignore the moral or ethical foundations of our discipline. Such recognition is clearly not new; Adam Smith was Professor of Moral Philosophy when he wrote *The Wealth of Nations* (1776). For much of the time since then, and certainly in most of this century, concerns by economists about moral sentiments and ethics have been at best muted. (The debate started by Titmuss in the 1970s about the nature of altruism in the context of blood donation is something of an exception. See Titmuss 1971.) Outstanding in this context is the work by Hausman and McPherson (1993) who pose such questions as: 'What is the moral basis of a concern with efficiency? Is it really less controversial than the moral commitments that lie behind notions of equity? What do economists presuppose when they factor questions of economic welfare into questions of efficiency and questions of equity? Can these moral suppositions be sustained?'

There is also a need for economists to consider the questions of the origin and the formulation of preferences. Economists normally take preferences as givens and not the subject of inquiry; for example, as to whether they are rational or not. We argue from an assumption of completeness—an issue specifically in formation of health status preferences that Alan Shiell in SPHERe is currently investigating. Notably, preferences over beliefs are typically not investigated by economists (but see the discussion of Akerlof and Dickens 1982, below). It is this lack of concern with the formulation of preferences in general and over beliefs in particular that perhaps more than anything explains the relative lack of interest in moral and ethical matters by economists. As Hausman and McPherson point out: 'utility theory places no constraints on what individuals may want' and they argue that it cannot be viewed as a positive theory 'without further assumptions concerning the extent to which people are rational, and it is not merely a model or definition, because rationality is itself a normative notion'. The need to accept the importance of ethics in economics is also the focus of work by Hurley (1998) when he writes: 'economists . . . who conduct evaluative economic analyses must appreciate more deeply that such analyses are inherently exercises in social ethics . . . The development of methods for such . . . analyses needs to occur in conversation with the broader literature on social ethics and moral philosophy.'

In principle there are a number of possible ways forward here, all of which result in some questioning of utility theory. For example the work of Sen (1985a) on functionings and capabilities (and as partly reflected in the work of Culyer 1989 on extra-welfarism in health economics) is one. It is also to be noted that one clear potential advantage of utility theory which results in many economists hanging on to it is the measurability that it allows. Yet as Sen has remarked on this front, 'it is better to be vaguely right than precisely wrong'. The 'bounded rationality' of Williamson (1975) and others is another option, as are the multiple utility functions of Margolis (1982). Moving beyond consequentialism and taking account of process utility is also a possibility. Considering a more communitarian rather than an overtly individualistic liberal basis on which to build may prove useful (Mooney 1998a). Questions of rights to, claims over and needs for health care also require to be teased out—as do the links between them. Specifically concerning rights, as Hausman and McPherson (1993) state, 'On instrumental or consequentialist views, the problem of rights articulation can be formulated as one of selecting rules that maximise good consequences.' They go on to suggest, however: 'This is straightforward in principle, although difficult problems of strategic coordination may arise in devising effective rules.' This issue of devising effective values—what I have called 'a constitution' (following Kemp and Asimakopulos 1952)—is discussed in more detail below. Sen's approach to rights is also potentially useful—that the degree of goodness of a state of affairs varies with the perspective of the evaluator (Sen 1985b).

The work of Buchanan (1986) on 'constitutional' choices is highly pertinent with consideration of choices about setting the general rules of the game. As Brennan and Buchanan (1985) argue: 'if rules influence outcomes and if some outcomes are "better" than others, it follows that to the extent that rules can be chosen, the study and analysis of comparative rules and institutions become proper objects of our attention'. This notion of a 'constitution'—which (even if the language has changed) dates back to the 'laws and institutions' of Adam Smith (1759)—is central. As Vanberg (1994) describes it, 'the constitutional paradigm . . . reverses . . . the logic of the goal paradigm. Instead of concentrating on the 'goals that organizational action is supposedly *directed at*, it draws attention to the procedural foundations that organizational action is *based upon*'. A somewhat related point is made by Evans (1998): 'we can set up an analytical framework postulating that consumer behaviour can be represented as the outcome of maximizing some objective function, but the framework tells us nothing at all about the arguments of the objective function'.

This chapter is part of a wider programme of work which has the intention of investigating these various ideas (and others) to see what progress can be made in clarifying the value base for health economics. This programme, if not wholly comprehensive, is at least more cohesive and consistent than the body of ideas which currently exist. It is worth recalling the recognition that Adam Smith (1759) gave to the need for rules, essentially social or community rules. Smith wrote: 'without regard to . . . general rules . . . what would become of the duties of justice, of truth, of chastity, of fidelity . . .? . . . upon the tolerable observance of these duties, depends the very existence of human society, which would crumble into nothing if mankind were not generally impressed with a reverence for those important rules of conduct'.

Building more comprehensively

At least two forms of health economics are open to critique: that based on the market and, related to that, the form of health economics that has grown up with an acceptance that the market in health care fails. This latter school of thought can be placed under the umbrella of what is often referred to as 'extra-welfarism'—but only partly so. A major driving force of this chapter is a recognition that, first, the market fails in health care and, second, there is little systematic building of an alternative paradigm for health economics. This is not to discount the work of health economists but to point to the need to build more comprehensively on the work that has been done.

Agency issues

Most health economists would probably agree about the centrality of the agency relationship. There is disagreement however as to (a) who the decision maker is and (b) whether there is more than health in the patient's utility function. Indeed agency in health economics seems very much a descriptive technique rather than an analytical tool. It remains (oddly) a black box, recognized as central but analytically largely empty. Certainly it has provided a basis for much of the work by health economists on supplier induced demand (SID). While this is important in the discussion of whether markets fail or not—perhaps the litmus test—there are two problems with SID (Mooney 1994a). First, it is empirically almost impossible to provide proof of its existence; and second, even if that could be done, it is doubtful if such proof would be especially useful in informing policy. This is simply because the question of SID is secondary to that of what incentives more generally are needed to get doctors to behave in ways that the community wants them to behave. It is *this* which is a major issue.

There are two forms of agency present for health care professionals, especially doctors—the individual patient/individual doctor and the doctor on behalf of some wider grouping—the functioning of both of which will depend, at least in part, on the financing arrangements. As Evans (1984) states: 'Optimal resource allocation requires the physician to act as agent, not only of her patient, but of the wider society as well.' What is interesting at this wider level is how little concerned health economists have been with what the objective(s) might be that doctors (and other health care professionals) are supposed to be pursuing for that wider society.

At the individual agency level there may again be a need to depart from more standard analyses. For example, Akerlof and Dickens (1982) have suggested that the application of cognitive dissonance theory within an economic model may help to explain certain economic behaviour better than standard models. They argue: 'First, persons not only have preferences over states of the world, but also over beliefs about states of the world. Second, persons have some control over their beliefs.' In health care the formation of beliefs and perhaps also preferences can almost certainly be influenced by the agent doctor. Cognitive dissonance theory thus raises questions how best to formulate agency in health care. There is a basis here for reappraising agency as it has to date been used in health economics not just at the individual level but (even more so) at the wider level as well, i.e. in terms of preferences for what health care systems are about.

Preference issues

There has been perhaps too little concern with problems of 'fuzziness' in the formulation of the preferences for health. In general there is little recognition of the context in which the agency relationship takes place. There is a need to link agency more formally to issues of need, the problems of ill-formed preferences, the ideas of Frankfurt (1971) of different levels or different orders of preferences (see Mooney 1998a) and how preferences in health care are formed. Just how need relates to such considerations as rights to health care and rights to health and to the notion of 'claims' (see below) also needs to be teased out.

Extra welfarism shares with welfarism the idea that tastes are given. In a more general context, Boulding (1969), in an AEA presidential address, disputes this: 'personal tastes are learned, in the matrix of a culture or a subculture in which we grow up, by very much the same kind of process by which we learn our common values. Purely personal tastes . . . can only survive in a culture which tolerates them, that is, which has a common value that private tastes of certain kinds should be allowed.'

He continues: 'One of the most peculiar illusions of economists is a doctrine that might be called the Immaculate Conception of the Indifference Curve, that is, that tastes are simply given, and that we cannot inquire into the process by which they are formed.' He suggests also that while too often economics ignores other values, such as 'the larger issues of malevolence and benevolence, the sense of community and so on', there is no technical reason why these values could not be embraced.

Boulding argues that there is a second criticism of the economic ethic. This one would appear to me to be yet more worrying. He states that, in making decisions, 'we are faced with two very different frameworks of judgement. The first of these is the economic ethic of total cost benefit analysis. It is an ethic of being sensible, rational, whatever we want to call it. It is an ethic of calculation . . . an ethic which depends on the development of measurement and numbers.' He continues: 'This type of decision making however does not exhaust the immense complexities of the human organisms and we have to recognize that there is in the world another type of decision making in which the decision maker effects something, not because of the effects that it will have, but because of what he "is", that is, how he perceives his own identity.' He concludes: 'The attack on economics is an attack on calculatedness.'

Much legitimate effort has gone into the development of the measurement of health status and in particular quality-adjusted life-years (QALYs). Unfortunately, measuring health seems largely to have precluded measuring almost all other possible outputs or outcomes of health services (although this is beginning to change—see for example Ryan 1998 and Salkeld 1998). QALYs are determined according to individuals' stated preferences for extensions of life vs. improved quality of life. The finer details of QALYs do not matter in the context of this chapter but two points do need to be made. First, individual preferences are used to elicit such weights. Second, when QALYs are used, then some averaging of the emerging preferences is made and variations in preferences for own health states are not allowed to count. (This is based on some 'external judgment' although it is not clear where this 'external judgment' comes from.) This means that in most instances it is assumed that a QALY is a QALY is a QALY. Work by Williams (1978), Nord (1994) and Mooney et al. (1999) has begun to question whether the weights attached to such QALYs might vary according to *social* preferences depending on who the recipients are (e.g. rich vs. poor).

Underlying such work and assumptions are two key questions: whether individual preferences are to count and, more fundamentally, whether society has a preference for such preferences to count. As Rice (1998) has put at least part of the question here: 'do people know what is good for them?', and implicitly asks: 'isn't it time we found out?' Yet more to the point perhaps is the question: do people want their preferences to count? Research by economists on this matter seems overdue. (One of my SPHERe colleagues, Virginia Wiseman, is about to investigate this in various different contexts.) If people as patients do not want their preferences over individual health care choices to count, does that not again pose the question of whether, nonetheless, people as a community might not as a minimum want to be involved in determining the decision rules or constitution which might be used to guide the allocation of health care resource allocation?

As Culyer (1989) acknowledges, extra-welfarism is based on some of the ideas from Sen. Culyer's interpretation of Sen's work, however, appears somewhat conservative and there is scope for taking yet more facets of Sen's theories and incorporating them more fundamentally in health economics. These aspects include his concepts of commitment and capabilities; his critique of utilitarianism and of consequentialism more generally; and especially the issue of some individuals' inability to manage desire adequately. Extra-welfarism also includes the notion of maximization of something. Sen (1992), however, expresses reservations about the attempted all-embracing pursuit of quantification. First, he argues against what he calls 'over-completeness', suggesting that '"waiting for toto" may not be a cunning strategy'. Second, it remains consequentialist. Third, there is no agreement (because the question is not asked) as to whose preferences are to count in determining the 'legitimate' objectives of any health care system or specific intervention. Originally extra-welfarism appeared 'monist' (to use the terminology of Hurley 1998), with only health being considered relevant, but a broader form of extra-welfarism now seems capable of incorporating more into the objective function of both patients and health care systems (Culyer 1998). Fourth, extra-welfarism does not reflect adequately on the social or community or—more fundamentally still—'communitarian' (see below) concepts of either health or health care. Fifth, it plays down the question of individuals' differing preferences and at the same time does not acknowledge the potential problems associated with overruling such individual preferences. (For example, *ceteris paribus*, people who attend for screening are likely to value their health differently from those who do not.)

Health economists have tended to assume or postulate objectives which, while they may seem eminently reasonable, are seldom validated. It is difficult to defend the idea that it is for health economists to set the objectives of the health services which we seek to evaluate. We may want to persuade and cajole others to set objectives. To progress far without that is problematical. Also, even if it is accepted that health services are about health—and that seems difficult to argue against!—there is a jump then in moving to argue (a) that they are about health *only* and (b) that they are about health *maximization*. While a quantifiable objective for the purposes of monitoring whether progress is occurring is desirable, it is less clear that such an operational goal should take precedence over what might otherwise be seen as the true goal—even if not quantifiable—of health services. There is a danger that the desire for quantification and supposed rigour becomes the thief of truth.

Looking forward

Communitarian claims

A non-consequentialist—it may be better to dub this 'beyond consequentialist'—approach is needed in reappraising the value base of health economics. Various possibilities are available. In the rest of this chapter I want to concentrate on just one: the notion of a constitution for health services. Leading into this is, I think, best done through 'communitarian claims' (Mooney 1998a), although other routes are possible. Communitarians, not surprisingly, place the community at the centre of their analyses and their value system. Community can be defined in various different ways but perhaps most satisfactorily as a group of people with some common life through reciprocal relationships. This can be a physical or geographical community but it can also be a professional one, a particular pressure group and, indeed, many social organizational structures would fit the definition of 'community' in communitarianism. Communitarians emphasize the social and community aspects of life, arguing in essence that life, identity and relationships are all communally based. Communitarianism is at odds with the atomism of modern liberalism and its idea of a 'disembodied' self. There is a value to the community per se and a value in being a part of—being embodied in—the community.

Communitarianism can be both prescriptive and descriptive. It is prescriptive in that it assumes that life will be better if we allow communitarian and public values to guide our lives. It is descriptive in the sense that communitarians believe that this social self is a truer reflection of how individuals actually are. In their understanding of the construction of society, communitarians reject both a bottom-up approach—an aggregation of atomistic discrete individuals—and a top-down one—an imposed authoritarian regime—on the grounds that both fail. Social institutions can be valued for themselves and not just for what they produce as outcomes or consequences.

With respect to the notion of claims, Broome (1991) has proposed that a claim to a good involves a duty that a candidate for that good should in fact have it. His analysis concentrates on claims as a basis for fairness. I have previously suggested (Mooney 1998a) that this notion can be extended to include concerns for both efficiency and fairness and that the concept of 'communitarian claims' may be helpful in deciding how best to allocate society's scarce resources in the specific context of health care. Such communitarian claims 'recognise first that the duty is owed by the community of which the candidate is a member and secondly that the carrying out of this duty is not just instrumental but is good in itself' (Mooney 1998b).

Anderson's expressive theory

The expressive theory of Anderson (1993) may also provide a useful base on which to build. She argues:

> An expressive theory defines rational action as action that adequately expresses our rational attitudes toward people and other intrinsically valuable things. According to the rational attitude theory of value, something is valuable if and only if it is rational for someone to value it, to assume a favorable attitude toward it. And to adequately care about something requires that one express one's valuations in the world, to embody them in some social reality. This is a demand of self-understanding.

Anderson suggests that the social aspect of the expressive theory

> reflects not a conventionalist but an anti-individualist theory of rationality. It claims that individuals are not self-sufficient bearers of practical reason: they require a context of social norms to express their attitudes adequately and intelligibly in action, to express them in ways others can grasp.

In her theory, as compared with consequentialist theories, she states that the latter 'recognize just one norm for action—that it maximize intrinsic value' while, by contrast, 'expressive theories recognize a wide variety of norms, which have several features that are puzzling from a consequentialist point of view: they are intentional, backward looking, distributive, and non-instrumental'.

What emerge from this theory are a number of important issues, three of which will be highlighted here as particularly germane to the value base of health economics. First, the idea of an expressive theory understands values in terms of what might be described as the embeddedness of communitarianism and the 'atmosphere' of the institutionalists. Second, and related to the first point, the theory is clearly non-consequentialist. Third, it supports the view that a greater element of democratization is needed than currently obtains in economic evaluation in health care (under the banner of either

CUA—cost-utility analysis—or CBA—cost-benefit analysis). Part of the problem here is that insufficient thought has been given to the value base of CBA when we allow for the presence of an agent in health care; it has been assumed that market failure is based only on information asymmetry and (as discussed earlier) these assumptions do not extend to take account of the problems of preferences—and indeed ill-formed or even unformed or unformulated preferences for health. A wider problem with CBA at present is that while many analysts are prepared to argue that greater democratization in the evaluation process would be 'a good thing', so that there could be more participation and also a possibility of extending the value base beyond simply an 'imposed' willingness-to-pay model, such an option is often dismissed as being too costly and too time consuming.

Institutionalist economics

The 'institutionalist' economics school appears to provide a basis for allowing Anderson's theory to be translated into practice. A suitable marriage is possible, as that institutionalist school echoes Anderson's theory (although it seems that they have not previously been linked in the literature). This is especially true with respect to the importance of process and context (or 'atmosphere' as Williamson 1975 calls it), i.e. that the institutions in which economic activity occurs are not to be considered neutral in the evaluative processes.

That branch of institutionalist economics which has been called 'constitutional economics' is highly pertinent. This is normally seen in the context of organizations where there is, as Vanberg (1994) describes it, 'an exchange of commitments among the contracting parties to accept certain constraints on their future choice options'. Even more directly relevant is what Vanberg calls the 'constitutional perspective'. This, he suggests, emphasizes 'the fact that two different aspects of the issue need to be separated: first, the question of to whom the organization's constitution assigns rights to take part in organizational decisions, and, second, the question of whose interests are de facto taken into account by those who are authorized to make organizational decisions'. He continues: 'The first question refers to the procedural rules by which decisions on organizational matters are made, in particular, decisions on how the pooled resources are to be used . . . The second question refers to the factual constraints faced by those who are entitled . . . to take part in organizational decisions.' (It is interesting to note here, given the recent tendency to refer to patients as 'customers' or 'consumers', that Vanberg argues that, in this context, 'the customers of a firm typically are not members of the organization and have no constitutional rights to be included in the firm's decision making process'. Yet, nevertheless, their interests are an obvious major constraint on those to whom the constitution of the firm assigns decision making rights.

Using communitarian claims accepts that more democracy is 'a good thing' but not necessarily concerning the whole value system or the whole set of values to be used. Rather, these claims can be used to allow a democratic setting of the principles of health care (essentially what it is that citizens or the community wants from its health service—as I have previously argued: Mooney 1994b). They can then be used as a guide for the policy makers to pursue the objectives and operational goals of the health service with whatever resources society puts at their disposal. Specifically on this point about the basis of social choice, Bergson (1954), one of the fathers of welfare economics states (a sentiment endorsed by Arrow 1963): 'the problem is to counsel not citizens generally but public officials . . . [The official's] one aim in life is to implement the values of other citizens as given by *some rules of collective decision making*' (emphasis added). This does not mean that citizens need to be asked to express their values or preferences for every public service good but, rather, to be involved in setting the rules for collective decision making or what I have described above as a constitution. The key here relates to the question that economists in welfare economics have been grappling with for generations, i.e. the nature of the social welfare function.

It would appear too that there is a basis here for a rational consideration of how best to fund health services. This is an issue that ought to be resolved *subsequent* to sorting out the objectives of health care and not, as seems too often to be the case, in Australia at least, *prior* to that debate and decision. I do not mean to suggest that there has been no work done in looking at what citizens might want from their health services—for example, in Australia the work of Nord and Richardson on this front is highly relevant (see, for example, Nord et al. 1995). That research is limited and in some other instances not well based. It is also the case that the questions of whether we can get at 'community' values, and whether (as, for example, communitarians would tend to argue) these are different from the aggregation of individual citizen values, are very much under-researched.

Individualism and community

The dominant paradigm in health economics remains individualistic, whether welfarist or extra-welfarist. For the former this needs no explanation, but for the latter it may. The extra-welfarist perspective is individualistic in the sense that individuals are approached in an individual context to indicate how they value different dimensions of health. Aggregation of these individual values does occur but only through some averaging procedure. The nearest one gets to a 'constitution' in this context is assumptions about the maximization of health: it is simply the sum of the parts. There is certainly some external notion that it is only health that is in the constitution and then, in turn, that health is to be maximized. It is not clear in extra-welfarism whence this posited 'constitution' is derived.

There can be little doubt that the only possible source of values, or at least of valuing, is people. I make this (possibly rather obvious) point because, since I embarked on critiquing health economics from this standpoint, I have met with puzzlement over some of my ideas. At least some of that puzzlement arises from a concern that I am arguing against the notion of people being the valuers.

The issue, however, is not whether people are to be the valuers. They must be. It is *which* people and, perhaps as important, *in what context*. The communitarian would argue for individuals being valuers as long as these individuals are allowed to reflect their history and their community (however they define them). Values, in other words, are context specific. (The quotes used at the beginning of this chapter attempt to reflect on this from, first, the perspective of liberal individualism—even atomism—expressed by Constant 1988 and, second, the more communitarian perspective of Rousseau 1968.)

Vanberg (1994) distinguishes between three paradigms in studying organizations: the exchange paradigm, the goal paradigm and the constitutional paradigm. The market is the best example of the exchange paradigm. On the goal paradigm (which is one that I have been tending to support in recent years but, I now think, perhaps somewhat inappropriately or unhelpfully), Vanberg makes the following point:

> What gives the [goal] paradigm its apparent plausibility is probably the fact that it is for us the natural and unquestioned way of interpreting the actions of an individual human actor. Just as we take it for granted that a person's actions can be understood in terms of his or her goals we are inclined to suppose that organized collective action can equally be understood in terms of goals pursued by such action. Yet, whatever may be said about the fruitfulness of the goal paradigm in the study of individual human behaviour . . . it is of questionable value when applied to organized collective action . . . The seemingly solid agreement on the relevance of the concept [in the relevant literature] appears to become meaningless as more serious efforts are made to specify its content . . . Advocates of the 'goal paradigm' seem to face a dilemma: they insist that the concept of an organizational goal is indispensable, but are unable to define clearly the concept without reifying the organization.

Of late I have tended to advocate the setting of goals. Increasingly, however, I recognize that such setting is certainly difficult and perhaps almost impossible for health services—at least on an informed and rational basis. The constitutional paradigm takes as its value base the idea of 'the procedural foundations that organizational action is based upon'. This shifts the emphasis away from the setting of goals, and also allows the community to be involved with a relatively low information base in determining, according to their preferences, the social rules on which the policy makers are to run the service.

It is worth quoting Buchanan and Vanberg (1994) at length on informational requirements, as it is this essentially empirical matter that is, perhaps, most commonly put forward as a reason for not going down the road of eliciting the values from the community:

> As one moves from collective choice among alternative constitutions, to collective choice among constitutional experts to, finally, individual choice among alternative constitutional arrangements, not only are the informational requirements for an intelligent choice dramatically reduced, the individual's incentives for making an informed choice significantly increase. While it may be very difficult to predict reliably the working properties of alternative constitutional rules, and also difficult to assess the true competence of constitutional experts, individuals will have fewer difficulties in assessing the relevant working properties of actually operating constitutional systems. And as they individually and separately choose their own 'constitutional environment' they also have much more reason to make an informed choice, compared to their participation in a collective choice among constitutional rules or among constitutional experts.

We have here a way out of the dilemma of wanting to bring public preferences into health service decision making without all the complexities and costs of an Athenian-style democracy. We can use the community voice to set the constitution and leave the 'experts' to operationalize the constitution.

Where the dividing line comes is at best fuzzy. What is covered by the operationalization experts is in a sense the 'nitty gritty' of policy. What constitutes the nitty gritty needs to be established in the constitution. It is interesting to note, when set out like this, that so little work has been done by economists in looking at the context of preferences in health care—especially in the area of health status valuation where most work on valuing has been done. There is some, especially in the work of Nord (1994) and in the more general, if limited, research on the relationship between objective and subjective measures of health, where context—especially social context—is brought into the equation.

Again, the issue of the context in which individuals might want their values to count is too little researched. The question of when individuals' or community preferences are to count is best determined by the individuals or the community. In SPHERe we are currently planning a study which will do two things. First, it will examine whether individuals in different contexts want their preferences and the community's preferences to count.

Second, in the light of what these preferences are, the individuals and the community will again be asked if and when they want the community's preferences to count. It is studies like these that will assist in determining what is 'constitutional' and what is 'operational'.

There is a 'fudging' in what I have said so far in this chapter, with regard to any distinction between community and the aggregation of individuals. It is my hypothesis that, ideally, the community is defined as more than simply the sum of its parts. Yet, while I suspect that many would agree, the question of how to elicit and measure community preferences remains at best unresolved. The worry is that it is unresolvable.

There is a prior question. What do we mean by community? It is noteworthy that economists all too seldom address this question. When we do, we restrict our efforts to some rather simplistic 'economies of one', or a Benthamite social welfare function which is simply the sum of the parts where each counts as one. If we look at other social sciences and, indeed, other disciplines the situation is different. A central plank of philosophy lies in balancing the claims of the individual with those of society; the raison d'être of sociology seems to lie in the same question. Social work attempts to deal not only with the problems of individual clients but also with the society which creates those problems. Health promotion recognizes the tension between individual risk-factor interventions and risk conditions as they arise in society (Shiell and Hawe 1996).

Amir Ahmadi (1999) argues that because of the functional differentiation of social life and the extreme specialization of social roles, it has become more and more difficult for individuals to identify with intermediate groupings (such as communities). He suggests that it may be less apposite to speak of 'communities of values' than of 'communities of causes'. While I believe it is too early to forsake the notion of a 'community of values', seeing health services as a cause has a certain appeal to it.

In the context in which I seek to use the term 'community', the definition —or, more accurately, clarification—of community by Alan Shiell and Penny Hawe (1996) goes a long way towards what I seek, even if not the whole way. Nonetheless this chapter is not the place to dwell overly on the precise definition of community. Shiell and Hawe suggest that there is a need to

> recognise the communitarian view that community relations are a feature of individual identity and well-being. Community means more than association or shared location. It also means more than the inclusion of interpersonal effects (externalities) in the individuals' utility function. The intrinsic and not just the instrumental value of social relationships is important.

How to capture this wider view of community, to elicit the preferences of such a community and to measure such preferences I will leave for another day. I could argue this on grounds of space. The reality, however, is that, as yet, I have no idea how to go about it. There is a potentially helpful body of literature. The question that worries me in this context is, quite simply: how will I or anyone else know when we have captured community preferences?

In any analysis of the community and the individual, the question of the position (and protection?) of individual rights is likely to arise. This, in the context of a communitarian value basis for health care, will be the subject of a later paper. Suffice it to say here that, generally, any system of rights restricts the unilateral power of the state or other social institution. To achieve this there is a need for a constitution, an independent judiciary, bicameral legislation or something of that ilk. Health services are strangely devoid of, and even deny, the need for such an institution to protect individual rights.

Constitutionalism

The implications of a constitutional approach are potentially many. We can see some of this in the work of Stone (1993). She writes of the differences between social and commercial insurance as follows: 'Social insurance operates by the logic of solidarity. Its purpose is to guarantee that certain agreed-upon individual needs will be paid for by a community or group.' With private insurance the logic is different. 'Those who are sick and need care would come forward to purchase it, but among the sick, only those who could afford it would actually receive care . . . People who could not afford to buy care would not receive any, regardless of their need for it or ability to benefit from it.'

Such a distinction, which readers might take as so obvious as not to require making, nonetheless raises an important question: How do we choose between these two? Which needs are to be insured against in social insurance? How and by whom are they to be 'agreed upon'? While over the years we have as a sub-discipline argued forcefully (especially Culyer 1995 and Williams 1978) about the meaning and value of the concept of need, beyond the designation of the valuer as a 'third party' the who-is-to-agree-upon-need question is not asked and certainly not answered. It would be the job of the constitution to answer these questions and then to help to decide what formulation of health care system and institutions a society might seek to embrace.

My SPHERe colleague Stephen Jan (1998) has examined the merits of a more holistic approach to economic evaluation which is in essence constitutionally based. He argues that 'broader "non-health" factors ultimately alter the social environment of the community in which these programs are set and, in turn, impact on health'. Jan gives the example, taken from Evans and Stoddart (1990), whereby genetic endowment, physical environment and individual response, as well as the social environment, are incorporated as relevant attributes in the evaluation.

Jan's work is aimed primarily at the issues involved in attempting to use economic evaluation in a different culture, in this case the culture of Aboriginal Australians. He writes of one study examining a screening programme for otitis media in Aboriginal infants. In addition to the impact on the hearing of children, he claims that 'two other potential outcomes were the training and employment given to the Aboriginal health worker and the window of access into the health care system provided to the mothers and families affected by the service'. He adds: 'Importantly such sources of value were defined by the type of existing problems faced by the community rather than being assumed beforehand.'

Shiell, Hawe and Seymour (1997) endorse the views of 'some health economists, most notably Erik Nord, who [have] suggested that respondents should be told of the policy implications of the answers they give and allowed to revise their answers accordingly'. They go on to argue that 'the process of values elicitation can be used to help respondents construct their preferences in the first place'. While these authors are dealing with ex post considerations or, at most, concurrent ones, the equivalent ex ante might be seen as a constitution. It is thus possible to see the idea of a constitution as being a form of preference formation and elicitation.

All of this makes life messy for health economist researchers, although I doubt that it does for health policy makers who, in my limited experience of exposing such ideas to them, seem to take some comfort from them. We lose some rigour or—more accurately, and not the same thing—some powers of quantification in adopting this constitutional road. Largely, such a loss is due to the decreased neatness of the 'objective function' that is then likely to emerge. Of course, health will be there in the health care constitution. That is what society expects. But I suspect they want more than simply health, and the only way—the only legitimate way—to find this out is to ask them. Amir Ahmadi (1999) has suggested that there is a need for citizens to 'lay siege' (Habermas 1997) to the existing institutional machinery, not so as to take it over, but in order to influence its decision making criteria and processes.

A constitutional context matters. As Jan describes the context for his holistic approach: 'a number of themes are constructed out of possibly disparate sources of evidence, e.g. previous case studies, survey data, personal observation. Such themes are then meshed into patterns into which the evaluator seeks to build a holistic picture of reality.' Wilber and Harrison (1978), however, draw attention to the fact that this 'technique of contextual validation can never produce the rigorous certainty espoused by logical positivists'.

There is a sense in which we have allowed quantification to drive our analyses in health economics. There is a need to rethink and 'to let the question drive the analysis', as Hurley (1998) has suggested, 'rather than simply imposing a pre-determined framework and making the question fit the framework in procrustean fashion'. By implication, Hurley is stating that *we*—health economists—have pre-determined the question. This is not to oppose the rigour provided through quantifiability. Nor is it to argue that what has been valued and quantified to date by health economists has been a waste of our time. Rather, it is to make the case for establishing a constitution which then sets up the questions that we as health economists (as well as others) need to address.

Preliminary empirical work

Within SPHERe we have begun some preliminary work to investigate this notion of a constitution. To date we have mostly looked at policy makers' interpretation of what the community understands by 'constitution,' although in one instance we have looked beyond at community preferences. I would like to report on tentative findings to date.

We have attempted to work with health policy makers at various levels in the Australian health care system—at state, area, general practice and hospital levels. At the state level in South Australia (SA) a questionnaire was issued to the senior members of the Health Commission (the state health department). The results of that questionnaire were used as a basis for building, with the same staff, a workshop discussion on the subject of a constitution, or what were described as principles for setting the direction for purchasing health services (given that South Australia was adopting a form of purchaser–provider split).

Two key things emerged from these discussions. First, given the opportunity to discuss the idea of a constitution for the SA health services, the participants grabbed it with both hands. There was a stimulating debate. In their evaluation of the process, the participants indicated that just to have the debate was in itself very worthwhile. Second, an agreed set of principles emerged. Leaving aside the details, it was clear from these principles that the group wanted more than some simple health maximization. They wanted equality of access (i.e. equal opportunity to use services), where access was defined in terms of the perceived height of barriers, and they wanted to weight health gains to some recipients above health gains to others. They wanted more than health gains: for example, respect for the autonomy and dignity of patients. They wanted to be seen to be making wise and transparent decisions on behalf of the community. And they wanted, ideally, that the community's preferences be used to establish the principles of the constitution—perhaps the most fundamental part of the constitution concerns who should establish it.

A similar exercise has been used with a committee concerned with the guidance to general practitioner divisions in Australia (where such divisions provide the glue for individual practices and individual practitioners in a geographical area). Results here are not available at the time of writing.

In South Australia we have also conducted a community survey using conjoint analysis to elicit individuals' preferences for health services, both at a hospital level and at a general practitioner level (Mooney et al. 1999). Here we distinguished between the preferences of individuals as individuals, and individuals in the role of state planners. As before, we will not focus on the details. There was, however, support for the principle of equity—not only horizontal equity, but also vertical equity. This was to be applied to groups which differed by age, existing health status, socio-economic status, smoking status or Aboriginality. The following was also relevant at the level of principles: the questionnaire which investigated vertical equity indicated that those randomly given information about the very poor health status of Aborigines attributed greater weight to health gains in this group than did those who were not given this information (although the difference was not statistically significant). There is clearly a need to ensure that any use of preferences, for the purpose of establishing principles, is informed. Among other principles that emerged were: keeping costs low at the point of consumption, and targeting those people with greater health problems.

We are continuing this process in general practice in Sydney. We are also planning to develop the work in different contexts—including individual hospitals and all the health services for a community of about 25,000.

Conclusion

The key point of this chapter is that there is a need to build a more comprehensive framework as a value base for health economics. For those who agree that the market fails, bits of that framework are there, but it is somewhat patchy and needs more cohesion. There are holes to be plugged but also a need for some overarching theory.

I have concentrated on the idea of a constitution for health services, arguing that the exchange paradigm of the market needs to be replaced with either a goals paradigm or a constitutional paradigm. While defining the goals or objectives of health services is important, it seems that too little progress has been made in that direction. Better, perhaps, to settle initially for the setting of a constitution, out of which operational goals might follow. A constitution has the added advantage that the community can express its preferences for what goes into it. This retains an important element of community involvement or democracy, without getting into the costs and repercussions of an Athenian-style democracy in health care. Much remains to be done, not least in establishing where the constitution ends and the operational concerns begin.

Acknowledgements

I am grateful to SPHERe colleagues—Amir Ahmadi, Steve Jan, Glenn Salkeld, Alan Shiell and Virginia Wiseman—for comments on an earlier draft of this paper.

References

Ahmadi, A. (1999) Personal communication.

Akerlof, G.A. and Dickins, W.T. (1982) The economic consequences of cognitive dissonance, *American Economic Review* 72: 309–319.

Anderson, E. (1993) *Value in Ethics and Economics*, Cambridge MA: Harvard University Press.

Arrow, K. (1963) *Social Choice and Individual Values*, New York: Wiley.

Bergson, A. (1954) On the concept of social welfare, *Quarterly Journal of Economics* 68: 233–252.

Boulding, K.E. (1969) Economics as a moral science, *American Economic Review* 59(1): 1–12.

Brennan, G. and Buchanan, J.M. (1985) *The Reason of Rules—Constitutional Political Economy*, Cambridge: Cambridge University Press.

Broome, J. (1991) *Weighing Goods*, Oxford: Blackwell.

Buchanan, J.M. (1986) *Liberty, Market and State: Political Economy in the 1980s*, New York: New York University Press.

Buchanan, J.M. and Vanberg, V.J. (1994) Constitutional choice, rational ignorance and the limits of reason, in V.J. Vanberg (ed.) *Rules and Choice in Economics*, London: Routledge.

Constant, B. (1988) *Liberty of the Ancients Compared with That of the Moderns*, Political Writings, Cambridge: Cambridge University Press.

Culyer, A. (1989) The normative economics of health care finance and provision, *Oxford Review of Economic Policy* 5: 34–58.

—— (1995) Need, the idea won't do, but we still need it, *Social Science and Medicine* 40: 727–730.

—— (1998) How ought health economists to treat value judgments in their analyses? in M.L. Barer, T.E. Getzen and G.L. Stoddart (eds) *Health, Health Care and Health Economics. Perspectives in Distribution*, Toronto: Wiley.

Evans, R.G. (1984) *Strained Mercy*, Toronto: Butterworth.

—— (1998) Toward a healthier economics, in M.L. Barer, T.E. Getzen, and G.L. Stoddart (eds) *Health, Health Care and Health Economics. Perspectives in Distribution*, Toronto: Wiley.

Evans, R.G. and Stoddart, G.L. (1990) Producing health and consuming health care, *Social Science and Medicine* 31: 347–363.

Frankfurt, H. (1971) Weakness of the will and the concept of a person, *Journal of Philosophy* 68: 5–20.

Fuchs, V. (1996) Economics, values, and health care reform, *American Economic Review* 86: 1–24.

Habermas, J. (1997) Interview on questions of political theory, in Habermas, *A Berlin Republic*, Lincoln, NE: University of Nebraska Press.

Hausman, D.M. and McPherson, M.S. (1993) Taking ethics seriously: economics and contemporary moral philosophy, *Journal of Economic Literature* 31: 671–731.

Hurley, J. (1998) Welfarism, extra-welfarism and evaluative economic analysis in the health sector, in M.L. Barer, T.E. Getzen, and G.L. Stoddart (eds) *Health, Health Care and Health Economics. Perspectives in Distribution*, Toronto: Wiley.

Jan, S. (1998) A holistic approach to the economic evaluation of health programs using institutional methodology, *Social Science and Medicine* 47(10): 1565–1572.

Kemp, M.C. and Asimakopulos, A. (1952) A note on 'social welfare functions' and cardinal utility, *Canadian Journal of Economics and Political Science* 18: 195–200.
Margolis, H. (1982) *Selfishness, Altruism and Rationality*, Cambridge: Cambridge University Press.
Mooney, G. (1994a) *Key Issues in Health Economics*, Hemel Hempstead: Wheatsheaf.
—— (1994b) What else do we want from our health services? *Social Science and Medicine* 39: 151–154.
—— (1998a) 'Communitarian claims' as an ethical basis for allocating health care resources, *Social Science and Medicine* 47(9): 1171–1180.
—— (1998b) Economics, communitarianism and health care, in M.L. Barer, T.E. Getzen, and G.L. Stoddart (eds) *Health, Health Care and Health Economics. Perspectives in Distribution*, Toronto: Wiley.
Mooney, G., Jan, S., Ryan, M., Bruggemann, K., and Alexander, K. (1999) What the community prefers, what it values, what health care it wants. A survey of South Australians, Sydney: SPHERe, Department of Public Health and Community Medicine, University of Sydney.
Nord, E. (1994) The person trade-off approach to valuing health care programs, *Medical Decision Making* 15: 201–208.
Nord, E., Richardson, J., Street, A., Kuhse, H., and Singer, P. (1995) Maximising health benefits versus egalitarianism: an Australian survey of health issues, *Social Science and Medicine* 41: 1429–1437.
Reinhardt, U. (1992) Reflections on the meaning of efficiency: can efficiency be separated from equity? *Yale Law and Policy Review* 10: 302–315.
Rice, T. (1998) *The Economics of Health Reconsidered*, Health Administration Press, Chicago.
Rousseau, J.-J. (1968) Letter to M. D'Alembert on the theatre, in J.-J. Rousseau, *Politics and the Arts*, Ithaca NY: Cornell University Press.
Ryan, M. (1998) Using conjoint analysis to go beyond health outcomes: an application to in vitro fertilisation, *Social Science and Medicine* 48: 535–546.
Salkeld, G. (1998) What are the benefits of preventive health care? *Health Care Analysis* 6: 106–112.
Sen, A. (1985a) *Commodities and Capabilities*, Amsterdam: North-Holland.
—— (1985b) Ethics and economics, *Social Philosophy and Policy* 2: 2.
—— (1992) *Inequality Re-examined*, Oxford: Clarendon Press.
Shiell, A. and Hawe, P. (1996) Health promotion, community development and the tyranny of individualism, *Health Economics* 5: 241–247.
Shiell, A., Hawe, P., and Seymour, J. (1997) Values and preferences are not necessarily the same, *Health Economics* 6: 515–518.
Smith, A. (1776) *The Wealth of Nations*, Edinburgh.
—— (1759) *Theory of Moral Sentiments*, Edinburgh.
Stone, D. (1993) The struggle for the soul of health insurance, *Journal of Health, Politics and Law* 187(2): 287–317.
Titmuss, R. (1971) *The Gift Relationship: From Human Blood to Social Policy*, New York: Random House.
Vanberg, V.J. (ed.) (1994) *Rules and Choice in Economics*, London: Routledge.
Wilber, C.K. and Harrison, R.S. (1978) The methodological basis of institutionalist economics: pattern model, story telling and holism, *Journal of Economic Issues* 12: 61–89.

Williams, A. (1978) 'Need'—an economic exegesis, in A.J. Culyer and K. Wright (eds) *Economic Aspects of Health Services*, London: Martin Robertson.
Williamson, O. (1975) *Markets and Hierarchies: Analysis and Antitrust Implications*, New York: Free Press.

3

SOCIAL CHOICE AS THE SYNTHESIS OF INCOMMENSURABLE CLAIMS

The case of health care rationing[1]

Paul Anand

Introduction: rationing in the UK

Economics (and its literature applied to health) is—or used to be—fundamentally consequentialist. As a result, economists, with growing exceptions,[2] and support from philosophy, tend to be concerned about states of affairs and less concerned about process issues, except to the extent that free choice is instrumental in bringing about desirable states of affairs. Those who have advocated the use of the QALY (quality-adjusted life-years) maximization rule have, however, been advocates of explicitness as well: their argument was that implicit rationing led to an allocation of health care that was not consistent with normative criteria, a point on which philosophers might be expected to agree. Indeed, one might see QALY proponents as advocates of a more extensive approach to the use of explicit normative criteria—the principle is not new as explicit statistical formulae are already used to establish a measure of geographical equity in the distribution of funds in the UK.

The Oregon experiment in explicit rationing with all its pitfalls and subsequent modifications is now (in)famous, but the UK experience is also interesting. Rationing is said not to be explicit in the UK and certainly is not co-ordinated at the national level, but the introduction of the NHS internal market has provided an opportunity for priorities to be set more explicitly. Within the system as it operated until recently, health authorities were given fixed annual budgets which they used to purchase health care on behalf of populations within their geographically specified catchment areas. The move to an explicit purchasing system necessitated that consideration was given to what was purchased and why. Potentially, this was a golden opportunity for advocates of explicit rationing, though an examination of

Table 3.1 Numbers of health authorities planning to ration by treatment

Rationed treatment	*Possible rationale*
Cosmetic plastic surgery (9), varicose veins (4)	Health care need
Homeopathy (3), alternative therapies (3)	Effectiveness
Reversal of sterilization (7), reversal of vasectomy (6)	Patient choice
Gender reassignment (5)	Minority voter support
Assisted conception (5)	Weakness of claims rights
Dental implants (3) removal of asymptomatic un-erupted wisdom teeth (2), aesthetic orthodontics (2)	Unclassified

Note
The figures in parentheses indicate the number of health authorities, out of a sample of 66, who were planning to withdraw purchasing support for patients with the conditions mentioned.

sixty-six health authority purchasing plans in Redmayne (1995) suggests that change was limited. In Table 3.1 we summarize the numbers of health authorities indicating that they would not be purchasing certain kinds of treatments. We have excluded a longer list of treatments that were going to be cut by only one health authority on the basis that they are statistical outliers.

The evidence shows just how few health authorities were excluding classes of treatment and just how few classes are excluded. On the right hand side of the table, we have postulated some possible justifications for these exclusions. For each case, there is a possible normative justification but the *overall* picture suggests that treatments have been selected for cutting where there might be least effective 'political' support either from the population at large or from within the medical profession. If this interpretation is correct, it may be that the implicit approach to rationing is allowing the wrong sort of preferences to be taken into account—i.e. ones which exist but have inappropriate moral significance (Dolan, Cookson and Ferguson 1999).

Some people have argued that implicit rationing would better suit the NHS approach to decision making but the evidence seems to suggest that, without formal criteria, there could be little change and much of that would be ineffective. Even if rationing could be effected in an implicit way, the question needs asking as to how we should evaluate different implicit rationing schemes, or help those operating them. Our argument is based on the idea that rationing does, and should, reflect different types of moral claims which, because resources are scarce, are in competition with each other. The integration of these different kinds of moral claims is the fundamental problem facing those who want to calculate who is entitled to what. However, this observation leads to the view that it is the integrative, some call it synthetic, task of which we need an account. Most theories in economics and philosophy, by contrast, currently provide us with an account of one aspect of this task.

The structure of the rest of the chapter runs as follows. In the second section we draw on ideas from decision analysis and philosophy of science to make a distinction between the QALY as a measure, and QALY maximization as a decision rule. We develop the idea that objections to the QALY approach are often most naturally thought of as objections to the decision rule (QALY maximization) as well as the consequentialist foundations which underpin it. The third section surveys a shortlist of non-consequentialist claim types which, we argue, specify concerns that should be taken into account when setting health care priorities. We note also that at conceptual and practical levels, the QALY measure can be used to indicate when some of these claims have not been met. In the fourth section we examine the question of description in a formal sense, which is a primary concern to economic theorists. We develop a simple, but new *non*-linear programming model and show that the kind of non-consequential claims surveyed can indeed be incorporated into a formal model designed to assist in the setting of health care priorities. The fifth section introduces a survey designed to explore voter support for the normative ideas previously discussed. In the sixth section we present the results of a number of statistical analyses of the survey data, while section seven offers some summary remarks.

Remarks on the conceptual framework

It is common to hear reference to the 'QALY approach'. Sometimes this is helpful, but it is useful for our purposes to acknowledge that this is an abbreviation which obscures an important distinction. On the one hand, the QALY measure is a measure of health gain. There are different proposals for how this measure should, in practice, be constructed, but these differences are ones that concern only the metric of benefit. There is also a second sense in which the term has come to be associated with the idea that we should set health care priorities so as to maximize the sum of the benefits. This use alludes to a decision rule, as opposed to a measure, and any serious discussion does need to recognize this distinction—the literature appears to be divided into pro- and anti-QALY camps, in which the distinction receives short shrift. It is perfectly possible to advocate the use of the measure and the decision rule at the same time, but this is not necessary. For example, one might think that the measure of benefit was normatively correct but that sum maximization across people was not appropriate because it is blind to the distribution of benefits. Such a move is, for example, part of a standard argument against utilitarianism and it is worth keeping track of the reasons why particular theories are rejected when we are interested in moving on to develop theories that are improvements.

There is also a potential source of confusion because it seems acceptable to talk about weighted QALY maximization as if this were just another, more general form of QALY maximization.[3] The justification is that the weighting process adds little to the mathematical formulation: mathematically the point is correct. However, it is not obvious that one should closely tie theories to their mathematical structure, even in economics. For example, decision theorists do not now say that all violations of subjected expected utility theory can be interpreted within the expected utility framework. Rather they have sought to provide non-expected utility models of violations of expected utility. My preference, and it has to be only that as we are talking about choice between conventions, is to say that weighted QALY maximization, whether it is appealing or not, represents quite a different decision rule, mathematical similarities notwithstanding. To maximize QALYs weighting children under 2 at zero is going to lead to a very different health care system to that suggested by unweighted QALY maximization, for instance. Such a rule is more in keeping with insights generated by quite different, non-utilitarian philosophies. In what follows, we shall find two ways in which the measure-rule distinction is helpful. To anticipate, it is possible to show that the QALY *measure* is more consistent with non-consequentialist *decision rules* than has been suggested hitherto. Furthermore, the formal framework of maximization we show to be capable of incorporating a significant range of non-consequentialist issues.

The second set of distinctions that needs to be made concerns the link between QALYs, utilitarianism and consequentialism. In the past, some health economists have viewed QALY maximization as the application of utilitarianism in the health field. Clearly a QALY is not a measure of desire satisfaction, so a simple equation is not possible. Utilitarianism and QALY maximization are both sum maximizing social choice rules, but there are differences that show the two doctrines to be more distant relatives than their common maximizing ancestry might indicate. For one thing, it is fundamental to the logic of the utilitarian doctrine that we take account of all preferences when evaluating a state. Typically, and by contrast, the QALY maximization rule depends on a more constrained informational input that derives from the expected health care gain of the patient him- or herself. Furthermore, estimates of QALY potential in a patient are reasonably objective and therefore offer the promise of social agreement between citizens and the state. Utilities, and interpersonal comparisons of utility more so, are inherently subjective and make a poor basis for solving social conflicts over scarce resources, even if one does not accept the extreme position which holds interpersonal comparisons of utility to be impossible.

In some senses, the QALY is better off for being the distant cousin of utilitarianism, but it does appear to be a species of consequentialism. However, consequentialism itself is subject to a number of profound inadequacies and these, we suggest, apply in health as they do elsewhere. The fact that QALY maximization fails to deal with issues of equity because it is insensitive to distributive fairness questions has been noted elsewhere and extensively (for example Wagstaff 1991). Being sensitive to distribution does not, however, require a rejection of consequentialism. Here, we want to draw attention to a number of issues, beyond distributive equity and related to lacunae in consequentialism which also need to be reflected in the rationing algorithm.

What needs to be integrated

The main part of our proposal has its roots in Amartya Sen's critique of conventional welfare economics and his development of an alternative, so-called capability rights theory, in which he offers a theory of social choice that integrates consequences and deontology. However, we want to suggest that the integration of needs in health care priority setting might be even more extensive than Sen's theory indicates. Specifically, we want to claim that a complete account of the rationing process needs to integrate five types of moral claims: consequences, social contracts, rights, votes and community values. The notion of claim types proposed is close to the discussion of claims in health care prioritization that can be found in Mooney (1998). However, the list proposed here implicitly suggests a role for, and conception of, theoretical discussion about the integrative project which is slightly different to that which has prevailed in the literature up to now. One way of putting this is to say that our proposal suggests that theorists should think not about the arguments for and against theories of particular claim types but more about the way in which these different claim types should be incorporated into the overall rationing scheme. In the discussion that follows, it should be remembered that we are advocating a decision rule which integrates these different claim types but which includes consequences and which provides, as a result, a role for the QALY measure. As we allow—with the QALY camp—that benefits and costs should play a role in the integrative project, we move on to consider the four remaining issues that stand outside consequentialism.

Social contracts

Within welfare economics and moral philosophy, one of the most interesting, analytical innovations in recent times has been Rawls' development of the counterfactual social contract. In a sense, the QALY maximization rule depends for its support on a similar distancing from one's own known needs. If everyone were to pursue their own self-interest they would argue for the profile of health treatments most likely to benefit them directly or otherwise. On the other hand, the QALY maximization rule suggests that some people—the old, and those who are unable to generate many health care benefits for instance—should abstract from their own known position in life and accept the QALY maximization rule. Indeed, it has always been a part of the QALY maximization story that many elderly people would support the rule, and that it was possible to drive a wedge between preferences for the design of the health system on the one hand, and personal self-interest on the other. Perhaps the elderly were expected to say to themselves: '*If we had* sat down and talked this through from the start, we would have *agreed* that a health care system which maximizes health is best.'

Whether this is appealing or not, we should note that there are actual social contracts that have been made by politicians with members of the public, and that these carry considerable weight with those who expect the state to do something for them, as a result. The question of residential-care funding exemplifies this: many of the growing number of elderly people for whom residential care is necessary do not see what grounds there are for making individuals pay, if they can. They remember an actual social contract neatly summarized by the phrase 'from cradle to grave' used at the time of NHS's establishment, some fifty years ago. These people would seem to have a point. They have paid taxes and crucially not invested in private health care insurance on the basis that the system would look after them in old age. Some people say that the general taxation system is not a savings scheme, but it does make intergenerational transfers and no government, up to now, has advocated that people should make provision for such care in old age.

Social contracts rarely have explicit termination dates but it is still unrealistic to think of them as never being subject to change. Further, they tend to be difficult to enforce, but this is a general problem that the public sector must address, if it is to survive. If promises made on behalf of the state are not enforceable, the public sector is undermined and this can only be the aim of a state determined to wither away, as Marx or Nozick (1974) have indicated. The basic point is that even if QALYs—or healthy year equivalents (HYEs) for that matter—measure health gain, their maximization must be tempered by an acceptance that some contingent, temporally specific aims are also legitimate.

Rights

The right of all members of society to adequate health care is one that is recognized almost universally.[4] However, even if we accept this fundamental right, experience suggests it does not take us very far in setting priorities within society. It tells us nothing about what proportion of resources should go on health care and little about how those funds should be distributed. The problem with rights is that of chronic under-determination. Allowing that people might have rights to health care—see for instance Buchanan (1984)—doesn't tell us very much about what precisely it is they are entitled to.

The literature has also allowed the suggestion—that rights and QALYs are incompatible—to persist. If we make a clear distinction between the rule and the measure, then it is apparent that this is not necessarily so. For example, we could monitor the expected QALYs different ethnic groups achieve for different kinds of treatments: evidence of much lower expected QALYs might indicate that the rights to equal treatment and/or access were being challenged. This is a simple point which undercuts the opposition between consequentialism and deontology at the practical level—the informational basis suggested by one can play a major role in monitoring the success of the other. In practical settings, where social decision making is driven by the information available, it is helpful to run through the impact on information systems that different conceptual frameworks will have. Note also that even though consequentialism and deontology may draw on the same kinds of information, the impact in terms of priority setting could be reversed depending on which conceptual framework one supports. In the consequentialist framework, expected QALYs are used to direct health care resources to those who could generate most benefit. In a deontological framework, expected QALYs can be used to highlight pockets of need and move resources in an opposite direction. We suggest that even most of those in the QALY camp would say that black people should not suffer fewer opportunities to health care for similar conditions because they have a lower life expectancy, which in return results naturally from lower incomes. Many people would find taking the differential QALY benefits an infringement of black and white rights to equal treatment.

Votes

The study of social choice in economics is centred around issues to do with the aggregation of preferences and the analysis of voting behaviour, and it is easy to show that the QALY maximization rule will not, in general, be consistent with basic rules like majority voting. For example, assume a healthy population in which the life expectancy is the same for all members at some time, t. The population can be partitioned into two groups, *a* and *b* (of size n(*a*) and n(*b*) where n(*b*) is greater), depending on the ages at which some life-threatening but completely curable disease strikes its members, y(*a*) and y(*b*) respectively. Suppose that y(*a*) is less than y(*b*): then QALY maximization will recommend treating all of group *a* first before moving on to treat group *b* members. However, majority voting (by rational egoists) yields the opposite result. So QALY maximization is incompatible with majority voting, and in many situations we think that majority voting is the proper way to determine social choices.

However, we argue that the choice between votes and QALYs is not dichotomous—it isn't an either/or kind of problem. For example, some voters might think that there should be less support for gender reassignment because they don't approve of homosexuals and lesbians and think such operations are somehow part of the deviant approaches to sexuality of which they disapprove. Given the evidence in Redmayne (1995), this is not fanciful, and yet there seems to be a perspective from which we might think that such votes should not be counted. Explicit rules and guidelines might well rule the inclusion of prejudice-based voter intentions out of consideration and indeed even voters who held such views might not realistically expect that they would be taken into account. Part of a full account of the rationing process will, therefore, have to say something about when we do, and when we don't, take votes into account. For that reason, we are not faced with a straight either/or choice—in this sense, we can think of integration as involving, inter alia, a decision about when certain things should be considered, and when they should not. In other words, votes pose a challenge for the designers of a decision rule (or process), not the QALY measure.

Increasingly, expectations concerning public consultation and deliberation mediate the relative weight given to expertise, and lay preferences about many social choices. In many areas of science and medicine this is well accepted. For example, work by psychologists on the acceptance of hazards in particular areas has shown that narrow sender-receiver models of risk communication are giving way to more broadly based models of communication in which risks are the subject of public deliberation where experts and policy makers both listen and talk. Complementing this, work by Swiss economists shows that in the location of nuclear waste facilities, negotiation receives support from over 70 per cent of the population, while measurements of economic value (like minimum reservation prices) receive support from only 20 per cent of the population (Oberholzer-Gee et al. 1997). Further, survey evidence suggests that UK voters find the fairest procedures are those that *combine* technical (economic and scientific) expertise with some form of public consultation. Currently, views about the significance we should attach to expert opinion are changing and this has implications for the social deliberative processes that people find acceptable. When it comes to health care rationing in the UK, the evidence seems to be that many voters still place considerable faith in medical judgment. Perhaps they do not value transparency as highly as the public sector reform rhetoric about transparency suggests they do or should, and perhaps the American public sector experience lends some support to their scepticism.

Communitarianism

Many of the insights that communitarians pull together might be handled in the building blocks we have tried to identify here. However, their views are sufficiently distinctive, novel and in some sense holistic that it is worth giving attention to them without parcelling those views out. Key to this approach is that individual identity has an important social element and that communities, real social communities, play an important role in social choice (Bell 1993; Etzioni 1995). For example, there are societies in which respect for the elderly is an important social value. Such societies might want their health care systems to look after the old, though the QALY maximization rule gives this a rather low priority.

Etzioni has memorably said of North American society that, as with whaling, there should be a 10-year moratorium on the creation of new rights. Instead, communitarians point to the responsibilities and duties that people have to the communities and units within which they live. If we have certain duties, they may include forgoing behaviour which recklessly puts our own health or that of others at risk. Smoking, heavy drinking, driving at 35 miles per hour in a built-up area and unsafe sex are everyday examples. Some cases are difficult to deal with, but others are not: the French, for instance, *require* that skiers take out personal insurance. These duties suggest that some conditions or patients should attract no entitlements even if the patients are not elderly and however fully they might recover if treated.

Formulation—a simple non-linear programming example

In the previous section, we noted that, conceptually, the QALY could be used as an indicator of performance in terms of equity and rights. In itself the remark seems to suggest a conceptual link between the deontology and consequentialism which are often discussed in such a way that they appear to be completely incompatible. However, economists are drawn to the question of formulation and there is a tendency for issues to be downplayed if we don't know how to formulate them formally. Nonetheless, researchers have argued that at least some factors mentioned could be incorporated into a super QALY and that the QALY is therefore saved. Given what we have said so far, there is reason to think that such claims reveal a combination of different priorities and some muddled thinking. In this section, we want to discuss how some of the considerations that lie outside the QALY maximization decision rule can be formalized. Specifically, we shall use the tools and example below to formulate a general approach to health care priority setting within a non-linear programming framework. Table 3.2 provides the information for a simple health care rationing problem in which 50 people are divided into four types.

Assume that cost of treatment equals 1 unit for all groups and the budget, B, equals 10 units. Everyone treated recovers completely and those who

Table 3.2 Example of a simple health care rationing problem

Groups (g)	*A*	*B*	*C*	*D*
Age when affected	50	50	40	40
Life expectancy if treated	85	75	65	70
Numbers in group (all affected)	15	20	10	5
Responsible for condition	Yes	No	No	No

aren't die. In the following discussion, we use a decision rule that requires maximization subject to various constraints.

Maximand

$$Max\sum_{g} w.\hat{Q}$$ where $w = 0$ if responsible for one's own condition and 1 otherwise.

Constraints

$$b \leq B \tag{1}$$

$$n(g) = k\forall g \tag{2}$$

$$n(g)/\sum n(g) = l\forall g \tag{3}$$

where k and l are positive constants.

Using the example and framework above, it is easy to demonstrate how (at least some of) the distributive and non-consequentialist issues described above, and which lie outside the scope of the QALY maximization decision rule, can be operationalized with the constrained maximization framework provided by standard non-linear programming.[5] QALY maximization ranks the groups according to the difference between life expectancy and the age affected, which means a priority of A, D followed by BC. With only the budget constraint set and giving equal weight to all groups, 10 people from group A would be treated. However, if we were to say that each of the groups had a right to equal treatment, represented by the addition of constraint (2), then constrained QALY maximization leads to all groups being given equal priority and, depending on how one implements this, 2.5 people from each group being treated. This is a highly egalitarian approach, and from a technical viewpoint it is describable as a form of constrained maximization—however, such a description is somewhat misleading as it is the binding constraints which do the work. If one believes in equal but individually grounded *rights*, then the crude constraint (2) should be replaced with something like (3) which, in effect, weighs the group members according to group size. This gives individuals in the population an equal probability of being treated, regardless of which group they belong to. QALY maximization subject to (1) and (3) leads to treatment of 4 individuals from B, 3 from A, 2 from C and 1 from D. Again, this is an egalitarian result and the general principles should now be clear. One can use and extend this framework to reflect many of the moral concerns that have been discussed above, as well as others who take a non-monist view. For example, if one wants to maximize health care benefits but exclude those responsible for their own conditions (see Anand and Wailoo 1999, for evidence of such preferences), then it is possible to maximize QALYs, using the weighting system given, subject only to the budget constraint. Members of group A would lose any entitlements, so the ranking would be D followed by BC. It is therefore possible to incorporate responsibility (or causes) into the health care priority setting process, as well as rights. Or again, suppose one did not want to penalize group C members compared with group D members—both groups contract the condition at the age of 40 and yet the QALY maximization rule favours D members because they have a longer lifespan. One could replace the actual life expectancies measured by some national average: the argument of the maximand would no longer be $\hat{Q}$ and the link between entitlements and final life expectancy would be removed. In any case, and to repeat, these comments are intended to shed light on how certain kinds of phenomena can be incorporated into a formal framework.

Survey methods and results

Health care entitlements, we have argued, should be functionally dependent on consequences, rights, votes, actual social contracts and community values. The decision rule of health maximization focuses on just one of these, which is why, we contend, the doctrine seems so alien to many. In the following sections we test the validity of our criticisms of health maximization, and the level of support for alternative frameworks which we have advocated, using a self-administered, anonymous questionnaire. It identifies elements of frameworks that the public believe are important and that we believe should be integrated with health outcomes to form an acceptable health care rationing mechanism.

Our empirical results relate to a number of the conceptual links between QALY maximization, its problems, and the alternative frameworks we have discussed. First, we shall provide evidence relating to the problem of arbitrary exclusion and people's concern for equal treatment for those in equal need. Second, we shall provide evidence which shows that many people believe that extending the health care benefit to incorporate various utilities, as utilitarians would want, is inappropriate. Third, we provide evidence which indicates that many people are sensitive to information about causes and duties, as non-consequentialist theories suggest might be appropriate. Fourth, we provide evidence that sheds light on the extent to which people believe health care rationing is a social choice about which vote-related information should be collected.

Specific framing issues are dealt with separately in subsequent sections but some general points about the survey design are appropriate here (see also note 6). The survey was piloted using three variations of the questions before arriving at the final version. These pilots were used mainly to address individual question wording (see for instance Moser and Kalton 1971, and

Dillon 1990) but issues such as the order of questions and response rates were also examined.[6] It was decided that none of the questions should mention costs directly but control for this by making it clear that potential patients differ only in terms of the criteria mentioned in the situation descriptions. This approach was decided on in order to avoid overly complex descriptions while still controlling for this obviously crucial component in decision making. Feedback at the pilot stage supported this approach.

The final version of the survey was sent out to a sample of Leicestershire residents drawn from the electoral register. This was considered the most reliable and up-to-date sampling frame with postal addresses available. A usable response rate of 31 per cent was achieved ($n = 144$). A covering letter was also sent which introduced the concept of rationing/priority setting. As a result of feedback from the pilot surveys it also explicitly stated that the study was not related to the level of funding for the National Health Service. In addition to this, respondents were asked for a small number of socio-economic details. Exact, binomial confidence intervals (CIs) are reported where appropriate (Armitage and Berry 1994).

Socio-economic characteristics of sample

Respondents were asked to report details on four dimensions of socio-economic status in order for checks to be made on the degree to which respondents were representative of the population (Leicestershire residents). Responses to these questions are reported in Table 3.3. Also included as a means of comparison are results from the 1994/95 General Household Survey (GHS). These calculations were made after excluding all respondents aged under 16. Due to the facts that an individual must be aged 16 or over to appear on the electoral register, and that the list used was compiled in October 1996, nine months previous, there is a slight under-representation of those aged under 18 in our sample. Our sample also shows a lower proportion of respondents in the age range 26–45 years and a higher number in the range 46–64 years, in comparison with the GHS. There is a significant under-representation in our sample of those in the highest income category (over £25,000) while other income categories reflect a relatively close alignment with respondents in the GHS. Notable differences occur within occupational categories, the most prominent of which is the proportion of retired persons, which is lower in the GHS. Differences in other occupational categories do not exceed 5 per cent. Further information included in Table 3.3, for comparative reasons, is from the 1997 general election results for Leicester. Our sample indicates a proportion of 57 per cent of respondents voted for the Labour Party in the last election, while only 11.1 per cent and 10.4 per cent voted for the Conservatives and Liberals respectively. While this would appear to be a major bias in the sample, election results indicate that this is not excessive. Labour voters are over-

Table 3.3 Socio-economic details of sample

	Male		*Female*		*Total*		*GHS*[7]
	N	*(%)*	*N*	*(%)*	*N*	*(%)*	
A. Age (years)							
<18	0	0	2	1.4	2	1.4	3
18–25	5	3.5	12	8.3	17	11.8	10.8
26–45	23	16	14	9.7	37	25.7	38
46–64	25	17.4	31	21.5	56	38.9	27
>65	18	12.5	14	9.7	32	22.2	19.9
B. Gross household income (£s per annum)							
<5,000	12	8.3	23	16	35	24.3	18.8
5,000–16,000	30	20.8	31	21.5	61	42.4	37.9
16,000–25,000	15	10.4	13	9	28	19.4	19.6
>25,000	10	6.9	4	2.8	14	9.7	23.6
C. Occupation							
Employed	37	25.7	32	22.2	69	47.9	55.5
Self-employed	3	2.1	0	0	4	2.8	7.4
Unemployed	7	4.9	6	4.2	13	9	6.4
Retired	22	15.3	22	15.3	44	30.6	22.0
Other, e.g. student, housewife	2	1.4	12	8.3	14	9.7	14.7
D. Vote in 1997 election[8]							
Conservative	5	3.5	11	7.6	16	11.1	16.1
Labour	47	32.6	35	24.3	82	57	46.3
Liberal	9	6.3	6	4.2	15	10.4	7.7
Other	0	0	1	0.7	1	0.7	–
Total	71	49.3	73	50.7	144	100	

represented only by a 10 per cent margin while the variation between sample results and general election figures does not exceed 5 per cent for the other parties. While the decision to return a usable questionnaire was a self-selected action, the authors believe that there are no major biases in this sample on the four socio-economic dimensions tested.

Prioritization issues

QALY maximization and arbitrary exclusion

In this section of the survey we test the extent to which respondents agree with QALY maximization as a rationing device by using age differences between groups of patients as a proxy for health gain. While there is existing evidence to suggest that there is limited support for rationing by age[9], questions here explicitly test health maximization by controlling for factors such as prognosis after treatment.

Respondents were asked to consider how funds should be allocated between two kinds of disease, if it were not possible to treat all those affected, when patients differ only in age. While uncertainty may be characteristic of medical decision making in practice, it was decided to abstract away from this for reasons of simplicity. QALY issues were further exaggerated in the decision problem by equating treatment with full recovery, including normal life expectancy, and lack of treatment with death. Four options were presented.

- 'QALYMAX' (QALY maximization) is where all resources are used to treat those in the lower age group first, with those in the older group receiving treatment only if there are funds left over.
- 'FAVYOUNG' entails allocating more resources to the treatment of the disease which affects the younger group. It gives a degree of preference to the younger group and consequently reflects a concern for health outcomes, but does not necessitate the complete exclusion of a patient group from health care entitlements on grounds of age, which may be seen as somewhat arbitrary, as would occur with a health maximizing approach.
- 'EQUAL' indicates the option of equal allocation of resources between the two diseases.
- 'DON'T KNOW' was also included for the undecided.

Initially, respondents were asked to choose between groups where age differences were large (80 years vs. 40 years). This differential was gradually reduced until groups differed by just one year (41 years vs. 40 years). We would expect support for health maximization to be more likely where age differences are largest and, given the potential for respondent anchoring, this was the first question presented. If anchoring does prevail in this context, the question format will therefore favour QALY maximization. Results are shown in Table 3.4.

Some of the more obvious, or at least commonly used, statistical tests (chi and z) are not strictly applicable in this situation, as responses to questions are not independent. We therefore used a replicated measures test, the Cochran Q test for differences between proportions in *k* (greater than two) related samples with categorical or naturally dichotomous data (Siegel and Castellan 1988: 171). Using *p* to denote the proportion of subjects choosing in a way that is consistent with QALY maximization, and subscripts in an obvious fashion, we conduct the test, $Ho : p_{80} = p_{70} = \ldots = p_{41}$ *vs* Ha : *Ho false*. The test statistic, Q, has a value of 58.9 and is approximately chi-squared distributed

Table 3.4 QALY maximization

Age differentials (years)	*MEAN*[10]	*95% CIs*	*QALY max.*		*Favyoung*		*Equal*		*Don't know*	
			N	%	N	%	N	%	N	%
80 vs. 40	0.8357	0.7638–0.8929	23	16.0	27	18.8	90	62.5	4	2.8
70 vs. 40	0.8865	0.8223–0.9337	16	11.1	27	18.8	98	68.1	3	2.1
60 vs. 40	0.9650	0.9203–0.9886	5	3.5	15	10.4	123	85.4	1	0.7
50 vs. 40	0.9930	0.9617–0.9998	1	0.7	4	2.8	138	95.8	1	0.7
41 vs. 40	0.9930	0.9617–0.9998	1	0.7	0	0.0	142	98.6	1	0.7

with $k-1$ degrees of freedom when $n \geq 4$ and $nk \geq 24$. As $n = 144$ and $k = 5$, these conditions are met. We can, therefore, reject the possibility that the answers to the different versions of the question are drawn from the same population.[11] A more approximate approach to our data here would be to note that in all variations, the percentages of those choosing in a manner consistent with QALY maximization, as evidenced by the confidence intervals and as we discuss below, are always closer to 0 per cent than 100 per cent.

Those concerned purely with health maximization must choose option one in all situations, irrespective of the size of age differences. The decision problem was described such that even where the age differences may be small, failure to choose this option involves a deliberate sacrifice of QALYs. Results show that support for such an approach is limited. Even in the first scenario, where one would expect support for QALY maximization to be strongest since the age difference between the two groups of patients is largest, 95 per cent confidence intervals indicate that the proportion of those rejecting this approach ranges from 76 to 89 per cent. Furthermore, as age differences are reduced, the proportion of respondents not agreeing with QALYMAX increases. This reaches a maximum range of 96 to 100 per cent at a ten-year age gap. These figures indicate an overwhelming rejection of the health maximizing approach. Respondents generally do not agree that age should be used as a rationing device even when there are large differences between groups and therefore large differences in potential life years saved (or lost). A similar pattern is found when examining the number of respondents opting for the intermediate FAVYOUNG option with a significant level of support (19 per cent) where age differences are largest, falling to zero when ages differ by just one year.

While these results indicate a rejection of the health maximizing approach to rationing, they should not be seen as demonstrating a complete lack of concern over health outcomes, particularly when age differences are large. The sample mean, indicating the proportion of respondents rejecting any skewing of resources based on age, is 0.6429 (95 per cent CIs, 0.56–0.72) when the first group are aged 80 years old. Although sample means increase dramatically as the age of the first group of patients is reduced, responses indicate that the proportions of those indicating any concern for health outcomes is also significant. To further understand these data, we conducted a confirmatory cluster analysis[12] of the responses to these questions. We hypothesized that there might be three groups of respondents: strict QALY maximizers who preferred to treat the youngest in all cases; strict 'equal righters' who preferred to allocate funds equally between diseases affecting younger and older groups; and 'trade-offers' who would increasingly prefer QALY maximization to equal priority setting as the QALY difference got larger. The results of this analysis appear in Figures 3.1 to 3.5. What we find is that the largest of these three groups is in fact one that looks like our postulated 'equal righters' group. Two smaller clusters can also be identified,

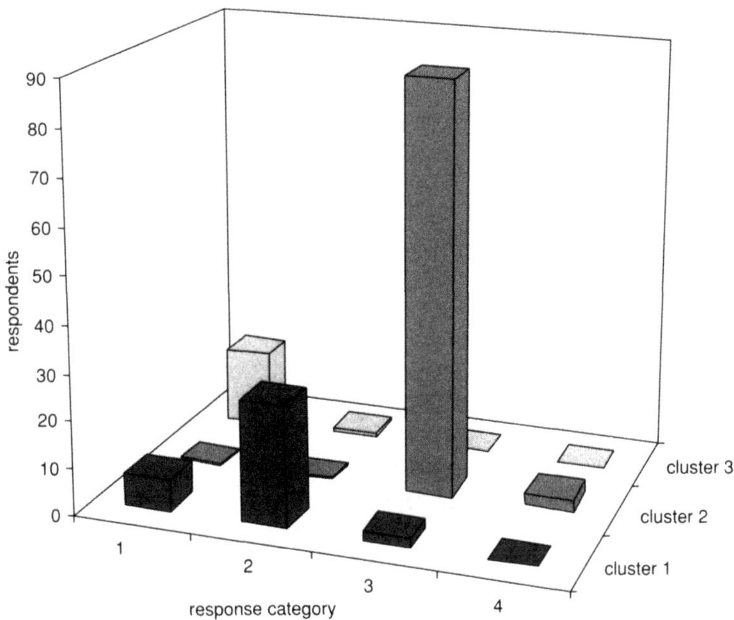

Figure 3.1 80 vs 40 years

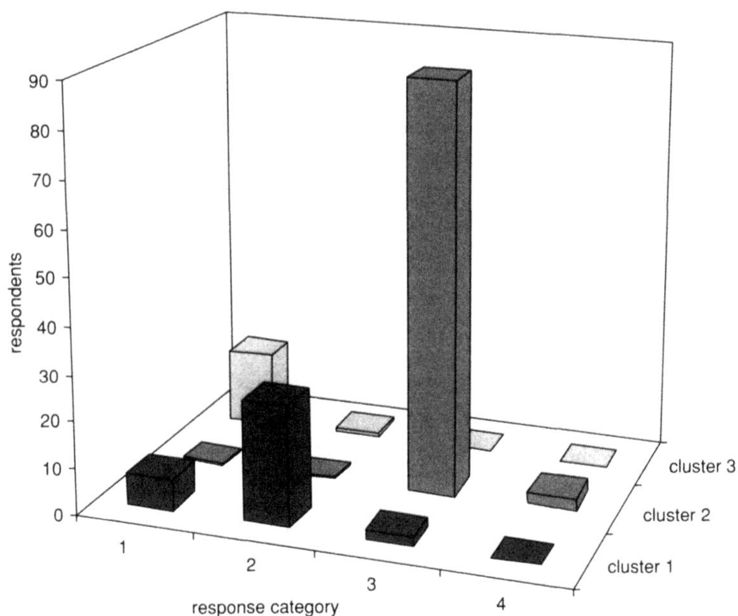

Figure 3.2 70 vs 40 years

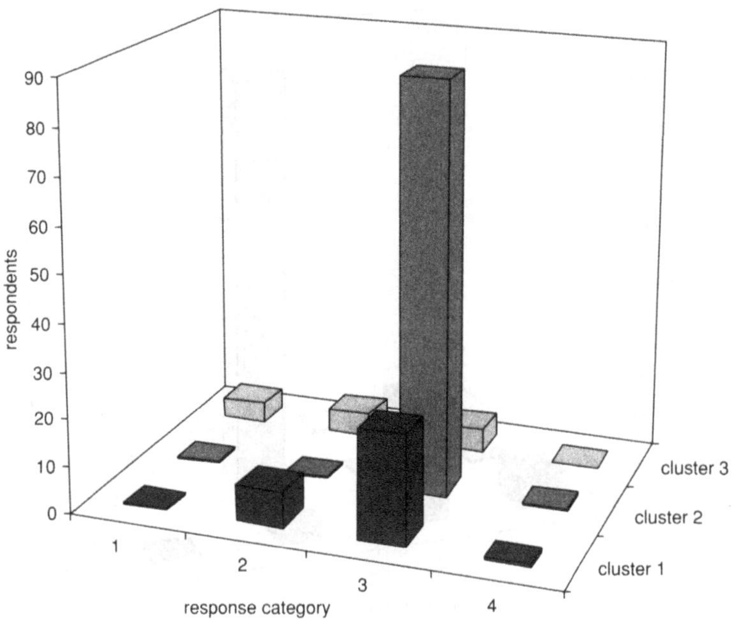

Figure 3.3 60 vs 40 years

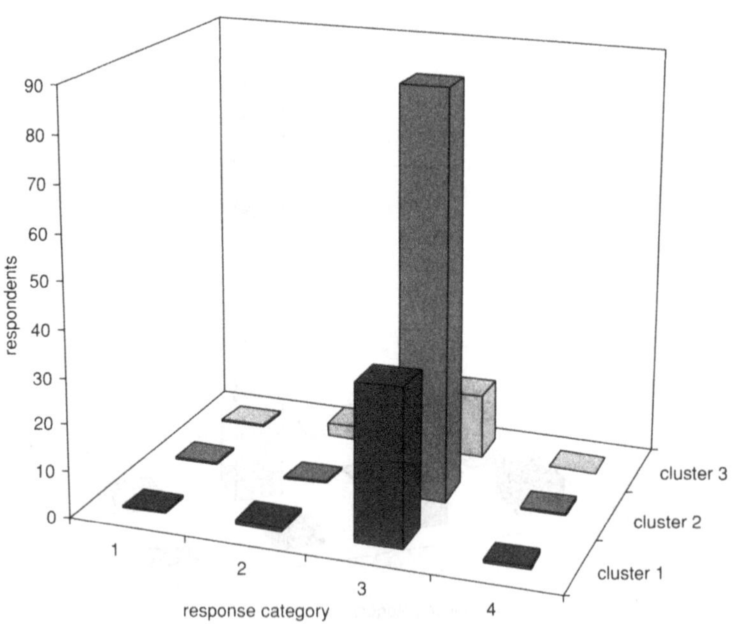

Figure 3.4 50 vs 40 years

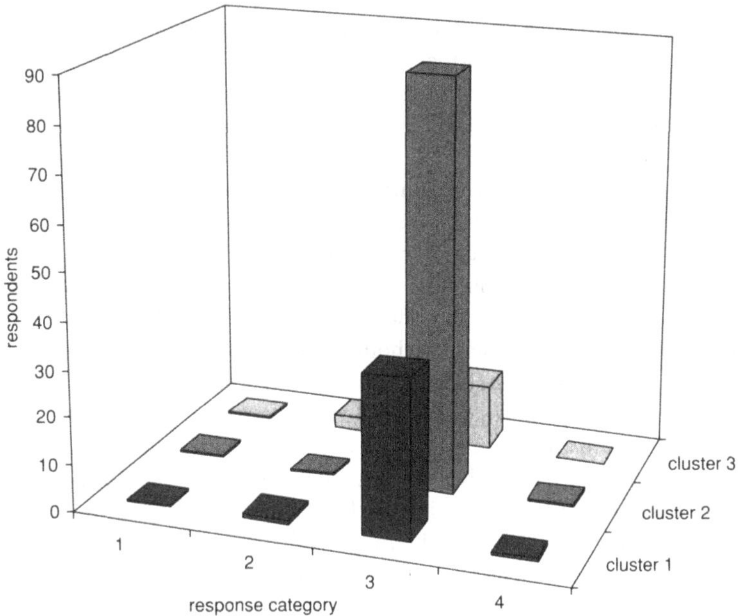

Figure 3.5 41 vs 40 years

although these two groups only depart significantly in their choices from equal priority when the QALY difference is large. Cluster 1 comprises a distribution of people, though the modal choice is to allocate resources to both diseases but more to that which affects the younger patients. Cluster 3, which is slightly smaller and more homogenous than cluster 1, comprises mainly people who support QALY maximization when the QALY difference is great. However, notice that this cluster is not equivalent to our postulated QALY maximization group, as members of it switch to equal priority as the QALY differences between the groups diminish. Using a non-parametric (chi-squared, contingency table) test, we also examined whether there were any socio-economic differences (age, sex, employment status, income category and voting behaviour) between these three clusters, but were unable to find any of statistical significance.

Limited appeal of forms of consequentialism

The decision rule of QALY maximization is a variant of consequentialism, since alternatives are judged only in terms of the health outcomes produced. There has been a tendency to use the term in a positive prescriptive sense, despite the fact that there is not the same philosophical tradition of argument for health maximization as there is for utilitarianism, upon which traditional economic tools are based. This section tests four competing types of consequentialism that are derived from utilitarianism in that they widen concern away from the individual's health (which is the concern of QALY maximization) towards a more utilitarian metric, which would include the welfare of all actors affected by a medical procedure, rather than the individual patient.

As noted earlier, potential confounding influences were controlled by an explicit instruction to subjects to treat patients as being equal in all respects other than those which appeared in the question. However, included from the beginning of this section was the general statement that patients are similar in all aspects other than those specified. This served as a security measure against response bias without making the questions excessively repetitive or lengthening the survey. Results are shown in Table 3.5.

The first question in this section asks whether a broader measure of outcome than the health or utility of an individual patient should be used in determining entitlements to health care. Results indicate a sample mean of the proportion of people disagreeing with personal utilitarianism of 0.88 (95 per cent CI, 0.81–0.93). Despite the magnitude of responses favouring equality of access for patients irrespective of the effect on personal utility, there is still a greater degree of support for this type of consequentialism than the other more inclusive types tested in this section.

The three other questions included in this section were concerned with consequences outside the individual sphere. Choices were offered between patients who differ only in marital status (spouse utility), whether they have children (family utility), or income (economic utilitarianism). Options presented corresponded with a consequentialist ideology, an anti-consequentialist view, and an egalitarian view.

First, when faced with a choice between a married and an unmarried person, the proportion of those who disagree with giving priority for treatment to the married person, as indicated by the sample mean, is 0.97 (95 per cent CI, 0.92–0.99), indicating an overwhelming rejection of this type of consequentialism. Another criticism of the health maximizing approach to prioritizing health services is that it does not incorporate the effects on a patient's dependants. Respondents were therefore presented with a choice between patients with and without children. A proportion of over 0.93 of respondents disagreed with the view that those with children should be given a higher priority than childless patients (95 per cent CI, 0.88–0.97), opposing the choice advocated by a consequentialist decision rule. Economic welfare was the broadest consequence respondents were asked to consider. In this question, a choice between high- and low-wage patients was presented. In the absence of market failures, economic consequentialism advocates prioritizing services for high-wage earners, yet our estimates show confidence intervals of the proportions rejecting this approach between 96 per cent and 100 per cent. Interestingly, the option to give priority to low-wage

Table 3.5 Varieties of consequences*

Types of outcome	*Mean*[13]	*95% CIs*	*Consequentialist*		*Anti-consequentialist*		*Egalitarian*		*Don't know*	
			N	%	N	%	N	%	N	%
Personal utility	0.8810	0.8113–0.9318	15	10.4	n/a†		111	77.1	18	12.5
Spouse utility	0.9650	0.9203–0.9886	5	3.5	1	0.7	137	95.1	1	0.7
Family utility	0.9301	0.8752–0.9660	10	6.9	2	1.4	131	91	1	0.7
Economic utilitarianism	0.9859	0.9500–0.9983	2	1.4	14	9.7	126	88	2	1.4

Notes

* Though our main interest is in the fact that mean proportions, as indicated by the confidence intervals, are nowhere near 0, as they would have to be if 'consequence maximization' held, we also test $Ho : p_{PU} = p_{SU} = \ldots = p_{EU}$ *vs* $Ha : Ho$ *false* using the Q test previously discussed. In this case, $Q = 15.47$ with 3 degrees of freedom, which is highly significant (i.e. $p < 0.01$). We can reject the hypothesis that the proportions choosing the 'consequence maximization' consistent choice are the same for four conditions summarized in the table.

† This option was not considered relevant to this question.

earners received a significant degree of support (10 per cent). Not only does this reinforce the strength of opinion against rationing by economic consequence but may also indicate that the concept of access to health services according to need should incorporate the ability to pay for such services privately.

Results in this section indicate that attempts to find a publicly acceptable rationing device based solely around a utilitarian philosophy will be inadequately based. Indeed, when compared to results concerning the QALY maximizing approach (where age differences are largest), each of these alternatives based on broader consequences receives a lower level of support. It therefore appears that QALY maximization is not deficient due to the nature of the consequence (health) that is its sole concern, but because of its consequentialist nature per se. An acceptable rationing framework must incorporate broader concerns than QALY maximization, but these concerns are not consequential in nature. Subsequent sections of the survey test the acceptability of such alternative frameworks that may complement concerns for outcomes such as health gains.

The relevance of causes

Health maximization focuses only on outcomes in terms of health. In common with all brands of consequentialism, it is blind to the underlying reasons for these outcomes. We focus here on the extent to which health care entitlements are affected by how treatment-needs came to be generated. Questions are asked both in terms of specific conditions and with respect to risky behaviour in general.

In each of the scenarios presented we ask about priority setting between groups of patients suffering from the same condition, such that the expected health gain from receiving treatment would, on aggregate, be the same for both groups. Results are shown in Table 3.6.

Question one asks if priorities for treatment should differ between HIV-positive persons who have become infected through the use of illegal intravenous drug use (and *may* be seen as responsible for their condition), and those infected through contaminated blood transfusions. Confidence intervals at the 95 per cent level indicate that the proportion of those advocating preferential treatment for those infected through contaminated blood transfusions (and therefore rejecting a pure health maximizing policy) ranges from 50 per cent to 68 per cent. A slightly lower proportion of respondents accept that cause is relevant in scenario two, which presents choices between smokers and non-smokers requiring treatment for lung cancer (see Persaud 1995, for a normative discussion of some issues relating to smoking and rationing). Confidence intervals in this situation indicate that the proportion of those choosing for non-smokers to receive a higher priority for treatment than smokers ranges from 38 per cent to 56 per cent. These results show that,

Table 3.6 The importance of responsibility and cause*†

Condition and cause	*Mean*[14]	*95% CIs*	*Relevant*		*Not relevant*		*Don't know*	
			N	%	N	%	N	%
HIV/AIDS: illegal drugs vs. blood transfusions	0.5954	0.5062–0.6802	78	54	53	37	13	9
Lung cancer: smokers vs. non-smokers	0.4706	0.3845–0.5580	64	44	72	50	8	6
Mountain rescue	0.8529	0.7821–0.9078	116	81	20	14	7	5
General disease: risky lifestyle vs. caution	0.4031	0.3177–0.4930	52	37	77	54	13	9
			QALY max.		*Anti-QALY max.*		*Equal*	
Life expectancy: socio-economic group	1	1	0	0	12	8	130	92
Life expectancy: lifestyle	0.9236	0.8674–0.9613	11	8	6	4	127	88

Notes

* We tested $Ho : p_{HIV} = p_{LC} = \ldots = p_{RL}$ *vs* $Ha : Ho$ *false* as before. In this case, $Q = 67.40$ with 3 degrees of freedom, which is highly significant (i.e. $p < 0.01$).

† We tested $Ho : p_{SEG} = p_L$ *vs* $Ha : Ho$ *false*. For related *pairs* of responses the McNemar test is used and the sample size is sufficiently large to justify using a chi-square approximation. The value of the test statistic is 9.09, allowing for a continuity correction, and carries 1 degree of freedom. The null is rejected at the significance level, $p = 0.01$.

in these specific situations, health maximization is unpopular as it is blind to how health gains are generated.

Question three presents a similar situation in very general terms. Two groups of patients require medical treatment in a situation where there are insufficient funds to treat all those in need. One group require treatment as a result of engaging in risky behaviours while the other group are suffering as a result of events beyond their control. Respondents are asked to consider whether or not the cause of disease is relevant to the priority for treatment that patients should receive. In this general situation there is a slightly higher level of agreement with the viewpoint that patients in each group should receive an equal priority, as consistent with consequentialism. The proportion of respondents indicating that the cause of disease is relevant in this general case, as indicated by the sample mean, is 40 per cent (95 per cent CI, 0.32–0.49).

In order to provide a comparison, question four frames the problem in an area outside the health service. Respondents were asked to consider whether mountaineers should be obliged to take out insurance to cover the costs of any rescue services they may require. This situation mirrors that faced in the health service, but was included to identify differences in opinions between the NHS and other services supported by resources provided by a combination of public and voluntary sources. Results show that there is a far greater level of support for non-equal access to such services than in the health sector. The sample mean of the proportion of the sample supporting compulsory insurance is 0.85 (95 per cent CI, 0.78–0.91).

Results in this section as a whole indicate that there is a moderate level of support for allocating priorities to patients on grounds other than expected health gains. Respondents are concerned with how health care needs are generated and are prepared to discriminate against those who fail to take precautions to protect their own health. The significance of this rejection of consequentialism, and therefore QALY maximization, is particularly important given the framing of the questions. In each of the scenarios presented, equality of opportunity for patients equated to a health maximizing viewpoint. Given what we know about attitudes to the NHS, this meant that the questions were biased in favour of the health maximization standpoint. This effect is apparent from the results gained in question four, which show a greater level of rejection for the QALY maximizing approach outside the immediate health service. Yet despite this, results indicate a high level of support for cause relevance. Two supplementary questions in this section address this bias by framing the issue in an alternative manner. Both questions present a situation where two groups of patients are suffering from similar conditions but have differing life expectancies. In the first instance this is due to economic status, with those from a wealthy background enjoying a higher life expectancy. In the second case the patient group with lower

Table 3.7 Majority vs expert opinion and political affiliation

	Conservative	*Labour*	*Liberal Democrat*	*Other*
Popular opinion (provide)	6	46	1	0
Expert opinion (don't provide)	8	19	11	1
Don't know	2	17	3	0

life expectancies lead lifestyles that are generally considered to be risky for health. In each of these scenarios, QALY maximization advocates allocating priority to the group with the higher life expectancy. Results, however, show an overwhelming rejection of the QALY approach. Not one respondent opted to allocate a lower priority to the lower income group in order to generate greater health gains, with the majority opting for equal treatment of both groups. There were, however, a small proportion (8 per cent) who expressed a preference for the opposite view, that is, to give a higher priority to the low income group.

Similarly, in the second question in this section, there is little evidence of a willingness to adhere to the position advocated by the health maximizing approach when this entails giving priority to a group of patients with healthy lifestyles. CIs of 95 per cent indicate that the proportion of persons holding a view that contradicts QALY maximization is in a range from 87 per cent to 96 per cent.

Finally, we conducted an analysis of the impact of socio-economic variables on responses and found evidence only of a link with political affiliation—see Table 3.7.

Given that three cells in Table 3.7 have expected values of less than 1, a chi-squared test on the raw table is inappropriate. Further, given the meaning attached to each of the categories, it would be inappropriate to collapse cells. However, dropping the 'other' category involves losing information from only one observation and seems a small cost to pay for the appropriate hypothesis test (*Ho* is that the distributions are independent while *Ha* is just the negation of *Ho*). For the truncated 3 × 3 table, chi-square is 18.4 with 4 df, which is significant at the $p = 0.001$ level (though strictly two out of nine—22 per cent—of the cells have expected values of less than five, while the commonly quoted rules for applying the chi-squared require that no more than 20 per cent of the cells have expected values below five).

Overall, a strong rejection of the QALY maximizing decision rule has been demonstrated. While these questions cannot isolate the reasons for this rejection, it seems reasonable to suggest that this is due to concern with the way in which expected health gains are generated. The most likely confounding factor in this section is the egalitarian nature of public attitudes to the NHS, which has been addressed both by including a scenario dealing with a similar issue outside the NHS and by equating QALY maximization variously with equality and inequality of access.

Votes/public opinion

Table 3.8 shows responses to questions concerning citizens' procedural rights in health care. Respondents were asked to consider the extent of their agreement/disagreement with three types of consultation process. The first two of these refer to methods of measuring public opinion, namely public consultations such as citizens' juries and voter surveys. The third question asked if health services should aim to mirror a private-insurance-based system as traditionally advocated by economists, on the grounds that this is the most effective method of representing individual preferences.

Results show that there is general support for both forms of public consultation with point estimates around 2.4 (95 per cent CI, 2.3–2.6), where 3 is equal to neutrality and lower numbers represent agreement. This indicates that there is general support for health authorities involving the public in rationing decisions and that the form of consultation does not significantly alter the level of this support. Average opinion is slightly against distributing resources in a manner similar to private markets, with results indicating a point estimate of 3.3 (95 per cent CI, 3.2–3.5). Finally, note the non-parametric test for the entire 3×5 contingency table is highly significant: chi-square = 61.117 which with df = 8, is significant at less than the $p = 0.001$ level.

Relevance of votes and rights

Table 3.9 shows results relating to two questions,[16] which ask respondents to consider how health priorities should be decided when there is a conflict between health maximization, voter opinions and the rights of individual patients. We are concerned here with the identification of rights-based entitlements to health care without necessarily involving a trade-off with health outcomes and indeed, as previously suggested, it may be possible to judge outcomes in terms of their rights-based implications.

The first of these questions presents a situation where a health authority must decide on the priority for a disease which affects only members of an ethnic minority group, meaning that there are relatively few voters advocating a high priority for this condition since they are unlikely to be at risk. The question does not directly specify the efficiency of available treatments, since pilot studies revealed that this did not influence responses and only complicated the question. There are no grounds for rejecting treatment provision on health maximization grounds. Confidence intervals of 95 per cent

Table 3.8 Voter opinion

Role of consultation	*Mean*[15]	*95% CIs*	*Strongly agree*		*Agree*		*Neutral*		*Disagree*		*Strongly disagree*	
			N	%	N	%	N	%	N	%	N	%
Consultation exercises	2.4406	2.2688–2.6123	25	7	58	40	38	26	16	11	6	4
Surveys of voters	2.4861	2.3075–2.6647	26	18	55	38	37	26	19	13	7	5
Private insurance mirror	3.3287	3.1556–3.5017	6	4	27	19	41	28	52	36	17	12

Note
We tested $Ho : p_{ce} = p_{sv} = p_{pim}$ *vs* $Ha : Ho$ *false*. In this case, as the underlying response measure is ordinal (clearly agree to clearly disagree), we use the Friedman two-way analysis for k related samples. The test statistic has an approximate chi-squared distribution when the number of either observations or treatments is large, which is the case as $n = 142$ (allowing for incomplete observations which had to be removed for the analysis). The value of the test statistic, F, with 2 degrees of freedom, is 46.82, which is highly significant (i.e. at $p < 0.01$). A correction for ties is available but may not be unbiased—the uncorrected statistic is biased but known to be conservative, so gives an unambiguous underestimate of the significance level.

Table 3.9 Voting and rights

Reason for difference	*Mean*	*95% CIs*	*Health max.*		*Public opinion*		*Don't know*	
			N	*%*	*N*	*%*	*N*	*%*
Minority population	0.1318	0.0787–0.2026	112	78	17	12	15	10
Popular treatment	0.5897	0.4950–0.6798	48	33	69	48	27	19

Note
We tested $Ho : p_{MP} = p_{PT}$ *vs* Ha : *Ho false* using the McNemar test for related pairs. The value of the test statistic is 46.15, allowing for a continuity correction, and carries 1 degree of freedom. The null is rejected at the significance level, $p = 0.01$.

indicate that the proportion of those who think the health authority should respond to public opinion and give this condition a low priority ranges from 8 per cent to 20 per cent. There is therefore general agreement with the option supported on health maximization grounds, although we suggest a rights-based argument below for these responses.

The second question presents an alternative decision problem in which voter opinion is in direct conflict with clinical opinion. Respondents are asked to consider whether a health authority should provide a treatment which has a very low expected health gain and is therefore not supported by doctors, but which the public have said should be provided. In this scenario, results illustrate a much higher tendency for respondents to disagree with health maximization, with confidence intervals ranging between the 50 per cent and 68 per cent levels.

The difference (statistically significant) between the results gained in these two questions yields important implications for the role of rights in the rationing debate. It is clear that health maximization or voting, alone, cannot explain these results. Our suggestion is grounded in health care rights. First, broad support for a rights-maintenance approach to rationing is exhibited. Respondents are generally willing to reject the option favoured by voters in question one, when this would entail the violation of the rights of a specific group (an ethnic minority). This trend is reversed in the second question, where there is a much higher level of agreement with voter opinion rather than health maximization, since the former option entails the provision of the service. Second, we argue that the results suggest a possible judgment of outcomes in terms of their implications for group rights. Question one in particular is demonstrative of Sen's theory of capability rights, where the outcome of providing treatment may reflect concerns for equality of access for different groups, specifically ethnic minorities, rather than a concern with health maximization as a value in itself.

Summary and concluding remarks

This chapter has provided an overview of a project that has, in the course of a number of papers, looked at the links between new approaches to welfare economics and the development of policy instruments for rationing health care. We began by looking at evidence relating to health care rationing in the UK, conducted in the absence of formal policy, and found it to be haphazard and politically driven (not in a benign sense) from a welfare/ethical standpoint. The paper then went on to look at the proposal that we should ration so as to maximize QALYs, and found the supporting literature somewhat cryptic and in need of clarification. We made an explicit distinction, first, between the QALY as a measure (which most people would now accept as useful) and QALY maximization as a decision rule (which many have always rejected). We also argued that QALY maximization is not necessarily a form of utilitarianism but that it certainly is a form of consequentialism, and that it must therefore suffer from all the problems that any welfare analysis based purely on consequentialist considerations must suffer. In section 3, we argued that a comprehensive and normatively acceptable analysis of social choice in policy settings must take account not just of consequences, but also of rights, actual social contracts, and norms about procedural justice (e.g. the role of voting vs. the opinion of experts): this puts integration, rather than aggregation, at the centre of social choice (Arrow 1951). These claims have sometimes appeared to be resisted by health economists on the grounds that such claims had not been formalized, so in section four we showed just how this can be done. Many of the considerations from new welfare economics (i.e. the sort being developed by Sen and other social-choice theorists) that have been referred to in the literature can be handled within a non-linear programming framework, a framework that has the advantage of showing QALY as the special case it is, formally. To explore the extent to which the new welfare-economics issues identified are supported by voters, a survey was conducted. In most respects, voters were more consistent with ideas from non-consequentialist welfare economics than the older approach. For example, we found support for QALY maximization ranged from 16 per cent down to 0.7 per cent of the sample: on the other hand, up to 34.8 per cent of the sample voted for choices that relied on the use of the QALY measure. This supports the view that QALYs have a role as performance indicators (Smith 1990) even if the maximization rule attracts very little support.

We also argued that the reasons for conditions and capacity to benefit had a substantial impact on rationing attitudes, though reasons lie, at present, outside the formal framework of decision theory or social choice and welfare economics. Between 37 per cent and 81 per cent of our sample thought the reasons for a particular condition should be taken into account. On the other hand, 0 per cent of our sample thought QALY differences should be taken into account when these resulted from socio-economic inequalities between potential patients. Our population frame consisted of voters in a particular area of the UK (the Midlands), but the sample was random and its profile reasonably close to the national average, so that we have little reason to believe that the qualitative conclusions would not be replicated in other areas too. It is these different, non-consequentialist cards that members of society throw up for consideration in the social consideration of their claims on resources. Understanding how these claims are or should be integrated still throws up a wide variety of theoretical and empirical avenues for future research—perhaps along the behavioural decision-analysis or multivariate lines indicated in von Winterfeldt and Edwards (1988). In this sense, health care problems highlight the limits of consequentialism just as experimental evidence has encouraged decision theorists to favour non-expected utility theories (Anand 1993).

Alan Williams (1992, 1996) has done more than anyone, possibly in the world, to articulate the need for all health systems to devote much more attention to the development and use of information on the benefits of medical interventions. This project is a modest tribute to his work.

Notes

1 Most of the material for this chapter first appeared in two articles: QALIES and the integration of incommensurable claims, *Health Care Analysis*, 1999, and Utilities vs. rights to publicly provided goods: arguments and evidence from health-care rationing, *Economica*, 2000.
2 See Rawls (1971), Nozick (1974), Scanlon (1977), Hart (1979), Sen (1979, 1985), Raz (1982), Korsgaard (1993), Scheffler (1988), Sugden (1993), Kolm (1994, 1995), Pattanaik (1994), Fleurbaey and Gaertner (1996) and Suzumura (1999). For non-consequentialist treatments of health care rationing, see Harris (1987), Burrows and Brown (1993), Nord (1993, 1994), Nord et al. (1995), Singer et al. (1995) and Ryan (1999).
3 Wagstaff (1991) and Birch and Gafni (1992) seem to concur with the possibility of the distinction made here.
4 See Dworkin (1977) for a general account of rights. Broome (1991, 1993), by contrast, adopts a neo-utilitarian defence of entitlements to health care, grounded in what he calls the good.
5 In this case the non-linearity refers to the form of the constraint.
6 The questionnaire was designed to minimize the impact of a number of potential problems discussed in literature on survey design. First we ensured that question words were as neutral in the description of options as possible. In some cases, we used the phrase 'some people argue that . . .' to reduce bias due to perceptions of what might be socially acceptable answers—though we noted also that in many cases, because different welfare/moral theories prescribe different courses of action, all responses could be argued to be socially desirable. We also sought to describe options in as symmetrical a way as possible. By contrast, open-form questions have been shown to elicit (Dillon 1990: 118) more reports of socially undesirable behaviour, but we felt that this was not a major concern here and that the demands of quantitative analysis more than justified our use of

closed-form questions. We included 'don't know' and 'equal preference' response options wherever possible, as we did not want to force a preference where none existed. Introduction of 'don't know' options has been shown to reduce agreement with other substantive options, but we found that very few respondents checked this item when given the option. In their discussion of the particular problems associated with opinion surveys, the statisticians Moser and Kalton (1971) identify two kinds of responses: the first tries to estimate (and put bounds on) the proportion of a population who agree with a particular opinion, while the second asks individuals a series of questions in order to provide an overall measurement of attitudes. As our empirical analysis is driven by the theory of QALY maximization, and as we have collected (ex ante and ex post) information establishing the relation of our sample to its population, our work, especially the confidence intervals we provide, primarily illustrates the former strategy. That said, the fact that most people seem to believe that patients should be given equal priority, with some diminution of the effect when age differences are very large, indicates evidence of overall attitudes also.

7 Figures for age, income and occupation are taken from the General Household Survey of 1994/95 (n = 18,237). Voting behaviour taken from 1997 general election results, Leicester wards.

8 Source: Press Association.

9 See for example Nord et al. (1995) for survey work in Australia, and Kuder (1993) for focus group evidence in the USA. Bowling (1996) includes the topic of age in her survey work based in the UK, but questions are not controlled in such a way that implications for QALY maximization can be drawn.

Lewis and Charny (1989) offered a sample of Welsh voters' choices between individuals differing only by age and found that, in two of the three examples, there was support for treating the younger patient. However, respondents were discouraged from choosing equal priority. Furthermore, in the example which had the smallest difference in age between the two individuals (35-year-old vs. a 60-year-old), over half of those who chose to allocate resources to the younger patient reported doing so only with difficulty. Interestingly, in their third example, voters preferred to treat an eight-year-old in preference to a two-year-old.

10 Means and confidence intervals are based around a coding of QALYMAX = 0, other responses = 1.

11 We are grateful to one of the referees for pressing us on this point.

12 We used commonly employed techniques (Everitt and Dunn 1991). Ward's technique for assigning members to clusters is used to avoid the problem of 'chaining'—that is, the construction of artificial clusters that can arise if nearest elements to a cluster boundary are selected, regardless of their relation to the cluster centre. Distances between members were operationalized using the Euclidean distance—in the case of cluster analysis, the Euclidean distance is the *n* dimensional equivalent of the shortest distance between two points as specified by a straight line between them.

13 Mean and confidence intervals for responses that correlate with a consequentialist approach are coded as 0, alternatives are coded 1.

14 Means and confidence intervals are calculated on the basis of health maximization = 0, alternatives = 1.

15 Means and confidence intervals are based on strongly agree = 1, . . ., strongly disagree = 5.

16 For exact questions see Appendix 1E.

References

Anand, P. (1993) *Foundations of Rational Choice Under Risk*, Oxford: Oxford University Press.

Armitage, P. and Berry, G. (1994) *Statistical Methods in Medial Research*, 3rd edn, Oxford: Blackwell.

Arrow, K.J. (1951) *Social Choice and Individual Values*, New York: Wiley.

Bell, D. (1993) *Communitarianism and Its Critics*, Oxford: Oxford University Press.

Birch, S. and Gafni, A. (1992) Cost-effectiveness/utility analyses: do current decision rules lead us to where we want to be? *Journal of Health Economics* 11: 279–296.

Bowling, A. (1996) Health care rationing: the public's debate, *British Medical Journal* 312: 670–674.

Broome, J. (1991) *Weighing Goods*, Oxford: Blackwell.

—— (1993) QALYs, *Journal of Public Economics* 50: 149–167.

Buchanan, A. (1984) The right to a decent minimum of health care, *Philosophy and Public Affairs* 13: 55–78.

Burrows, C. and Brown, K. (1993) QALYs for resource allocation—probably not and certainly not now, *Australian Journal of Public Health* 17: 278–286.

Dillon, J.T. (1990) *The Practice of Questioning*, London: Routledge.

Dolan, P., Cookson, R., and Ferguson, B. (1999) Effect of discussion and deliberation on the public's views of priority setting in health care: focus study group, *British Medical Journal* 318: 916–919.

Dworkin, R. (1977) *Taking Rights Seriously*, London: Duckworth.

Etzioni, A. (1995) *The Spirit of Communitarianism*, London: Fontana.

Everitt, B.S. and Dunn, G. (1991) *Applied Multivariate Data Analysis*, London: Edward Arnold.

Fleurbaey, M. and Gaertner, W. (1996) *Admissibility and Feasibility in Game Forms*, Discussion Paper, Osnabruck: University of Osnabruck.

Harris, J. (1987) QALYfying the value of life, *Journal of Medical Ethics* 3: 117–123.

Hart, H.L.A. (1979) Between utility and rights, *Columbia Law Review* 65: 828–846.

Kolm, S.-C. (1994) Rational normative economics vs. 'social welfare' and 'social choice', *European Economic Review* 38: 721–730.

—— (1995) *Moral Public Choice*, Paris: Institute for Advanced Studies in the Social Sciences.

Korsgaard, C.M. (1993) The reasons we can share, in E.F. Paul, F.D. Miller and J. Paul (eds) *Altruism*, Cambridge: Cambridge University Press.

Mooney, G. (1998) Communication claims on an ethical basis for allocating health care resources, *Social Science and Medicare* 47: 1133–1198.

Moser, C.A. and Kalton, G. (1971) *Survey Methods in Social Investigation*, 2nd edn, Aldershot: Gower.

Nord, E. (1993) The relevance of health state after treatment in prioritizing between different patients, *Journal of Medical Ethics* 19: 37–42.

—— (1994) The QALY—A measure of social value rather than individual utility, *Health Economics* 3: 89–93.

Nord, E., Richardson, J., Street, A., Kuhse, H., and Singer, P. (1995) Maximizing health benefits vs. egalitarianism: an Australian survey of health issues, *Social Science and Medicine* 41: 1429–1437.

Nozick, R. (1974) *Anarchy State and Utopia*, New York, Basic Books.

Oberholtzer-Gee, F., Bolhnet, I., and Frey, B.S. (1997) Fairness and competence in democratic decisions, *Public Choice* 91: 89–105.

Pattanaik, P.K. (1994) Rights and freedom in welfare economics, *European Economic Review* 38: 731–738.

Persaud, R. (1995) Smokers' rights to health care, *Journal of Medical Ethics* 21: 281–287.

Rawls, J. (1971) *A Theory of Justice*, Cambridge MA: Harvard University Press.

Raz, J. (1982) Rights based moralities, in J. Waldron (ed.) *Theories of Rights*, Oxford: Oxford University Press.

Redmayne, S. (1995) *Reshaping the NHS*, Birmingham: NAHAT (National Association of Health Authorities and Trusts).

Ryan, M. (1999) Using conjoint analysis to take account of patient preferences and go beyond health outcomes: an application to invitro fertilisation, *Social Science and Medicine* 48: 535–546.

Scanlon, T.M. (1977) Rights, goals and fairness, *Erkenntnis* 2: 81–94.

Scheffler, S. (1988) *Consequentialism and Its Critics*, Oxford: Clarendon Press.

Sen, A.K. (1979) Personal utilities and public judgements: or what's wrong with welfare economics, *Economic Journal* 89: 537–558.

—— (1985) *Commodities and Capabilities*, Amsterdam: North-Holland.

Siegal, S. and Castellan, N.J. (1988) *Non-Parametric Statistics*, New York: McGraw-Hill.

Singer, P., McKie, J., Kuhse, H., and Richardson, J. (1995) Double jeopardy and the use of QALYs in health care allocation, *Journal of Medical Ethics* 21: 144–150.

Smith, P. (1990) The use of performance indicators in the public sector, *Journal of Royal Statistical Society* 153: 53–72.

Sugden, R. (1993) A review of Inequality Re-examined, *Journal of Economic Literature* 31: 1947–1962.

Suzumura, K. (1999) An axiomatisation of non-consequentialism, mimeograph, London: London School of Economics.

Wagstaff, A. (1991) QALYs and the equity efficiency trade-off, *Journal of Health Economics* 10: 21–41.

Williams, A. (1992) Cost-effectiveness analysis—is it ethical? *Journal of Medical Ethics* 18: 7–11.

—— (1996) QALYs and ethics: a health economist's perspective, *Social Science and Medicine* 43: 1795–1804.

von Winterfeldt, D. and Edwards, W. (1988) *Decision Analysis and Behavioral Research*, Cambridge: Cambridge University Press.

4

ACCOUNTING FOR FAIRNESS AND EFFICIENCY IN HEALTH ECONOMICS

Joshua Cohen and Peter Ubel

Introduction

The use of economic reasoning to analyze health care is a comparatively recent development. However, the seeds for this development were sown long ago. Highly influential neoclassical economists like Paul Samuelson, emulating the success of the natural sciences in employing calculus, derived behavioral rules from mathematically tractable first-order principles. Post-war neoclassicals wanted to reduce the ambiguity of certain economic concepts and remove value ladenness from economics. It was thought that by increasing the hardness of economics, they could do both. Formulating economic theory mathematically undoubtedly increased hardness, which in turn made certain concepts less ambiguous. Theoretical claims that did not lend themselves to mathematical translation were even cast aside by some neoclassicals: '[A]ny sector of economic theory which cannot be cast into the mold of such a [mathematical] system [of equations] must be regarded with suspicion as suffering from haziness' (Samuelson 1947: 9). Samuelson admitted that the degree of hardness in economics could only be considered 'intermediate,' but that 'when one descends [in degrees of hardness] lower . . . say to certain areas of sociology . . . [they] are almost completely without substantive content' (1947: ix).

Post-war neoclassicals were often critical of the methods being used in the 'softer' social sciences. Neoclassicals attempted to impose more rigorous economic methods on these other social sciences, a practice that became known as *economics imperialism*. The neoclassical view that economic theory studies the allocation of scarce means with alternative uses (Robbins 1932) did not preclude the study of scarce noneconomic means with alternative noneconomic uses. Perhaps the most successful example of economics imperialism is found in Gary Becker's work. In the 1960s and 1970s, Becker revolutionized the study of sociological phenomena such as family, race, and class, using a neoclassical apparatus of analytical tools (Becker 1976).

Health economics is a relative newcomer to the economics profession. It became a subdiscipline (with its own peer-reviewed journals and professional associations) in the 1980s. Health economics fits neatly under the rubric of economics imperialism as health economists generally analyze health care using a neoclassical model of behavior. In the process of subjecting health care to economic analysis, health terms are translated into economics jargon; health becomes a product, patients consumers, doctors health care providers, the hospital a product delivery system, and care managed.

As the field of economics has become increasingly quantitative, it has become less likely for health economists to focus attention on ethical values such as *fairness* that are presumably less quantifiable. This said, the need to emphasize the ethical dimension associated with economic decisions is perhaps more evident in health care than in other sectors of the economy. Certainly, the ethical issues raised by possible tradeoffs between fairness and efficiency in health care illustrate the risks of relying too much on quantitative economic approaches, such as Paretian welfare analysis, that ignore ethical considerations.

Health economists may see themselves solely as engineers, offering technical solutions to technical problems. However, they are at least indirectly concerned with ethical issues. When a health economist is asked to evaluate the *kind* of health output to be produced—longer life expectancy, increased quality of life, fewer sick days—answers to this question presuppose a certain ethical view about what is best for society. Furthermore, when health economists deal with questions of distribution such as 'To whom should Medicaid funds be allocated?' they are concerned with fairness. Even if supposedly value-neutral Pareto distribution rules are used in the name of improved efficiency, a certain fairness norm is implied. The Pareto definition of efficiency *implies definite value judgments* about fairness.

This chapter describes how ethics and economics interact in the area of health care rationing. This section has explored the advantages and limitations of using Paretian welfare economic analysis to evaluate the fairness-efficiency implications of health care rationing. The second section explains how the possibility of a fairness-efficiency tradeoff needs to be assessed both within the dollars domain and between the dollars and rights domains. The third section evaluates a practical case of explicit health care rationing, the Oregon health care initiative. This initiative is assessed in terms of how it has promoted fairness and efficiency.

Conventional wisdom on the fairness-efficiency tradeoff

'The market needs a place, and the market needs to be kept in place' (Okun 1975).

Rights and dollars domains

Okun (1975) distinguishes *rights* and *dollars* domains in society. The chief distinguishing characteristics of the rights and dollars domains, according to Okun, are *equality*[1] and *efficiency*, respectively. In the rights domain, political and judicial institutions provide universally distributed rights and privileges that proclaim the equality of all citizens. However, in the dollars domain, society's economic institutions rely on market-determined incomes that produce substantial disparities among citizens in material well-being. Hence, some degree of inequality, unequal spread of wealth, is guaranteed by virtue of the competitive aspects of the market process. There are winners and losers in the marketplace where motives to maximize profits and consumer utility reign. Under an ideal set of assumptions, utility- and profit-maximizing behavior lead to the most efficient outcomes.

It seems that the two domains can be further distinguished by the *inexchangeability of rights* for other rights, as opposed to the *exchangeability of dollars* for commodities with dollar value and vice versa. Rights may not be bought and sold, whereas dollars can (either for commodities with dollar value or for other convertible currencies). For example, every citizen has a right to vote, and each citizen's vote is counted equally. No one has to pay for this right, nor is the wealthier citizen's vote weighed more than the poor citizen's. Furthermore, no one is supposed to sell their vote.[2]

Policymakers can intervene in both domains. In the rights domain, policymakers help to establish and fortify citizens' rights. In the dollars domain, they can mitigate for the possibly negative side effects of an unregulated market distribution of dollars.[3] The unregulated market evidently promotes economic growth, but does this unevenly across the population.

Policymakers appear to be faced with two types of *tradeoffs*. On the one hand, within the dollars domain, efficiency can be traded off for a more equal distribution of dollars, or vice versa. On the other hand, efficiency can be traded off for an enlargement of the scope of rights, or vice versa.

Consider how this general discussion of the rights and dollars domains applies to health care as it is organized in the United States. In the United States, health care occupies both domains. On the dollars side, health care is a major industry accounting for more than 15 percent of the nation's Gross Domestic Product. Health care has all the attributes that we associate with big business—corporations, stockholders, mergers, bankruptcies, etc. However, a certain circumscribed area of health care is protected from the dollars domain. This area occupies the rights domain, where, for instance, a number of *constitutionally* grounded health care rights are *universally* distributed to citizens such as the right to refuse treatment, and the right to emergency treatment.[4] Additionally, a number of *legal* rights to health care are specifically targeted at certain subpopulations such as Veterans, the elderly, and the very poor. Programs such as Medicare and Medicaid establish inalienable legal rights to the provision of health care services to those who qualify for them. These programs serve in part as a buffer against the vagaries of the market, making sure that inability to pay for health care services does not prevent eligible citizens from access to health care.

Equality and efficiency

Equality as a proxy for fairness appears to be the guiding principle behind decisions made in the rights domain, whereas efficiency (mediated by utility- and profit-maximizing behavior) appears to guide the decision making process in the dollars domain. Equality in this context implies that it is our duty to treat each other *as if* we are equal, disregarding certain characteristics that make us different such as race, gender, and socioeconomic status. This idea hinges on the Aristotelian principle that 'like cases be treated like.' The principle 'treat like cases like' seems to underlie many, if not all, notions of fairness. But, it begs the question 'Which characteristics do we consider morally relevant likenesses?' The various notions of fairness differ not in whether like cases should be treated like, but instead with respect to *what* are considered morally relevant likenesses. For example, when we have life saving treatments that could either save the life of someone who could be returned to perfect health, or the life of someone who will have a disability, are both types of patients alike because they are human beings, and therefore deserve life saving therapy? Or, are they unlike each other in that one will have a disability and the other will not (see Nord et al. 1999)?

It would be presumptive to suggest definitive answers to the latter questions. However, we can say that unless everyone is equal with respect to the likenesses that we may consider to be morally relevant, which of course is not the case, providing everyone with the same amount of health care would not make much sense.

Efficiency in this context comprises a *technical* element: Pareto-efficient and production and consumption; and a *social* element: the Pareto principle. Technically, a number of marginal conditions must apply. The first condition is that the marginal rates of substitution between any pair of distributable commodities, resources, or outcomes (for example, health care outcomes) must be the same for all individuals who consume both commodities or are beneficiaries of both resources or outcomes. The second condition is that the quantity of each commodity, resource, or outcome produced conforms with consumer (or beneficiary) preferences. That is, the marginal rate of transformation in production must equal the marginal rate of substitution in consumption for every pair of commodities, resources, or benefits. If these conditions do not hold, a shift in the patterns of production and/or consumption is possible which would benefit some without injuring others. These technical conditions imply the social element associated with Pareto efficiency, namely, the widely cited Pareto principle which says that a change (for instance, a health care policy change) is desirable if it makes some individual(s) better off without making any others worse off.

It should be noted here that the Paretian form of distributive justice merely accounts for a *preference-satisfaction* view of human well-being. It is far from clear whether such a view suffices as an adequate account of well-being—especially in the context of health. The preference-satisfaction view would appear in certain instances to assume too tight a connection between choices and preferences and, in turn, too tight a connection between preference-satisfaction and well-being. Visible acts of choice are supposed to accurately reflect preferences. But, in fact, important choices in health care, choices made by patients and health care providers alike, may be more reflective of certain moral constraints than they are of preferences. As for preference-satisfaction, it may fail to improve well-being if the preferences being satisfied are irrational, poorly cultivated, or simply based on incomplete or false information.

Equality-efficiency tradeoff

As noted above, equality (as a proxy for fairness) and efficiency are presumed to relate inversely. The inverse relationship between equality and efficiency can be depicted using the indifference curve tool. In Figure 4.1 below, following Rawls (1971: 37–39), the indifference curves (I and I′) represent possible combinations of equality and efficiency that are considered by society to be *equally just*.[5] Society can attach weights to equality and efficiency

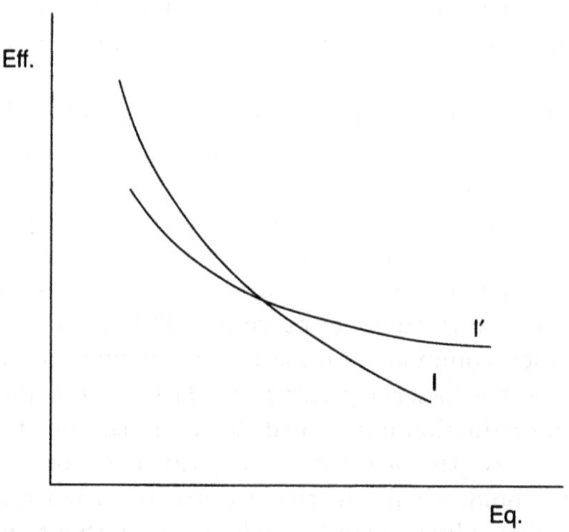

Figure 4.1 Two hypothetical indifference curves representing possible combinations of equality and efficiency

given its respective notions of distributive justice, whether these are egalitarian, Rawlsian, utilitarian, or libertarian. The slope of an indifference curve at any particular point expresses the relative weight allotted equality and efficiency. A more vertical curve (I) gives relatively more weight to equality, while a more horizontal curve (I′), allots more weight to efficiency. The more important and/or the more poorly satisfied a value such as equality or efficiency is, the greater the increase in another value required for compensating a loss. In this context, equality can be broadly measured by evaluating the variance in, for instance, wealth or health outcomes across the population. Efficiency can be broadly measured by assessing the total production of wealth or health outcomes divided by the inputs needed to produce them.

Now imagine a three-person world, one impartial distributor and two beneficiaries, X and Y. The impartial distributor distributes health care resources necessary[6] to produce certain health outcomes. These outcomes can be measured in terms of decreases in morbidity and mortality—life expectancy discounted for the quality of life expected, or quality-adjusted life-years (QALYs). Suppose that there is a line, MN, that represents the locus of possible Pareto-efficient points (see Figure 4.2 below). At each point on the MN curve a Pareto-efficient allocation of health outcomes (for example, QALYs) exists. A Pareto-efficient allocation of health outcomes is one in which no individual can be made healthier—for instance, in terms of QALYs —without making some other individual less healthy. In other words, there is no redistribution possible that makes either individual healthier without making the other less healthy.

The Pareto distribution rule appears to ignore the relative (in)justice of the status quo. From a Paretian perspective, for instance, a distributive policy that increases health outcomes of a few already healthy individuals,

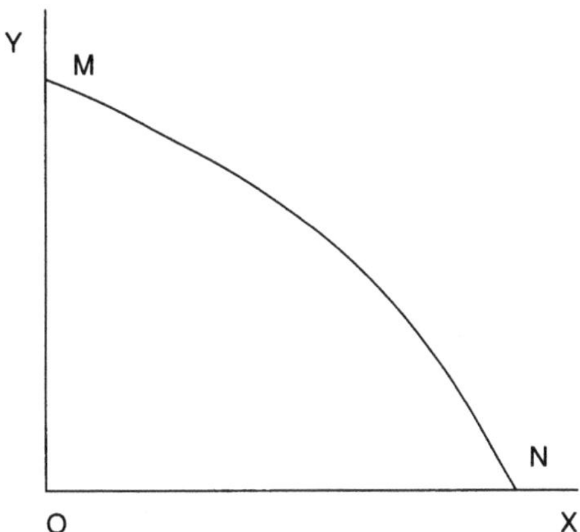

Figure 4.2 Pareto-efficient locus

even if this increase is only marginal, while leaving many unhealthy individuals just as unhealthy, would be considered a Pareto improvement. 'A state can be Pareto optimal with some people in extreme misery and others rolling in luxury, so long as the miserable cannot be made better off without cutting into the luxury of the rich' (Sen 1987: 32).

From the Paretian perspective, the locus of points, MN in Figure 4.2, *is not ranked in terms of equality or fairness, but only according to efficiency.* Giving M to Y is considered *just as efficient* as giving N to X, but we do not know whether it is fairer to give N to X, or M to Y. The only thing we do know is that if we give N to X, and nothing to Y, Y's well-being would stay the same, while X's would improve—a Pareto improvement. Needless to say, it could be that Y has an intense need for M, while X's need for N is only slight. In this case, Y stands more to gain from getting M than X stands to lose from not getting N. But, since the Paretian viewpoint precludes the possibility of interpersonal comparisons of need intensity, we cannot compare X and Y's needs. This is an enormous limitation. In fact, the only thing we can definitively say is that all points below MN are inferior distributions in terms of Pareto efficiency.

If we add the 45-degree line representing a simple equal division of health resources, and we assume simplistically that resources and outcomes are proportionate, we *can* rank points on MN in terms of how much or little equality they denote (see Figure 4.3 below). For example, compare point C to point D. If we place weight on an equal division of health outcomes, D would be considered a 'better' distribution than C, despite the fact that they are both *technically* just as Pareto-efficient.[7]

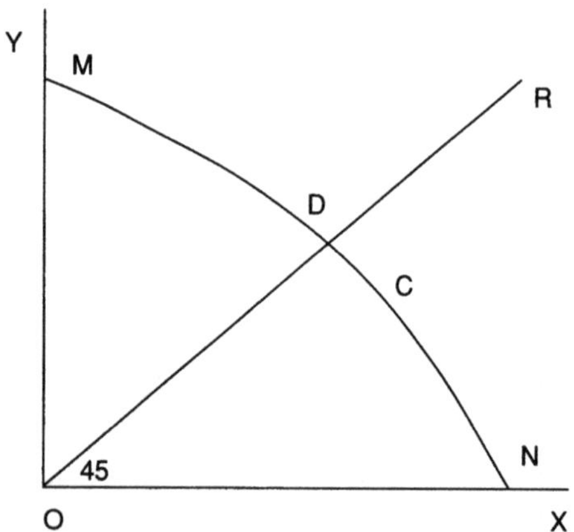

Figure 4.3 Adding 45-degree line

Tradeoffs inevitable?

Notice how in the case of the C–D comparison in Figure 4.3, the presumption that there is *necessarily* an equality-efficiency tradeoff is demonstrated to be false. Efficiency and equality *do not always have to be balanced against each other*. Moving from C to D improves equality while we remain on the same Pareto-efficient locus.[8]

There are in fact a number of other rules of distribution that do not have tradeoff implications—are not zero-sum games. Positive- as well as negative-sum games are possible between equality and efficiency. One such rule —*resource equalization*—is described in Culyer (1990). On the basis of a hypothetical case of global-budget health care rationing, Culyer illustrates the *tradeoff* implications of three different distributive rules. Culyer shows the effects the different rules have on the degree of efficiency, measured in terms of population health outcomes per resource unit expended, and the degree of equality, measured in terms of variance in population health outcomes. The first rule Culyer considers, the *radically egalitarian* distribution rule, equalizes health outcomes across the population. Given differing individual health care needs, such a distributive rule implies allocating the medically neediest a disproportionate share of resources. It may even imply allocating all resources to the medically neediest depending on the initial dispersion of health care needs across the population. A completely even spread of health outcomes raises the health outcome levels for some (the initially sickest) while possibly lowering the outcomes for others (the initially healthiest) as this rule implies actively lowering the latter's health to the lowest common denominator. The population's overall health outcome level may drop as the initially healthiest may stand more to lose than the neediest stand to gain. Culyer states, therefore, that radical equality comes at a price: an inefficient allocation of resources.

Culyer next considers the *utilitarian* distribution rule which aims to maximize aggregate health outcomes. This rule is maximally efficient, given Culyer's definition of efficiency, as the outcomes per unit of input are maximized. However, the gain in efficiency is offset by a loss of equality; the variance in health outcomes across the population increases, leaving the initially sickest even sicker, while the initially healthiest either remain healthy or get healthier. Culyer states therefore that utilitarian efficiency comes at a price; an unequal allocation of both resources and outcomes.

The third and most interesting case Culyer considers is a compromise between the utilitarian and egalitarian rules. He calls this compromise *resource equalization*. This egalitarian rule is less radically egalitarian than outcomes equalization. It is inspired by Dworkin's equality-of-resource-endowment rule (see Dworkin 1985). The point of this rule is to give everyone an equal 'minimally adequate' share of scarce health care resources. People can do what they want with the resources at their disposal, in line with their health-related preferences. As a result, societal health care resource utilization will reflect differing preference and initial health endowment patterns among people. If people start out with equal resources, a health care market allocation will result in some people benefitting more, and others less from their initial resource endowment, depending on their initial health status and their preferences. Access to health care *resources* is spread evenly across the population. But health outcomes are unevenly distributed, both because individuals' needs and preferences are different to begin with, and because each individual's capacity to benefit from resources is different. However, the unevenness of distribution is less than it would have been in the utilitarian case. Additionally, resource equalization is more efficient than a radically egalitarian distribution. This compromise case of resource equalization does not necessarily imply a tradeoff between equality and efficiency. Compared to initial degrees of equality and efficiency, resource equalization may improve both.[9]

The Oregon initiative

The first and second sections above describe in abstract terms the relationship between fairness and efficiency, against the backdrop of Paretian welfare analysis. These two sections also theoretically describe how the fairness-efficiency tradeoff plays itself out both within the dollars domain and between the dollars and rights domains. In this section we evaluate a practical case of explicit health care rationing, the Oregon health care initiative. This initiative is assessed in terms of how it has promoted fairness and efficiency both within the dollars domain and across the dollars and rights domains. The inevitability of a fairness-efficiency tradeoff is called into question.

In 1983, the President's Commission for the study of ethical problems in medicine and biomedical and behavioral research asserted health care's special status among 'goods' that 'society has a role in distributing as equitably as possible.' Evidently, there is something special about health care. In a way different from other kinds of services, health care services allow us to pursue important life goals that could not be pursued without them (Daniels 1985). Because of health care's special place in society, it is often argued that health care should not be distributed solely according to either ability, or willingness, to pay. Given health care's unique status, the Commission suggested that 'all Americans should have adequate access to health care resources,' access being defined by the Commission as the ability each citizen has to secure necessary health care without being barred for reasons of social status, income, ability to pay, place of residence, or other factors extraneous to the appropriate delivery of health care services.[10] For all intents and purposes, however, the federal government has since abandoned fairness as a goal of health care policy (Caplan 1997: 148). If there is a common purpose to government health care policy today, it appears to be *cost containment* which, if viewed charitably, is supposed to be synonomous with efficiency. The growth in health expenditures has been contained over the last 8 years following increased enrollment in managed care. Managed care has managed to control costs somewhat by way of *capitation*, or prospective payments of lump sums to health care providers per patient, rather than retrospective payment per medical intervention as under fee-for-service.

The exponential rise in health care costs over the last three decades, from 7 percent of GDP in 1968 to over 15 percent of GDP in 1998, raises the specter of a health care system out of cost control. However, this cost problem should not mask the problems related to lack of fairness in the health care system. Despite more money being pumped into health care during the last three decades, the numbers of uninsured (more than 44 million in 1998, or 17 percent of the American population) and underinsured have risen dramatically while population-wide health-outcome measures have not improved significantly during this time period.[11]

Rising costs related to the Medicaid program, together with federal Medicaid budget cuts in the 1980s, led many state governments to arbitrarily limit Medicaid eligibility by lowering the income threshold level by as much as 35 percent. On the face of it, this seems to be grossly arbitrary. Limiting eligibility on income grounds rather than medical necessity does not even seem rational, given that one of the original goals of the Medicaid program was to protect the poor from being in financial dire straits due to the costs of health care. In fact, this way of rationing seems to institutionalize rationing according to ability to pay rather than medical necessity.

In 1989, John Kitzhaber, a physician, community leader, and then state senate chairman in Oregon,[12] launched an initiative designed to reduce the arbitrariness associated with Medicaid rationing. Kitzhaber was fundamentally opposed to rationing according to ability to pay. Instead, he wanted to construct a 'rational,' publicly accountable rationing system. Kitzhaber gathered the support of many local politicians, community activists, physicians, patient representatives, and state Medicaid officials to push the initiative through the state legislature. The initiative's main purpose was to improve the poor's access to Medicaid by adding as many uninsured people to the Medicaid rolls as possible. All residents with incomes below the federal poverty level would become eligible for Medicaid, not just the very poor. As a result, the option of arbitrarily rationing people out of the health care system no longer existed. Rather than rationing by excluding people, the initiative proposed rationing by way of exclusion of health care services.

The Oregon initiative constitutes an effort to develop an integrated social policy approach, not strictly a health care policy approach. Dollars spent on health care imply an opportunity cost in terms of forgone alternative spending outlets. Resource allocations for health care are balanced with allocations in related areas which also affect health, such as education. The Oregon initiative proposes a system of resource allocation that recognizes scarcity and opportunity cost, and hence the need to allocate funds and resources among many competing social programs including health care, education and infrastructure.

It may be helpful to consider the Oregon initiative as analogous to Culyer's resource equalization distribution rule. This is because, with the Oregon proposal, access to resources is equalized according to medical need across a clearly defined subpopulation (all residents with an income below the federal poverty level).

For the purpose of rationally excluding a number of health care services, the Medicaid benefit package had to be overhauled and reduced. The method Oregon chose to accomplish this was the *prioritized list*. In the prioritization process, two key questions need to be answered. First, given the Medicaid budget allocated Oregon, the number of people covered has to be established. Second, the health care services for which people are covered has to be determined. So-called *condition treatment pairs* are the building blocks of the prioritized list. Each medical condition (for example, appendicitis) is linked specifically with a treatment (appendectomy).[13] Rather than eliminating types of services (such as prescription drugs), Oregon's prioritized list would eliminate specific relatively ineffective treatments for specific conditions. A prioritized list would guarantee that health care benefit reductions would eliminate only the least effective treatments. In 1991, Oregon ranked more than 700 diagnoses and treatments in order of importance. The Oregon Health Services Commission decided to draw a line below which everything would be covered, and above which nothing would be covered.[14] Treatments that prevent death and lead to full recovery ranked first in priority. Treatments that prevent death without full recovery are ranked next. Treatments that result in minimal or no improvement in the quality of life ranked last.

The Oregon initiative targets both the rights and dollars domains. In the rights domain, it aims at establishing for all Oregonians a legal right to a basic, though comprehensive, health care package.[15] The Oregon plan also intervenes in the dollars domain by enforcing community rating of health insurance premiums, thus limiting the ability of health insurance companies to risk-rate premiums. It is in this sense comparable to the resource equalization rule. Those below the federal poverty level are guaranteed access to the Oregon Medicaid program, those above are guaranteed access to an employment-based policy that provides at least as beneficial a package as the Medicaid program. What Oregonians do with this access benefit is up to them. How they spend their health care resources depends first and foremost on their initial health status, but also on their health-related preferences and those of their health care providers.

One of the initiative's objectives is to improve efficiency by moving the Medicaid population out of fee-for-service and into the prepaid system of *managed care*. By commissioning the services of cost-conscious, privately run managed care companies, coverage for the poor and uninsured could be made more affordable to the state than if traditional indemnity plans were commissioned. Furthermore, Oregon legislated mandatory community-rating of health insurance premiums in order to prevent health coverage exclusion by managed care companies owing to preexisting conditions. Since managed care companies contain costs by limiting available services and restricting patient choice, the state came up against a federally imposed hurdle that normally applies to state Medicaid programs: federal regulations prohibit rationing of services to those eligible for Medicaid. Oregon requested an exemption from these regulations. Specifically, Oregon requested permission to reduce the number of medical services covered to accommodate for a greater number of enrollees. Oregon obtained federal waivers and eventually passed its initiative through the state legislature, implementing it in 1994.

A task for health economists is to evaluate the efficiency implications of the Oregon initiative. From an apparently middle-of-the-road perspective on efficiency, the Pareto perspective, the Oregon initiative is *socially* inefficient. This is because some will lose benefits as a result of the initiative's implementation. Efficiency appears to be sacrificed for the sake of improved fairness in terms of increased access to and use of the Medicaid system.[16] The Paretian perspective does not, however, consider the possibility of *net* social gains or losses in terms of *both* efficiency and fairness. The Paretian perspective narrowly focuses on the comparatively few Medicaid recipients who lose coverage of unprioritized treatments as a result of health service rationing, and not on the accruing net gains of the entire population of Medicaid recipients. If the social gains in terms of *both* fairness and efficiency outweigh the losses, then a positive-sum game is feasible.

To judge whether there is a positive-sum game, economists would have to examine both efficiency and fairness indicators. On the efficiency side, health economists must evaluate whether covering the uninsured poor is effective without substantially raising the costs of the state's Medicaid program. Empirically, the benefit side of efficiency comprises at least three separate indicators: *access* to health care services, *use* of state health care services, and *health outcomes* related to use. Of these three indicators, data unequivocally confirm improved access. Oregon has added more than 100,000 people to the Medicaid program (Bodenheimer 1992, Blumstein 1997). All persons under the poverty level are now eligible for Medicaid. Before the plan was instituted, only 57 percent of these people were eligible. Furthermore, the initiative mandates health care access for *all* Oregonians to a basic (though comprehensive) health care package. Data also suggest limited improvements in both the use of health care services and health outcomes among the Medicaid population (Blumstein 1997, Oregon State Health Commission Report 1997). On the cost side, the crucial parameter to measure is the difference between actual costs of the currently covered Medicaid population and projected Medicaid costs if the poor uninsured population were not covered. Actual costs have remained within the state's Medicaid budget. However, a better indicator of efficiency cost, opportunity cost, and the cost of alternative ways of improving access, has not been calculated. This makes it difficult to state unambiguously whether the Oregon proposal is or is not cost-effective.

The Oregon initiative appears to promote a *fairer* state Medicaid health care system on two counts. First, if we judge fairness in terms of 'like cases being treated like,' with the only morally relevant likeness being medical need, the Oregon initiative appears fair because, across the entire poor population, equal resources are being expended for equivalent medical needs, regardless of ability to pay. Second, the Oregon initiative enforces community rating of health insurance premiums. As a result, it protects those with preexisting conditions from having to pay exorbitantly high insurance premiums.[17] The Oregon initiative does, however, limit explicit rationing to Medicaid recipients. For this reason, it has been labeled by some as unfair. Critics attack the plan for making the poor bear the burden of providing universal access. Despite it being true that rationing falls on the shoulders of the poor,[18] the plan has not led to a widening of the gap between the health outcomes of the rich and poor (see the Oregon State Health Commission Report 1997). It has improved the poor's *relative* health status compared to the wealthy, even though some current Medicaid recipients are worse off than they were before. As Daniels (1991) predicted, 'the loss of less important services by [some] recipients is more than counterbalanced by the gains of the uninsured. As a result, the plan reduces overall inequality between the poor and the rest of society' (2234).

In brief, Oregon, in theory, shows how fairness and efficiency can work together. In addition, Oregon illustrates a unique opportunity for the private sector, managed care companies, to cooperate with the state's regulatory bodies in mandating access to health care services. This said, in practice, physicians and policy analysts have to learn to accept that increasing access to as many as possible comes at the price of withholding services from some. We therefore need measures of fairness that take account in a sophisticated way of issues such as access, so tradeoffs between fairness and efficiency can be identified. We also need to be able to identify situations where tradeoffs between fairness and efficiency do not occur—situations which have generally been ignored in the economics literature.

Notes

1 In this context, equality is used as a proxy for fairness. Needless to say, equality and fairness are not the same thing. Under certain circumstances, being fair may imply actually treating individuals unequally.

2 Okun distinguishes between the rights and dollars domains. However, the line between the two domains is semi-permeable. Notably, property rights are part and parcel of the dollars domain.

3 Of course, in some instances, policy makers may actually deregulate sectors within the dollars domain to promote efficiency, as has been done throughout the 1980s and 1990s.
4 Most health care rights are termed negative rights. Other than a right to emergency treatment, United States legal statutes do not guarantee a citizen's positive right to health care services.
5 Rawls uses Pareto efficiency as a measure of efficiency, while his concept of equality indicates an equal division of 'primary goods' across the population. Since Rawlsian primary goods include rights as well as commodities, the equality-efficiency tradeoff suggested by Rawls occurs across the rights and dollars domains.
6 Health care resources are necessary, though not sufficient, conditions for producing health benefits. Other resources such as education also contribute to better health outcomes.
7 Note that any move from point to point along the Pareto-efficient locus MN would be socially suboptimal in terms of the Pareto principle. That is, moves from point to point along MN imply a zero-sum game where one person wins while another loses. Since Pareto only allows for ordinal comparisons between persons, the balance of losses and gains cannot be assessed.
8 Of course, the move from C to D implies that one beneficiary gains while the other loses; a Pareto-inefficient move. But both C and D are technically Pareto-efficient points.
9 Whether resource equalization is fair or not depends on the initial dispersion of medical needs across the population. If needs are similar across the population, then resource equalization leads to a fair distribution. If needs are dissimilar, it will have to be judged whether the resulting variance in health outcomes is fair or not. To make it fair, the resource-equalization rule may have to be supplemented by the establishment of a 'necessary minimum' level of resources, below which no subpopulation is allowed to fall.
10 The 1983 Commission was careful not to suggest that the government should establish health care as a constitutional or legal right.
11 Empirical evidence strongly suggests that lack of (adequate) insurance decreases health care access leading to significantly worse health outcomes. A person's condition upon hospital admission, his use of resources during hospitalization, and likelihood of death all vary according to the person's health insurance status (see Hadley et al. 1991, Lefkowitz and Monheit 1991).
12 Kitzhaber is now Governor of Oregon.
13 Of course, for certain conditions, there may be more than one therapy involved.
14 The line was drawn at 587 on the original list of 700 condition-treatment pairs.
15 It must be noted that in Oregon, before the initiative, one third of the uninsured were Medicaid eligible, while twice that many were the working poor and their dependants—people not eligible for public assistance, yet who could not afford their own health insurance.
16 Technically, however, the overhauled Oregon Medicaid system may be just as efficient as before. To illustrate this, see Figure 4.3. Suppose X represents that part of the population who loses some benefits as a result of the overhaul. Y represents that part of the poor population who gains benefits. Assuming that the Pareto-efficient locus does not shift in- or outwards, we could depict the gain accruing to Y and the loss to X as a move along the MN curve from point C to point D.
17 The Oregon Medicaid program is also a popular program. In a survey carried out by the Oregon State Health Commission, 88 percent of Medicaid patients

said they were satisfied with the health care services provided to them (Oregon State Health Commission Report 1997).

18 This situation is not new. Before implementation of the initiative, health care to the poor was rationed by way of ability to pay.

Bibliography

Aday, L., Andersen, R., and Fleming, G. (1980) *Health Care in the US: Equitable for whom?* Beverly Hills CA: Sage Publications.

Arrow, K. (1951) *Social Choice and Individual Values*, Oxford: Oxford University Press.

Beauchamp, D. (1989) *The Health of the Republic*, Philadelphia PA: Temple University Press.

Becker, G. (1976) *The Economic Approach to Human Behavior*, Chicago: University of Chicago Press.

Blumstein, J. (1997) The Oregon experiment: the role of cost-benefit analysis in the allocation of Medicaid funds, *Social Science and Medicine* 45: 545–555.

Bodenheimer, T. (1992) The Oregon Health Plan—lessons for the nation—part one, *The New England Journal of Medicine* 337: 651–655.

Caplan, A. (1997) *Am I My Brother's Keeper*, Bloomington IN: Indiana University Press.

Churchill, L. (1994) *Self-Interest and Universal Health Care*, Cambridge MA: Harvard University Press.

Cohen, J. (1996) QALYs, needs, and preferences, *Journal of Medical Ethics*: 267–272.

Culyer, A. (1990) Commodities, characteristics of commodities, characteristics of people, utilities and the quality of life, in S. Baldwin, C. Propper, and C. Godfrey (eds) *Quality of Life Perspectives*, London: Routledge.

Daniels, N. (1985) *Just Health Care*, Cambridge: Cambridge University Press.

—— (1991) Is the Oregon rationing plan fair? *The Journal of the American Medical Association* 265: 2232–2236.

Dworkin, R. (1985) *A Matter of Principle*, Cambridge MA: Harvard University Press.

Hadley, J., Steinberg, E., and Feder, J. (1991) Comparison of uninsured and privately insured patients: condition on admission, resource use, and outcome, *The Journal of the American Medical Association* 265: 374–379.

Kitzhaber, J. (1990) Speech before the Oregon Senate.

Klappholz, K. (1972) Equality of opportunity, fairness, and efficiency, in M. Peston and B. Corry, *Essays in Honor of Lord Robbins*, London: Weidenfeld and Nicolson.

Lefkowitz, D. and Monheit, A. (1991) Health insurance, use of health services, and health care expenditures, *National Expenditure Survey Research Findings* 12, AHCPR Pub. No. 92-0017, Rockville, Maryland.

Mitchell, L. (1998) *Stacked Deck*, Philadelphia PA: Temple University Press.

Nord, E., Pinto, J., Richardson, J., Menzel, P., and Ubel, P. (1999) The value of DALY life: problems with ethics and validity of disability adjusted life years, *British Medical Journal* 319 (27 November): 1423–1425.

Office of Technology Assessment Study (1992) *Evaluation of the Oregon Medicaid Proposal*, US Government Printing Office.

Okun, A. (1975) *Equality and Efficiency: The Big Trade-Off*, Washington DC: The Brookings Institution.

Oregon State Health Commission Report (1997).

President's Commission for the study of ethical problems in medicine and biomedical and behavioral research (1983) *Securing Access to Health Care*, US Government Printing Office.

Rawls, J. (1971) *A Theory of Justice*, Cambridge MA: Harvard University Press.

Robbins, L. (1932) *An Essay on the Nature and Significance of Economic Science*, London: Macmillan.

Rowley, C. and Peacock, A. (1973) *Welfare Economics: A Liberal Restatement*, London: Martin Robertson.

Samuelson, P. (1947) *Foundations of Economic Analysis*, Cambridge MA: Harvard University Press.

Sen, A. (1987) *On Ethics and Economics*, Oxford: Oxford University Press.

Ubel, P., Arnold, R., and Caplan, A. (1993) Rationing failure: the ethical lessons of the retransplantation of scarce vital organs, *The Journal of the American Medical Association* 270: 2469–2475.

Ubel, P., DeKay, M., Baron, J., and Asch, D. (1996) Cost-effectiveness analysis in a setting of budget constraints: is it equitable? *The New England Journal of Medicine* 334: 1174–1178.

Part II

RESISTANCE TO MARKET-BASED REFORM OF HEALTH CARE SYSTEMS

5

THE NATIONAL HEALTH SERVICE, THE 'INTERNAL MARKET' AND TRUST

Robert McMaster

Introduction

The UK's National Health Service (NHS) was founded fifty years ago as a central element of the welfare state arising from the post-war Beveridge reforms. The NHS was to provide universal, high-quality medical care, free at the point of consumption. General taxation was, and remains, the source of finance for the NHS. Arguably, it is this method of financing that is both the strength and weakness of the UK's health service. Commentators continually refer to the low percentage of GNP expended on health services in the UK relative to other industrialized states, particularly the USA. This is viewed as evidence of the comparative efficiency of both the NHS in providing health care, and its financial arrangements. Moreover, the NHS is popularly judged to be equitable in the provision of treatment and facilities, although this perception is subject to considered challenges (see, for example, Goodin and Le Grand 1987; Klein 1995). Simultaneously, taxation-based finance represents a weakness as it entails obvious consumption inefficiencies for the neoclassical economist, and relies on the continued positive disposition of taxpayers towards service users in the context of accelerating costs and fiscal parsimony. It is the combination of increased demand, the projected income elasticity of health care, and significant technological cost inflation that has led to issues of funding arrangements, and popularized discussions on a funding crisis in the NHS.

Previous Conservative governments argued that the growth of expenditure on the NHS required greater cognizance of the efficiency and efficacy of this expenditure. Indeed, this is consistent with the wider view of those governments that the market afforded a more efficient mechanism for allocating resources than state bodies. Arguably, their attempts to resolve the efficiency and fiscal concerns of health provision were influenced by the Griffiths Report of 1983 (Klein 1995), which stressed the need for greater cost-effectiveness, and Alain Enthoven's (1985) paper on 'improving efficiency' in the NHS. His argument was advanced in the context of the perceived failure of previous reforms in arresting the efficiency concerns of an expansive expenditure-demanding institution.[1] Enthoven asserted that the creation of an 'internal market',[2] where bureaucratic fiat is substituted for the price mechanism, would improve the allocation of resources. His case, and the wider advocacy of an internal market, is based on the theoretically complementary analyses of the Public Choice model of bureaucracy, and Williamson's transaction cost economics, embedded in the ideology of neoliberalism (see Keaney, this volume).

Both approaches share four crucial features: the standard economic behavioural tenet, a principal-agent model of interaction, informational asymmetries between parties, and the primacy of the market. These characteristics are more evident in the Public Choice approach, where it is readily recognized that the models employ standard assumptions, and are grounded in perfect competition (Mueller 1996). By contrast Williamson (1996: 6) attempts to differentiate transaction cost economics from strict orthodoxy on a host of grounds. Notwithstanding these efforts, Williamson himself considers that the transaction-cost framework both complements and extends orthodox analysis (Williamson 1996: 8).[3] Moreover, Williamson's (1975, 1985) analysis tacitly invokes a Smithian invisible hand when he asserts that markets are a natural state of affairs. Witness his biblical-style claim that 'in the beginning there were markets' (Williamson, 1975: 20), and his more recent stance that hierarchy 'is the organization(al) form of last resort' (Williamson 1993a: 131).

The overriding concern here is not the specific normative stance adopted by Williamson or Public Choice authors, but the tacit nature of this adoption under the guise of objective, value-free analysis. This is a criticism frequently levelled by heterodox analysts, and the arguments will not be repeated. However, of relevance here is that the advocacy of market reforms in the NHS is based on the insistence that the resolution of principal-agent type problems associated with informational asymmetries will necessarily enhance systemic efficiency. This presumes rather narrowly constituted modes of human behaviour and economic interaction. As other, non-standard economic and multidisciplinary, assessments of aspects of the evolution and operation of the 'internal market' demonstrate, the issues are a good deal more complex than mainstream economic conceptions would suggest. While this chapter reviews those assessments, it endeavours to measure the impact of the initial market-oriented reforms, and subsequent policy initiatives of the new Labour government on trust between contracting parties in the NHS.

Trust is recognized as being a neglected concept in economics. Arguably, this is not confined to neoclassical analysis, since Institutionalists are often remiss in their accounts of the role of trust in directing and influencing behaviour. However, there has been an increase in the attention devoted to trust, particularly, in the UK context, under the auspices of the recent ESCRC Contracts and Competition Programme (see, for example, Burchell and Wilkinson 1997; Flynn et al. 1997; Lyons and Mehta 1997a, b). Those contributions emphasize the importance of trust in ensuring the effective conduct of economic activity, and present empirical evidence of cultural distinctiveness in the types of trust important to commercial contractual relations. Such an exercise has not been as extensively applied to the evolving contracting culture of the NHS. A possible exception is the recent paper by Goodard and Mannion (1998). However, they adopt a Williamsonian position that effectively rules out any evolutionary perspective. This chapter attempts to address this to some degree, drawing on theoretical developments, and the growing empirical literature analysing the effects of market-oriented reforms in the health service.

The process is complicated somewhat by more recent reforms enacted by the new Labour government. In its legislation,[4] the government claims to have abandoned the 'internal market' in preference for a 'third way': clinical governance-integrated care. However, this chapter argues that while the most recent reforms emphasize collaboration through the termination of competition, they retain elements of the internal market by maintaining the client-contractor split established in the 1990 reform package. Consequently, the incentive structure of actors may still portray market-oriented influences. The chapter asserts that, in effect, the previous reforms contributed to a principal-agent division in the provision of health care, and the nature of the present reforms does not fully address this. Elements of trust subject to erosion will not be fully re-established by the maintenance of formal client-contractor splits.

The following sections set out the salient features of the 1990 and 1997 reforms. Following this, the chapter critically reviews the economic literature on trust, which emphasizes the importance of embedded institutional factors in the role and levels of trust in economic activities. The penultimate section conjectures how both reforms may affect trust in the health service. A conclusion follows.

The NHS and the 1990 reforms

Previous legislation, *Working for Patients*, specified two rather neutral objectives: to provide better health care for patients, and to successfully respond to patients' needs and preferences. However, the paper asserted that in order for those objectives to be attained the NHS must be subject to the most radical institutional change since its inception. This involved opening the service to market-oriented incentive structures, while maintaining the general funding of the service intact, i.e. through general taxation. The legislation introduced market-oriented interactions between actors in the health service by imposing a contractual relationship between different bodies in the NHS. The centrepiece of the reforms was the division between purchasers and providers, and the devolution of budgetary responsibility from health authorities. Change focused on hospital service, general practice and community care.

More specifically, the legislation established the purchasers of health care as General Practitioners (GPs) and District Health Authorities (or health boards in Scotland), whereas the providers were hospital units. The government endeavoured to increase the number of actors in the field by encouraging hospital units to seek NHS Trust status and GP practices to seek fundholding status, which involved greater autonomy from health authorities and increased budgetary responsibility. Trusts were encouraged to compete for contracts for secondary patient care. The obvious aim here being to reduce the perceived rigidities associated with monopoly bureaucratic supply. Thus, the rationale suggested that those Trusts, or hospital units, not offering a sufficiently responsive service would experience diminished revenues and consequent financial difficulties. There are clear incentives for management to engage in practices that ensure consumer satisfaction and, in a competitive market, to achieve this efficiently. The ultimate sanction for the management of such 'inefficient' bodies would be loss of occupation. The relevant Secretary of State had the power to replace the management of poorly performing units.

The parallels with the 'market' discipline of the Williamsonian M-form construct are apparent. According to Williamson (1985) the corporate headquarters of an M-form firm acts as a capital market in the allocation of resources. Management in poorly performing divisions will, at best, have comparatively less opportunities to advance their careers.

On the demand-side, the reforms effectively transferred influence from hospitals and consultants to GP fundholding practices, by empowering fundholders with the right to switch referrals to alternative suppliers, including the private sector. Under the fundholding arrangements, finance for services flowed from the purchaser's budgets (both GP fundholders and health authorities). Thus, in theory at least, dissatisfied purchasers could ultimately seek alternative suppliers and, as a result, funds are transferred to this new supplier. Contracts between commissioning bodies and Trusts were negotiated on an annual basis: arguably, a relatively short duration for the complex nature of some of the activities involved. In some cases specific individual treatment(s) represented a contractual agreement funded on a cost-per-case basis. This further enabled purchasers to exert influence over providers, given that in the case of dissatisfaction an alternative supplier would be sought for the following case.

Moreover, the influence of GP fundholders was increased further by the concomitant movement from health authority to fundholding purchasing of certain forms of patient care. The rationale for this was based on a variation of Arrow's (1963) thesis on the information problems associated with consumer choice in health care. Not only do patients experience informational deficiencies regarding health status and appropriate actions, so do health authorities. GPs are judged to be in the best position to evaluate patient welfare. This was reflected in a further clause in the legislation imposing contracts on GPs tailored to enhance patient choice of GP, and to furnish GPs with incentives to offer a greater range of primary care services, including minor operations.

Thus, while the reforms enhanced the purchasing role of GPs, they were also subject to constraints in the form of the ability of patients to substitute their source of primary care. Given that funds were allocated on the basis of the number of people registered with a practice, GPs perceived not to be offering quality services would experience declines in registered patients and revenues. Further, conventional agency theory indicates that partnership dynamics can constrain individual free-riding and inefficiencies, given suitably defined property rights. Under both the 1990 and 1997 reforms, GPs' independent contractual status was preserved. However, whether those twin sources of competitive pressure actually materialized is highly debatable.

More generally, the separation of functions and devolution of budgetary responsibility was intended to stimulate competitive pressures at both primary and secondary care levels, and in this manner enhance cost awareness, while simultaneously improving the quality of care (Chalkley and Malcolmson 1996a; Flynn and Williams 1997). Equity was not a prominent issue in the reforms, although equity considerations were not ignored entirely. Indeed, the legislation had several references about the importance of tailoring services to need as opposed to ability to pay. However, despite those references the previous Conservative government's reform package represented a considerable shift in the culture of NHS activities (Flynn and Williams 1997; Hughes et al. 1997; Montgomery 1997; Keaney, this volume). Contracting formalized relationships between actors across the so-called *purchaser-provider* split. Communication between parties was inevitably drawn into recognized channels, as opposed to informal arrangements. Indeed, this was the experience of contracting in the NHS for ancillary activities, such as catering and domestics, introduced by earlier legislation, and in other state bodies subject to similar patterns of vertical disintegration (McMaster and Sawkins 1996). However, despite this, adjustment contracts carried no legal recognition. Instead, arbitration of any disputes, and regulatory enforcement was conducted by central NHS management in the relevant ministry (for example, the Department of Health in England, or the Scottish Office in Scotland). Thus, while the shift to contracting is clearly a market-oriented alignment, it does not represent full-scale privatization in that contracting bodies do not possess the property rights to seek judicial arbitration, and are subject to administrative fiat. It is, perhaps, more appropriate to view the reforms as a means of performance management (Montgomery 1997), or 'new public management' (Brereton and Temple 1999) redolent of the broader 'Great

Capitalist Restoration' (see Keaney, this volume). Nevertheless, this legal distinction notwithstanding, a number of issues are raised by institutional change of this nature:

1 whether the new value structure is concordant with the established one founded on the Hippocratic ethos, and senior clinician dominance;
2 whether the change in value structure generates or resolves agency issues, and its effects on trust between parties;
3 whether the institutional change is commensurate with the objectives of the reforms;
4 whether the new system can generate sufficiently reliable information to address the means of achieving stipulated objectives.

This set of issues is rather different from the 'efficiency' emphasis of conventional economics and health economics, and to some extent this is also the case with the evaluatory criteria advocated by Le Grand and Bartlett (1993). In the *King's Fund Institute* evaluations Le Grand and Mays (1998) specify quality, efficiency, choice and responsiveness, and equity as principal evaluatory parameters. Much of the commentary on efficiency is based on Williamson's static transaction cost framework. There are inherent dangers in this, the predominant one being Williamson's assumption that governance change can be separated from institutional 'shift parameters' (Williamson 1993a: 113), which are presumed to remain constant.[5] This implies that not only is exchange impervious to the institutional environment, but that organizational change of this magnitude occurs within a vacuum: there is no value change or trust distortion. Nevertheless, despite this potentially considerable criticism, the evaluatory criteria advanced by Bartlett and Le Grand has been adopted by many studies.

Evaluations of the 1990 reforms

At the time of the earlier review of the NHS, most prominent health economists were broadly in favour of introducing some form of competition in the provision of health services (see, for example, Culyer et al. 1990). He noted that the 'great weight' of professional advice was to maintain the tax-based funding arrangements, but to accompany this with the standard neoclassical perspective that supply-side competition was a prerequisite in enhancing 'efficiency' (Barr et al. 1989; Chalkley and Malcolmson 1996a). However, despite this initial optimism the evidence on the efficacy of the 'internal market' is inconclusive. Arguably, this is hardly surprising given the complexity of the reforms and the hybrid arrangements engendered, the intractable difficulties attached to measuring health care processes and outcomes, and the time frame since the imposition of the initiative (see Keaney, this volume). Moreover, the reforms were implemented during a period when there was a substantial increase in funding, thus generating further measurement difficulties for the analyst endeavouring to disentangle the effects of the reforms from the increase in resources. Finally, assessment may be subject to bias since the initial wave of NHS Trusts tended to be atypical in that they were more comparatively efficient than non-trust bodies (Propper 1996). Nevertheless, a considerable literature has been spawned, employing eclectic empirical techniques from mainstream econometric regressions to case studies, although the latter constitutes the bulk of analysis. Further, due to the profound magnitude of the institutional change, analysis tended to concentrate on specific aspects or ramifications.

For example, Propper (1996) conducted one of the few conventional econometric studies of the effects on the pricing of specific clinical treatments. In her sample of first wave NHS Trusts she found that prices for certain treatments (ENT and gynaecology) were forced downwards, although the UK's small private sector was active in those areas. Other treatments, such as general surgery, did not demonstrate this pattern. Nevertheless, Propper concluded that her results were consistent with the hypothesis that 'market forces' did have an impact on provider behaviour, but emphasized that this was only an initial finding given that her results were only for a small part of the 'internal market'.

Other studies have also emphasized the exercise of caution in evaluating the reforms. Nevertheless, there is some tentative support for central elements of the legislation—principally the 'purchaser-provider' split—from reviews undertaken under the auspices of the King's Fund Institute (Robinson and Le Grand 1994; Le Grand et al. 1998).

Some reports have been more forthright in their support. In their survey of fundholding practices across various disparate regions, Glennerster et al. (1994) found that fundholders recorded cost savings relative to non-fundholding practices in, for example, drugs budgeting and hospital referrals. The authors also emphasized less quantifiable efficiency sources in contracting activities. Specifically, they believed that fundholding offered informational advantages concerning patient requirements and preferences, and incentives to improve service standards as GPs were (financially) penalized for delays or patient dissatisfaction. Importantly, Glennerster et al. also considered that a two-tier service resulting from fundholding would be transitory. Concisely, concerns were expressed that GP fundholding would create substantial differences in the quality of care offered and access to this care. Arguably, fundholders would have the incentive to screen potentially expensive patients (such as the elderly) from their practices in order to protect their budgetary expenditure: so-called cream-skimming. In competing for patients, Trusts may be financially impelled to offer patients registered with fundholders treatment as a priority regardless of clinical factors, producing obvious inequities. In a review of pertinent studies, Le Grand et al. (1998) found that two-tier standards had been exacerbated.

A number of commentaries have been more sceptical of the benefits of the reforms, but again they stress the intrinsic difficulties in accurately assessing the impact, let alone the efficiency effects, of the new arrangements. Methodological criticisms also question the usefulness of many economic approaches (for a general critique of neoclassical health economics, see Keaney 1997). Flynn and Williams (1997) note that the reforms demonstrated inherent contradictions, as the objectives of competitive efficiency had to be reconciled with other goals, such as equity of access. Indeed, this 'contradiction' is evident in the evaluatory parameters employed by researchers: witness the possible trade-offs in Le Grand and Bartlett's (1993) and Le Grand and Mays' (1998) criteria. The source of this 'inherent contradiction' may be due to the superimposition of market-oriented norms onto a preexisting institutional structure, where non-contractual incentives are manifest (Montgomery 1997). Despite the optimism expressed by advocates of market reform, clinician incentives are not entirely driven by economic factors. Clinicians are heavily influenced by professional bodies, which are frequently perceived to constitute anti-competitiveness by reducing contestability and increasing economic rent through the erection of entry barriers and restriction of purchaser choice. The argument is analogous to that presented against labour unions by free-market economists. By the same token, however, professional bodies stipulate behavioural parameters that may enhance patient welfare in addition to acting as a self-serving (and preserving) apparatus. In this respect the imposition of the 'new public management' represents a potential clash of value structures and not merely an adjustment to economic incentives. The point will be developed below.

Methodologically, considerable issues are raised in attempts to assess the impact of the reforms. For example, McHale et al. (1997) question the uncritical adoption of even less orthodox economic theories of contract, such as relational exchange. They state:

> The crucial role of regulation in the NHS internal market suggests that contract models developed in the context of commercial practice have only limited utility for understanding the NHS system. Though the[se] models . . . suggest some useful contrasts and insights, individually none provides an adequate [basis of] analysis of the NHS.
>
> (McHale et al. 1997: 206–207)

This point cannot be exaggerated in its importance. Analyses predicated on the tenets of mainstream economics are impaired in their ability to examine the *nature* and *evolution* of the reforms. In particular, mainstream approaches tend to be predicated on the principal-agent assumption that agents will extract a stream of (utility-maximizing) benefits potentially at the expense of the principal. This presumes, as later sections argue, a specific view of trust that may not be robust within the context of health service provision. Some analysts have explicitly noted this, engaging and drawing on other models of behaviour and process (see, for example, Hughes et al. 1997; Kitchener 1998; Lapsley 1993; McHale et al. 1997; Montgomery 1997, *inter alia*). These approaches are noted in the penultimate section, and to some extent support the chapter's conjectures in respect of trust and health service reforms.

Indeed, it may be argued in some quarters that the new Labour government's reform package is some official recognition of the context-specific assumptions of the case for market-oriented reforms and their collision with reality. The 1997 reforms stress the need for co-operation between bodies in the NHS, and so, albeit tacitly, raise the analytical role of trust (Goodard and Mannion 1998) and reconsider the ubiquity of the principal-agent model. However, all is not as it may seem.

The 1997 reforms

The newly elected government claimed to be committed to abandoning the 'internal market' for health care. Certainly the White Paper, *The New NHS* (Secretaries of State 1997), emphasizes integrated care and co-operation as opposed to the competitive imperative previously sought. New primary care groups and clinicians from provider Trusts are to be encouraged to collaborate with NHS authorities in planning the local patterns of service provision within the new, centrally determined clinical governance, Health Improvement Programme.

Within the context of this programme, services are to be assessed according to benchmark performance against other provider Trusts as measured on a six-dimensional framework. Among the dimensions specified are health improvement (such as variations in death rates across population groups); fair access (equity); effective delivery (compliance with agreed stipulations); efficiency (cost effectiveness); patient/carer experience (some measure of satisfaction); and health outcomes (success in increasing survival rates). This new framework replaces the previous evaluatory framework—the Purchaser Efficiency Index—that was driven by cost effectiveness and the number of 'completed consultant episodes'. The government claims that this represents a considerable advance in ensuring the 'efficient' quality of health care, and indeed there may be sound reasons for concurring, but there are a number of outstanding issues concerning measurability and incentive effects, outlined more fully in the following sections, that may counter the government's contentions (see also Keaney's insightful critique of clinical governance and evidence-based medicine in this volume).

The reorganization further empowers GPs, despite the cessation of GP fundholding in preference for newly established, and larger, primary care groups. These groups are to be GP-led, and to have greater budgetary responsibility than GP fundholders, as they will be the principal commissioning or purchasing body for secondary health care. As noted, under the 1990 reforms this function was mainly retained by health authorities, with fundholders adopting a less prominent purchasing role. However, the trend was to increase the purchasing activities undertaken by fundholders—the 1997 reforms may have merely accelerated this process.

The creation of primary care groups by, effectively, amalgamating existing fundholding practices (from April 1999) is a prominent organizational innovation of the reforms. This is reflected in the present government's attempts to end the 'fragmentation' of the service by rationalizing structures through the horizontal integration of existing, secondary care Trusts and, at an administrative and regulatory level, NHS authorities—the objective being the promotion of strategic co-ordination between those bodies. By reducing the number of players in the game, and charging them with the duty to co-operate in the process of planning and commissioning services, the legislation assumes that the perceived dysfunctional behaviour engendered by market-orientation will be overcome. The trilateral arrangement envisages authorities acting in a regulatory capacity, and primary care groups and Trusts in a co-operative relationship. For this reason the duration of any 'commission' has been extended from one to up to three years.

Nevertheless, there are aspects of the new reforms that suggest that not only has the 'internal market' apparatus not been entirely abandoned but, in some respects, it has been reinforced. Arguably, any abandonment is more likely to be de jure as opposed to de facto for political reasons. Apart from any resemblance to relational exchange there are a number of clues buttressing this contention, the principal one being the retention of the purchaser-provider split. This was the centrepiece of the 1990 reforms, and the sine qua non of any market arrangement. Moreover, in *The New NHS* the Department of Health states: 'Primary care groups will grow out of the range of *commissioning* models that have developed in recent years' (Secretaries of State 1997: 34, emphasis added). And: 'The Government *will retain the separation* between the *planning* of hospital care and its *provision*. This is the best way to put into practice the new emphasis on improving health' (12, emphasis added).

These statements endorse the core organizational framework of the previous legislation. The employment of the term 'commissioning' is a euphemism for the persistence of contracting interfaces. Contentiously, by separating the demand (planning) of secondary care, as articulated through the commissioning process, from its provision, the reforms maintain not only the integral structure of the previous arrangements, but also the divergence of incentives of agents within it. Even in an atmosphere of co-operation, as the government insists the reforms will engender, the flow of funds from primary to secondary care groups suggests that actors will at least be influenced by considerations of appropriation. In other words, it is conceivable that secondary providers may perceive it to be to their advantage to press for an upward adjustment in the funding for activities provided, whereas purchasers may be motivated by the converse. The reforms place considerable emphasis on decentralized management, characteristic of other market-oriented initiatives of the previous Conservative government, and even greater emphasis on devolved budgeting (Montgomery 1997; Bartlett et al. 1998; Le Grand et al. 1998). Primary care groups will possess considerable budgetary discretion, in line with that advocated by pro-market reformers such as Glennerster.

If the foregoing is the case, then far from abandoning the principles of market orientation the current reforms have amended, as opposed to overhauling, the 1990 framework. The number of players may contract through horizontal integration, and regulatory procedures strengthened through broader performance indicators and joint 'co-operation', but the centrality of formalized exchange is retained. Indeed, this has drawn support from Le Grand et al. (1998: 141) who state: 'Overall the [legislation] deserve[s] a guarded welcome, not least because [it] has preserved some of the features of the internal market that, as best as can be determined, have been demonstrated to work.'

The importance of this should not be underestimated: as Bowles (1998) convincingly argues, markets effect the framing of decision making, motivations, values and culture. It is conceivable that the 1997 reforms are not as radical in adjusting those factors as may be supposed from the claim that the 'internal market' has been abandoned. Drawing from Bowles, of particular interest is how the establishment of market-oriented norms, and their subsequent reform, have impacted not only on those factors, but on the ubiquitous influence on all those features: trust.

Trust: a brief overview

It is commonly acknowledged that much of the economics literature does not document the characteristics, impact and levels of trust on economic activity. Famously, Arrow called on analysts to recognize trust as both a necessary and sufficient condition for economic activity, by emphasizing that 'There is an element of trust in every transaction' (Arrow 1973: 23). However, despite Arrow's attempts to map out the sine qua non of trust, in terms of its efficiency properties, and non-tradability and externality features; he was less successful in fashioning any robust definition.

Trust can be defined in terms of some form of co-operation between parties, where there is some reliance on another's goodwill, even if this is minimal (Baier 1986). Further,

> When I trust another, I depend on her good will toward me. I need neither acknowledge this reliance nor believe that she has either invited or acknowledged such trust since there is such a thing as unconscious trust, as unwanted trust, as forced receipt of trust, and as trust which the trusted is unaware of.
>
> (Baier 1986: 235)

Thus, to trust implies that there is some diminution in behavioural uncertainty (Fox 1974; Zucker 1986). Parties orient behaviour on the basis of the expectations of the behaviour of others (Lyons and Mehta 1997a), and their motivations. This draws on John Locke's considerations of *entrustment*. Concisely, not only is the identity of the individual who is trusted of paramount importance, so is the question: what is to be trusted to them? (Baier 1986: 236). Arguably, the extent of entrustment, especially in employment relationships, is influenced by shared values and loyalty (see Fox 1974; Zucker 1986, *inter alia*; Simon 1991; Fukuyama 1995), and may be considered as an integral part of social capital. In this respect Sako's (1992) delineation of trust is useful in that it reflects certain types of behavioural 'risk' in commercial contracting. He defines three categories of trust in exchange relations. First, contract trust, where a party is trusted to carry out a task as specified. Second is competence trust. Here there is a belief in the party's ability to provide commodities of a certain quality. Third, goodwill trust pertains to the extent of discretion and initiatives a party can exercise in her/his task(s), without seeking undue advantage or moral hazard. Hence, the foregoing reflects contract, competence and goodwill risks respectively. Sako's schema emphasizes how trust not only relates to behavioural uncertainties and individual motivations, but also to their abilities, and beneficial use of knowledge.

Much of this is not contentious, but there is considerable variation in accounting for trust across disciplines. This goes some way to explaining the lack of rigorous models of the mechanisms sustaining trust (Burchell and Wilkinson 1997; Lyons and Mehta 1997a, b). There is a contrast between the calculative self-interested trust of mainstream economics and the socially-embedded trust of anthropology, sociology and heterodox economic approaches.

Since Arrow, conventional economists, who explicitly recognize trust, tend to encapsulate it in the rational choice framework.[6] Witness, for example, Dasgupta (1988), and Leibenbstein's (1987) employment of game theoretic techniques to illustrate the economic efficiency of trusting. In the absence of trust, self-interested individuals will not transact, whether in single or repeated games. By applying George Akerlof's 'market for lemons', Dasgupta demonstrates that trust has beneficial externalities. Since producers will only invest in trust for personal rather than social benefits there is an underinvestment in trust formation. Leibenstein's application of the prisoners' dilemma reinforces the argument that self-interested behaviour will generate a sub-optimal outcome.

Mainstream economists' persistence in maintaining the assumption that individuals are motivated to trust for calculated, self-interested reasons has been the subject of some debate within the discipline. Williamson (1993b) is generally dismissive of the notion of calculative trust. Instead, he contends that this is a more general phenomenon of calculative behaviour redolent of opportunism. Thus, '*The study of economic organization is better served by treating commercial contracts without reference to trust*' (Williamson 1993b: 99, emphasis added).

Following Williamson, it would be irrational for individual A to depend on individual B, when A knows that B will be inherently exploitative. Trade, or any other economic activity, would, at best, be severely impaired without appropriate enforcement mechanisms, or governance structures. Ironically, Williamson's case is both appealing and repellent. Voluntary trading occurs between parties where both information and power are extremely unevenly distributed, without the sophisticated governance arrangements Williamson's analysis infers. David Hume recognized this as long ago as 1738 in his *Treatise of Human Nature*, when he argued that the exploitation of power in market exchanges was constrained by reputation effects. Failure on the promisor's part carries, at worst, the penalty of never being trusted again. In other words, Williamson fails to appreciate institutional sources of trust.

To reject trust from the narrow neoclassical model is not the same as rejecting more general conceptions of trust. Herein lies the rub with Williamson: his rejection of trust throws the baby out with the bath water. He adopts an excessively Hobbesian orientation. By presuming that opportunism is innate human behaviour, and simultaneously discounting trust, he presents no more than a grotesque variant of the Humean knave. Aspects of trust must be innate (Baier 1986), or else the human race would be reduced to a hermit-like existence.

More recently, Burchell and Wilkinson have dismissed narrowly conceived self-interested trust in *market* transactions. They argue:

> Trading partners derive mutual benefits from cooperation in production from which their incomes are ultimately derived, but they compete over the proceeds of production because what one gets the others cannot have. Every business relationship is therefore by its nature both rivalrous *and* cooperative.
>
> (Burchell and Wilkinson 1997: 219, original emphasis)

The evidence presented by Burchell and Wilkinson (1997) and Lyons and Mehta (1997a, b) shows that many firms display what Burchell and Wilkinson term 'enlightened self-interest'.[7] Firms recognize that tendencies towards exploiting gains from rivalrous behaviour could impair the sustenance of co-operation, and undermine mutual long-term benefit flows. However, both sets of authors refer to the importance of cultural factors in fostering trust, and in providing a rich variety of enforcement mechanisms. This is a common finding in an extensive literature, although Choi et al. (1994) argue that trust can arise and be sustained on positive feedback alone. Generally, Fukuyama's (1995) survey highlights cultural differences between low-trust individualistic, and high-trust collectivist societies and performance. Moreover,

Zucker's (1986) insightful analysis suggests that trust has to be supported by stable institutions (such as the law and money), and within this she also cites the role of professional associations in signalling (competence and goodwill variants of) trust.[8] In this respect trust arises from positive feedback, but there is some role for enforcement mechanisms in supporting trust. This also appears to be the case in the relational-exchange literature. For example, Macaulay (1963), Goldberg (1980) and Macneil (1982) stress the importance of parties' identities, and the establishment of a 'contract constitution' (Goldberg 1980). By contrast, the survey of inter-firm relations in Britain, Germany and Italy conducted by Arrighetti et al. (1997) and Deakin et al. (1997) suggests that trust is both buttressed and reproduced by contract law to a greater extent than suggested by the relational-exchange literature.[9] Nevertheless, the literature recognizes both the fragility of trust, and the role of customs in providing a vehicle for trust.

Custom (or conventions) legitimizes the entitlements of actors, and the exercise of enforcement mechanisms in the event of behaviour incompatible with established norms (McMaster and Sawkins 1996). In this respect Schlicht's (1993) 'journey' in a taxi is an excellent example of trust buttressed by custom. Payment is made after the journey, frequently without receipt. Custom prevents the driver from aggressively endeavouring to extract further payment since (s)he is not *entitled* to pursue this course of action. However, should the passenger attempt to leave the taxi without having made the appropriate payment the taxi driver could legitimately attempt to extract payment more insistently (due to an infringement of contract trust). In effect, parties entrust each other to adhere to custom-established behavioural parameters. In essence, customs convey both contractual and competence (the passenger assumes that the licensed driver is competent at her/his job) variants of trust. The extent of entrustment does not usually go beyond this; for example, the passenger will not usually entrust the driver with keys to her/his home. In effect, goodwill trust is not a major aspect of the interaction. Arguably, trust in this context is 'unacknowledged' (Baier 1986), since the exchange is of a relatively simple nature. It is trust supported by custom that simplifies exchanges which may be vulnerable to both adverse selection and moral hazard. There is usually little requirement for (potentially expensive) direct third-party involvement.

Thus, the argument presented here suggests not only that custom is important in establishing and supporting the various hues of trust, but that both custom and trust influence and are influenced by human behaviour. In their papers, Lyons and Mehta (1997a, b) usefully attempt to analyse the role of trust in commercial exchanges by drawing on Weberian notions of behavioural orientations. Four behavioural orientations are identified. First, instrumental rationality, where the individual is purposefully calculative, and in the extreme acts in a moral vacuum. Second, value rational behaviour, where the individual is influenced by some belief system, is committed to this system, and acts in ways consistent with it. Third, affectual behaviour refers to states of feeling and emotion. Fourth, traditional behaviour refers to habituated behaviour patterns (routines), such as those which form part of a firm's corporate culture.

Instrumental rationality, value rationality and traditional behaviours are of greatest interest for our purposes. Obviously, *homo economicus* (and indeed the Williamsonian variant) resembles the Weberian conception of instrumental rationality.[10] It is well recognized that one of the most important shortcomings of conventional theory is its failure to take cognizance of institutions. Thus, the rationality of *homo economicus* suggests, at best, a low-trust environment between parties. Clearly, instrumental rationality corrodes trust since, as noted, the assumption is that individuals will be innately exploitative, subject to exogenous constraints. This is manifest in the agency-theory approach to organization, tacitly employed in many evaluations of NHS reforms (witness Chalkley and Malcolmson 1996a, b, 1998). Concisely, the extension of the market mechanism is claimed to resolve the agency problem, by generating information and curtailing shirking potential.

The whole basis of the findings of agency theory is predicated on an absence of trust between actors, and narrowly conceived behavioural assumptions (see the excellent critique in Simon 1991). If actors are not assumed to be instrumentally rational, or Humean Knaves, then the simplistic market-oriented conclusions of the agency approach are not as compelling (McMaster and Sawkins 1996). Instead, other behavioural orientations may dominate instrumental rationality in its crudest sense. Specifically, the Weberian suggestion that behaviour can be 'traditional' and/or 'value rational' follows Thorstein Veblen's thesis that human behaviour is habit driven—habits being sanctioned and legitimized by institutions, and transmitted by routines (Nelson and Winter 1982). This raises the possibility of an interesting distinction between inter-firm trust (across a market interface) and intra-organizational trust.

Routine, as a manifestation of customary practices, can be a vehicle for stability, especially in *intra*-organizational interactions. Here contracts (should they exist formally) are less tangible than relational exchanges of long duration between firms, and actors are interacting within an authority, as opposed to a market, power structure. Intra-organizationally, routines can operate on at least two levels. First, as a means of preserving and enhancing the cognitive performances of individuals—as a knowledge store (Nelson and Winter 1982). Second, by establishing bounds of toleration, thereby conveying trust.

Fox's (1974: 24) observations on the instruction to 'sweep the floor' is an excellent example of this. He correctly indicates that the instruction is highly routine, yet involves some individual discretion as to what constitutes an appropriate performance (and even effort) level. The instructor trusts that the sweeper will undertake the task, and perform it to some satisfactory level. Thus, trust is being expressed in both a contractual and competence manner, but, again, this may be 'unacknowledged'. The sweeper's behaviour may be oriented by 'traditional' influences, which may underwrite performance, and (goodwill) trust in the legitimacy of the instruction. Here, it may be argued, the degree of entrustment between the parties is heavily, although not exclusively, influenced by institutional factors, such as the power structure as sanctioned by the authority relation and routine.

Fox's observations also reveal much about the depth of trust in the employment relationship. Concisely, there is an obvious association between the degree of trust required when parties possess considerable discretion in the execution of tasks. Similarly, where the degree of discretion is considerable there is likely to be less rigidity in chains of authority and routines (see Ouchi 1980).[11] However, where the degree of entrustment is less apparent, and routines buttress the low level of trust between actors, it is possible that these routines can be confined to extremely narrow parameters by 'the dikes of vested interest' (Nelson and Winter 1982: 111). The rigidity of arrangements can engender considerable resistance to change. Arguably, routine can be viewed as being analogous to a property-rights bundle, where any breach of the established bounds of toleration is viewed as an attenuation of a particular party's property rights: witness the demarcation disputes of the 1970s in British heavy industry. The foregoing can also be expressed in terms of a demand for equity, not necessarily equality, between the parties (Ouchi 1980). Routine in these circumstances represents a truce (Nelson and Winter 1982), where routine, albeit demonstrating rigidities, conveys the limited goodwill trust between the parties.

Thus, the Weberian conception of traditional behaviour can be sensitive to perceptions of whether change in enduring relationships, such as the employment relation, impacts asymmetrically upon groups of actors. The lower the degree of trust, the greater the sensitivity. Yet, even in high-trust environments change can lead to actor disorientation and *dis*trust. Laggardly, some neoclassicists are gradually recognizing this. The most prominent examples are Frey's (1993) and Whynes' (1993) contributions. Frey, in particular, contends that some hierarchical change that involves increased recourse to vertical monitoring throughout the organization—as in performance measurement—can be interpreted as acts of *dis*trust by actors who are committed to the values of the organization. In Weberian terms, the benchmark of value rational behaviour is corroded, as goodwill trust diminishes. Accordingly, actors become disenchanted and reduce effort in non-monitorable activities. There may be a perception that actors have effectively been disengaged from the core values of the organization by management. In effect monitoring *crowds out* effort (Frey 1993: 665), and generates inefficiencies inefficiently (Whynes 1993: 446). Fox's sweeper no longer feels obliged to exert effort beyond some enforceable minimum. Commensurate gives way to perfunctory effort. Indeed, Simon's (1991) assertion that conventional agency theory misses the point with its emphasis on free-riding and shirking has some resonance here. Simon inquires:

> The question is not whether free riders exist—much less employees who exert something less than their maximum—*but why there is anything besides free-riding.*
>
> (1991: 34, original emphasis)

Of course, the foregoing represent considerable generalities and conjectures. What are central to the examination, however, are the importance of trust, and the complexity of feedback mechanisms that can reinforce variants of trust, as well as diminishing it. The mainstream reliance on a reductionist perspective of human behaviour and motivation, confines conventional analysis to the status of a 'special case' (see Hodgson 1998). The effect of change on trust and the conduct of activities in the NHS are reviewed in the following section.

The NHS reforms and the corrosion of trust

Prior to the 1990 reforms, the NHS was considered to be characterized by a high degree of clinician autonomy (Flynn 1992; Klein 1995; Keaney, this volume). Clinicians retained the ultimate authority over the allocation of resources, usually based on professionally defined criteria of need. Since the 1960s, at least, there has been a gradual 'bureaucratization', which has tended to shift the balance from an administered to a managed service (Reed and Anthony 1993). This process accelerated with the 1990 reform package. The literature suggests that this process of centralization was a result of government attempts to contain the growth in NHS expenditure: concisely, all reforms were fiscally-driven, founded on the 'fiscal crisis of the state' (see Keaney, this volume).

However, as noted, the 1990 reform, for the first time since its inception, introduced specifically market-oriented mechanisms into both the allocation of resources and the organization of the NHS. Obviously, from an Institutionalist perspective this represents substantial change that will impact not only on the constraints to actors' preferences, but on the *moulding* of those preferences (Bowles 1998; Hodgson 1998). The patterns and extent of trust between parties cannot be isolated from such change. Yet there is little direct empirical evidence tracing out the nature of this change and how it impacts on the ability of the health service to meet its ultimate objectives.

Prima facie, the ideological basis of the NHS is egalitarian, and the underlying value structure in any health service is governed by the Hippocratic ethos. Following Glennerster et al. (1994), noted earlier, and Williams (1990) the introduction of market-oriented reforms would seem to suggest that the drive for 'efficiency' would inevitably generate some, or exacerbate existing, inequalities in the provision of care. In sum, there is scope for potential conflict between the established ethos and the value structure associated with a more market-aligned incentive structure. The previous Conservative government, exhibiting political sensitivities, argued that the reforms represented a continuing evolution of, as opposed to an alteration to, the fundamental principles of the NHS. However, the dynamic of the market does represent a tension in the NHS, especially since the reforms were superimposed on existing routines (Montgomery 1997). In short, the 1990 reform represented a significant institutional change, and change can result in instability and deterioration in the degree of entrustment.

More specifically, the pre-1990 NHS operated on a basis of high-value congruence. The dominance of the clinical profession and the prevailing Hippocratic ethos was further accompanied by considerable performance ambiguity, and actor discretion. However, this dominant value structure was subject to constraints in the form of, albeit subservient, bureaucratic administrative and fiscal influences. Lapsley (1993) usefully demonstrates the subservience of these influences in the operation of financial management. Finance officers conducted budgetary affairs by employing 'crude control techniques', such as adjusting the rate of payments for materials, stock control, and delaying the replacement of vacancies (Lapsley 1993: 387). The fluidity of this system of financial management emerged as a means of accommodating the dominance of clinicians in planning the provision of activities. Yet, arguably, the openness of the system was based on the resemblance of the NHS to an Ouchian clan (Lapsley 1993). Certainly, the dominance of clinicians was recognized as the source of legitimate authority, but beyond the core group of clinicians other groups shared in the same belief set. For instance, Ascher (1987) has documented the co-operative atmosphere pervading the relationship between clinical staff (especially nurses) and non-clinical staff (such as domestics and porters) in the delivery of care to patients. Indeed, Ascher further contends that non-clinical staff are frequently perceived to be part of a team delivering post-operative care.

The clan resemblance of the system generated, and reinforced, considerable degrees of trust (Reed and Anthony 1993; Montgomery 1997). In particular, extensive degrees of competence trust were invested in the professional code of practice of clinicians. Certainly, performance ambiguities were tolerated *if* a clinician had training accreditation as ratified by the Royal Colleges. This was (and remains) the principal means of expressing competence trust in physicians and other clinical staff. However, there is a perception that the professional accreditation remains a constraint on the market mechanism—analogous to an entry barrier that inflates costs by encouraging the potential pursuit of 'Rolls Royce' services standards without any awareness of costs (see Hartley 1990). It was this perception of a lack of accountability that shaped aspects of the 1990 reforms. Essentially, this can be interpreted in a number of ways. First, the pre-1990 NHS exhibited *too much* entrustment in the ability and incentives of clinicians. The absence of robust accountability mechanisms permitted clinicians, who had the opportunity, to free-ride, and insulated senior clinicians from the need to consult the preferences of patients. Second, the extensive degree of entrustment invested in clinicians was allocatively inefficient. Thus, by introducing more market traits into the activities of the health service, accountability and efficiency would be enhanced. Little was said regarding the ramifications for trust.

There are a number of points which indicate that a necessary prerequisite for the reforms was a diminution in the degree of entrustment. Theoretically, some advocates of marketization of state services have explicitly argued for such a diminution. Vining and Weimer (1990) argue that trust in state activities is essentially an entry barrier that reduces the contestability of state services. They claim that by increasing contestability the efficiency in the provision of state services will improve. Thus, by deduction, acting in a manner that erodes the 'stock' of trust will increase contestability and hence efficiency. Arrow's argument is completely turned on its head. It is obvious from the thrust of their argument that Vining and Weimer adopt a highly reductionist perspective in respect of human motivations, behaviour and trust. Individuals are no more than shirking, utility maximizers, and trust is tacitly assumed to be a mechanism for ensuring the pursuit of bureaucratic utility maximization. Arguably, the narrowness of this conception denigrates the attractiveness of their assertions.

Montgomery indicates that the pre-1990 NHS had an array of quality-control mechanisms, ranging from the Audit Commission to community health councils. The 1990 legislation created an additional body, the Clinical Standards Advisory Group, to oversee standards of care, access to, and availability of services. Nevertheless, Montgomery claims that

> The importance of these quality control mechanisms is largely political rather than direct. In practice, however, the need to avoid adverse comment from official bodies is an important constraint. Yet these mechanisms work through contracts as much as on them.
> (1997: 180–181)

In this respect, Montgomery highlights a report from the Clinical Standards Advisory Group on the treatment of diabetes: the government's response was to note that the responsibility for this lay with local purchasers. Montgomery's example illustrates the adjustment in the pattern of activities encouraged by the 1990 reforms.

The division between planning and delivery created by the market-oriented arrangements, combined with a prominent role for the NHS Executive in setting contract guidelines and regulating the conduct of providers and purchasers, has increased the role of managers in the health service.

Moreover, the role of management further increased through the deployment of the Purchaser Efficiency Index as an evaluatory benchmark for relative performance. This acted as a limited constraint on the discretion of clinicians in that NHS trust performance was (partially) judged on the throughput of patients. Trust managers could legitimately insist that clinicians adopt practices that were conducive to increasing the number of 'consultant episodes'. The relative positions of NHS managers and clinicians had been subject to adjustment. Moreover, this process was compounded by the recruitment policy of managers. NHS trusts were encouraged to actively recruit managers with private sector experience, and to further their positions of responsibility.[12] Again, this can be interpreted as a weakening in the Hippocratic ethos as the dominant value structure. The external recruitment of managers with little previous knowledge of the pre-1990 health service implies that such staff will be less influenced by, and more disengaged from, the prevailing value structure.

GP fundholding also represents a movement in the pattern of activities, and a similar incursion by a more (narrowly conceived) cost-conscious belief structure. As noted previously, GPs' increased budgetary responsibility alters their legitimized decision making frame: there is an increased emphasis on prudence in their financial management. However, Barker et al. (1997) contend that the common ownership patterns across any exchange interface imply that actors are likely to share objectives rather than pursue independent and conflicting goals. Nevertheless, it must remain a possibility that, even if this new behavioural influence is superimposed on the existing value structure, the orientation of behaviour will change: tensions will arise. The very nature of any sort of contract relationships implies that while actors may share some commonality in beliefs, they are extracting differing benefit flows (see Macneil 1982). Despite the Barker et al. claim, which has some attraction, the 'internal market' through a creeping market-oriented value structure may produce potentially conflicting objectives, and will certainly weaken trust bonds.

What empirical evidence there is on the changing aspects of trust since the inception of the 1990 reforms has tended to be indirect. There has been no study similar to those undertaken by Arrighetti et al. (1997), Burchell and Wilkinson (1997), or Lyons and Mehta (1997a, b), into trust patterns in the commercial sector. Therefore, conjectures are necessarily tentative. However, studies into the process of contracting in the NHS by Hughes et al. (1997), McHale et al. (1997) and Kitchener (1998), revealed not only organizational change based on medical-cost centres, but on the 'rising importance of the language and style of corporate activity in UK hospitals' (Kitchener 1998: 89). Moreover, Hughes et al. and Kitchener trace instances of considerable deteriorations in the relationships between contracting parties (usually trusts and contracting health authorities). The common feature between the two was that disputes were more likely to arise where a 'harder' (or more formal) contracting frame was adopted. In the Hughes et al. study on contracting in the NHS in Wales, there were instances where central authority had to be exerted to resolve disputes.

What these studies do suggest is that while the 1990 reforms may not have affected the level of trust between patients and the health service, certainly in terms of competence (indeed it may have been encouraged by the Patients' Charter). However, more recent events have acted to question this stance. As Keaney (this volume) notes, the nature of market-oriented change has partially refocused the relationship between patients and NHS bodies. Contentiously, Keaney suggests that recent malpractice in an NHS hospital in Bristol has been permitted by the reality of market-oriented norms. The degree of competence trust between patients and NHS bodies, as opposed to *individual* clinicians per se, may well have diminished somewhat.

Within the NHS the division between purchasers and providers may have been at the source of declines in goodwill and contract trust. By emphasizing a contractual relationship on a more formal basis, contracting parties become less engaged in reciprocating shared values in an informal manner. The nature of interaction changes, and routines become less fluid. This *creates* contractual uncertainty in the Sakoian sense. The superimposing of potentially conflicting values, and the formalization that is a prerequisite of market orientation leads to a weakening of the Ouchian clan structure: ironically, just as private firms are seeking change that promotes it (Lapsley 1993). Certainly, any attenuation in an Ouchian clan structure may be expected to diminish goodwill trust. Although actors may not be entirely disengaged from shared beliefs, the pattern of expressing those beliefs has been altered. Indeed, Hughes et al. found some evidence of sluggish compliance, and other forms of professional resistance. In effect, the 'internal market' may have produced counterproductive results by *inducing agency-type problems* of the nature found by Hughes et al. (1997), McHale et al. (1997) and Kitchener (1998), and therefore adversely affect the narrow efficiency targets sought by the previous Conservative government.

This raises the issue as to whether the current reforms will redress any trust deterioration experienced by the health service. As noted earlier, trust received no attention in the government's legislation. The promotion of trust between parties in the NHS may thus be considered not to be a priority of the 1997 reform. However, it may be argued that the programme's emphasis on 'softer' (or relational) contracting models and increased co-operation between bodies will provide a basis for fostering both contract and goodwill trust. Goodard and Mannion (1998) certainly consider this in their commentary on the 1997 legislation. They also argue that the latest reforms represent more of an 'evolution [to the 1990 scheme] rather than revolution', and continue by noting that the 'third way' reforms 'attempt to tread the line between competition and co-operation in an effort to squeeze benefits from each' (Goodard and Mannion 1998: 117). Yet Goodard and Mannion present this claim, attractive as it may be, on the basis of the static transaction-cost framework. They do not, and indeed given their adopted framework cannot, make cognizance of the nature of institutional change, and the adjustment this involves in value and belief systems (Bush 1987; Edgren 1996; McMaster 1999). These aspects are fundamental to any analysis of trust.

Nevertheless, the question remains open, since the current reform package maintains the central elements of the 'internal market', and devolves more budgetary responsibility to the successors of GP fundholding (primary care groups). Moreover, the imposition of a six-dimensional evaluatory framework may be the source of tension: what are the priority dimensions? How will they be interpreted? Will the formalized monitoring of clinical activities in this way make clinicians more accountable, or more resistant to the imposition of the government's package? It appears that the government has not fully appreciated the role of trust in economic activity, and is as culpable as many conventional economists in sensing the potential importance of trust within a complex organizational system, such as the NHS. Clearly, there is a need for more research into the impact of trust in the UK's health care system.

Concluding comments

The imposition of market-oriented arrangements, of necessity, has led to some erosion of trust between internal actors in the NHS. The loosening of Ouchian clan structures, and the creeping imposition of a differing value structure has resulted in considerable flux within the NHS. The stability that fosters and nurtures trust has been diminished, and is unlikely to be re-established for some time.

Of course, the importance of trust and entrustment within the NHS is an underdeveloped research area. Therefore, it is difficult to gauge the impact of diminished trust between parties on the ability of the NHS to meet its hybrid objectives. The Hippocratic ethos underpinning clinical activity within the health service may be insulated from any climatical change in the degree of trust between actors. However, there may be an indirect qualitative influence on the ability and motivation of staff to perform their tasks effectively. There is no doubt that the 1990 reforms introduced more rigidities, via the contracting process, into the system. However, it did pose clinicians with important questions as to the efficacy of many treatment methods, but perhaps in a rather alien fashion that engendered resistance and distaste. It is questionable if the 1997 reforms will radically alter this pattern. What is clear, though, is that there is no way that the 1997 reforms represent the status quo ante.

Policy makers and economists have been rather myopic as to the potential role of trust in general, and with respect to the provision of health care in particular. The unique nature of the NHS presents an opportunity for redressing this oversight. Unfortunately, to date there does not seem to be any movement in this direction.

Notes

The helpful comments of John Davis and Michael Keaney are acknowledged. Of course, the standard disclaimer applies.

1 The NHS had, prior to 1990, been subject to two structural reforms. In 1974 regional and area health authorities were created, in England, to better co-ordinate and plan activities. District management teams and family practitioner committees were the lowest level of authority, and implemented policy. The 1982 reforms, in England, eliminated area health authorities, and established district health authorities as the lowest tier of authority. Family practitioner committees were made accountable directly to the Department of Health and Social Security (central government), as opposed to regional authorities. The structure of the NHS in other parts of the UK demonstrated some differences. For example, in Scotland health boards fulfilled the roles of English district authorities and certain regional functions. These reforms gradually increased the non-clinician managerial input into the planning of services, thereby diminishing the influence of clinician consultants (for a discussion see, for example, Flynn 1992; Klein 1995; Keaney and Lorimer 1999; Keaney, this volume).

2 The use of scare quotations around the term internal market is a reflection of the institutionalist-based critique of the absence of a rich analytical conception of the market as an institutional arrangement within the neoclassical literature. There is a lack of any etymological appreciation of the term in neoclassicism, judging by the tacit assumption that markets are ubiquitous.

3 Williamson endeavours to place transaction-cost economics at the frontier of orthodoxy. By investigating the 'black box' of organization, and representing organizations, specifically firms, as more than a Cobb-Douglas production function, Williamson claims to advance an eclectic approach incorporating law, sociology and organizational theory. Moreover, Williamson claims that one of the prominent 'antecedents' of transaction-cost economics was the Old Institutionalist John Commons. Despite those claims, many commentators consider that Williamson's approach is dominated by neoclassicism (see, for example, Pratten 1997). Indeed, Williamson (1996: 8) himself gives the game away when he states, 'transaction cost economics subscribes to and works out of what I see to be the core commitments of orthodoxy'.

4 As published in the government's White Paper for England, *The New NHS: Modern, Dependable*, (Secretaries of State 1997). Scottish legislation was along very similar lines.

5 This aspect of Williamson's framework has received considerable attention in the institutionalist literature. Moreover, there has been a distinct recognition of this weakness in the new institutionalist literature, primarily by Douglass North. In his Nobel Prize lecture, North emphasized the relationship between organizational performance and institutional environment, especially cultural factors. To date Williamson persists with the ceteris paribus clause.

6 Coleman (1990) is a notable sociologist who has documented the development of trust based on social norms where an individual will only adhere to these norms (and hence trust) when the balance of costs and benefits suggest that it is beneficial to do so.

7 Arrighetti et al. (1997), Burchell and Wilkinson (1997: 221) and Deakin et al. (1997) surveyed firms in three selected European countries (Germany, Italy and the UK) engaged in vertical trading relationships. A total of 62 firms were questioned in two industrial sectors (mining machinery and kitchenware). The aim of Burchell and Wilkinson's survey was to explore the nature of contractual relationships, and indicate institutional influences, such as the social and organizational context of contracting. Arrighetti et al. and Deakin et al. aimed to disclose the importance of contract law in establishing and supporting trust.

Lyons and Mehta's (1997b) survey produced qualitative data from a sample of firms located in the Midlands and south of England. Their sample was randomly selected, and included firms from a wide range of industries. As with Burchell and Wilkinson, Lyons and Mehta's survey attempted to analyse firms' contracting relationships, but in this case by endeavouring to test Williamson's contract-type hypothesis. Their findings were broadly supportive of Williamson's central analysis of exchange, although they conclude that 'more attention needs to be given to identifying the conditions necessary to create and sustain relational contracting' (Lyons and Mehta 1997b: 64).

8 Interestingly, Zucker observes that the development of socially oriented trust not only frequently rests on a stable institutional environment, but can arise out of long-standing relationships (process-based trust) and common characteristics, such as family, religion or ethnicity. She maintains that institutional stability is the key to the fostering of trust.

9 Deakin et al. (1997) claim that this finding is contrary to Macaulay's (1963) and Williamson's (1985) contentions that firms are not reliant on formal contract as a means of moulding inter-firm co-operation. Arguably, the Deakin et al. study is more damaging to Williamson's case than to Macaulay's. Macaulay explicitly recognises that economic interactions do not occur in a cultural vacuum, whereas Williamson's insistence on employing the institutional 'ceteris paribus' clause implies that in his view exchange does occur, de facto, in a vacuum. Perhaps Deakin et al. exaggerate the impact of their findings on Macaulay's conclusions. However, they are on firmer ground by pointing to the weaknesses in Williamson's 'private ordering' hypothesis (see also Hodgson 1998: 178).

10 Lyons and Mehta's commentary assumes that homo economicus is instrumentally rational according to the Weberian delineation. However, this is not as straightforward as it may seem. The Weberian conception infers individual intentionality. It is not clear that homo economicus exhibits this trait. Thorstein Veblen's critique despaired at the passiveness of *homo economicus*. He famously states that neoclassical man is no more than a 'lightening calculator of pleasure', and a 'homogenous globule of desire of happiness under the impulse of stimuli that shift him about the area, but leave him intact' (Veblen 1898: 389). There is no intention per se, only a reaction to exogenous changes.

11 Related to this, in his critique of the Public Choice model of bureaucracy, Dunleavy (1991) maintains that senior bureaucrats have preferences for small working teams with a highly collegiate atmosphere, where there is considerable individual discretion.

12 It was also the view of (the small number) of pre-1990 NHS administrators I contacted, that the promotion prospects were substantially enhanced if an individual had private sector experience.

References

Arrighetti, A., Bachman, R., and Deakin, S. (1997) Contract law, social norms and inter-firm cooperation, *Cambridge Journal of Economics* 21: 171–195.
Arrow, K.J. (1963) Uncertainty and the welfare economics of medical care, *American Economic Review* 53: 941–973.
—— (1973) *The Limits of Organization*, New York: Norton.
Ascher, K. (1987) *The Politics of Privatization: Contracting Out Public Services*, Basingstoke: Macmillan.
Baier, A. (1986) Trust and antitrust, *Ethics* 96: 231–260.
Barker, K., Malcolmson, J., and Montgomery, J. (1997) Contracting in the NHS: legal and economic issues, in R. Flynn and G. Williams (eds).
Barr, N., Glennerster, H., and Le Grand, J. (1989) Working for patients: the right approach? *Social Policy and Administration* 23: 117–127.
Bartlett, W., Roberts, J.A., and Le Grand, J. (eds) (1998) *A Revolution in Social Policy: Quasi-Markets in the 1990s*, Bristol: Policy Press.
Bowles, S. (1998) Endogenous preferences: the cultural consequences of markets and other economic institutions, *Journal of Economic Literature* 36: 75–111.
Brereton, M. and Temple, M. (1999) The new public *service* ethos: an ethical environment for governance, *Public Administration* 77: 455–474.
Burchell, B. and Wilkinson, F. (1997) Trust, business relationships and the contractual environment, *Cambridge Journal of Economics* 21: 217–237.
Bush, P.D. (1987) The theory of institutional change, *Journal of Economic Issues* 21: 1075–1116.
Chalkley, M. and Malcolmson, J.M. (1996a) Competition in NHS quasi-markets, *Oxford Review of Economic Policy* 12: 89–99.
—— (1996b) Contracts for the National Health Service, *Economic Journal* 106: 1691–1701.
—— (1998) Contracting for health services with unmonitored quality, *Economic Journal* 108: 1093–1110.
Choi, C.J., Grint, K., Hilton, B., and Taplin, R. (1994) Achieving co-operation: contracts, trust and hostages, *Journal of Interdisciplinary Economics* 5: 221–236.
Coleman, J. (1990) *Foundations of Social Theory*, Cambridge MA: Harvard University Press.
Culyer, A.J., Maynard, A.K., and Posnett, J.W. (eds) (1990) *Competition in Health Care: Reforming the NHS*, Basingstoke: Macmillan.
Dasgupta, P. (1988) Trust as a commodity, in D. Gambetta (ed.) *Trust: Making and Breaking Co-operative Relations*, Oxford: Blackwell.
Deakin, S. and Michie, J. (eds) *Contracts, Co-operation, and Competition: Studies in Economics, Management, and Law*, Oxford: Oxford University Press.
Deakin, S., Lane, C., and Wilkinson, F. (1997) Contract law, trust relations, and incentives for co-operation: a comparative study, in S. Deakin and J. Michie (eds).
Dunleavy, P.J. (1991) *Democracy, Bureaucracy and Public Choice: Economic Explanations in Political Science*, London: Harvester Wheatsheaf.
Edgren, J. (1996) Modelling institutional change: some critical thoughts, *Journal of Economic Issues* 30: 1017–1029.
Enthoven, A.C. (1985) *Reflections on Improving Efficiency in the National Health Service*, London: Nuffield Occasional Paper.

Flynn, R. (1992) *Structures of Control in Health Management*, London: Routledge.

Flynn, R. and Williams, G. (eds) (1997) *Contracting for Health: Quasi-Markets and the National Health Service*, Oxford: Oxford University Press.

Flynn, R., Williams, G., and Pickard, S. (1997) Quasi-markets and quasi-trust: the social construction of contracts for community health services, in R. Flynn and G. Williams (eds).

Fox, A. (1974) *Beyond Contract: Work, Power and Trust Relations*, London: Faber and Faber.

Frey, B.S. (1993) Does monitoring increase work effort? The rivalry with trust and loyalty, *Economic Inquiry* 31: 663–670.

Fukuyama, F. (1995) *Trust: The Social Virtues and the Creation of Prosperity*, London: Penguin.

Glennerster, H., Manos, M., Owens, P., and Hancock, H. (1994) GP fundholding: wild card or winning hand? in R. Robinson and J. Le Grand (eds).

Goldberg, V.P. (1980) Relational exchange: economics of complex contracts, *American Behavioral Scientist* 23: 337–352.

Goodard, M. and Mannion, R. (1998) From competition to co-operation: new economic relationships in the National Health Service, *Health Economics* 7: 105–119.

Goodin, R. and Le Grand, J. (1987) *Not Only the Poor: The Middle Classes and the Welfare State*, London: Allen and Unwin.

Hartley, K.J. (1990) Contracting out in Britain: achievements and problems, in J. Richardson (ed.) *Privatisation in Britain and Canada*, Dartmouth: Institute for Research on Public Policy.

Hodgson, G.M. (1998) The approach of institutional economics, *Journal of Economic Literature* 36: 166–192.

Hughes, D., Griffiths, L., and McHale, J.V. (1997) Do quasi-markets evolve? Institutional analysis and the NHS, *Cambridge Journal of Economics* 21: 259–276.

Keaney, M. (1997) Can economics be bad for your health? *Health Care Analysis* 5: 299–305.

—— (2001?) Proletarianizing the professionals: the populist assault on discretionary autonomy, in J. Davis (ed.) *The Social Economics of Health*, London: Routledge.

Keaney, M. and Lorimer, A.R. (1999) Clinical effectiveness in the National Health Service in Scotland, *Journal of Economic Issues* 33: 117–139.

Kitchener, M. (1998) Quasi-market transformation: an institutionalist approach to change in UK hospitals, *Public Administration* 76: 73–95.

Klein, R. (1995) *The New Politics of the NHS*, London: Longman.

Lapsley, I. (1993) Markets, hierarchies, and the regulation of the National Health Service, *Accounting and Business Research* 23: 384–394.

Le Grand, J. and Bartlett, W. (eds) (1993) *Quasi-Markets and Social Policy*, Basingstoke: Macmillan.

Le Grand, J. and Mays, N. (1998) Methods, in J. Le Grand et al. (eds).

Le Grand, J., Mays, N., and Mulligan, J. (eds) (1998) *Learning From the NHS Internal Market*, London: King's Fund Institute.

Leibenstein, H. (1987) On some economic aspects of a fragile input: trust, in G.R. Feiwel (ed.) *Arrow and the Foundations of the Theory of Economic Policy*, Basingstoke: Macmillan.

Lyons, B. and Mehta, J. (1997a) Contracts, opportunism and trust: self-interest and social orientation, *Cambridge Journal of Economics* 21: 239–257.

—— (1997b) Private sector business contracts: the text between the lines, in S. Deakin and J. Michie (eds) *Contracts, Co-operation, and Competition: Studies in Economics, Management, and Law*, Oxford: Oxford University Press.

Macaulay, S. (1963) Non-contractual relations in business: a preliminary study, *American Sociological Review* 45: 55–69.

McHale, J., Hughes, D., and Griffiths, L. (1997) Conceptualising contractual disputes in the National Health Service internal market, in S. Deakin and J. Michie (eds).

McMaster, R. (1999) Institutional change in UK health and local authorities, *International Journal of Social Economics* 26: 1441–1454.

McMaster, R. and Sawkins, J.W. (1996) The contract state, trust distortion and efficiency, *Review of Social Economy* 54: 145–167.

Macneil, I.R. (1982) Economic analysis of contractual relations, in R. Burrows and C.E. Veljanovski (eds) *The Economic Approach to Law*, London: Butterworth.

Montgomery, J. (1997) Control and restraint in National Health Service contracting, in S. Deakin and J. Michie (eds).

Mueller, D.C. (1996) Public choice theory, in D. Greenaway, M. Bleaney and I. Stewart (eds) *A Guide to Modern Economics*, London: Routledge.

Nelson, R.R. and Winter, S.G. (1982) *An Evolutionary Theory of Economic Change*, Cambridge MA: Harvard University Press.

Ouchi, W.G. (1980) Markets, bureaucracies, and clans, *Administrative Science Quarterly* 25: 129–141.

Pratten, S. (1997) The nature of transaction cost economics, *Journal of Economic Issues* 31: 781–803.

Propper, C. (1996) Market structure and prices: the responses of hospitals in the UK National Health Service to competition, *Journal of Public Economics* 61: 307–335.

Reed, M. and Anthony, P. (1993) Between an ideological rock and an organizational hard place: NHS management in the 1980s and 1990s, in T. Clarke and C. Pitelis (eds) *The Political Economy of Privatization*, London: Routledge.

Robinson, R. and Le Grand, J. (eds) (1994) *Evaluating the NHS Reforms*, London: King's Fund Institute.

Sako, M. (1992) *Prices, Quality and Trust: Inter-firm Relations in Britain and Japan*, Cambridge: Cambridge University Press.

Schlicht, E. (1993) On custom, *Journal of Institutional and Theoretical Economics* 149: 151–169.

Secretaries of State (1997) *The New NHS: Modern, Dependable*, Cm 3807, London: HMSO.

Simon, H.A. (1991) Organizations and markets, *Journal of Economic Perspectives* 5: 25–44.

Veblen, T.B. (1898) Why is economics not an evolutionary science? *Quarterly Journal of Economics* 12: 373–397.

Vining, A.R. and Weimer, D.L. (1990) Government supply and government production failure: a framework based on contestability, *Journal of Public Policy* 10: 1–22.

Whynes, D.K. (1993) Can performance monitoring solve the public services' principal-agent problem? *Scottish Journal of Political Economy* 40: 434–446.

Williams, A. (1990) Ethics, clinical freedom and the doctors' role, in Culyer et al. (eds).

Williamson, O.E. (1975) *Markets and Hierarchies: Analysis and Antitrust Implications*, New York: Free Press.
—— (1985) *The Economic Institutions of Capitalism: Firms, Markets, Relational Contracting*, New York: Free Press.
—— (1993a) Transaction cost economics and organization theory, *Industrial and Corporate Change* 2: 107–156.
—— (1993b) Opportunism and its critics, *Managerial and Decision Economics* 14: 97–107.
—— (1996) *The Mechanisms of Governance*, New York: Oxford University Press.
Zucker, L.G. (1986) The production of trust: institutional sources of economic structure, 1840–1920, *Research in Organizational Behavior* 8: 53–111.

6

PROLETARIANIZING THE PROFESSIONALS

The populist assault on discretionary autonomy

Michael Keaney

As its name implies, a social economics of health care is not simply concerned with the distribution and allocation of service provision, although these are undoubtedly of major importance. Issues of equity and justice would inform the treatment of these, however, in contrast to the distorted, and distorting, preoccupation with 'efficiency' characteristic of neoclassical economics. As Glen Atkinson (1995: 94) points out, the enabling myth facilitating the latter is 'based on the notion that efficiency can be objectively discovered, but equity is simply a matter of subjective tastes'. The dualism of subjective and objective supports the false dichotomy of efficiency vs. equity. Equally, it contends that objectivity is synonymous with neutrality, whereas subjectivity is hopelessly shackled with bias. Other scholars have gone to great lengths to rid our institutionalized model of 'science' of this fallacy, which has been so harmful to the cause of a democratically founded social inquiry (for instance, see Lynd 1939; Mills 1959; Dowd 1966: 58; Haskell 1998; Tool 1998: 8–10).

The social economics of health care, therefore, is just as concerned with human relationships. Traditionally, the patient-doctor relationship has been the subject of most investigation, because of the doctor's ultimate responsibility for the treatment of the patient. This emphasis, though understandable, has perhaps been at the expense of the relationships patients have with other professionals, including nurses, pharmacists, those in professions allied to medicine, and even the clerical and ancillary staff whose work is vital to the proper, co-ordinated functioning of a modern, complex health care service. Then there are the inter-professional relationships that comprise the politics of health care organizations. And, given the inexorable rise in importance of health care as a public good, there is the consideration due to the role of government and the public regulation of health care services.

While the latter topic has hardly been ignored as matter for debate, its subject-matter has undergone a substantial shift in recent years in Great Britain. The British government has increasingly sought to regulate the decision making behaviour of health professionals, most especially doctors, in response to fiscal pressures resulting from a number of parallel developments, each of which acts to intensify the other. In a nutshell, in order to control spiralling costs of care the National Health Service (NHS) has been transformed from an organization governed by a bureaucratic and medically authoritarian ethos into one that is managerialist, fiscally constrained and in perpetual crisis.

This chapter examines why this has come to be. It does so by framing these changes in the context of a global phenomenon—the New Right ascendancy and its entrenchment via the ideology of neoliberalism. This has had very specific consequences for states and governments, with the latter shrinking in contrast to the expansion of the former. As a result, more avenues of democratic accountability have been closed off, while state power is wielded more and more according to 'evidence-based' verities whose apparent scientific (and therefore authoritatively value-neutral) legitimacy belies the thoroughly political ends for which they are the means. In common with other parts of the state sector, the NHS has been reformed to take account of the new conventional wisdom that has seen the idea of a distinct practice of public administration make way for the elevation of 'business values' and the emulation of supposed private sector efficiency and effectiveness. The impact of these reforms upon patients will affect not only the financial provision for health care services, but also their relationships with their doctors and other health care professionals. The resulting impoverishment of the vast majority of citizens in no way serves the goals of equity and justice. A perverse, utterly regressive, sort of efficiency is the most that could be claimed for it.

The fiscal crisis of the state

James O'Connor's detailed examination of the pathologies of the state in late modern capitalism remains a lucid, compelling account. Building upon the work of Baran and Sweezy (1966), O'Connor identified those tendencies inherent in capitalism that would work—indeed, did work—to undermine the Keynesian economic policies and the social democratic settlement of the post-1945 period. His basic thesis bears repeating:

> Every economic and social class and group wants government to spend more and more money on more and more things. But no one wants to pay new taxes or higher rates on old taxes. Indeed, nearly everyone wants lower taxes, and many groups have agitated successfully for tax relief. Society's demands on local and state budgets

> seemingly are unlimited, but people's willingness and capacity to pay for these demands appear to be narrowly limited.
>
> (O'Connor 1973: 1)

Meanwhile,

> although the state has socialized more and more capital costs, the social surplus (including profits) continues to be appropriated privately . . . The socialization of costs and the private appropriation of profits creates a fiscal crisis, or 'structural gap', between state expenditures and state revenues. The result is a tendency for state expenditures to increase more rapidly than the means of financing them.
>
> (O'Connor 1973: 9)

The answer to this dilemma of the early 1970s was the 'Great Capitalist Restoration' of the Thatcher-Reagan era (Stanfield and Stanfield 1996), which ushered in a set of policies whose ground had been cleared by the multitude of academics investigating the twin problems of governability and overload (see Parsons 1982). Put simply, these asserted that because governments were taking on too many (economic) tasks, such as the ownership and control of whole industries, strategic macroeconomic planning via Keynesian demand management and, of course, the provisioning of the welfare state, economic performance as a whole suffered (Bacon and Eltis 1976). This, in turn, was a threat to social order (Huntington 1975). This potentially fractious coalition of conservatives and classical liberals accumulated sufficient momentum to displace a regime at the end of its intellectual tether regarding seemingly intractable economic stagnation. Although influential prior to the rise of Thatcher and Reagan, inasmuch as the Callaghan and Carter administrations had already accepted the basic logic of monetarism (if not its finer detail), the ideological assault of the New Right achieved full intensity as the 1980s progressed. By the end of that decade, with the collapse of the Berlin Wall and the overthrow of communist regimes throughout Eastern Europe, the full-blooded capitalism advocated by the classical liberals seemed triumphant. Backed by a battery of academically respectable research 'showing' the futility of state intervention in economic matters, the 'free market' was fast becoming the only game in town.

Nevertheless, the subsequent fiasco of 'shock therapy' in the former Soviet Union demonstrated the utter inadequacy of the ideologues' 'understanding' of how their own beloved system actually works. The formal separation of economy and polity—of market and state—that is central to classical liberalism is, like its conception of the relationship between efficiency and equity, a false dichotomy. To some extent this has been recognized by the World Bank, which had previously been an enthusiastic advocate of 'structural adjustment' aimed at the replication of 'market conditions'. Its 1997 World Development Report attempted to reinstate the state as a valid, indeed essential, component of a healthy economy. As Panitch (1998) notes, however, the primary function of the state remains the facilitation and legitimization of accumulation.

The major emphasis placed upon rendering state organizations and public services more 'business-like' in the wake of the New Right ascendancy was both an attack on older notions of public administration and a specifically public service—and therefore non-market—ethos, and a more intensely aggressive (than had hitherto been the case) legitimization of accumulation. British state sector reforms typically involved the imposition of managerial hierarchies emulating textbook models of business behaviour whose relevance was not a primary consideration, even where these had been rejected as unworkable by private sector enterprises. Once managerialism had become sufficiently embedded, the introduction of quasi-markets could proceed. Both of these developments required the acquiescence, co-operative or otherwise, of professions which had enjoyed considerable autonomy in determining and enforcing standards of service quality. Where that acquiescence has not been so readily forthcoming, the state has employed a variety of means to achieve the desired end of greater control.

The Great Capitalist Restoration has involved the aggressive reassertion of the state's facilitation and legitimization functions. It is even more true now than in 1973 to say that 'nearly every state agency is involved in the accumulation and legitimization functions, and nearly every state expenditure has this twofold character' (O'Connor 1973: 7). Tax breaks, regional policies, the imposition of a national schools curriculum, stringent rules for the funding of higher education—including the promotion of 'external' sources of income—are just some of the more recent developments underpinning a culture characterized primarily by a market sensibility. Citizens become consumers whose primary function is to purchase goods and services in order to serve the needs of monopoly capital, with the social economy a minor consideration at best. And, where the social economy is considered, it is as the result of an ongoing process involving the displacement of the burden of costs from capital to the state. Kapp (1971: xiii) observed that

> a system of decision-making operating in accordance with the principle of investment for profit cannot be expected to proceed in any way other than by trying to reduce its costs whenever possible and by ignoring those losses that can be shifted to third persons or to society at large.

With governments now, more than ever since the 1930s, tied to policies of balanced budgets, and public expenditure per se a thing to be viewed with suspicion, more and more losses inherent in late modern capitalism are being shifted by the state itself to third persons and to society at large. Thus, for example, the costs of child care continue to be borne overwhelmingly by women, whose career opportunities are inevitably blighted by a system geared towards the extraction of surplus-value from labour that, at best, will not 'disappear' owing to inconveniences such as pregnancy and family obligation. It is no accident that, as with other measures of equal opportunities, tailored flexibility of employment for women is relatively more common in the state sector—though even there by no means adequate.

As Parsons (1982) documents, during the 1970s a vast literature grew supporting the idea of more limited government. Parallel to this was an increase in a political rhetoric of low expectations. Government could no longer be expected to undertake those tasks previously assigned to it. The reasons proffered for this about-turn centred mostly on inefficiencies, the ineffectiveness of public bureaucracy, and the insensitivity of public servants—all had a degree of plausibility. This scaling down of government commitment was, however, mainly a response to this structural gap or fiscal crisis. Electorates were sold such policies on the basis of tax cuts. Lower government expenditure meant higher disposable income. This highly effective political device sounded the death knell of old-fashioned social democracy as a viable electoral proposition, and facilitated the transformation of the state into the energetic facilitator and legitimizer of accumulation that it now is, as compared with its rather more ambivalent (by comparison) predecessor.

This was portrayed most vividly by John Kenneth Galbraith in his depiction of the 'culture of contentment', in which the majority of the electorate in liberal democracies work to exclude the wider economic and political enfranchisement of the poor for fear of the consequences for their own disposable incomes:

> It would be an exercise in improbably charitable attitude were the fortunate to respond warmly to expenditures that are for the benefit of others. So government with all its costs is pictured as a functionless burden, which for the fortunate, to a considerable extent, it is. Accordingly, it and the sustaining taxes must be kept to a minimum; otherwise, the liberty of the individual will be impaired.
>
> And politicians faithfully respond. To run for office promising better services for those most in need at even higher cost is seen by many, if not quite all, as an exercise in political self-destruction.
>
> (Galbraith 1992: 46–47)

Where services retain the approval of the contented majority who, nevertheless, do not wish to pay more for them, improvements in service quality and extra funding must be generated via 'efficiency savings'. Among the methods employed to achieve these are pay freezes, 'downsizing', tighter budget allocations, and more stringent auditing of expenditures and measurement of outcomes. Given the length of time in which greater efficiencies have been wrung out of state sector enterprises, there is now far less potential for such savings to be made without severely impairing the performance of public services. Not surprisingly, this serves to heighten the political sensitivity surrounding these. There is some evidence that suggests that, while voters may not yet be ready to countenance overt increases in taxation to finance more government expenditure, they are no longer convinced of the desirability of an inexorable decline in taxes. Present efforts by Thatcherite standard-bearers to indict the Blair government for enacting 'stealth taxes' is not generating much by way of public indignation—at least, not yet (Brittan 1999). No less an organ of business sensibility than the *Financial Times* reckons this is indicative of 'a pretty seismic shift in the terms of political trade' (Stephens 2000). The response of policy makers to this changed electoral environment is pathological—even more auditing, standard setting, rules compliance and outcomes measurement. The guru of the 'Third Way' himself advocates continued reductions in income tax and capital gains tax, together with increased tax credits for small business start-ups and the provision of 'further incentives for the IT sector' (Giddens 2000).

In Britain, the NHS retains the strong support of the electorate as a desirable and eminently practical arm of the welfare state, contrary to the market libertarianism of Thatcherism. In common with health care globally, nevertheless, the cost of maintaining a viable NHS that meets its basic goals of a comprehensive, equitable provision of health care that is free at the point of access, is in danger of spiralling. One reason for this is, in some measure, the result of the NHS's own success. An ageing population, many of whom would not, prior to the existence of universal health care, have lived as long, is placing new demands upon the system. In parallel, new developments in health care technologies are similarly intensifying the pressure on budgets.

The British government's answer to this problem has been to apply the same principles of what has come to be known as the New Public Management (NPM) to the NHS, as it has done elsewhere in the state sector. In a sense, this programmatic transformation of the state sector has evolved sufficiently for some commentators to note the move away from traditional hierarchical forms of *management* towards structures and regimes of *governance*, emphasizing standards setting, rules compliance and performance measurement (Rhodes 1997). The remainder of this chapter examines how the 'New Governance' has been, and is being, implemented in the NHS, and what effects this will have upon patients and, specifically, the quality of patient care. Thereafter, an alternative model of health care will be posited—one that rejects both traditional, paternalistic modes of delivery and the current 'evidence-based' authoritarianism characteristic of the NHS reforms.

Old market, new governance, same old problem

One of the key architects of the newly implemented regime of clinical governance in the NHS is Liam Donaldson, the Chief Medical Officer for England and Wales. Another is Muir Gray, a senior figure in the NHS Executive. Together they described the pre-Thatcher NHS as

> administered rather than managed. Change and development occurred by a predominantly 'command and control' system of planning. Delivery of services to patients was governed through a mixture of statutory regulations, guidance, operating instructions, and local freedoms. Quality was seen as inherent in the system, sustained by the ethos and skills of the health professionals working within it.
>
> (Donaldson and Gray 1998: S37)

Despite various administrative reforms undertaken by previous governments, the problem of cost containment simply intensified. The 'lack of clarity in the overall accountability for service performance at local level' (1998: S37), itself a perception premised on traditional business management notions of accountability and performance, led the Thatcher government to initiate more fundamental changes. The managerialism inherent in the Thatcher administration's initial efforts to tame the NHS budget was best expressed by the Griffiths Report, produced by the committee of inquiry set up to investigate the management of the NHS. According to this group of men, chaired by the managing director of Sainsbury's, a supermarket chain, 'if Florence Nightingale were carrying her lamp through the corridors of the NHS today she would almost certainly be searching for the people in charge' (Department of Health and Social Security 1983: 12). On the basis of this verdict, the government instigated a reorganization of the NHS which, emulating business practice, established an executive board whose chief was envisioned by Griffiths' team as the Secretary of State for Health and Social Security's 'right hand man' (sic). Tiers of management were added further down the newly constructed hierarchy, and the following six years were spent embedding general management in the NHS. In the words of Strong and Robinson (1990: 3):

> Down the tatty corridors of the NHS, new and dedicated heroes would stride—the general managers. Inspired by their leadership a new sort of staff would arise. Armed with better information and new techniques from the private sector, much more closely monitored yet working as a team, they would at last take collective pride in their work—and responsibility for it.

The reality was inevitably more complex. The model of management promoted by the Griffiths Report and, implemented thereafter in the first wave of reforms, was 'an example of the kind of instrumental rationality in which profoundly political questions of priority and value are transposed into apparently scientific or technical issues' (Pollitt et al. 1991: 79). As we shall see, this model continues to inform the ongoing structural changes, with the same consequences. This clashes with the goals of health care professionals. Of particular importance in this regard is the medical profession, whose power and status within the NHS has been under continuous attack ever since 1983. While there are good reasons for changing this set of circumstances, crude consumerist populism married to managerialist economism is possibly the very worst basis for reform.

As was observed at the time, the Griffiths reforms could only provide a basis for further, more fundamental change:

> Even among professions, doctors are unusual in the scope of their autonomy. In the NHS hospital consultants can, broadly speaking, admit whichever patients they choose, treat them in whatever way they wish, discharge them when they see fit, and leave it to others to sort out the resource and staffing consequences of these 'clinical' decisions. They cannot be instructed to alter any of these decisions by a manager, and the Griffiths reforms did nothing to alter this.
> (Pollitt et al. 1991: 80)

Despite attempts to assert themselves politically, sometimes by co-opting health care professionals on to management boards, managers remained unable to control medical decision making. The financial constraints placed upon the NHS during the 1980s added to the tensions between managers and doctors, since the latter did not consider the former to have assumed new responsibilities since the implementation of the Griffiths reforms, despite the government's—and managers'—intentions (Harrison et al. 1992: ch. 4). Indeed, because of the intensifying politicization of the NHS, managers became 'much more *externally focused*; they were increasingly compelled to respond to governmental agendas and were consequently less able to respond to internal professional agendas' (Harrison 1999: 53).

A major drawback, however, was the managers' inability to define problems and effect solutions that could be appraised as effective. This has been attributed to a fundamental flaw in the conception of management, both at the heart of the Griffiths Report and most commonly informing state sector reform throughout this period:

> NHS managers work in an arena where a profuse and unstable range of values and priorities must be considered. Success is a concept that has multiple meanings for different groups of actors. The Griffiths model seems to view the manager as a technician whose practice consists in applying the principles derived from management sci-

> ence to the problems of his or her own organization. In contrast the art of management cannot be reduced to such explicit rules. In a setting such as the NHS, where there are contradictory objectives and multiple perceptions of problems, managers had in the past become more sensitive to the phenomena of uncertainty and ambiguity.
>
> (Pollitt et al. 1991: 79)

As a result, formulating objectives and measuring their attainment or otherwise is made difficult. But because of the political requirement that there should be explicit measurement of performance, those aspects of the NHS activity that could most easily be monitored—input and process data—facilitated the 'slide towards a lop-sided emphasis on narrower notions of *efficiency* and *economy*' (Pollitt et al. 1991: 79). Given the climate of hostility towards certain types of government expenditure, such lop-sidedness was not discouraged by the Conservative administration.

Nevertheless, having embedded structures which defined, on paper, chains of command, and having facilitated the development of accounting technologies that enabled more detailed costings of expenditures, the stage was set for the introduction of the 'internal market' in 1991. This was assisted further by the burgeoning field of inquiry known as health economics, which applied the theory and techniques of neoclassical economics to health care. Re-creating market conditions within the NHS provided an even surer platform for the further development of this sub-discipline. Whether or not health economists have made major contributions to patient welfare, however, is another question entirely (see Keaney 1997; Seedhouse 1997; Keaney and Lorimer 1999a: 123–126).

As is well documented by Hildred and Watkins (1996), there are unique problems in accounting for the costs of health care. Economies of scale vary between hospitals, the identification and allocation of indirect costs is inherently discretionary, and overhead loads can be assigned to service charges on widely varying bases. The most serious difficulty lies in the subjectivity of costing procedures, contrary to the popular image of cost as objectively determined. And 'objectivity' here is not being confused with neutrality. For in the calculation of indirect costs is involved the identification of cost drivers, the 'elements of activities that are thought to "cause" the indirect costs to vary . . . Managers *choose* cost drivers; there is no objective standard that dictates a specific selection' (Hildred and Watkins 1996: 758). 'Objectivity is observed when scientific procedures are followed; but neutrality, i.e. indifference to results, is neither possible nor desirable' (Dowd 1966: 58). Scientific procedures of peer review and public scrutiny are far from the normal practice of business accounting. 'It is safe to assume that few firms would be eager to make known to outsiders the content of the cost accounts, or even the nature of the costing practices; these are proprietary concerns' (Hildred and Watkins 1996: 759). The state is no less opaque in its costing practices.

All of this is to say that the re-creation of market arrangements presupposes a set of circumstances in no wise replicated empirically:

> Because neoclassical microeconomic theory treats price movements as the essential guidance mechanism for a market economy, the manner in which they are determined comprises the central concern of the discipline, and market structures are the key explanation of variations. The price that measures a commodity's value to society is rooted in two valuations: the assessment by individual buyers of the personal benefit that will accrue from its purchase, and the calculations by sellers (using the most efficient production processes) of the costs of production that must be covered. The former leads to willingness to pay for various quantities of the commodity and the latter to willingness to offer amounts of the commodity at various prices.
>
> (Hildred and Watkins 1996: 759)

Aside from the obvious crudity of the depiction of the patient-professional relationship in such a utilitarian manner, the crux of the entire model—the accuracy of price as a measure of value—is patently fictitious. No one can deny that health care costs are spiralling. But there is as yet no accounting technology that can provide a 'true and fair view' of the costs of health care provision owing to the secrecy, and therefore subjectivity, of the costing procedures employed.

The basic premise of the internal market was that a brake on cost increases could be achieved via the recasting of relationships on an exchange basis. The purchasers of health care, as agents for patients, were the general practitioners and health authorities. The former were given the option of a direct budget allocation which they could thereafter spend at will. It was presumed that they would 'shop around' hospitals in order to locate the most 'competitive', or cheapest, form of appropriate secondary care. Theoretically, this included care provided by non-NHS hospitals. Those general practitioners who did not opt to become 'fundholders' remained wedded to the older system of primary care funding, whereby health authorities were billed for the cost of services employed. The trouble with this arrangement was that the capping of health authorities' budgets, coupled with their diverse spending requirements, meant that non-fundholding general practices often faced harsher financial circumstances than did fundholders. Accusations arose of a two-tier NHS developing as a result of the advantages enjoyed by fundholding practices in affluent areas compared to the difficulties of non-fundholding practices in economically deprived locales. Incentives were such that it was in general practitioners' financial interest to have registered relatively healthy patients. Reports of practices 'losing' patients on the basis of cost were not uncommon (see Dixon and Glennerster

1995). Even now, supposedly post-internal market, evidence of discrimination against costly patients—especially those with poor mental health—is still emerging (Boseley 1999).

Hospitals, designated the 'providers' of care (based on a particularly narrow concept of care), were to meet the challenge of this new environment by responding in typical market-inspired fashion. Costs were to be cut in order to provide the most efficient, cost-effective care possible, since referring general practitioners could no longer be relied upon simply to continue long-established relationships with consultants on grounds of professional reputation alone. Hospitals were invited to 'opt out' of health authority control and become free standing 'Trusts' with their own annual budget allocations which, together with 'earnings' from services provided, would have to cover all financial needs for the fiscal year.

Almost as an afterthought, the legislation enacting these changes stipulated that contracts between purchasers and providers should include conditions concerning the practice of systematic clinical audit to ensure the quality of patient care. The structures facilitating such activities evolved slowly at first, given the lack of any prior blueprint (Hopkins 1996: 423–424). As a result, the practice of clinical audit was unevenly spread, and of varying quality itself. In certain cases this was to have significant consequences.

The internal market was officially buried by Tony Blair's Labour administration in 1997. It had always been unpopular as a policy, if only for the simple reason that the motives of Blair's Conservative predecessors towards the NHS were always suspect. Repeatedly they had to reassure the public that the NHS was 'safe in our hands'. But the quiet disposal of the internal market was driven by more than simple triumphalism. The main premise of re-creating competitive market arrangements was cost control. This had failed to materialize, and even more damagingly for its proponents, the internal market had added to costs by effecting a redistribution of NHS spending away from care towards the administration required to support it (Paton et al. 1997). Meanwhile there arose a high profile case involving the provision of paediatric cardiac surgical care in Bristol, where under-qualified surgeons were, for a period of several years, conducting operations with a markedly high fatality rate. Their practice was inadequately audited—and even when it was properly monitored, the results were kept secret, thus continuing the unnecessarily high proportion of deaths. As well as the more traditional protections afforded by the medical profession closing its ranks, a crucial incentive prolonging this awful affair was the internal market itself, which encouraged secondary care providers to compete in order to win 'customers'. By keeping their poor results quiet, the hospital authorities concerned could 'sell' their services at irresistibly low rates to cash-strapped general practitioners driven to accept the best 'bargain'.

These consequences of 'marketization', on both the demand and supply sides of the notional split, bear witness to Kapp's prescient warning of the consequences of reordering state sector agencies according to models of private business behaviour:

> Some of the current attempts to render public decision-making more 'rational' in terms of market costs and returns carry the danger that this disregard of some or all of the negative effects of decisions may become even more general and typical. Instead of reducing the incidence of social costs, such attempts are likely to increase them.
>
> (Kapp 1971: xvi)

In Bristol, the internal market had combined with traditional medical prerogative to produce the worst possible results. Other, admittedly less dramatic, cases of a similar nature came to light, and merely added to the momentum for change. The new Labour government did not take long to grasp the nettle of NHS reform. Within seven months of coming to power, it published three separate White Papers outlining the nature of that reform for the NHS in England, Wales and Scotland. While nominally autonomous to varying degrees, each NHS unit was to be subject to the implementation of a new regime, known as clinical governance.

Clinical governance

Ostensibly the reassertion of clinical criteria over the failed managerialist and market exchange models of decision making, clinical governance in fact represents a continuation of the effort to limit professional autonomy. This it does by its emphasis upon standards and rules compliance, where these are based upon 'best available scientific evidence'. Like the internal market, clinical governance attempts to remove resource allocation decisions from the political sphere. In so doing, it renders these far less accountable than might otherwise be the case.

Governance has been distinguished from government as being 'activities backed by shared goals' as against those that are 'backed by formal authority' (Rosenau 1992). This is only partially accurate, however. Increasingly, governance is about activities backed by shared goals which are also backed by formal authority of one kind or another, right up to and including legal authority. It is generally agreed that the accountability of public service providers, especially where these are members of traditionally powerful professions, is most desirable. Quality of service from the user's point of view ought to be of paramount importance, and is certainly acknowledged to be so. But what opportunities are there for users and the wider public to have a say in the design and delivery of health care services? Just how accountable are standards-setting processes? And to what extent is professional expertise in the delivery of care being supplanted by statistical prowess beyond the reach of conventional public scrutiny, let alone that of the patient?

The new regime of 'clinical governance' is the successor to that of clinical effectiveness, launched in 1996 (NHS Executive 1996, Keaney and Lorimer 1999a). That had brought together a number of separate policy initiatives which had been running in parallel until then. In doing so, policy makers not only rendered policy more coherent, but attempted to enact 'an elegant solution to the problem of matching demand for healthcare technologies to the level of resources available' (Harrison 1998: 22). Put simply, the clinical effectiveness agenda was, and remains, the practical application of a doctrine known originally as 'evidence-based medicine' (EBM)—most initiatives begin in the medical sphere—and now applies more broadly to health care of all kinds wherever possible. Evidence-based health care is the attempt to ensure that all health care professionals practice care that is based on best available scientific evidence. Just as the clinical effectiveness agenda sought to render health care decision making more accountable to best evidence, so the clinical governance initiative seeks to embed that agenda by putting in place the structures to support it.

These developments are both coincident and compatible with the evolution of New Public Management (NPM). Ferlie et al. (1996: 10–15), in their taxonomy of NPM styles, chart the way in which the initial emphasis upon managerialism has, in some cases, given way to a more participatory approach to decision making and evaluation. NPM1 is characterized as, in essence, an efficiency drive. Emphasis is placed upon 'business-like' hierarchical modes of decision making with managers appropriating authority previously exercised by autonomous professionals. Value for money and efficiency audits are undertaken with a view to getting more from less. NPM2 involves the institution of quasi-markets, a shift from management by hierarchy to management by contract, and downsizing and decentralization. NPM3, in contrast to the preceding models, concentrates on organizational culture change, whether this is achieved via bottom-up or top-down modes of implementation. The latter has been the more common, with its emphasis upon corporate identity and mission, although professional autonomy remains under pressure from managerial prerogative. Finally, NPM4 features a greater focus on service quality as defined by users, as opposed to customers. There is greater scepticism over the efficacy of market 'solutions' and a resultant shift towards greater local accountability and democratized decision making. So far, the NHS has traversed the pathway of reform from NPM1 to somewhere in between NPM3 and NPM4. For while clinical governance stresses the importance of patient views and feedback, and especially complaints, the consumerist model of health care that is being fostered—within the wider context of a culture of consumerism—gives patients the illusion of choice while rendering it more difficult for professionals to exercise the judgment essential to good quality care.

Clinical governance was first mooted in the NHS White Papers of 1997. In the Scottish White Paper, it was mentioned only briefly, but nevertheless quickly built up a momentum in the period preceding its full implementation on 1 April 1999. In its conception, it retained the managerialist ethos of its predecessors. But it also represented the most serious attempt to circumscribe clinical freedom in accordance with the British government's goals.

> The Government's new emphasis on the quality of services to patients must be reflected in the responsibilities and management of Trusts. The Government will amend Trusts' statutory duties to make explicit their responsibility for quality of care. This will need to be taken every bit as seriously as the existing financial responsibilities. Trust Chief Executives will carry ultimate accountability for the quality of care provided by their Trust, in the same way as they are already accountable for their Trust's proper use of resources. Trust Chief Executives will be expected to ensure there are suitable local arrangements to give them, and the Trust board, the assurance they need that this duty is being met. The intention is to build on existing patterns of professional self-regulation and corporate governance principles, but offer a framework for extending this more systematically into the local clinical community, and ensure the internal 'clinical governance' of the Trust.
>
> (Scottish Office Department of Health 1997: para. 68)

According to Donaldson and Gray (1998: S38), clinical governance is important because 'it brings clinical decision making into a management and organisational framework'—an acknowledgment of the failure of both the Griffiths reforms and the internal market to do the same. The previous notion of quality as 'doing things right' is insufficient, and needs to be broadened to take account of whether the NHS is doing the right things. Now quality is to be defined 'as doing the right things, for the right people, at the right time, and doing them right first time' (1998: S39). Doing the right things is to be determined according to organizational goals, as opposed to clinical judgment. Doing them right first time, meanwhile, demands detailed prescription—and proscription—based upon rigorous evaluation of the available scientific evidence.

Before examining the shortcomings of clinical governance, it is as well to highlight its positive aspects. Not the least of these is the recognition that in many instances there exist work systems that place 'far too much responsibility on the shoulders of the individual doctor, often a young and unsupported clinician' (1998: S40). Donaldson and Gray cite the study by Lucian Leape (1997), who adapted risk management techniques employed in the airline industry and pilot training to hospital management in order to minimize errors. There is little question that some traditional modes of organization—if these could be so described—invite error rather than prevent it.

'Expecting young clinicians to manage everything correctly at 2 o'clock in the morning without systems support is . . . an unrewarding task for both manager and clinician' (Donaldson and Gray 1998: S40). As Leape (1997: 215) highlights, the role of system design—or the lack of it—can be crucial in the prevention of errors.

Nevertheless, Leape makes a crucial admission prior to his main discussion: 'Systems that rely on perfect performance by individuals to prevent errors are doomed to fail, for the simple reason that humans are incapable of perfect performance' (Leape 1997: 214). Clinical governance's emphasis upon error prevention and getting things right first time threatens to disregard this essential point. Aside from the potential for patients' unrealistically high expectations of professionals' performance, prescribing what is 'right' depends upon a static view of the world. If, as is often told in the health care literature, health care technologies are proliferating at an accelerating rate, thereby placing increased pressure on costs, then the world of health care provision is anything but static. Yet the emphasis upon clinical practice guidelines, which can feature detailed prescriptive guidance on specific treatments, and whose ambiguous medico-legal status is a matter of legitimate concern among professionals, threatens to render the NHS less capable of flexible response just at the period of its existence where this is most required. The body established to produce clinical practice guidelines for the NHS in Scotland is committed to revising its guidelines every two years. But as the number of guidelines grows, the work required to support their formulation, dissemination and implementation, before even revision, increases exponentially. As a result, guideline implementation has, up to now, been patchy at best (Keaney and Lorimer 1999b).

The traditionally authoritarian role of hospital consultants faces a welcome challenge from clinical governance. The emphasis upon the satisfactory resolution of patients' complaints is certainly better than the lack of accountability that characterized older models of the doctor-patient relationship. 'Clinical freedom' was often unfortunately interpreted as licence to disregard patients' concerns, however unfounded these might have been. Poor interpersonal skills do not normally endear some individuals to others. Recent tragic events such as the Bristol episode have added to the sense of urgency among policy makers for a more 'customer-driven' ethos to be engendered within the NHS. The problem, however, lies with the conception of patients as *consumers* of health care (Keaney 1999).

The matter of choice

According to Zygmunt Bauman, individual choice is framed by two sets of constraints. The first of these is what he calls the *agenda of choice*: the range of options available for selection. 'All choice means "choosing among", and seldom is the set of items to be chosen from a matter for the chooser to decide' (Bauman 1999: 72). Consumers typically have no input into the design and manufacture of consumer products. What choice they can exercise is circumscribed to the extent that competing pre-packaged manufactures vie for purchase. Participation is limited to the selection and acquisition of goods in exchange for money and, possibly, remonstration and recompense (itself not always guaranteed) in the event of an unsatisfactory transaction. At best, consumer 'sovereignty' is a very limited, and limiting, notion, whether as expressed theoretically in the model of perfect competition, or empirically as it is enshrined in consumer protection legislation and facilitated via the necessarily more complex 'imperfect' forms of competition that exist in reality. It is patently fictitious as a description of empirical market conditions (Galbraith 1985). Moreover, to conceive of patients as consumers does not represent a major redistribution of power within the patient-doctor relationship. Rather, the relative equalization is achieved via the constraints placed upon professional autonomy. Though patients can now express dissatisfaction more freely than before, and indeed have greater access to information than before through such media as the internet, their apparent empowerment is largely illusory. The important issue of knowledge asymmetry, itself an inevitable consequence of the division of labour, is ignored.

It is not clear why doctors who are more beholden to managerial prerogative and cost constraint, and so less able to exercise professional discretion, should, of necessity, be *better* for patients. Implicit is the assumption that where discretion may be exercised, it will be either vindictive or inadequate. Admittedly, recent episodes within the NHS, like those mentioned earlier, have not added to the organization's reputation for effective, patient-centred health care. But the second of Bauman's criteria, the *code of choosing*, as manifest in clinical governance, risks an unnecessary and undesirable truncation of clinical autonomy, ostensibly as a protection for patients, but no less consistent with the fiscal constraints bearing down heavily upon the NHS. Patients and clinicians alike are being directed towards those treatments that are validated according to the tenets of evidence-based medicine wherever possible. And where these do not readily apply, managerial consent for treatment procedures can be withheld.

The matter of evidence

The assumption informing this drive towards 'evidence-based everything' (Fowler 1997) is that the evidence validation procedures are themselves valid. The controversies surrounding scientific testing and the interpretation of statistics are not acknowledged. And the implication that, prior to this latest innovation, doctors and other health professionals paid little, if any, attention to 'evidence' is patently absurd. 'The presumption is made that the practice of medicine was previously based on a direct communication with God or by tossing a coin' (Fowler 1997: 240).

The first question concerns just what is meant by 'evidence'. What information is relevant to health care professionals in their respective practices? Clearly, the knowledge imparted to professionals during their apprenticeships is going to be of central importance. So, too, will the experience gained, both prior to final qualification and subsequently, as a practising, registered professional. This is especially important at a time of ever more rapid change. One of the chief arguments behind the EBM doctrine is the idea that the best informed doctors are usually those straight out of medical school, since these are more likely to have been paying close attention to the relevant journals and information outlets: 'We become out of date and our patients pay the price for our obsolescence' (Sackett et al. 1997: 10). Other sources of information include peer review and multidisciplinary collaboration. But a major source of relevant information is surely patients themselves. They remain largely unacknowledged in the current debates surrounding EBM and health service reform.

As to validation, especially in such a politically sensitive situation as that of the NHS, policy makers are, for whatever reason, refusing to recognize the malleability of evidence. The NHS is not alone in its incorporation of the EBM ethos. Throughout the Blair administration, policy is being informed by specially commissioned research that is 'good' because it is empirically founded. Taken at face value, this concern with 'relevant' research—a clear repudiation of the sort of research championed famously by Milton Friedman —is to be welcomed. But who defines what is 'relevant'? The research director of the Joseph Rowntree Foundation has been quoted as saying that '"evidence led" may mean "what we want for our own political purposes"' (Walker 2000). Without appropriate democratic transparency and accountability, ends can be established and the means to their accomplishment identified without recourse to the public in whose name all of this is being enacted. As with neoclassical economics, the undiscussed issue is that of power.

Even putting aside the issue of power, there remains the problem of the lack of consensus in health care decision making. The production and dissemination of clinical guidelines is an effort to overcome this difficulty, but this involves the elevation of one epistemological model over its rivals. As Harrison (1998: 26) concludes, it is naïve to assume that there need only be widespread dissemination of validated guidelines in order to produce the desired changes to clinical practice. Secondly, given the reliance of EBM upon a particular form of epistemological model, which Harrison describes as both probabilistic and empiricist, disputes about the probability of an intervention's effectiveness are not uncommon. Thirdly, EBM does not resolve the efficiency/equity dichotomy, as it can support the pursuit of either health gain maximization or equitable distribution.

The main difficulty with EBM is its identification with an epistemological model whose validity is not unquestioned. Indeed, as Harrison (1998: 26) observes:

> clinical doctors are more likely to be influenced in their practice by their own (and close colleagues') experience with similar types of patient, and by their own reasoning and treatment logic, than by the publication of meta-analyses of large numbers of cases.

According to the tenets of EBM, good clinical guidelines are founded upon randomized-controlled trials (RCTs),

> in which the effects of two or more treatments, usually including one which is regarded as the control or standard treatment, are studied by allocating each group of patients one of the different treatments available at random. The *control treatment* provides a standard against which the new treatments can be compared. The object of randomising is to have groups in which the different possible factors which might affect the outcome, such as age and severity of disease, are distributed independently of the treatment given. From a randomised controlled trial one can calculate an unbiased estimate of the difference between the effect of the new and control treatments.
>
> (Hutton 1996: 96)

RCTs are costly, however, and normally require financial backing of the kind most usually afforded by pharmaceutical companies. Given the limitations placed upon any RCT, much effort has gone into producing meta-analyses of RCTs that produce supposedly definitive statistical statements on the efficacy of the treatment concerned. Problems arise, however, with the selection of appropriately similar RCTs for inclusion in the meta-analysis, and the statistical aggregation involved. These have been well documented elsewhere (see Keaney and Lorimer 1999a: 121–123). Despite this controversy, the epistemological hierarchy central to evidence validation in EBM has been only slightly revised, with single, large RCTs now deemed as reliable as meta-analyses, as opposed to having superior weight (Scottish Intercollegiate Guidelines Network 1999: 20).

A more fundamental problem with EBM, alluded to earlier, is the dominance, in practice, of a different kind of clinical reasoning, characterized by Harrison (1998: 26) as both '*deterministic* (that is, it assumes that clinical events necessarily have causes which can be identified and, in principle, modified) and *realist* or *naturalist* (that is, it entails a belief in a world of objectively real entities whose nature can be observed)'. While both epistemological models are employed to some degree in practice, and both depend upon past experience for the validation of clinical knowledge, EBM by its nature is the more conservative because of its assumption of inherent uncertainty and exclusive reliance upon statistical inference. Some view it as 'a built-in method for rejecting or delaying medical advances' (Fowler 1997: 241).

The development of integrated clinical pathways (ICPs) follows directly from practice guidelines (Campbell et al. 1998). ICPs are care plans that adapt guideline recommendations in formulating prescribed multidisciplinary care procedures. On the positive side, they give explicit recognition to the importance of the roles played by non-medical professionals in patient care. Not surprisingly, they have won strong support from nursing professionals eager to gain a status in large measure unjustifiably denied by the older regime of medical authoritarianism. ICPs also facilitate better communication with patients, who can be provided with a structured care plan and information regarding their progress over time. But ICPs suffer from the same problem of obsolescence as that of guidelines except that, in so deeply embedding certain procedures as matters of organizational policy, they render change and the improvisation necessary in unforeseen circumstances more difficult to accomplish. To use Ayresian terminology, they are technologies prone to rapid ceremonialization.

Nevertheless, politically speaking, EBM serves the purpose of concentrating the ownership of clinical decision making. Though it largely remains the property of the clinical profession concerned, it is being moved 'away from the clinical practitioner and towards the academic/epidemiologist/health services researcher' (Harrison 1998: 21). As with research disconnected from the world of practice elsewhere, this results in the use and abuse of results for ends quite apart from the benefit of patients: 'Unhampered by any knowledge of bedside care, many non-clinicians, economists and politicians speak with clarity on a difficult subject' (Fowler 1997: 241).

The concentration of decision making power, even within health professions, makes that decision making more malleable to the prerogatives of senior NHS management, given that, in order to be implementable, clinical practice guidelines must make recommendations commensurate, theoretically at least, with resource allocations. This is not to say that guideline implementation is cost-neutral. Systematically implementing and auditing the implementation of guidelines is a resource-consuming enterprise. A hospital-wide implementation of just one clinical guideline will have resource implications throughout the organization. Having produced forty-one guidelines to date, were SIGN (Scottish Intercollegiate Guidelines Network) and its masters to insist upon immediate implementation of all relevant guidelines the service would undoubtedly collapse. Newspaper reports have echoed the findings of studies that 'the organisational costs of delivering health care "look set to increase"' (Timmins 1999). Given the commitment to measurement and monitoring entailed in the clinical governance regime, this should come as no surprise. Just as the internal market engineered the re-allocation of resources away from patient care towards administration, so the new governance demands a similar redistribution in favour of oversight, prescriptive and proscriptive, and always limited by the measurement technologies employed.

Proletarianization and the state

With the decline of mutuality and the rise of oversight (Davies and Mannion 1999), the discretionary autonomy of health professionals, especially that of doctors, has been challenged as never before. Admittedly, doctors have not helped themselves and their peers by their actions. The old, authoritarian model of health care provision that was medically driven was flawed in several respects. First, doctors could, and often did, ignore the insights of other caring professions in the design, implementation and evaluation of interventions. The emphasis upon curative and invasive technologies, rather than caring and palliative methods, for instance, reflected the narrow interpretation of what exactly constituted 'care'. This had ramifications for the treatment of various conditions, including pregnancy, where even today, in a nominally more participatory environment, too many women are being subjected to Caesarian sections as a matter of course by male obstetricians. This is symptomatic of the generally unsympathetic way in which the male-dominated medical profession has tended to treat women, both in the past and, in certain respects, even now. Not surprisingly, a substantial body of feminist literature has emerged on the subject (for example, Ehrenreich and English 1973; Connell 1987). As Chalmers (1995) points out, greater involvement of women in the design and administration of procedures before, during and after childbirth would have prevented much of the needless suffering and loss caused by the high-handed lack of basic consideration of another person's humanity, based purely upon wholly inappropriate gender assumptions.

Another undesirable feature of the medical profession, but consistent with the experience of other key occupational groups, is its power to dictate remunerative compensation. Few would deny the value of a doctor's contribution to individual and communal well-being. Nor would they underestimate the years of effort involved in becoming a registered, practising professional. But the medical profession has not won public sympathy in its commandeering of resources that might otherwise be spent on patient care. The establishment of the NHS in 1948 was preceded by heated and involved negotiations between the British Medical Association and the government. The latter was forced to accede to a number of demands which have since contributed to the relatively poor esteem accorded to the medical profession as a whole, as opposed to individual doctors. As detailed by Webster (1998), the post-war Secretary of State for Health, Aneurin Bevan, ran up against a brick wall of vested interest of a kind, to use Thorstein Veblen's memorable description, 'whose sole and self-seeking interest converges on the full dinner-pail' (Veblen 1983: 151). As a result, hospital consultants became salaried NHS employees entitled to have their own private practices, while general practitioners remained self-employed contractors, remunerated on the basis of the number of patients registered in their practices. In the

United States, this sort of rent-seeking behaviour has resulted in a system in which doctors are handsomely remunerated on the basis of the number of procedures administered, rather than the length of time and level of skill involved in 'physical examinations, thinking about solutions to medical problems, talking to patients, or "just" prescribing medicines' (Dowd 1997: 97). Such is the distorting effect of this system that new technologies are often introduced in much the same way as a new consumer product, without proper scientific and public appraisal of its efficacy, resulting in unnecessary and undesirable interventions: 'there is little doubt that the market system has the potential to exaggerate the diffusion of medical technologies that are expected to be profitable' (Blank 1996: 322). This point is better understood in Britain following the tragedy of Bristol.

A key aspect of the New Right ascendancy was its populist attack on the 'professions' as bastions of privilege. Given the above, there was ample material to exploit in the pursuit of this agenda. Once in power, the Thatcher administration set about reining in the various professions one by one. Politically this was astute, for a blanket curb on the professions would have aroused much more intense opposition. Nevertheless, the power exercised by each profession derived in part from the very nature of the enterprise in which they were involved. This was, and remains, especially true of the medical profession. Doctors carry the ultimate responsibility for patients' welfare, as it is they who must first of all diagnose the condition, and thereafter prescribe the appropriate treatment. Transferring this responsibility, even in part, to unidisciplinary or multidisciplinary committees, or to the chief executive of the hospital management board, as under clinical governance, does not change this. Nor does the encouragement of patients to view themselves as consumers of health care products, possessing the same statutory rights as in a department store. Few would be likely to assert their 'rights' as consumers when their lives depend upon the clinical skill and judgment of the emergency room doctor.

Part of the agenda of control has been to foster the public's suspicion of professionals as primarily self-interested individuals who treat their clients as means to the end of utility maximization. This, of course, is the crude psychology of classical liberalism and neoclassical economics. Sophisticated models of principal and agent, moral hazard, adverse selection and rent-seeking are built upon this crucial assumption regarding human behaviour. If only the theorists concerned had considered the possibility of greater complexity in human motivation. Not least among the human characteristics neglected here are altruism, trust and pride. All of these are significant contributors to the professional ethos.

Intrinsic to the notion of professional conduct is 'service above and beyond the call of contractual duty'. Yet the assumption of rational utility maximization dictates the use of contracts which become ever more precise —hence complex—in their specification, prescription and proscription of tasks. The result of this is a proportionate decrease in goodwill and trust, and a consequent reduction in the 'intangible' (i.e. immeasurable) value added by professionals to the service in question. Trust itself is important because it is undoubtedly more efficient to be able to rely upon the performance of necessary tasks that could not have been anticipated in any contractual negotiation but which, nevertheless, require completion for service quality to be of a high standard. For patients, trust is especially important. Given the ever-deepening division of labour in modern society, all of us rely upon the expertise and care of myriad professionals of whom we are only aware when something goes wrong. We are accustomed to investing an implicit trust in our society, based upon our experience of societal order and our expectation that it will continue, regardless of whether we approve of that order. Singling out doctors or any other professional group as deserving of suspicion serves to corrode that wider trust, as much as it corrodes the trust traditionally invested in specific professions. Pride in a job well done is integral to the professional ethos. As human beings, our identity in large measure derives from what we *do*, as opposed to an abstracted *being*. This notion has informed the work of writers such as Marx, Veblen, John Dewey, Clarence E. Ayres and C. Wright Mills. With regard to the work of the academic, Mills (1959) propagated a model of intellectual craftsmanship that depended upon the conscientious application of what Veblen would have termed the instincts of idle curiosity and workmanship in the never-ending effort to enact meaningful emancipatory change. Ayres' conceptualization of human life as 'the tool process' was predicated upon the view of human beings as inherently problem-solving beings, forever trying to narrow the gap between the 'is' and the 'ought' (Tool 1979: 165). Professions are associative bodies of people engaged in similar problem-solving activities. Together, members of a profession define—at least in part—the problem, and the manner or method of its amelioration or solution. The professional body also, as a collective entity, defines to a large extent the nature and function of that profession. It oversees the education and formation of apprentices, and accredits these as full professionals once appropriate experience and standards of performance are attained. This attainment is itself a matter of pride, and membership of a profession, one's peers' recognition of one as a suitably qualified practitioner, is a worthy aspiration. The retention of that public status depends upon the profession's ability to maintain the provision of a high quality service dependent upon the exercise of specialist skill. As the division of labour intensifies, the ability of such associative bodies to fulfil these functions becomes ever more significant.

As stated earlier, one means of undermining the status of the professions is to cast doubt upon their raison d'être, to suggest that in fact they are rent-seeking cabals of the rationally self-interested. On this view, professions are characterized, to use Adam Smith's famous words regarding merchants and master manufacturers, as 'an order of men, whose interest is never exactly the same with that of the publick, who have generally an interest to deceive and even to oppress the publick, and who accordingly have, upon many occasions, both deceived and oppressed it' (Smith 1981: 267). The importance of the professions and what is often referred to as the 'public service ethos' in late modern capitalism, through the workings of the welfare state, are necessarily diminished in a programme of economic retrenchment designed to alleviate the fiscal crisis. By attacking the very basis of the social economy in this way, the regressive redistribution of income, achieved through the privatization of profit and the socialization of costs, can be intensified.

Among the unintended consequences that arise in such circumstances is the intensification of the unease resulting from other sources of instability acting in combination with this destabilizing attack on the institutions of civil society. The economic restructuring resulting from the related forces of technological change and globalization has rendered as outdated the older notions of a steady career path for adults and guaranteed employment prospects for future generations. The unsettling effects upon individuals and communities are compounded by the retreat of the social security mechanisms that were designed to alleviate these just at the period where they are most required. The intense uncertainty that is characteristic of late modernity produces among individuals and communities what Bauman (1999: 5) terms *unsicherheit*:

> the German term which blends together experiences which need three English terms—uncertainty, insecurity and unsafety—to be conveyed. The curious thing is that the nature of these troubles is itself a most powerful impediment to collective remedies: people feeling insecure, people wary of what the future might hold in store and fearing for their safety, are not truly free to take the risks which collective action demands. They lack the courage to dare and the time to imagine alternative ways of living together; and they are too preoccupied with tasks they cannot share to think of, let along to devote their energy to, such tasks as can be undertaken only in common.

Of the three facets of *unsicherheit*, only unsafety is being addressed through the imposition of ever greater state regulation. But the manner in which this is supposedly to be achieved runs contrary to its stated aim of increased public safety. By attacking the institutions of civil society the populist state only serves to corrode further what remains of the social cohesion not already lost.

In his classic analysis of work under capitalism, Harry Braverman charts the proletarianization of the work force as the autonomy of craftsmen is transformed into methods of mass production:

> Insofar as these changes have been governed by manufacturing rather than marketing considerations (and the two are by no means independent), they have been brought about by the drive for greater productivity: that is, the effort to find ways to incorporate ever smaller quantities of labor time into ever greater quantities of product. This leads to faster and more efficient methods and machinery. But in the capitalist mode of production, new methods and new machinery are incorporated within a management effort to dissolve the labor process as a process conducted by the worker and reconstitute it as a process conducted by management . . . It is in the age of the scientific-technical revolution that management sets itself the problem of grasping the process as a whole and controlling every element of it, without exception. 'Improving the system of management', wrote H.L. Gantt, 'means the elimination of elements of chance or accident, and the accomplishment of all the ends desired in accordance with knowledge derived from a scientific investigation of everything down to the smallest detail of labor'.
>
> (Braverman 1974: 170–171)

Citing Gantt, Braverman highlights the EBM of an earlier age—evidence-based manufacturing. But it is precisely this same attention to detail via the decomposition of complex wholes into parts that can be measured that is threatening to overwhelm a National Health Service already stretched to the limits of 'efficiency'. The irony is that, far from controlling costs, such proliferating bureaucracy promises to increase them—a point not lost on the pharmaceutical-industry-financed Office of Health Economics (Timmins 1999).

Broadening ownership and control

Far from empowering patients, clinical governance leaves them in much the same position as did the internal market, and only marginally better off than in the earlier regime of medical authoritarianism. Unlike the United States, where the federal Agency for Health Care Policy and Research produced guidelines intended as much for patients as professionals (Hudgings 1995), guidelines in Britain have had no such commitment to patient participation. While at first there was little explicit attention paid to the input, potential and actual, of patients and the public to guideline formulation and implementation, more is now being done by way of facilitating patient participation in guideline development (Scottish Intercollegiate Guidelines Network 1999: 13). Yet it remains more of a 'bolt-on' addition to a model of health care that is still inherently authoritarian. All that has changed, from most patients' perspectives, has been the nature of that authority.

Yet, just as with the health professions, participation in guideline development and other decision making processes can yield potentially undesirable results if the nature of that participation is not itself open and accountable. As Doyal and Gough (1991) warn: 'It can advantage the already privileged through their ability to manipulate the information process and can sacrifice the common good to sectional interpretations of it.' And token representation in a system whose design was in no part subject to the input of a wider public cannot be expected to yield significantly different results than systems in which there is none. The rules of the game have already been established, prior to public participation.

In the NHS, there exist local health councils made up of lay representatives which act nominally in the interest of patients and the wider public. They were established in 1974 as part of a broader tranche of reforms that was superseded by the Griffiths reforms a decade later. The problem with the health councils is that no clearly defined role has been assigned to them, despite this statutory duty. Nor do they possess sufficient resources to make an impact greater than that presently achieved, in varying degrees, by those individuals sufficiently committed to making them work. Once again, they are a bolt-on addition to a system not designed to incorporate the sort of democratic input implicit in health councils' rationale. What is required is a fundamental reconstruction of the very concept of health care—one that places patients as active participants, and not simply passive recipients, in the process of care.

John Dewey's philosophy of inquiry encompasses the social, the political and the economic. It is rooted in a democratic ethos that assigns value to means and ends in accordance with the breadth of participation involved in their formulation and use. Contrary to the mainstream of Western thought, Dewey emphasized the symbiosis of means and ends—their mutually informative relationship. As a result, the pitfalls of deterministic progress (utopianism) and fatalistic reaction (nihilism and conservatism) are avoided. Instead, a politics of continuing reconstruction is envisaged, where technologies that improve social life are designed and implemented in such a way as to achieve 'minimal dislocation'. This is not to surrender all hope of progressive change in situations of institutionalized inequality and discrimination. Rather, it is 'to comprehend the related adjustments necessary to making an adjustment recognized as necessary'; otherwise they will 'simply increase the human incidences that initially motivated the adjustments' (Foster 1981: 933–934). As the shock therapists of the former Soviet Union discovered, to the cost of the unfortunate citizens of the countries concerned, establishing ends without sufficient reference to the available means is a recipe for maximal dislocation, and all the concomitant suffering and hardship that necessarily follows in its wake.

Medicine offers good illustrations of the importance of minimal dislocation. Cancer patients, when offered chemotherapy, must balance the likelihood of success with the diminished quality of life resulting from the treatment. Among the factors determining a patient's decision whether to undertake chemotherapy are considerations of longevity vs. activity. Given the uncertainty surrounding the outcome of any decision, the patient's choice will be the result of comparing the available means (relative health otherwise, quality of life) with the ends (longevity above all else, full and active participation in social life). Arbitrarily administered chemotherapy would result in maximal dislocation for those patients preferring to enjoy what time they have left instead of prolonging their lives (perhaps) but with a diminished range of activities in which they would be able to participate.

Authoritarian systems of governance are more likely to result in dislocation than are democratic, participatory modes of decision making. Despite the erosion of medical authoritarianism in the NHS, dislocation remains due to the elitist forms of decision making that have been introduced in its place. Whether by emulating so-called 'market norms' or the fallacy of a value-neutral technocracy, patients and the public remain vulnerable to the threat of dislocation. This is especially so in the context of the proletarianization of those whose skill and judgment are essential to the provision of high quality health care.

By way of contrast, consider Marc R. Tool's adaptation of an example employed by Dewey in the latter's *Logic: The Theory of Inquiry* (1938):

> Illustratively, consider the role and function of a medical diagnostician confronting a complex and difficult array of symptoms in a patient. The habitual diagnostic characterization appears not to apply; it does not fit or serve; the condition of physical impairment continues. Inquiry is invoked. New tools of disclosure may be employed. These new tests may themselves alter conditions and modify the causal complexities. Possible alternative explanations are conceptually reviewed. New diagnostic insights generate the need for a fresh selection and ordering of evidences. The process of juxtaposing hypotheses and observed reality continues. Each recasting is tested for its explanatory capacity. The diagnostic responsibility is concurrently to create and sensitively to explore more definitive explanations and more confirming factual information. Ultimately, but provisionally, the diagnostician selects the hypothetical explanation which most completely accounts for the observed impairment and treats the condition so diagnosed. Creativity is thus invoked internal to the inquiry process; it also leavens the process. It is reflective of the continuously evolving experiential and ideational acquisitions in the diagnostician's mind.
>
> (Tool 1995: 20)

Dewey himself was applying the crucial insight of Peirce regarding the formulation of hypotheses. According to Peirce, there are three types of inference: deduction, induction and abduction. Only abduction originates knowledge: 'Deduction reiterates what we know, and induction tests or generalizes knowledge that we already have' (Brent 1998: 349). Abduction, on the other hand, 'is the process of forming an explanatory hypothesis' (Peirce quoted by Tool 1995: 20). Hypotheses inform the design and conduct of inquiry, and contribute to the identification and evaluation of evidence. By turning clinical practice into a process of deduction based upon inductions packaged as guidelines, clinical governance ignores a crucial aspect of the process of care. Similar observations regarding the superiority of Peirce's method of inquiry have featured in the health care literature:

> The philosophy of C.S. Peirce . . . provides a promising framework in which to develop a theory of clinical reasoning that is both rigorous and probabilistic, yet able to recognize the uncertainties and particularities of day-to-day clinical practice.
>
> (Upshur 1997: 206)

But in empowering clinical professionals, a democratic health care system must also empower patients and the wider public it serves. A recasting of the patient-professional relationship as a partnership would be an effective means of achieving such an end. And Tool (1995: 189–195) provides a set of evaluative criteria by which a system of health care provisioning (among many other systems) can be appraised, from patient-practitioner relationships right up to and including the funding and organization of the service. As this implies, the reconstruction of the patient-professional relationship on a partnership model would have significant implications for the NHS as a whole, and beyond.

Postscript

At the time of writing, the NHS and the British public are recovering from the shock and revulsion arising from the conclusion of a lengthy criminal trial in which a general practitioner was found guilty of murdering fifteen patients. In all likelihood the total number of those he killed is significantly greater. In response, the government announced a full inquiry whose 'primary purpose will be to make recommendations on how best patients can be safeguarded in the future' (Milburn 2000). Concurrently, the medical profession's regulatory bodies are undertaking sweeping changes in an effort to reassure the public that all possible safeguards will be put in place to prevent such events from happening ever again (Boseley 2000). The British Medical Association is reported as 'hastily producing its own proposals . . . to head off punitive government action in response to the Shipman affair, even though no reform would of itself have prevented his crimes' (Brindle 2000). And there lies the rub. In the rush to prevent the freak incident the normal conduct of health care threatens to be impeded. There are, without doubt, reasonable measures that can be taken in the light of the lessons from this sorry affair. But ensuring it never happens again would be akin to evacuating San Francisco in order to prevent any future deaths from earthquakes. While in no wise a failsafe, only by increasing public accountability and democratic participation can professionals be allowed to practise conscientiously, and patients and the public be assured that the service is providing the nearest approximation to what is perceived as the best possible health care.

Note

The author gratefully acknowledges the helpful comments of John Davis, Robert McMaster and Marc Tool.

References

Atkinson, Glen (1995) Efficiency versus equity: a false dichotomy? in Charles M.A. Clark (ed.) *Institutional Economics and the Theory of Social Value: Essays in Honor of Marc R. Tool*, Boston: Kluwer Academic Publishers.

Bacon, Robert and Eltis, Walter (1976) *Britain's Economic Problem: Too Few Producers*, London: Macmillan.

Baran, Paul A. and Sweezy, Paul M. (1966) *Monopoly Capital: An Essay on the American Economic and Social Order*, New York: Monthly Review Press.

Bauman, Zygmunt (1999) *In Search of Politics*, Cambridge: Polity Press.

Blank, Robert H. (1996) The medical marketplace and the diffusion of technologies, *Health Care Analysis* 4(4): 321–324.

Boseley, Sarah (1999) Patients 'struck off by GPs for being uneconomic', *Guardian*, 13 September.

—— (2000) 'Cosy club' of doctors to go as GMC steps up ways to reassure public, *Guardian*, 10 February.

Braverman, Harry (1974) *Labor and Monopoly Capital: The Degradation of Work in the Twentieth Century*, New York: Monthly Review Press.

Brent, Joseph (1998) *Charles Sanders Peirce: A Life*, Bloomington and Indianapolis IN: Indiana University Press.

Brindle, David (2000) Doctors say 'vague' GMC is failing them, *Guardian*, 3 March.

Brittan, Samuel (1999) The overwhelming case for paying stealth taxes, *Financial Times*, 25 November.

Campbell, Harry, Hotchkiss, Rona, Bradshaw, Nicola, and Porteous, Mary (1998) Integrated care pathways, *British Medical Journal* 316 (10 January): 133–137.

Chalmers, Iain (1995) What do I want from health research and researchers when I am a patient? *British Medical Journal* 310 (20 May): 1315–1318.

Connell, R.W. (1987) *Gender and Power: Society, the Person and Sexual Politics*, Stanford CA: Stanford University Press.

Davies, Huw Talfryn Oakley and Mannion, Russell (1999) The rise of oversight and the decline of mutuality? *Public Money and Management* 19(2): 55–59.

Department of Health and Social Security (1983) *NHS Management Inquiry* (Griffiths Report), London: HMSO.

Dixon, Jennifer and Glennerster, Howard (1995) What do we know about fund-holding in general practice? *British Medical Journal* 311 (16 September): 727–730.

Donaldson, Liam J. and Gray, J.A. Muir (1998) Clinical governance: a quality duty for health organisations, *Quality in Health Care* 7 (supplement): S37–S44.

Dowd, Douglas F. (1966) *Thorstein Veblen*, New York: Washington Square Press.

—— (1997) *Against the Conventional Wisdom: A Primer for Current Economic Controversies and Proposals*, Boulder CO: Westview Press.

Doyal, Len and Gough, Ian (1991) *A Theory of Human Need*, Basingstoke: Macmillan.

Ehrenreich, Barbara and English, Deirdre (1973) *Complaints and Disorders: The Sexual Politics of Sickness*, New York: The Feminist Press.

Ferlie, Ewan, Ashburner, Lynn, Fitzgerald, Louise, and Pettigrew, Andrew (1996) *The New Public Management in Action*, Oxford: Oxford University Press.

Foster, John Fagg (1981) Syllabus for problems of modern society: the theory of institutional adjustment, *Journal of Economic Issues* 15(4): 929–935.

Fowler, P.B.S. (1997) Evidence-based everything, *Journal of Evaluation in Clinical Practice* 3(3): 239–243.

Galbraith, John Kenneth (1985) *The New Industrial State*, 4th edn, Boston: Houghton Mifflin.

—— (1992) *The Culture of Contentment*, Boston: Houghton Mifflin.

Giddens, Anthony (2000) A Third Way budget, *Guardian*, 29 February.

Harrison, Stephen (1998) The politics of evidence-based medicine in the United Kingdom, *Policy and Politics* 26(1): 15–31.

—— (1999) Clinical autonomy and health policy: past and futures, in Mark Exworthy and Susan Halford (eds) *Professionals and the New Managerialism in the Public Sector*, Buckingham: Open University Press.

Harrison, Stephen, Hunter, David J., Marnoch, Gordon, and Pollitt, Christopher (1992) *Just Managing: Power and Culture in the National Health Service*, London: Macmillan.

Haskell, Thomas L. (1998) *Objectivity Is Not Neutrality: Explanatory Schemes in History*, Baltimore MD: Johns Hopkins University Press.

Hildred, William and Watkins, Larry (1996) The nearly good, the bad, and the ugly in cost-effectiveness analysis of health care, *Journal of Economic Issues* 30(3): 755–775.

Hopkins, Anthony (1996) Clinical audit: time for a reappraisal, *Journal of the Royal College of Physicians of London* 30(5): 415–425.

Hudgings, Carole (1995) Guideline development and dissemination programme: Agency for Health Care Policy and Research, USA, in Michael Deighan and Sally Hitch (eds) *Clinical Effectiveness from Guidelines to Cost-Effective Practice*, Brentwood: Earlybrave Publications.

Huntington, Samuel P. (1975) The United States, in Michel Crozier, Samuel P. Huntington, and Joji Watanuki (eds) *The Crisis of Democracy: Report on the Governability of Democracies to the Trilateral Commission*, New York: New York University Press.

Hutton, Jane L. (1996) The ethics of randomised controlled trials: a matter of statistical belief? *Health Care Analysis* 4(2): 95–102.

Kapp, K. William (1971) *The Social Costs of Private Enterprise*, New York: Schocken Books.

Keaney, Michael (1997) Can economics be bad for your health? *Health Care Analysis* 5(4): 299–305.

—— 1999) Are patients really consumers? *International Journal of Social Economics* 26(5): 695–706.

Keaney, Michael and Lorimer, A.R. (1999a) Clinical effectiveness in the National Health Service in Scotland, *Journal of Economic Issues* 33(1): 117–139.

—— (1999b) Auditing the implementation of SIGN clinical guidelines, *International Journal of Health Care Quality Assurance* 12(7): 314–317.

Leape, Lucian L. (1997) A systems analysis approach to medical error, *Journal of Evaluation in Clinical Practice* 3(3): 213–222.

Lynd, Robert S. (1939) *Knowledge for What? The Place of Social Science in American Culture*, Princeton NJ: Princeton University Press.

Milburn, Alan (2000) The lessons of the Shipman case, *The Guardian*, 1 February.

Mills, C. Wright (1959) *The Sociological Imagination*, New York: Oxford University Press.

NHS Executive (1996) *Promoting Clinical Effectiveness: A Framework for Action in and through the NHS*, Leeds: Department of Health.

O'Connor, James (1973) *The Fiscal Crisis of the State*, New York: St. Martin's Press.

Panitch, Leo (1998) 'The State in a Changing World': Social-democratizing global capitalism? *Monthly Review* 50(5): 11–22.

Parsons, Wayne (1982) Politics without promises: the crisis of 'overload' and governability, *Parliamentary Affairs* 35(4): 421–435.

Paton, C., Birch, K., Hunt, K., and Jordan, K. (1997) Counting the costs, *Health Service Journal* 107(5567): 24–27.

Pollitt, Christopher, Harrison, Stephen, Hunter, David J., and Marnoch, Gordon (1991) General management in the NHS: the initial impact 1983–88, *Public Administration* 69(1): 61–83.

Rhodes, R.A.W. (1997) *Understanding Governance: Policy Networks, Governance, Reflexivity and Accountability*, Buckingham: Open University Press.

Rosenau, J.N. (1992) Governance, order and change in world politics, in J.N. Rosenau and E.-O. Czempiel (eds) *Governance without Government: Order and Change in World Politics*, Cambridge: Cambridge University Press.

Sackett, David L., Richardson, W. Scott, Rosenberg, William, and Haynes, R. Brian (1997) *Evidence-Based Medicine: How to Practice and Teach EBM*, New York: Churchill Livingstone.

Scottish Intercollegiate Guidelines Network (1999) *SIGN Guidelines: An Introduction to SIGN Methodology for the Development of Evidence-Based Clinical Guidelines*, Edinburgh: Scottish Intercollegiate Guidelines Network.

Scottish Office Department of Health (1997) *Designed to Care: Renewing the National Health Service in Scotland*, Edinburgh: The Stationery Office.

Seedhouse, David (1997) Tautology and value: the flawed foundations of health economics, *Health Care Analysis* 5(1): 1–5.

Smith, Adam (1981) *An Inquiry into the Nature and Causes of the Wealth of Nations*, Indianapolis IN: Liberty Fund.

Stanfield, James Ronald and Stanfield, Jacqueline Bloom (1996) Reconstructing the welfare state in the aftermath of the Great Capitalist Restoration, in William M.

Dugger (ed.) *Inequality: Radical Institutionalist Views on Race, Gender, Class, and Nation*, Westport CT: Greenwood Press.

Stephens, Philip (2000) No more tax cuts, thank you, *Financial Times*, 18 February.

Strong, Philip and Robinson, Jane (1990) *The NHS under New Management*, Buckingham: Open University Press.

Timmins, Nicholas (1999) NHS reforms 'could lead to increased costs', *Financial Times*, 7 April.

Tool, Marc R. (1979) *The Discretionary Economy: A Normative Theory of Political Economy*, Santa Monica CA: Goodyear Publishing Company.

—— (1995) *Pricing, Valuation and Systems: Essays in Neoinstitutional Economics*, Brookfield VT: Edward Elgar.

—— (1998) Instrumental inquiry and democratic governance, in Sasan Fayazmanesh and Marc R. Tool (eds) *Institutionalist Theory and Applications: Essays in Honor of Paul Dale Bush*, vol. 2, Northampton MA: Edward Elgar.

Upshur, Ross (1997) Certainty, probability and abduction: why we should look to C.S. Peirce rather than Gödel for a theory of clinical reasoning, *Journal of Evaluation in Clinical Practice* 3(3): 201–206.

Veblen, Thorstein (1983) *The Engineers and the Price System*, New Brunswick NJ: Transaction Publishers.

Walker, David (2000) You find the evidence, we'll pick the policy, *Guardian*, 15 February.

Webster, Charles (1998) *The National Health Service: A Political History*, Oxford: Oxford University Press.

7

CANADA

More state, more market?

Terrence Sullivan and Cameron Mustard

Canada has a unique history in the development of health policy and has attracted a wide interest from a range of commentators. These include seminal historical studies by Evans (1984), Taylor (1987), and Naylor (1992); and comparative contributions from Gray (1991), Drache and Sullivan (1999), and Tuohy (1999). The federal state role in the national health plan in Canada has been a pivotal one of conditioning provincial behavior through cost-sharing and a constitutionally acknowledged social spending power, notwithstanding clear provincial jurisdiction for health care. In Figure 7.1, we have characterized the national health care plan in Canada through five periods, differentiated by the manner in which changing patterns of state activism (expressed through federal-provincial transfer payments) have altered the scope of national health insurance and thereby the behavior of key actors in the delivery system.

These five periods include the pre-Medicare period prior to 1962, when there was no national plan, but a series of municipal and private plans leading up to a provincial introduction of Medicare in Saskatchewan; the early Medicare period from 1962 to 1975, which involved open-ended programs to expand the growth of hospitals and physician supply and insurance; the block grants period from 1975 to 1984, during which the federal government began to limit the open-ended transfers through the use of block grants with checks on unlimited growth; the Canada Health Act and Fiscal Retrenchment Era (1984–1994) represents the era in which federal cost sharing peaked in overall value (Deber 2000) and in which Canada conditioned further its provincial grants on the prohibition of so-called extra billing for medically necessary services. The consolidated transfer—the Canada Health and Social Transfer (CHST) period (1994–) into which we have recently entered—is one in which the federal government has consolidated two transfer grants into one, reducing rapidly its downstream obligations to allay debt pressures and significantly retreating as a major steering force for health reform. During the period of 1991–1996, average growth in

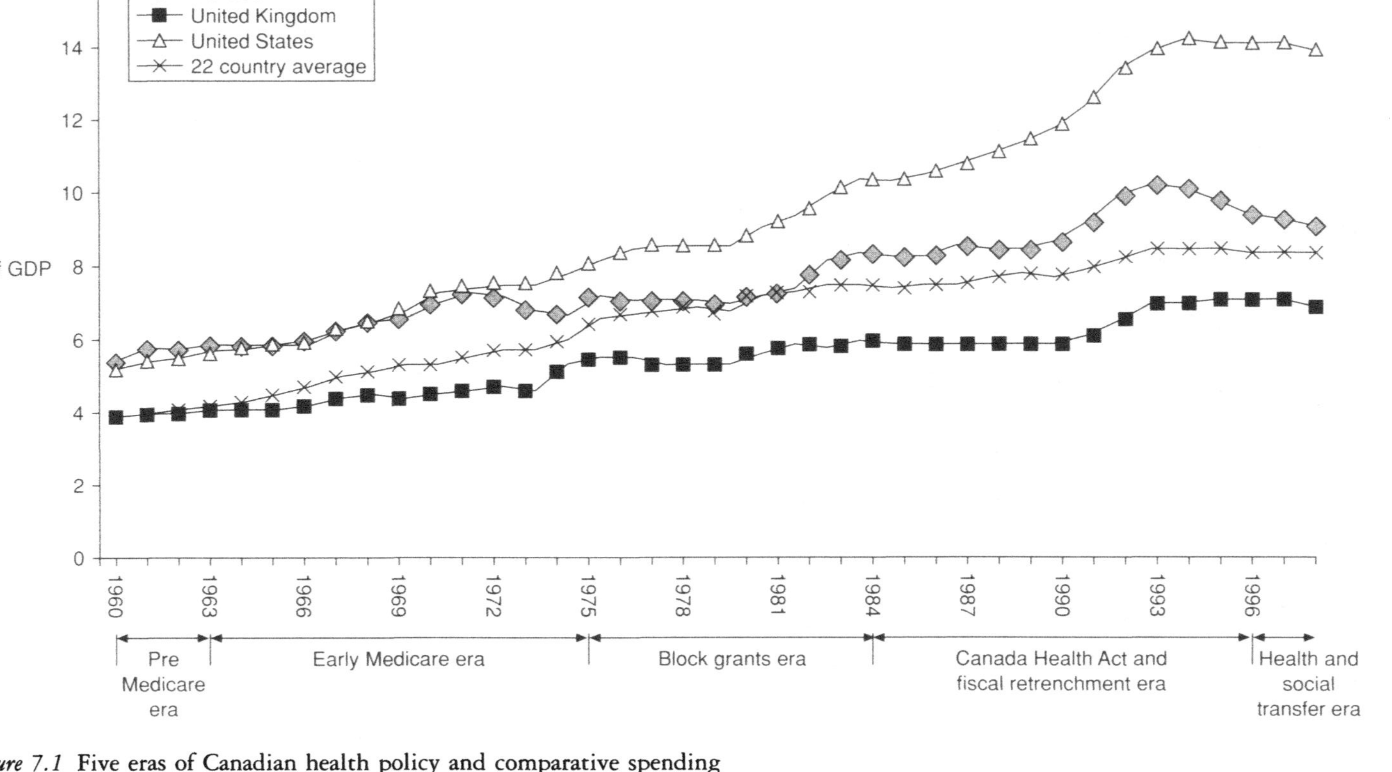

Figure 7.1 Five eras of Canadian health policy and comparative spending

Note

Adapted from Deber (2000) and the OECD health datafile. (The data include Canada, the US, and a '22 country average' of the values for: Australia, Austria, Belgium, Canada, Denmark, Finland, France, Germany, Iceland, Ireland, Italy, Japan, Luxembourg, Netherlands, New Zealand, Norway, Portugal, Spain, Sweden, Switzerland, UK, and US. Excluded are the Czech Republic, Hungary, Poland, Greece, Turkey, Korea, and Mexico, countries which are at a different stage of economic development.)

health spending was 2.6 percent, down from the previous 11.1 percent average of 1975–1991. In the new fiscally flush period since 1999, with a budget surplus available, the government of Canada has taken a balanced approach to debt retirement, tax relief and program spending increases. Health care is at the top of the lists of priorities for new federal program spending and a reassertion of federal spending power and activism appears possible. Indeed the most recent spending estimates for 1999 show creepback to pre-1991 growth levels with a 5.1 percent growth over 1998 (CIHI 2000).

In the pre-Medicare period, prior to the introduction of public health insurance, private financing of health care in 1960 in Canada was 58 percent of all spending (Hicks 1999). Canada's spending as a portion of GDP peaked in the recession of 1992 at about 10 percent of GDP when public spending also peaked at about 7.4 percent. In 1998, the public portion moved up slightly over 1997 at about 69.6 percent, and private spending was relatively stable at 30.4 percent of total health care spending (about 2.7 percent of GDP), which is where it has been for the last couple of decades (Hicks 1999). (See Figures 7.2 and 7.3 for public and total health expenditures comparing Canada with five OECD comparators.)

Distinct though Canada's history and policy legacies are, there are, in our view, two unique ideas which underpin the Canadian health care system at the turn of the century. First, like the majority of OECD nations, Canada ensures reasonably comprehensive health insurance for all citizens, regardless of capacity to pay, as a function of citizenship. Through a series of fiscal and administrative levers (and some legal bars), however, Canada remains the *only* jurisdiction in the OECD where there is no way to buy your way to the front of the line for medically necessary medical and hospital services, short of crossing the border into the United States. We refer to this idea as the 'solidarity of access' idea. Table 7.1 illustrates how this first idea is given expression via the conditioned transfer principles of the Canada Health Act.

Secondly, Canadian health policy has embraced—albeit with more rhetoric than substance—the growing evidence on the social and economic determinants of health, and the need to look beyond conventional health care spending for improvements in the health of the nation's population. We refer to this as the 'social production of health idea.' This embrace includes a long tradition of 'official' reports supporting action on the social determinants (Lalonde 1974; Ontario PCHS 1991; National Forum on Health 1997) as well as a strong scholarly tradition (Evans et al. 1994; Frank and Mustard 1994; Keating and Hertzman 1999). Both of these ideas face serious challenge in the marketized 'régime discursif' of health services consumption ideas which dominates in the US, just south of our border.

This chapter explores how these two ideas, which underpin the Canadian health care system and its policy discourse, are challenged by the ascendance of the market talk and market solutions which characterize health reform debates in the US. The US is Canada's largest trading partner—a country

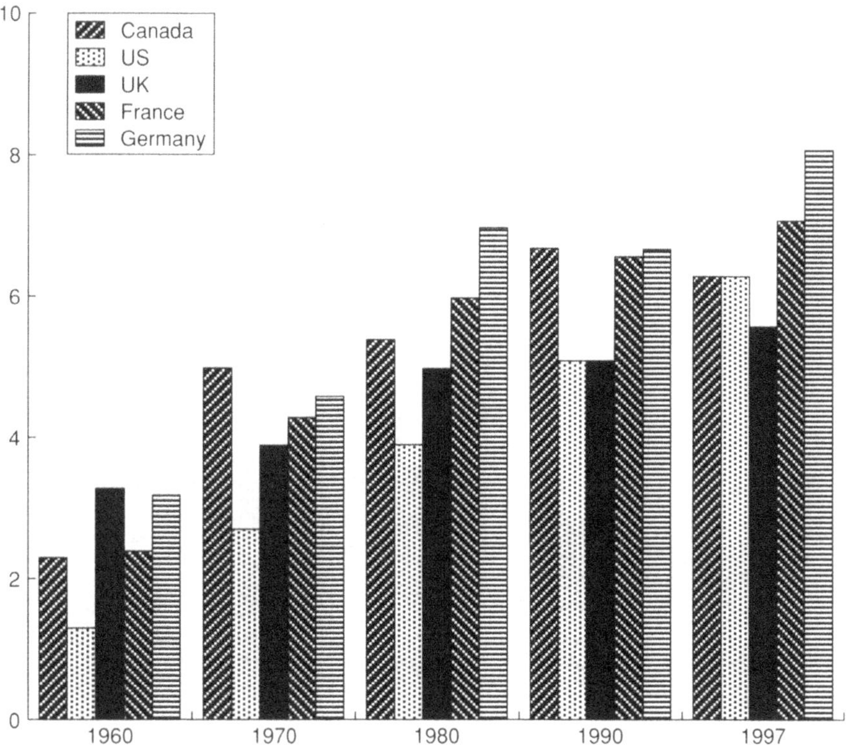

Figure 7.2 Public sector health expenditures as a percentage of GDP
(Source: OECD health data 1998).

ten times more populous and boisterous owing to the trillion dollar prowess of the American health market (Marmor 1999). Our economies are strongly linked through a set of integrated market structures and industries such as the automobile industry.

We will compare Canada's 'two ideas' with the three health policy imperatives faced by advanced economies, as suggested in Drache and Sullivan (1999): ensuring a comprehensive range of insured health services for all citizens; providing an efficient delivery system; and organizing social arrangements which produce health. Each policy imperative will be considered with reference to the public/private solutions in the evolution of the Canadian delivery system.

Ensuring a comprehensive range of insured health services for all citizens

In the last decade, Canada has emerged from a period of complete preoccupation with the growing national debt and weak economic performance, to a

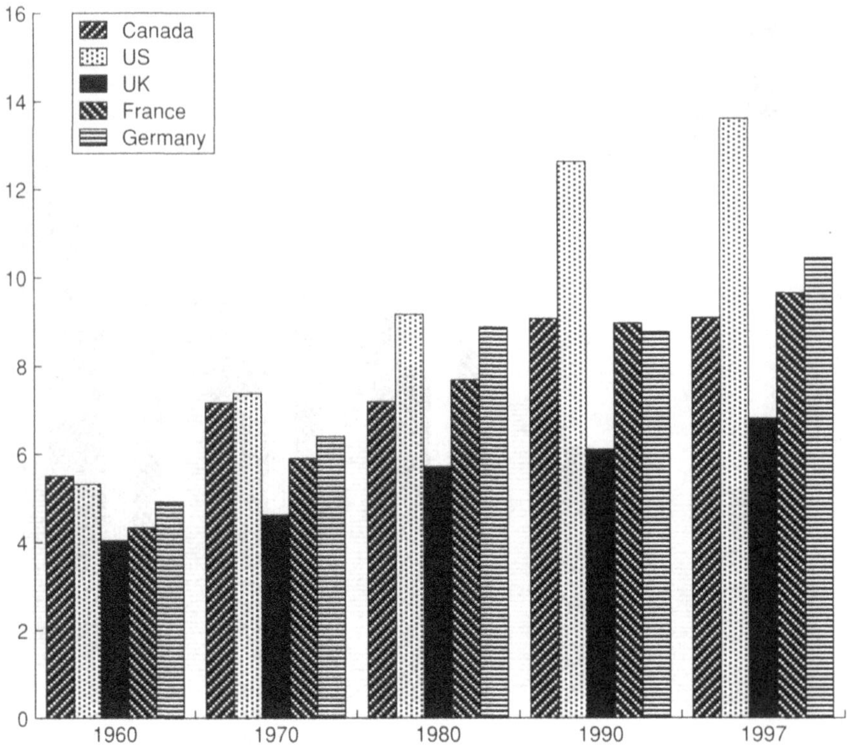

Figure 7.3 Total health expenditures as a percentage of GDP
(Source: OECD health data 1998).

period of modest optimism and slightly better economic performance. Unemployment is at its lowest level for two decades, and federal and provincial governments are making plans for large budget surpluses. During this period of time, spending on health care as a portion of all spending dropped for the first time and Canada moved from its position as second only to the US on a number of health spending indicators, to being somewhere just above the middle of the OECD average (Figure 7.1). This reduction came largely as a consequence of dramatic reductions in hospital spending. As a consequence there are serious pressures now on acute and chronic care beds and rhetorical talk about the 'death spiral' of the public system (Priest 2000).

The Canadian health insurance policy legacy has been strong on hospital and physician insurance programs, leaving vulnerable the range of health services and products required in the community including home care, long-term care, and pharmaceuticals. In the case of each of these three areas of health service, there is no equivalent to a national imperative for coverage.

Table 7.1 CHA principles and national goals*

CHA Principles	*Imputed national goals*	*Effects*
Portability	Horizontal equity; macroefficiency	Promotes labor mobility
Accessibility	Vertical equity; horizontal equity (e.g. no exclusion based on preexisting conditions)	Risk pooling; financial barrier or else reductions in federal transfers
Comprehensiveness	Vertical equity; horizontal equity; all necessary services covered	Non-comprehensive coverage Physicians and hospital covered some community ancillary services
Universality	Vertical equity; horizontal equity	All citizens have comparable access to medical and hospital services
Public administration	Vertical equity; macroefficiency	Progressive distributive consequence for taxation and health benefit

Note
* Adapted from Maslove 1997.

Quite different arrangements occur from province to province, and the national government has been encouraged in a set of recent recommendations to extend coverage in these areas. As Figure 7.4 illustrates, overall public spending is just under 70 percent of all expenditures, placing Canada once again in the middle of the OECD pack. The vast majority of physicians and hospital services are publicly paid, but pharmaceuticals and other providers are paid largely from private sector sources. Contrary to some views, the Canadian delivery system has never been a 'state-run' system, but a largely state-insured system. Canada always had a purchaser-provider split, with a strong role for private, not-for-profit delivery, and some for-profit delivery (Deber et al. 1998). (Figure 7.5 illustrates the rough separation of sources of revenue, purchase, and provision for the Canadian delivery system.)

Canada has made extensive use of consensus forums to develop elite accommodation vehicles to limit the problems of powerful stakeholder capture inherent in health departments (Lavis and Sullivan 1999, 2000). The most recent national consensus group, the National Forum on Health, produced in 1997 a five-volume set of recommendations dealing with issues in the evolution of the national health scheme which touched on both of the major

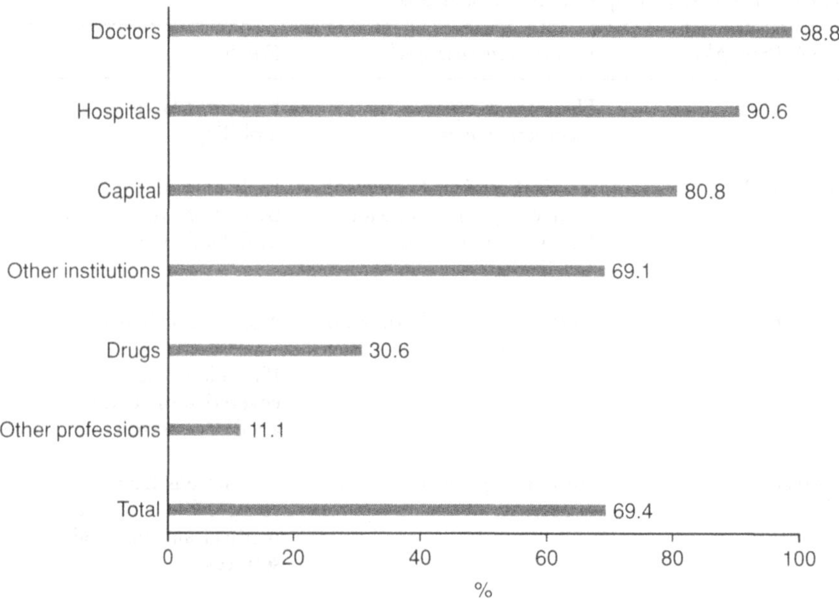

Figure 7.4 Public share of Canadian health spending
(Source: Canadian Institute for Health Information, 1997).

ideas noted above (National Forum on Health 1997). Most importantly for the purpose of this discussion, the reports recommended the creation of a federally coordinated pharmacare plan, and home care plan. Both of these areas have been historically absent in the policy legacy of Canada's public health insurance system built on hospital and physician services.

As hospital capacity has been steadily reduced in the last ten years in response to a dramatic fiscal crunch, pharmaceutical costs have been shifted out of the budget envelope of public hospital insurance and onto the private purse and employer payroll. Canadians, however, still pay significantly less for their pharmaceuticals than Americans, and in 1998 Canadian prices were about 88 percent of the median international price of drugs (PMPRB 1998). Hilary Clinton recently repeated calls for the US to allow its citizens to purchase drugs directly from Canada (Kenna 2000). Notwithstanding lower prices, pharmaceuticals nevertheless remain the fastest growing sector of public and private spending in the Canadian health care system (Lexchin 1999).

Currently, all provinces have some form of public pharmaceutical insurance from a residual scheme in Nova Scotia (covering under 35 percent of all costs), to a more comprehensive scheme in Saskatchewan (covering close to 90 percent). About one-half of Canada's $8B[1] drug expenditure bill is borne publicly, and the rest privately financed through payroll benefits and out-of-

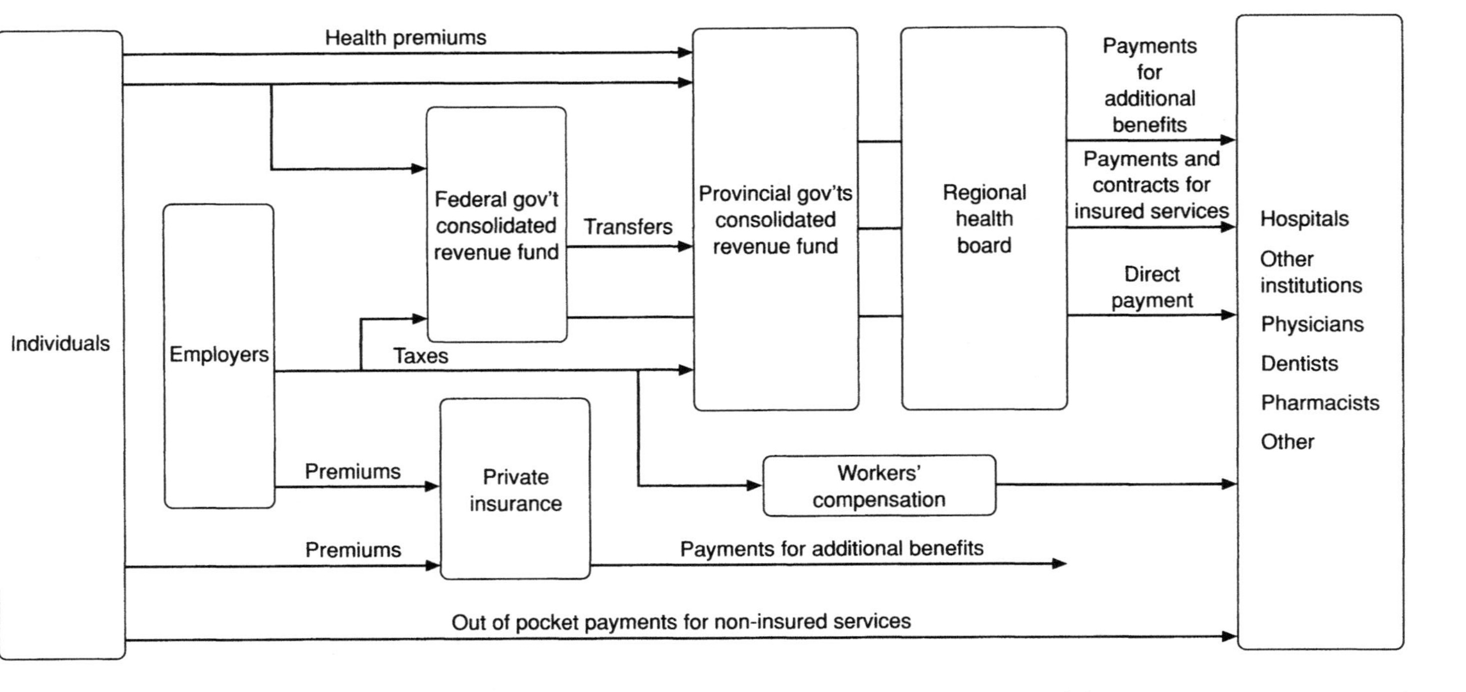

Figure 7.5 Financing of health care in Canada

pocket payments (Morgan 1998; Hicks 1999). Entering the new millennium, the government of Canada appears to have little appetite for launching the complex, large-scale checkerboard program necessary to build a national pharmacare program. Interestingly, the province of Quebec has moved ahead with a mandatory payroll-financed pharmacare program, with a significant user-pay component and a legal obligation for eligible employer groups to insure with private companies. Pressures to constrain the growth of pharmaceuticals nevertheless represent a major challenge for Canada, both on the public and the private side. At least one provincial government (British Columbia) has adopted reference-based pricing strategies and all are looking at better formulary management processes. The enthusiasm for integrated delivery systems in Canada at least allows the possibility of not-for-profit state management of disease (Leatt et al. 1996). Disease management is quite a lot more than managing pharmaceutical costs: it is a process which covers all aspects of health care from prevention through diagnosis and treatment to aftercare and monitoring. In the US, pharmaceutical companies have been at the forefront of the movement to state management of disease for a number of obvious reasons. In Canada, the notion of pharmaceutical drug adjudicators and managed care—managed for and by the pharmaceutical industry—is greeted with something less than enthusiasm (Evans 1997). Nevertheless, a number of companies have begun to develop inroads in this area in Canada. While the National Forum pressed for more coverage in the area of pharmaceutical care, there appears to be little federal interest in acting in this area. This is because the concentration of market interests is very large and the support for federal-provincial policy coordination very fragmented. These conditions in a federation amount to a recipe for little action (Pierson 1995).

In 2000, the federal health minister announced that he would be inviting direct discussions with provincial counterparts to advance models of federal-provincial cost sharing for expanding home care programs which were enriched in the 2000 federal budget. Public payment on home care programs in Canada has grown from an annual rate of increase of 1.2 percent of all public spending in Canada in 1980–1981 to 4 percent in 1997–1998. In the 1990s, as a consequence of shifting from acute to rehabilitative and long-term care, growth from all sources has been at an annual rate of increase of close to 11 percent with quite a lot of provincial variation (Health Canada 1999). Unlike medical and hospital services, careful estimates of private home care provision are currently not available, but the majority of provinces in Canada have some income testing for home care and especially long-term-care clients.

Calls from the National Forum for new state-level action in health reform and financing have had mixed results. On the one hand, a national pharmacare program has generated little response except from Quebec, which defines its own national (sic) plan. On the other hand, serious discussions are underway regarding a new cost-shared federal home care program. In both areas, public spending is growing rapidly.

To the extent that there is a private market voice in the reform debate, it presents itself in two forms. On the one hand private, the spirit of public finance is being tested by the Premier of Alberta, who supports for-profit *delivery* for hospital services as a way of introducing 'innovation' in the delivery system to make the delivery system more efficient. As noted earlier, private provision has always been part of the Canadian landscape but most (not all) private delivery in Canada is not-for-profit. The question of efficiency is very topical in the Canadian health reform debates. The second form of market discussion is an appeal to open up the federal legislative frame (Table 7.1), to allow competitive insurance financing to 'relieve the pressure on the public system' and reduce waiting times. Such calls are regular and repetitive, notwithstanding the abject failure of such a strategy in Britain and New Zealand (Flood 1997). Thus far most of these zombie-like ideas have been resisted (Deber 2000). Moreover, abandoning the solidarity-of-access idea associated with Canada's national health insurance may well affect the 'social production of health' idea in an adverse manner, as we will shortly argue.

Providing an efficient delivery system

At the turn of the millennium, Canada is near the top of the tables on life expectancy and in the middle of the OECD group in relation to health spending. In an interesting analysis of systems performance, Contandriopoulos (1998) developed a composite comparative indicator, using overall systems costs and national health outcomes, and concluded the following. First, the state of health of the Canadian population is among the best in the world. Second, there are fewer medical resources (numbers of beds and physicians) than the average for other OECD countries (attributed by the author to more efficient resource management than to scarcity); however, Canada is in a less enviable position with respect to overall spending and the price of its medical resources. The modest decline in GDP spending (Figure 7.1) in the last few years may have brought us slightly closer to the OECD middle and, at least on this composite indicator, raised our performance. However, it has also created enormous pressure on our delivery system with cries for greater private financing appearing regularly.

Canada, like most advanced economies, is challenged by the institutional rigidity of a health insurance scheme, which is the single largest pressure on provincial governments and which is very much subject to provider 'capture.' As Pierson (1999) observes, mature social programs like health insurance create persistent budget pressure and a marked loss of policy flexibility, making even small changes quite difficult. The consequence, in Pierson's terms, is the clash of 'irresistible forces' (post-industrial downward competitive pressure on government expenditures) with 'immovable objects' (very strong public support and political veto points exercised by concentrated interests).

Perhaps because health care is an enormously popular program in Canada, it has proved very resistant to major change, notwithstanding the recent and dramatic downward spending pressure as a function of the fiscal squeeze of the early 1990s. The most important state-initiated institutional change in the last two decades in Canada has been the rapid evolution of regional health authorities in all provinces except Ontario (Lomas 1999). The introduction of regional authorities at once shifted the blame for the effects of a large-scale reduction in the number and size of hospitals to sub-provincial regional authorities, while simultaneously reducing the traceability of spending cuts by federal and provincial governments.

The pressures on hospitals created as a consequence of the fiscal crunch of the early 1990s has generated a higher public concern regarding the quality and accessibility of services. Sixty-one percent of respondents to an Angus Reid poll in 1991 rated the system 'excellent' or 'very good,' a figure which fell to 52 percent in 1995, and to 24 percent in 1999 (Greenspon 1999). One feature of this reduced confidence has been the belief that waiting times for medical services were *increasing*. This belief is puzzling in the absence of solid evidence to support it. Like all jurisdictions with comprehensive health insurance who ration according to need rather than income, Canada has waiting lists (Maynard and Bloor 1998). Waiting lists are typically not an issue for urgent and emergent conditions. Elective procedures, however, are more problematic. Separate reports commissioned for the governments of Nova Scotia, British Columbia, and Manitoba showed that waiting lists for elective procedures had changed very little from the early to late 1990s and, if anything, median waits have *decreased* (Shortt 2000). In the last year, serious waiting problems associated with particular cancer conditions have arisen largely as a consequence of selected shortages of technical personnel. Affected patients are getting offers to go to US border cities to have immediate treatment. One comprehensive report for the Canadian government in 1998 concluded that more forceful management is certainly required to deal with waiting lists, but more money may or may not be useful (McDonald et al. 1998).

Notwithstanding this, there are a few in Canada who argue that waiting lists are an indication of the problems of 'command and control' medicine, which would be relieved not just through competitive for-profit delivery systems based on public financing, but through the use of competitive private, and privately financed, insurance markets. This latter solution has failed miserably to meet the first policy imperative of a comprehensive range of services for all citizens. In our view, the real debate is about what roles should be played by for-profit vs. not-for-profit firms in delivery, in the allocation of public money (to profits vs. to wages and worker benefits), and in the management of contracting within a largely publicly financed health care system (Flood 1997). It may be a fair assumption to say that all Western nations have enhanced some form of competitive contracting for health services as a way of driving efficiency. But these market tools have been used to promote quite different health goals, and to call this process convergent is to confuse ends and means, as Jacobs (1998) notes in relation to the different approaches in the UK, Sweden and Holland. European jurisdictions which rely on private insurance regulate benefits very heavily, while the companies themselves work in consortia to pool risk. Only the US system confirms the argument that competing and pluralistic health insurance markets do nothing more than add costs and reduce coverage; at the same time it proclaims itself as the best in the world (Kuttner 1997).

By the direct output measure of citizen health, Canada does reasonably well at delivering on the health of its citizens while spending just above the middle of the OECD pack. The contributions of overall health care spending to this effort, however, are less than obvious (Evans et al. 1994; Frenk 1998). Nevertheless, it may well be the case that the manner in which we organize our health financing arrangements does contribute to overall health status, not so much because of the benefits of medical technology, but because of solidarity effects arising from a range of pooled social resources (Mustard 1999; Ross et al. 2000).

Organizing social arrangements which produce health

It is now clear beyond any reasonable doubt that social arrangements contribute to health, beyond the effects of medical insurance. This is especially true in the developing world (World Bank 1993; Sen 1999) but also in advanced economies (Karasek and Theorell 1990; Evans et al. 1994; Amick et al. 1995; Blane et al. 1996; MacIntyre 1997). As Julio Frenk recently put it, progress in health improvement and reducing health inequalities will be achieved 'not so much by increasing access to medical care as by changing the social conditions and lifestyles that account for . . . such inequalities' (Frenk 1998: 419). The early, warm embrace of the Lalonde (1974) document on health determinants in Canada has not been matched by a series of clear policy responses directed at social conditions. This is true notwithstanding the fact that clear policy recommendations to achieve health have been made at the highest level in non-health care related areas of public policy (Ontario PCHS 1991; National Forum on Health 1998). Elsewhere we have tried to illustrate the significant institutional impediments to such action and the promising avenues for action on the non-health care related policy effects on the health of populations (Lavis and Sullivan 1999, 2000). Building the 'social production of health' intentionally into the design of the Canadian health system, or any health care system for that matter, turns out to be far from simple to achieve (Mustard 1999). For example, the public policies affecting labour markets, and their regulation and pervasive consequences for health, have often very little to do with health care services (Sullivan 2000).

One area associated with the social production of health that has attracted quite a lot of heat and at least a little light has been the relationship between income dispersion (degree of income inequality) and health. Wilkinson (1992) caught the attention of the policy community by arguing that Britain could add two years to its overall life expectancy if it were to adopt a more egalitarian income redistribution policy.

The relationship between income inequality and health status in advanced economies has moved from one of controversy and conflict to one of exciting empirical and theoretical work. Much of this originates in the UK, thanks to the efforts of Wilkinson and his colleagues (Wilkinson 1996), and more recent work in the US has replicated and refined the measurement issues: in particular, which measures of income inequality appear optimal for exploring the links (Kaplan et al. 1996; Kennedy et al. 1996; Kawachi et al. 1997). Nevertheless, there is still controversy over the nature of the relationship, although there is now good empirical data in favor of a relationship and against a hypothesis of measurement artifact (Wolfson et al. 1999). We would like to highlight two key areas worthy of consideration for the social production of health in Canada, since they touch on the market debate here, with consequences that perhaps militate against market solutions.

The first key area concerns a line of research being done by a group of Canadian and American researchers looking at income disparities and health, in Canada and the US. Ross et al. (2000) carefully examined the relationships between household income inequality and mortality rates in Canada and the US, using census metropolitan data and vital statistics. Among other things, they observed that Canadian provinces and census areas generally had less income inequality and better mortality rates than US states and census metropolitan areas. When age was considered, the relationship between income inequality and mortality was most pronounced for the working-age populations, where a 1 percent increase in share of income to the poorer half of households resulted in a decline of 21 deaths per 100,000. In fact, within Canada income inequality and mortality were not associated at either the provincial or metropolitan area levels.

One can easily see from Figure 7.6 that the slope of the gradient in income received by the less well off 50 percent of the population (the median share of income) is far steeper in the US than in Canada.[2] This very interesting finding does raise questions about the social arrangements and material conditions between the two countries which buffer (Canada) or exacerbate (US) the relationship between inequality and mortality. The authors (from both countries) explore two complementary hypotheses in relation to these findings. First, economic segregation in large US cities creates a mismatch between workers' housing and job locations, and also creates inequalities in locally financed public goods and services like schools,

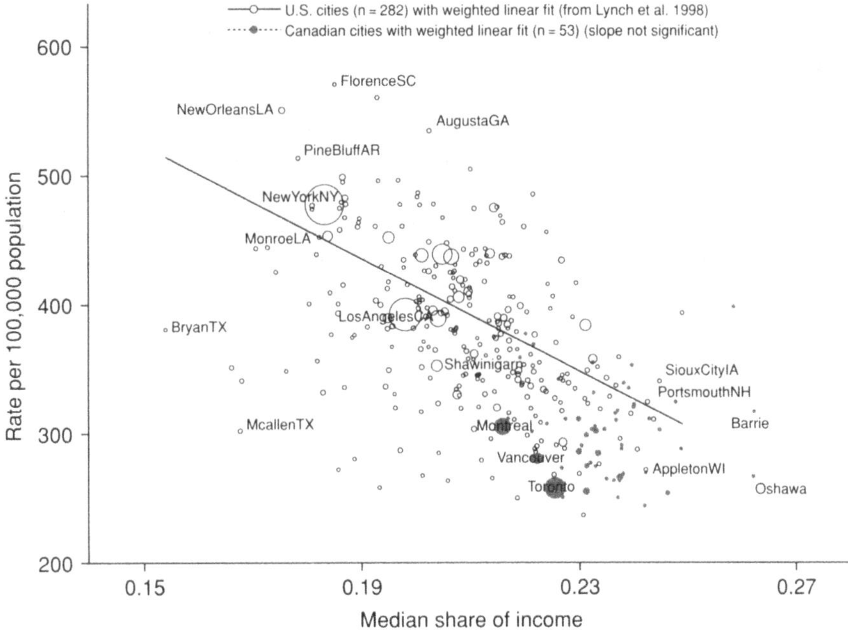

Figure 7.6 Working age mortality by proportion of income belonging to the less well off half of households, US (1990) and Canadian metropolitan areas (1991). Mortality rates standardized to the Canadian population in 1991. From Ross et al. (2000)

policing, recreation, etc., by pooling individuals with high social needs in municipal areas with poorer tax bases. Second, health care and high quality education are more sensitive to the marketplace and ability to pay in the US, whereas in Canada they are publicly funded and universally available. Public and social infrastructure can be argued to be more market sensitive (based on the ability to pay) in the US than in Canada, and this may go some way to explain the selective income disparity/mortality relationships between the countries. In the US, income appears to be a much stronger determinant of life expectancy—in both absolute and relative terms—than it is in Canada.

The second key area is one of the most significant features of the Canadian health care system: the distributive consequence of health care financing and health use. Work by Mustard et al. (1998) highlighted the net transfer of public health care insurance programs across income deciles, calculated from estimates of the incidence of household tax payments and the use of public insured health care services. Using a cross-sectional analysis of a stratified random sample of Manitoba households, Mustard and colleagues linked insured hospital services, long-term care, and medical services with 1986 census records at the individual level for 16,627 Manitoba households (representing about 5 percent of the Manitoba population). The study estimated only the benefit incidence of public expenditure on health care services, and full details of the sampling, estimation, and linking methods are described in the original paper (Mustard et al. 1998).

In 1986, 42.4 percent and 6.4 percent of the public portion of health expenditures were generated by tax revenues from the top and bottom income quintiles respectively. By contrast, health care services were distributed in an inverse fashion: 11.7 percent and 24.6 percent of health care service expenditures were received respectively by the top and bottom income quintiles. Figure 7.7 and Table 7.2 illustrate the incidence of tax and health care benefits by economic family income decile arising from this study based on 1994 data. The progressive redistributive effects of health care financing and benefits in Canada are significant.

This work stands in stark contrast to Rassell et al. (1993) and van Dooeslaer et al. (1993), who highlight the regressive effects of private insurance and

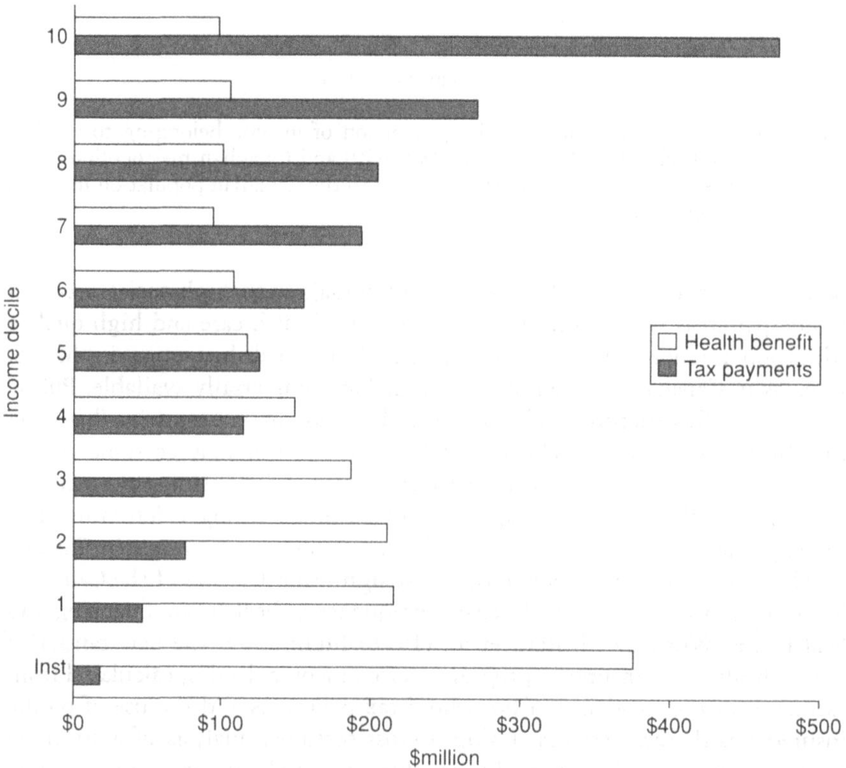

Figure 7.7 Incidence of taxation and incidence of health care benefits, by economic family income decile, Manitoba 1994

Table 7.2 Incidence of taxation and incidence of non-cash health benefits, by economic family income decile, 1994

Income decile	*Number of economic families*	*Number of persons*	*Taxes*		*A*		*B*	
			*Total tax**	*Total tax as percentage of total income*	*Total tax contribution to health*†	*Share of total*	*Estimated total insured health care use (including nursing homes)*	*Share of total*
			$000		*$000*		*$000*	
Institutional population	18,677	18,677	46,318.9	14.43	17,158.1	0.98	375,892.4	21.4
Household population								
1: $0–$15,600	81,093	105,838	125,694.1	14.25	45,687.3	2.61	215,089.7	12.2
2: $15,600–$23,3000	57,861	105,582	221,318.3	19.17	75,099.2	4.28	211,360.7	12.0
3: $23,3000–$29,800	45,950	105,797	265,223.4	21.89	87,393.8	4.98	186,319.4	10.6
4: $29,800–$36,2000	41,887	105,753	348,918.7	25.23	113,322.4	6.45	148,366.1	8.4
5: $36,200–42,3000	36,090	105,468	387,967.5	27.46	124,325.3	7.08	115,978.1	6.6
6: $42,300–$50,100	35,240	105,902	475,880.9	29.36	154,149.3	8.78	107,265.8	6.1
7: $50,100–$58,800	35,807	106,036	595,291.3	30.70	193.178.0	11.00	93,318.0	5.3
8: $58,800–$68,100	31,753	105,715	627,820.3	31.22	203,804.8	11.60	100,282.9	5.7
9: $68,100–$86,200	33,071	105,215	824,559.2	32.70	270,588.2	15.40	105,314.8	6.0
10: $86,200+	31,741	105,767	1,394,509.1	35.59	471,731.6	26.85	97,411.7	5.5
Total	449,170	1,075,750	5,313,502.0	28.92	1,756,600.0	100.00	1,756,599.7	100.00

Notes

* Total taxes include federal income and consumption taxes and Manitoba income and consumption taxes.

† In this model, household tax contributions are assumed to finance 100% of health care expenditures.

out-of-pocket payments in the US and Switzerland—the two OECD countries with predominantly private financing mechanisms.

While there continues to be much hopeful (some would say fanciful) talk in the Canadian reform debate on 'influencing' the social and economic determinants of health, it may be that national, provincial and local tax structures, and their effect on health care use, constitute the invisible hand which buffers the effects of income inequality on the health status of Canadians. One of the main 'influencers' on the health status of Canadians and health inequalities in Canada may well be the progressive tax and equalizing benefit structures of the Canadian state, relative to the US. Canadian health data show a strong relationship between health status and income, but, unlike the US and Britain, the apparent particular effects of income disparities may be muted, at least partially, by tax policies and health use benefit incidence which implicitly favor social equity!

Conclusion

How, then, do these two Canadian principles—the solidarity of access, and the social production of health—fare at the beginning of the twenty-first century? First, solidarity of access remains strong in Canada, although concerns regarding access are rising, even when the evidence points to better access for a range of procedures. The voice of key stakeholders, frustrated by a very stark and successful fiscal maneuver to reduce the downstream call on federal and provincial treasuries, has waked the sleeping dogs of professional interest and market opportunity. The current debates over health reform in Canada involve strong and conflicting partisan voices regarding the relative promise of the market and of the state in enabling health reforms. While stories of 'the death spiral' of the Canadian system may well be exaggerated, they do appear to be influencing the perception of health care consumers. One of the possible consequences of this 'death spiral' talk will be the weakening of the 'solidarity of access' idea by further introducing market elements in the financing of community and pharmaceutical services outside the policy legacy of the Canadian health care system. Stronger market elements and means testing are givens in the imminent home care debates on how to enrich federal transfers to the provinces. In the area of pharmaceuticals, market elements already dominate for all but the poor and aged, for whom residual provincial insurance exists.

The social production of health remains more of a promising idea, fostered by researchers and policymakers who wish to cultivate the hope of improved health through state and local action. Notwithstanding the triumph of markets, a recast role for the state in the production of national solidarity, social cohesion, and health requires such a resetting of the policy instruments of modern welfare states (World Bank 1997; Mustard 1999).

With a new and buoyant outlook because of budget surpluses, the government of Canada has taken a balanced approach to debt retirement, tax relief, and program spending increases. Each province has its own variant on these three with some emphasizing tax relief above all others. If one buys the argument for the salutary buffers of progressive taxation and program spending on behalf of the state, then the applications of tax cuts will need to be selective, as will the application of program spending. In either case we can look forward to more market and more state.

Notes

1 All dollar figures are in Canadian dollars unless otherwise specified.
2 Income for both countries included both earned income and income as a consequence of income from wages, salaries, self-employment, government transfers and investment income.

References

Amick, B., III, Levine, S., Tarlov, A.R., and Chapman Walsh, D. (eds) (1995) *Society and Health*, New York: Oxford University Press.

Blane, D., Brunner, E., and Wilkinson, R. (1996) *Social Organization and Health*, London: Routledge.

CIHI (Canadian Institute for Health Information) (2000) Health care spending on the rise, *CIHI Directions*, January.

Contandriopoulos, D. (1998) How Canada's health care system compares with other countries. An overview, in National Forum on Health, *Health Care Systems in Canada and Elsewhere*, vol. 4, *Canada Health Action: Building on the Legacy*, St. Foy, Quebec: Editions Multimondes.

Deber, R. (2000) Getting what we pay for: myths and realities about financing Canada's health care system, Dialogue on Health Reform, Toronto.

Deber, R., Narine, L., Baranek, P., Sharpe, N., Duvalko, K., Zlotnik-Shaul, R., Coyte, P., Pink, G., and Williams, P. (1998) The public-private mix in health care, in National Forum on Health, *Health Care Systems in Canada and Elsewhere*, vol. 4, *Canada Health Action: Building on the Legacy*, St. Foy, Quebec: Editions Multimondes.

Drache, D. and Sullivan, T. (1999) *Health Reform: Public Success, Private Failure*, New York: Routledge.

Evans, R. (1984) *Strained Mercy: The Economics of Canadian Health Care*, Toronto: Butterworth.

—— (1997) Going for gold: the redistributive agenda behind market based health care reform, *Journal of Health Politics, Policy and Law* 22(2): 427–465.

Evans, R., Barer, M., and Marmor, T. (1994) *Why Are Some People Healthy and Others Not: The Determinants of Health of Populations*, New York: De Gruyter.

Flood, C. (1997) Accountability of health service providers: comparing internal markets and managed competition reform models, *Dalhousie Law Journal* 20(2): 470–531.

Frank, J. and Mustard, F. (1994) The determinants of health from a historical perspective, *Daedalus*.

Frenk, J. (1998) Medical care and health improvement, *Annals of Internal Medicine* 129(5): 419–420.

Greenspon, E. (1999) Health care woes deemed provinces' fault, poll reveals, *Globe and Mail*, February 6, A7.

Gray, G. (1991) *Federalism and Health Policy: The Development of Health Systems in Canada and Australia*, Toronto: University of Toronto Press.

Health Canada (1999) *Provincial and Territorial Home Care Programs: A Synthesis for Canada*, Minister of Public Works and Government Services, Canada. Available at www.hc-sc.gc.ca.

Hicks, V. (1999) The evolution of public and private health care spending in Canada, 1960–1997, Canadian Institute for Health Information (CIHI), Health Action Coalition, Health Canada. Available at CIHI: www.cihi.ca.

Jacobs, A. (1998) Seeing difference: market health reform in Europe, *Journal of Health Politics, Policy and Law* 23(1): 1–33.

Kaplan, G., Pamuk, E., Lynch, J., Cohen, R., and Balfour, J. (1996) Inequality in income and mortality in the United States: analysis of mortality and potential pathways, *British Medical Journal* 312: 999–1003.

Karasek, R. and Theorell, T. (1990) *Healthy Work: Stress Productivity and the Reconstruction of Working Life*, New York: Basic Books.

Kawachi, I., Kennedy, B., Lochner, K., and Prothrow-Stith, D. (1997) Social capital, income inequality and mortality, *American Journal of Public Health* 87: 1491–1498.

Keating, D. and Hertzman, C. (eds) (1999) *Developmental Health: The Wealth of Nationals*, New York: The Guilford Press.

Kenna, K. (2000) First Lady blasts U.S. drug prices, *The Toronto Star*, February 9.

Kennedy, B., Kawachi, I., and Prothrow-Stith, D. (1996) Income distribution and mortality: cross-sectional ecological study of the Robin Hood Index in the United States, *British Medical Journal* 312: 1004–1007.

Kuttner, R. (1997) *Everything for Sale: The Virtues and Limits of Markets*, New York: Knopf.

Lalonde, M. (1974) *A New Perspective on the Health of Canadians*, Ottawa: Ministry of Supply and Services.

Lavis, J. and Sullivan, T. (1999) Governing health, in D. Drache and T. Sullivan (eds).

—— (2000) The state as a setting, in B. Poland, L. Green, and I. Rootman (eds) *Settings for Health Promotion: Linking Theory and Practice*, London: Sage.

Leatt, P., Pink, G., and Naylor, D. (1996) Integrated delivery systems: has their time come in Canada? *Canadian Medical Association Journal* 148: 803–809.

Lexchin, J. (1999) Controlling pharmaceutical expenditures in Canada, in D. Drache and T. Sullivan (eds).

Lomas, J. (1999) The evolution of devolution: what does the community want? in D. Drache and T. Sullivan (eds).

McDonald, P., Shortt, S., Sanmartin, C., Barer, M., Lewis, S., and Sheps, S. (1998) Waiting lists and waiting times for health care in Canada: more management!! More money?? www.hc-sc.gc.ca/iacb-dgiac/nhrdp/wlsum5.htm.

MacIntyre, S. (1997) The Black Report and beyond: what are the issues? *Social Science and Medicine* 44(6): 723–745.

Marmor, T. (1999) The rage for reform: sense and nonsense in health policy, in D. Drache and T. Sullivan (eds).

Maynard, A. and Bloor, K. (1998) *Our Certain Fate: Rationing in Health Care*, Office of Health Economics, London: Whitehall.

Morgan, S. (1998) Pharmacare: the pros and cons of Canada's National Drug Proposal, Occasional Paper 9, The Institute for Work and Health. Available at www.iwh.on.ca.

Mustard, C., Barer, M., Evans, R., Horne, J., Mayer, T., and Derksen, S. (1998) Paying taxes and using health care services: the distributional consequences of tax financed universal health insurance in one Canadian province, conference on the state of living standards and quality of life in Canada, Centre for the Study of Living Standards, Ottawa, October.

Mustard, J.F. (1999) Health, health care and social cohesion, in D. Drache and T. Sullivan (eds).

National Forum on Health (1997) *Canada Health Action: Building on the Legacy*, final report, Ottawa: Ministry of Health.

Naylor, C.D. (ed.) (1992) *Canadian Health Care and the State: A Century of Evolution*, Montreal: McGill-Queen's University Press.

Ontario PCHS (Premier's Council on Health Strategy) (1991) *Nurturing Health*, Toronto: The Queen's Printer.

Pierson, P. (1995) Fragmented welfare states: federal institutions and the development of social policy, *Governance* 8(4) (October).

——(1999) Coping with permanent austerity: welfare state restructuring in affluent democracies, paper presented at the European Forum on Recasting the European Welfare States, Florence: European University Institute.

PMPRB (Patented Medicines Prices Review Board) (1998) Annual report, Government of Canada, Ministry of Health, page 20. Available at www.pmprb-cepmb.gc.ca.

Priest, L. (2000) *Toronto Star*, February 8.

Rassell, E., Bernstein, J., and Tang, K. (1993) The impact of health care financing on family budgets, briefing paper (April), Washington DC: Economic Policy Institute.

Ross, N., Wolfson, M., Dunn, J., Berthelot, J.-M., Kaplan, G., and Lynch, J. (2000) Income inequality and mortality in Canada and the United States: a cross-sectional assessment using census data and vital statistics, *British Medical Journal* 320: 898–902.

Sen, A. (1999) Economics and health, *The Lancet* 354: 20.

Shortt, S. (2000) Waiting for medical services in Ontario: clarifying the issues in a period of health reform, prepared for the Dialogue on Health Reform, Toronto.

Sullivan, T. (2000) *Injury and the New World of Work*, Vancouver: University of British Columbia Press.

Taylor, M. (1987) *Health Insurance and Canadian Public Policy*, 2nd edn, Montreal: McGill-Queen's University Press.

Tuohy, Carolyn Hughes (1999) *Accidental Logics: The Dynamics of Change in the Health Care Arena in the United States, Britain, and Canada*, New York: Oxford University Press.

van Dooeslaer, E., Wagstaff, A., and Rutten, F. (eds) (1993) *Equity in the Finance and Delivery of Health Care: An International Perspective*. New York: Oxford University Press.

Wilkinson, R. (1992) Income distribution and life expectancy, *British Medical Journal* 304: 165–168.

—— (1996) *Unhealthy Societies: The Afflictions of Inequality*, London: Routledge.

Wolfson, M., Kaplan, G., Lynch, J., Ross, N., and Backlund, E. (1999) The relationship between income inequality and mortality is not a statistical artefact—an empirical demonstration, *British Medical Journal* 319: 953–957.

World Bank (1993) *Investing in Health*, World Development Report, New York: Oxford University Press.

—— (1997) *The State in a Changing World*, World Development Report, New York: Oxford University Press.

Part III

ISSUES SURROUNDING HEALTH CARE AND AGING

8

AGE, HEALTH AND MEDICAL EXPENDITURE

William A. Jackson

Introduction

Ageing poses problems for health economists. It affects everybody and has important consequences for health, yet it remains poorly understood and apparently beyond human control. Somehow, it manages to be both an obvious fact of life in its physical manifestations and an almost complete mystery in its underlying causality. The huge gap in our knowledge is perplexing for anyone hoping to organize efficient health care and promote human welfare. Under the circumstances, policy analysts will be tempted to abstract from ageing and regard it as outside the domain of health economics. Such abstractions are unwise, since ageing is intertwined with health and broaches fundamental questions about how health care fits into the wider social context.

Population ageing, a trend common to virtually all developed countries, has brought old age to greater prominence than ever before. Prior to the twentieth century, age patterns were stable, with only a tiny proportion of people in the upper age ranges; the rising proportion of old people seen during the twentieth century (and forecast to persist into the twenty-first century) is unprecedented and leads to novel policy issues. As populations age, the pressure on health care services seems likely to increase, forcing sensitive policy decisions. If current services are to be maintained or enhanced, then taxes and other payments may have to be raised. Alternatively, spending on services could be curtailed in order to hold taxes down. At the heart of these decisions lies the relation between age, health and medical expenditure.

The relation seems at first glance to be obvious: people grow older, their health worsens through biological ageing, and they make greater demands on the health care system. Old age should, it seems, be positively related to medical expenditures, in all times and places. Economists, especially those in the neoclassical mainstream, are usually happy to accept a simple, positive link between age and health care. People do not choose to grow old, so ageing does not fit comfortably into the neoclassical world of rational choice with fixed, well-defined preferences. Standard neoclassical models (even when 'intertemporal') ignore human ageing and thereby delegate its study to the other social and natural sciences. Where ageing cannot be avoided, it is kept at arm's length by using atheoretical, purely empirical methods centred on correlations between age and other variables. The narrowness of such methods can give a misleading impression of how age interacts with health care and medical expenditure.

This paper points out the depth, richness and complexity of the age–medical expenditure relation and argues for a broader treatment. Ageing is a prime example of an interdisciplinary topic requiring contributions from natural as well as social sciences. As a result, the economics of ageing cannot be handled satisfactorily by economic theory alone, even if this were to be expanded beyond the neoclassical frame. Nor can ageing be dealt with in a value-free ethical vacuum, since age differences and the ageing process will always invoke ethical problems. The following discussion highlights the biological, social and ethical background that often goes unnoticed in economic commentary on ageing and health care.

The age–medical expenditure relation

Old age does not in itself incur medical expenditure. Many people live through a lengthy retirement without receiving expensive medical treatments. Old age will eventually reduce people's physical capabilities and make them more vulnerable to disease, but the link with medical expenditure is far from immediate: increasing age reduces a person's physical capacities, which undermines health, which calls forth health care, which brings higher medical expenditure (see Figure 8.1). Age has no direct relation with spending, but the stages in the indirect relation are often assumed to be self-evident

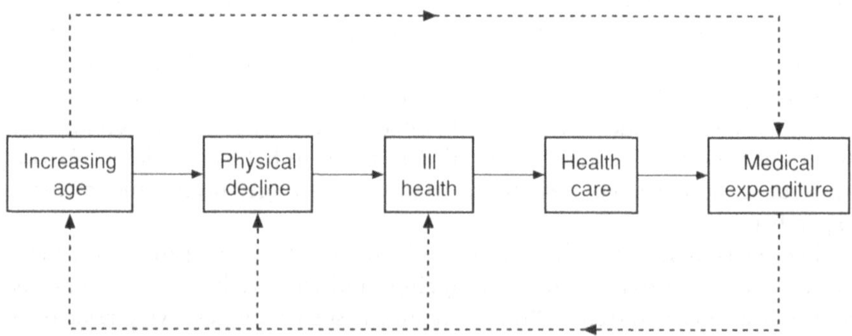

Figure 8.1 Causal links between age and medical expenditure

and universal. The logic of the age–medical expenditure relation, driven by apparent biological necessity, seems compelling. Other matters may intrude, though, and the several stages of Figure 8.1 merit more detailed consideration.

The first link, between age and physical decline, is less obvious than it may seem. Physiological ageing (senescence) can be distinguished from age-related disease. Old people may have no diagnosed diseases yet still have disabilities from their diminished physical strength and adaptability. In this case, old age is closely tied to disability, but not to any disease. On the other hand, old people may suffer from diseases that are age-related without being unique to them: major causes of death such as heart disease and cancer fall into this category. What is often described simply as ageing is a complex process involving the twin, interwoven elements of senescence and age-related disease. Moreover, physical decline in old age has always been related to a person's income and social background. The age-physical decline connection is by no means universal, natural and preordained.

The link between physical decline and ill health faces the prior difficulty of defining and assessing health. No single, observable yardstick exists whereby one can gauge the impact of ageing on a person's health and well-being. Health is a multidimensional entity, with qualitative aspects that cannot easily be captured on a quantitative scale. Attempts by health economists to produce output measures for health care have been fraught with problems and remain controversial, especially when used to guide health policy decisions. If health is a relative concept, then what we understand by 'full health' will vary among societies. Health as a policy target will embody value judgments (explicitly or implicitly) and require policy makers to take a stance on medical ethics. One cannot speak of health without summoning up many other social and ethical factors. Age may be unidimensional and easily measured, but health is not.

The next stage in Figure 8.1 links ill health with health care, on the assumption that those with illnesses will receive treatment. In a well-functioning health care system this should be true, although many obstacles can obstruct access to care. Some minor medical problems may go unreported and never get any treatment. Where patients bear part of the costs, financial hardship will limit access to medical care. Private health care will be biased towards people with greater ability to pay and may exclude retired and unemployed older people without reliable pension incomes. Even when health care is publicly subsidized and provided, access still tends to be slanted towards the higher socio-economic groups with superior information and greater willingness to claim their entitlements (Le Grand 1982). Health care will not be perfectly correlated with ill health, and other social and economic circumstances will play a part.

The last stage of Figure 8.1 links health care to medical expenditure. Once formal health care has been offered, it will bring expenditures, the size of which depend on how the health care system is organized. Large expenditures could indicate either plentiful, high-quality medical treatments or ineffective, superfluous ones. This last stage therefore relies upon health care efficiency, at both the micro level of individual treatments and the macro level of the whole health care system. Any connection between old age and medical spending must reflect the organization of health care. Especially relevant to older people is the division between formal and informal activities. Much non-specialized care of old people is provided informally, without payment, by relatives and neighbours; specialized medical care is nearly always provided formally by professionals. In some cases, the formal/informal boundary will be flexible, and any transfer of care from formal to informal sectors will reduce financial costs, while having a more ambiguous effect on real economic costs (Williams 1985). Governments keen to cut public expenditure have an incentive to replace formal care services with informal 'community care', whether or not this is the best option in a wider economic sense. The health care-medical expenditure link cannot be isolated from the various social and political factors underlying the health care system.

Figure 8.1 assumes that age stimulates medical expenditure via ill health and the provision of health care. This is the normal causal sequence, rooted in biological ageing, but it is not the sole possibility. Because health and disability cannot be easily defined and monitored, policy makers will find it convenient to use old age as a proxy for ill health and medical needs. Subsidized treatments and services may be triggered by old age alone, without the requirement for diagnosed medical complaints or disabilities. Age-related payments and services may also have a redistributive aim, given that older people on average have lower incomes than the younger, working-age groups. When policies are age-based, the middle stages in Figure 8.1 become redundant and age will act directly on medical expenditure (as shown by the top dotted line). Such links are institutional rather than biological; they serve as another reminder of the social aspects of ageing.

So far causality has been taken to work from left to right in Figure 8.1, from increasing age to medical expenditure. In practice, matters are not so simple, as causality could be reversed: medical expenditure and health care may influence health, which in turn should influence life expectancy. Population ageing is not an exogenous event to which health care must react; successful health care sustains population ageing, so that ageing becomes at least partly an endogenous variable (and causality in Figure 8.1 may go from right to left, as in the lower dotted arrow). Paradoxes can arise here. People cured of life-threatening diseases early in their life cycles may live on into old age and die from chronic diseases of affluence after prolonged and expensive treatment: medical successes may, as a result, bring higher morbidity rates and greater medical expenditure per head (Gruenberg 1977; Verbrugge 1984). If this circular causality holds, high medical expenditure will be self-reinforcing, via a strengthening of the ageing trend. An alternative possibility is that much medical expenditure on curative care is wasteful and inefficient; shifting expenditure towards preventive care might combine population ageing with lower medical expenditures, offsetting the usual assumption of a positive age–medical expenditure connection. The causality behind ageing and health care is complex, and the dominant influences may be hard to discern.

At the core of Figure 8.1 lies biological ageing, but the economic consequences of ageing depend heavily on social and ethical factors as well. To get a fuller view of how ageing interacts with health care, it is worth looking more closely at biological ageing, before moving on to social and ethical matters.

Biological factors

Our knowledge of biological ageing remains surprisingly sparse. So far, all efforts to discover the elixir of life and the fountain of youth (or their modern equivalents) have proved fruitless. The incentives to explain ageing could hardly be stronger, yet the causal mechanisms have resisted explanation. What does seem clear is that biological ageing is complex and emerges from our genetic make-up: it seems to derive from several parallel and interrelated processes that permit variability within an overall, predetermined scheme. Theories of biological ageing distinguish two main ways in which organisms age: programmed ageing, centred on genetic background, and unprogrammed ageing, centred on random lifetime events (for general discussions, see Hendricks and Hendricks 1977: ch. 4; Bond et al. 1993a). The two strands are not mutually exclusive and may coexist and interact.

Theories of programmed ageing look towards the reproductive strategy of complex organisms, which have a finite life span and must replace themselves with new members of the species if the species is to survive. The new members are similar but not identical to the old ones, giving scope for evolution and natural selection. Crucial to this account of ageing is the programmed development of an organism until it has reached its full reproductive capacity and produced offspring that survive and perpetuate the species. Once reproduction has been achieved, the further development of the organism has little evolutionary purpose. The growth programme runs out, and the organism's internal cells find it increasingly difficult to replicate themselves. Mistakes in cellular reproduction cause what is outwardly perceived as the natural process of biological ageing. All of this happens internally to the organism, at the genetic and cellular levels, although the genetics of ageing is as yet only imperfectly understood. The argument for programmed ageing rests chiefly on the evolutionary interpretation of why ageing occurs and what it involves. Since the evolutionary motive is the survival of the species, the genetic programme hinges on growth and reproduction, rather than ageing as such. Ageing is merely the decline that sets in after an organism has fulfilled its reproductive purpose and no longer needs to grow and develop. If ageing has a function, it is only the negative one of enfeebling and removing the older members of a species, so that they can be replaced by younger, more vigorous members.

Theories of unprogrammed ageing give greater weight to random events. Ageing is seen as a process of error accumulation, as against a programmed decline. Much of the damage to cell structures and functioning in an ageing organism seems to follow a random, unprogrammed pattern, not a fixed timetable. This applies to events within the organism, at the genetic, cellular and molecular levels and, more generally, to the external life events facing the organism. Individuals who age relatively quickly will have been exposed to a higher level of internally generated toxins and externally generated diseases and pressures. Actual damage to an organism will be largely random, even if vulnerability to damage has a genetic component. This opens up the prospect that ageing could be slowed down if some of the random damage to the organism could be avoided or delayed. If ageing is not entirely programmed, then hope persists of extending human life spans without having to rewrite the genetic programme.

Programmed and unprogrammed ageing, despite appearances, need not be contradictory and can be brought together as parts of a larger whole. Unprogrammed errors in reproduction provide the variety on which evolution depends. Perfect programming would eliminate errors and harm a species' ability to adapt—in the long term it could threaten the species' survival. Too many errors would also be counterproductive, by spoiling a well-adapted species' ability to reproduce. The ageing process, combining programmed and unprogrammed elements, can be viewed as a compromise between programmed and unprogrammed extremes. Ageing and eventual death mean that organisms are replaced by near-but-imperfect replicas of themselves and that most replication errors are concentrated innocuously among organisms who have already reproduced. Such a functionalist, evolutionary account of ageing finds a place for both programmed and unprogrammed ageing. Importantly for health care and social policy, the unprogrammed elements in ageing provide an entry point for social and ethical factors. Unprogrammed ageing precludes a genetic reductionism whereby human ageing is genetically predetermined regardless of its social context.

Another theoretical distinction sometimes made is between intrinsic and extrinsic ageing (Finch 1990: ch. 12). Intrinsic ageing refers to the hypothetical life course of an organism (or other entity) as determined by its own internal constitution, undisturbed by outside events. Extrinsic ageing refers to the external influences that act upon the organism and cause the actual life course to differ from the internal template. Observed ageing will consist of extrinsic factors superimposed on an intrinsic process governed by an organism's own internal make-up. Intrinsic ageing might seem to equate with genetic programming and extrinsic ageing with unprogrammed, random events, but this would be misleading. At the level of an organism, many intrinsic factors will be unprogrammed, for example the random errors in cellular reproduction. Intrinsic ageing can be said to embody genetic programming but it is not exhausted by it. Likewise, extrinsic ageing cannot be restricted only to random, unprogrammed events: some external influences on people will not be entirely random if one accepts that ageing is in part institutionalized and socially programmed. Consequently, the intrinsic/extrinsic and programmed/unprogrammed distinctions do not coincide, and can complement each other.

The intrinsic/extrinsic distinction suggests a stratified account of ageing. Usually applied at the level of the organism, it can also be applied at lower levels (genes, cells, organs) or higher levels (social groups or whole societies). This stratified account helps to draw out the complexity of ageing and the fact that it occurs simultaneously at several levels. A comprehensive study of ageing focused on any given level should include both intrinsic factors below that level and extrinsic factors above that level. Biological ageing cannot therefore be sealed off from its higher-level social context.

Social influences loom large in discussions of how health varies with old age. The traditional view is that the age-health relationship in developed countries has evolved during the twentieth century alongside changes in morbidity patterns and the causes of death. These changes, usually termed the 'epidemiological transition', involved a shift from infectious diseases as the main causes of death to the diseases of civilization, such as cancer and heart disease (Omran 1971). Success in preventing and curing infectious diseases has raised life expectancy but at the same time exposed people to a new range of degenerative diseases during an old age they would not previously have reached. Degenerative illnesses are less curable than infectious diseases and may result in chronic disabilities requiring long periods of treatment and care. Although morbidity is now being delayed, it may be spread out over longer periods, as shown in Figure 8.2(a). Greater longevity may be combined with high demands placed by old people on the health care system. As the population ages, other things being equal, medical expenditure is liable to increase on both a total and a per capita basis. Most commentators on population ageing and health care have adopted this cautious, pessimistic line (examples are Manton 1982; Schneider and Brody 1983; Brody 1985; Bebbington 1988). In this view, the price of greater longevity is an old age where one is vulnerable to chronic disease and heavily reliant on medical and social care.

Others have painted a more optimistic picture (Fries 1980, 1989; Fries and Crapo 1981). The diseases of civilization have as yet proved resistant to cures, but they may be preventable by changes in lifestyle, dietary adjustments, screening programmes and other measures. If so, then people might eventually live almost disease-free lives and die from natural causes rather than disease; the morbidity pattern would then be as shown in Figure 8.2(b). Since people would now be less prone to chronic, degenerative diseases, they

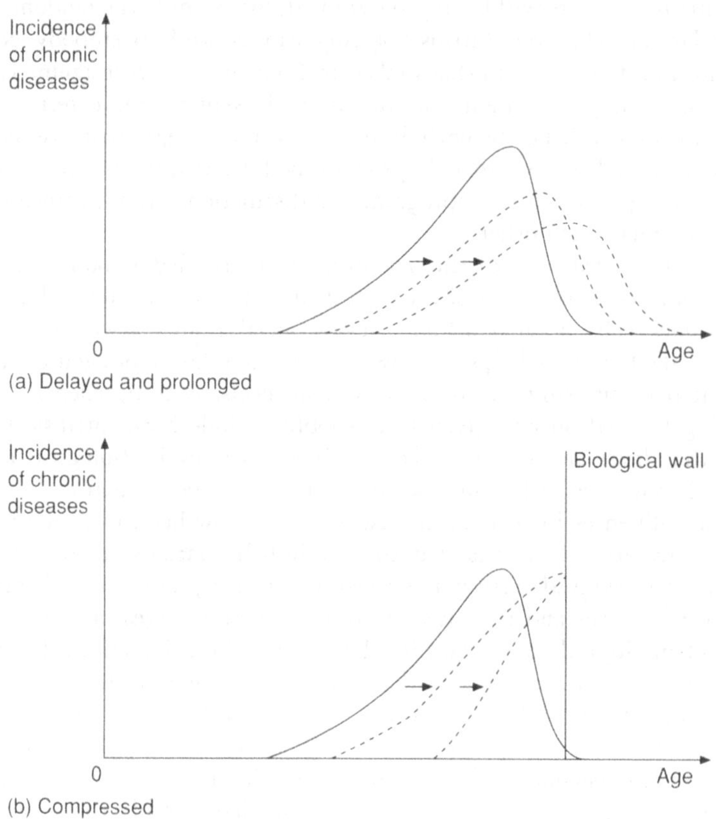

Figure 8.2 Morbidity patterns by age

would more often live through their full life span and die from natural causes ('natural death') or after a brief but severe period of illness in advanced old age. Morbidity would be concentrated into a shorter and shorter period at the end of people's lives; effectively, as in Figure 8.2(b), it would be compressed against the biological wall of natural death. The biological constraints on life span would become more visible, and most people would be able to live normal, active lives until their biological clock ran out.

With morbidity reduced and compressed, the effect of population ageing on medical spending would have diminished accordingly. As prevention replaced cure, many of the largest medical expenditures could be reduced or even avoided—health-promoting activity would be decentralized away from professional medical care to self-help, preventive activities (Fries et al. 1993). Arguments of this type have aroused controversy, on empirical and policy grounds. So far, there is little empirical evidence for compressed morbidity—chronic diseases are, if anything, becoming more prevalent among the elderly than previously. Given the empirical doubts, it could be dangerous to play down curative medicine and underestimate the effect of population ageing on health care. The optimistic view is a hypothetical portrait of what might happen if preventive care could be greatly expanded and developed.

Both the pessimistic and optimistic versions of the age-health relation rely heavily on the social environment. For the pessimists, the diseases of civilization will linger into the foreseeable future and so will the links between these diseases and modern lifestyles. Biological ageing will continue to work in tandem with chronic, age-related diseases. For the optimists, the diseases of civilization will ultimately be conquered, to reveal biological ageing in a purer form. This may seem to weaken the social influences on ageing, yet the outcome is attained through preventive social action. The optimists are not envisaging an exogenous, biologically based miracle cure but a programme of preventive health care; they differ from the pessimists in their expectation of success and their decentralized vision of health care, but their approach is nevertheless socially grounded. Conceivably, future developments may take a biological turn if geneticists learn how to reprogramme the biological clock towards greatly extended life spans or even immortality. As yet (fortunately, perhaps) the biological clock has not been tampered with and remains a constant—the major variations in 'biological' ageing are non-biologically determined.

Social factors

Social factors come increasingly to the fore as one moves from the ageing of an individual to the ageing of a population. At the aggregate level, the age–medical expenditure relation will depend on the age distribution of the population, as well as on the age-specific use of medical care, creating a second avenue by which social factors can come into play (as in Figure 8.3). Together, age-specific use rates and the age distribution will govern how medical expenditure evolves within an ageing population, although in neither case is causality unidirectional; medical expenditures can react backwards on to both use rates and the age distribution (as shown by the dotted line in Figure 8.3). The switch from individual to population ageing retains all the social factors present in individual ageing but adds extra ones working at the aggregate level on the age distribution. In particular, a population may be ageing for reasons other than the increased longevity of its members: a falling birth rate or outward migration of younger people can produce similar demographic changes. It is pertinent, therefore, to consider the social determinants of population ageing.

The standard pattern of demographic change in developed countries is summarized by the 'demographic transition'. Initially, in a pre-industrial society, mortality and fertility are constant and roughly equal; the age distribution is stable, with only a tiny proportion of people in the higher age

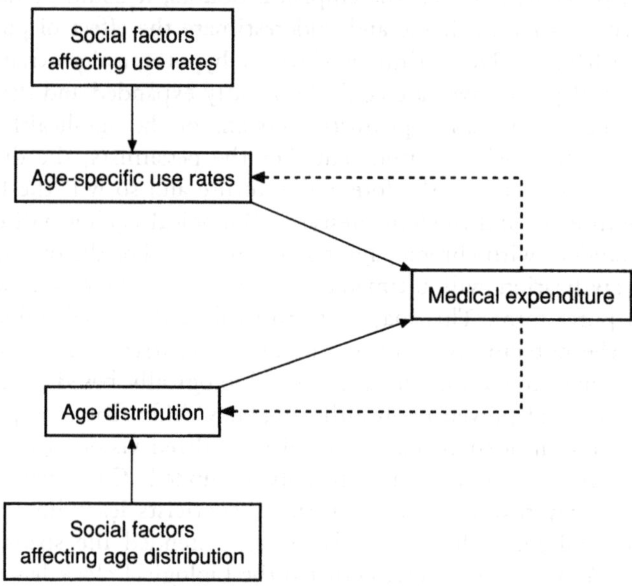

Figure 8.3 Population ageing and medical expenditure

groups. As economic development proceeds, mortality falls below fertility, causing rapid population growth at an accelerating rate. Later, however, the fall in mortality peters out and fertility begins to fall, so that population growth decelerates. Finally, fertility stabilizes and the population reaches a new steady state where mortality and fertility are again constant and roughly equal but the population now has a higher average age and a greater proportion of old people. The fall in mortality and fertility will both contribute to an ageing of the population that had never previously occurred. Net migration, because it is small relative to the total population, is generally assumed to have a negligible influence on the age distribution in most countries. This leaves mortality and fertility as the twin determinants of population ageing and its consequences.

Explanations of falling mortality can opt either for a socially based account, emphasizing improved social conditions and growing material wealth, or a more technological/biological account, emphasizing medical advances such as vaccination and cures for infectious diseases. Although the reduced mortality was linked with the decline in major infectious diseases (the epidemiological transition), the decline need not have resulted from curative medicine. Indeed, most demographers and other writers on mortality have pointed to improved nutrition and better living conditions as a more immediate cause of mortality decline: immunization campaigns postdated the fall in mortality for countries that were early to industrialize such as the UK

(McKeown and Record 1962; McKeown et al. 1975). Modern opinion sees increased longevity as having several causes, including improved nutrition, public health measures, and advances in medical technology (Livi-Bacci 1983). The mixture of causal influences is likely to vary among countries, according to when and how their decline in mortality took place. Within any given country, the social and economic causes of improved longevity lead to income and class biases, so that the rich end up living longer on average than the poor. There may be some forces acting against the rich (if, say, they smoke more than the poor, or undertake risky leisure pursuits), but on the whole the richer social groups will have lower mortality than the poorer ones. This shows up clearly in empirical studies of how mortality varies with social class (Marmot and McDowall 1986; Wilkinson 1986, 1992). The selection bias among elderly survivors means that the oldest age groups are disproportionately drawn from the wealthier social classes.

Perhaps counter-intuitively, fertility changes generally have a larger effect than mortality changes on a society's age distribution. Much of the current population ageing in developed countries is due to the general decline in fertility during the twentieth century (with the postwar baby boom as a temporary interruption of the long-run trend). As with mortality changes, the chief causes of fertility decline seem to be socio-economic developments rather than more technological matters such as improved birth control methods. Of key importance is the evolving economic role of women, as their greater participation in work and education has discouraged the raising of large families. These social trends are prominent even in economic theories of fertility based on utility maximization (Willis 1973). Alternative approaches give greater credence to normalized and socialized behaviour in explaining fertility, thus enhancing the social dimension (Easterlin et al. 1980; Donaldson 1991). Reduced fertility affects the age distribution through smaller birth cohorts and fewer children. The lower demand for health care and education services for children will at least partly counterbalance the higher demands on public services from the larger cohorts of old people. Fertility decline should offset the growing 'burdens' imposed by the elderly, dampening the effects of population ageing on medical expenditures.

The social background of the demographic transition shows that population ageing belongs to a larger process of economic development and is not merely an exogenous, random 'event' or 'shock' to which governments must react. Populations have begun to age in the twentieth century (after many thousands of years without ageing) because of fundamental social changes associated with industrialization and economic growth. Ageing and its attendant difficulties cannot be hived off from the broader trends towards economic development. The demographic transition suggests that economic growth will be correlated with population ageing, and that the countries with the fastest ageing populations will have the greatest capacity to support large numbers of retired elderly. Placing demographic change within its economic environment should temper exaggerated concerns over a special crisis coming apparently from nowhere to afflict the developed countries.

On top of the age distribution effects, social factors will have many other effects working through the individual life cycle. One such effect, discussed in the previous section, is the way that biological ageing is mediated through its social context and never appears in an undiluted, 'natural' form. Beyond the physical side of ageing, social factors will influence how old people are perceived and treated by other members of society. The very idea of old age is a social artefact. Any dividing line between 'old' and 'young' must be a somewhat arbitrary, artificial concept with little justification in human biology. Individual ageing, as a smooth, continuous process, does not divide the human life cycle into discrete, well-defined periods. The divisions within most people's life cycles—education, work, retirement—are socially constructed. This man-made periodization of ageing both reflects and reinforces social attitudes to the elderly; the retired are seen as being dependent on younger age groups even when physically capable and receiving no public pensions or health care. The low social status of older people may sap their self-esteem and render them less independent than they could be. Sometimes ageing becomes formally institutionalized, as when people become eligible for public benefits and social entitlements through their age alone, not their health or social circumstances. These social norms surrounding old age create an institutionalized ageing to be set alongside the physical processes of biological ageing.

The institutions defining old age have been discussed extensively in social gerontology, which adopts an interdisciplinary approach to ageing (for general introductions, see Hendricks and Hendricks 1977; McPherson 1983; Bond et al. 1993b; Binstock and George 1996). Writers on social gerontology have differed in the relative importance they attach to biological and institutional factors. Earlier work portrayed institutions as a means of accommodating biological ageing: the prime example is 'disengagement theory', where institutions disengage the elderly painlessly from their earlier working and social life, before they become physically incapable (Cumming and Henry 1961). More recent work has given institutions greater prominence and independence, so that they are no longer just responses to biological ageing and bring about their own normalized pattern of ageing. The strongest versions of this argument refer to the 'social construction of old age' and the 'structured dependency' of the elderly (Walker 1980; Townsend 1981; Estes et al. 1982; Phillipson 1982). From this perspective, institutions define the elderly as a group and assign them a lower, dependent status relative to younger age groups. Formal retirement is the most obvious case of such an institution; the statutory retirement age creates an artificial barrier between young and old, implying that older people are incapable of working or participating fully in society. Other institutions carry a similar message, notably centralized social care and the placement of old people in residential homes. Measures that supposedly help the elderly—pensions, formal care, and so forth—may reinforce their image as a dependent social group and damage their capacity or willingness to undertake a full range of social activities. The downgrading of older people can also be observed in the private sector, where corporate hierarchies push many employees into 'career failure' and premature retirement (Dugger 1999). Institutionalized ageing will have its own detrimental effects, only loosely connected with the physical consequences of old age.

Most of the literature on structured dependency concentrates on retirement policies and social care, rather than health care; the main reason seems to be that health care is highly institutionalized for both young and old alike, so that the contrast between them is less clear-cut. Health care may, nonetheless, reflect and contribute to the socialization of old age. The status of the elderly within the health care system has two main sources: how they are admitted into the system, and how they are treated once within the system.

If old people are admitted prematurely into hospitals or other institutions, this could reinforce their dependent status and add to the social construction of old age. Superfluous medical care for the elderly would be inefficient and possibly deny care to others in greater need. It is therefore important to compare specialist medical care in hospitals with other options such as residential or domiciliary care. The 'balance of care', as this comparison is often termed, could be decided either informally by the judgment of those with prior experience (say, social policy professionals or public sector managers) or formally by economic appraisal techniques such as cost-benefit analysis. Applying cost-benefit analysis will be difficult, because the informal care alternative is notoriously hard to evaluate and yet crucial to the comparison (Mooney 1978; Wright et al. 1981; Smith and Wright 1994). Recent policy reforms in several countries have appointed case (or care) managers to make this decision on behalf of old people, with the hope of finding the right balance of care and hence promoting efficiency and equity (Means and Smith 1994: ch. 5). Case management creates the administrative framework for more consistent balance-of-care assessments, but leaves open the role of formal economic appraisal as compared with less formal decision making methods.

Once within the medical system, the fate of old people hangs on whether their age determines the way they are treated. One strand of medical thinking has argued that they are best treated separately from other age groups, in geriatric wards (Hall 1988). The intention is to improve their treatment by catering for their special needs, but this might also foster a structured dependency of old people within the health care system. More generally, the prime question is whether a person's age should play a part in the allocation of health care. This raises some awkward issues in medical ethics.

Ethical factors

It might be argued that age is merely a personal characteristic, like gender or race, and not a legitimate basis on which to discriminate between people. Age differs from gender or race, however, in that it changes as people move through their life cycles: nobody is permanently attached to any particular age group. In a developed country, where life expectancies are high, most people will live through all the stages of the typical life cycle, and age discrimination need not entail a permanent bias against certain people. For this reason, age discrimination might be thought more tolerable than other forms of discrimination by personal characteristics. Age has special significance for health care, as it can make a big difference to the success and future benefits of medical treatments. A successful treatment of any given illness adds less to future life expectancy for an older person than for a younger person. If the aim of medical care is to preserve life, then this will imply giving scarce medical resources to the young before the old. A government wishing to maximize the total number of life years in a population should give priority to younger patients over older ones. The comparison becomes even less favourable to the elderly if one allows for the future offspring of younger patients (Broome 1992). Policy makers face a dilemma: they can either reject age discrimination and fail to maximize life expectancy, or maximize life expectancy and discriminate systematically against old people. The conflict between life preservation and an anti-discriminatory stance lies at the core of ethical debates over medical care for old people.

Ethical discussion of age discrimination often distinguishes between morally relevant and morally irrelevant discrimination (Daniels 1985: ch. 5). Empty age distinctions, unfounded on health or anything else, would be seen as morally irrelevant and thus unethical. Age discrimination would be rejected unless it could be justified as having moral relevance to the pursuit of some ethical objective. With health care, a person's age does have a bearing on whether they can undergo a certain treatment, the likely success of the treatment, and the quantity and quality of future life after the treatment. Raising the effectiveness of health care might require rationing schemes that favour younger people over older ones, other things being equal. Moral relevance means that age discrimination should not be written off as 'ageism' and might at times be ethically warranted

Once moral relevance is recognized as possible, there are three main alternative ethical positions: to rule out age discrimination in health care, to allow partial discrimination at some stages of the life cycle, or to allow complete age discrimination throughout the life cycle. Ruling out age discrimination in health care would be consistent with an anti-ageism argument applied everywhere in public policy. Anti-ageism is frequently defended on the basis that all people, regardless of their ages, have an equal desire to complete the rest of their life (Harris 1985: ch. 5). In this sense, the value of life would not vary with age, and age discrimination would be inappropriate. Anti-ageism can also be defended by considering the unsavoury consequences of discriminatory policies. An example of this is the 'double jeopardy' argument: old and sick people already suffer one major misfortune and to discriminate against them in the provision of health care would be piling injury upon injury. Hence, there may be ethical reasons to deny the moral relevance of age discrimination and allocate health care in an even-handed way, irrespective of age.

The case for partial age discrimination usually revolves around the idea of a normal or reasonable life span—a 'fair innings', as Harris (1985) terms it. By this argument, everyone is entitled to the normal life expectancy at birth for the society they live in (seventy-odd years in most developed countries), but anything beyond the norm is a bonus. Prevention of premature deaths will, as a result, have a higher weighting than preservation of life among the very old. Age discrimination will be marked out by a threshold set at the normal life expectancy: anyone below the threshold will not experience age discrimination but anyone above it will receive a lower weighting in the allocation of health care. The aim is to avoid premature deaths and give everybody the best possible chance of experiencing a full life cycle, including all the major stages of life. This would endorse partial age discrimination around the threshold age but not a generalized preference for younger over older patients. The argument can be augmented to allow for living standards as well as life expectancy—the aim would then be to ensure that as many people as possible experience the normal life expectancy at an acceptable minimum living standard. Prolonging later life would have a low value, especially if this brings declining quality of life. Setting minimum living standards would give a further reason to concentrate health care below the threshold of normal life expectancy.

The case for complete age discrimination usually stems from simple maximization criteria. If health care seeks to maximize the future life expectancy of patients (as life preservation would suggest), then it will be better to treat younger before older patients, as they bring a greater return in future life years. This holds true throughout the life cycle, so it is not restricted to comparisons between 'young' and 'old' people—even for people separated by only days or weeks in age, it would be better on average to give medical priority to the younger person. Similar conclusions follow from using quality-adjusted life-years (QALYs), the most common output measures adopted by health economists. Maximizing future QALYs will yield decisions even less favourable to old people than with the life years approach, because the quality weights for later life will be relatively low. Old people have a double disadvantage compared with the young: the quantity of their future expected life is smaller, and the quality will be lower, given their greater vulnerability to chronic illnesses and incapacity. Although complete age discrimination is more thoroughgoing than the partial version, it does not make the same dichotomy between young and old groups and its effects would be spread out more smoothly over the full life cycle.

Each of these ethical rules, if it informs policy decisions, will have implications for the age–medical expenditure relation. An anti-ageist rule would give doctors no freedom to hold back on medical treatments and expenditures devoted to the very old, whose future life expectancy and quality of life might be severely limited. Medical expenditure would be skewed towards older people, with their higher incidence of severe and chronic illness. Partial age discrimination would give special significance to the threshold age, above which discrimination occurs. Those past the threshold age, despite their vulnerability to age-related diseases, would be subject to rationing and denied the full treatments and expenditures normally associated with their ailments. The threshold age would become a prime focus of policy debates, akin to the role played by the statutory retirement age in pensions policy. Complete age discrimination would skew medical expenditure towards the young for any complaint suffered by both younger and older age groups. The old would still be receiving high medical expenditures because of their high incidence of disease, but their low priority in health care rationing would curb their share of medical expenditure. As older people are literally at the back of the queue under a complete discriminatory rule, many illnesses among the elderly might go untreated. The age–medical expenditure relation will be flatter than under anti-ageism or partial discrimination, though still likely to remain upward sloping.

Strict ethical rules may prove too strict to be valuable guides to policy. Any such rules can only rest on existing medical technology and life expectancies. Complete age discrimination, for example, appeals to experience with current medical technologies, where older people offer disappointing outcomes compared with their younger counterparts. Yet a lower quality of life among older people gives them more to gain from advances in medical technology; younger people, by contrast, are already troubled little with pain or disability and have lesser prospects for improved quality of life. Reluctance to dedicate medical resources to older people could discourage innovation and hamper medical progress in the areas where it is most needed. A similar result might also ensue from partial age discrimination, since an age threshold at current life expectancy would deter medical research on raising longevity; the long-term effect might be a satisficing strategy aimed at obtaining a fixed, universal life cycle. These problems reflect the general conservative bias inherent in static output measurement models founded on current technology. Age discrimination rules may impose a short-term outlook with a high discount rate inhibiting research on ageing and age-related disease. The results of future medical research are unknowable, but short-term gains from age discrimination might be bought at the expense of long-term costs from slower technical change.

Another drawback of age-discrimination rules is that they tend to be narrowly based on simplified equity criteria and take little notice of the wider context of health care policy. What seems in principle to be morally relevant age discrimination can spill over into a less worthy, 'morally irrelevant' discrimination. It is hard to see how systematic, publicly known rules discriminating against old people can avoid lowering their social status. Age discrimination rules, whether or not they are openly declared as such, will always potentially add to the social construction of old age. Unwittingly or not, they may be ratifying existing ageist attitudes: 'disinterested' ethical positions (based on, say, social contracts, individual preferences, or social welfare assessments) may be contaminated by the prevailing values of their society of origin. The quest for equity through morally relevant age discrimination could end up widening social divisions and increasing hardship among older age groups. Alternative policy objectives, founded on social solidarity, would be less willing to tolerate age discrimination.

Whatever position one takes about age discrimination in health care, one cannot escape ethics: if they are not made explicit, then they will be implicit in medical and policy decisions. But, while ethics are unavoidable, formal ethical rules can be avoided. Traditional approaches to health care rationing operate informally through the unco-ordinated clinical decisions made by doctors. This hidden rationing, without formal rules, has the advantage of flexibility and a low-key, decentralized handling of sensitive decisions. Ethics are still present, but they are not trumpeted or formalized. Health economists have sought to promote consistency and efficiency by having quantitative output measures and formal rules for health care allocation. Formal methods, when implemented, will encourage a higher-key, more managerial style of health care, with codified rules, top-down monitoring of employees and less freedom for manoeuvre. The formality forces hard choices over age discrimination, as it must be either officially blessed or outlawed. Rigid, centralized rules may endanger the subtlety that might be possible in a less formal, more decentralized approach. Besides the nature of ethical principles, it should remain an active policy question whether one should have formal contractual rules, as against informal, decentralized arrangements that leave room for trust and a common ethical culture.

Medical ethics are not the sole ethical factor involved in the age–medical expenditure relation. Decision making in health care is embedded within a wider set of policy decisions as to how many resources should be devoted to health care compared with other public services or private consumption.

Policy questions

Any government deciding its policy will have to assess both the internal organization of health care and the size of the total health care budget. These two items may be interdependent (if, say, a reorganization of health care leads to higher or lower total spending), though much economic discussion avoids the macro budgetary issue by considering economic efficiency within a fixed total budget. Setting the health care budget is a further area where numerous social and ethical factors will intrude. Ideally, perhaps, a government would have some overall normative goal and allocate its public spending accordingly. Likewise, the tax level, which determines the division between public and private activities, would be aimed at the same normative goal. In practice, of course, public decision making is exposed to a vast range of external pressures and sectional interests arguing simultaneously for general tax cuts and raised public spending in health care and elsewhere. Public decisions will depend on the political power of the competing interest groups and are unlikely to reflect a single, easily discernible welfare goal. Health care spending on the elderly is only a subset of total health care spending, which is itself only a subset of the larger budgetary decisions made by the government.

Discussions of ageing invoke another budgetary distinction, between spending devoted to younger age groups and spending devoted to the elderly. With pensions policy, the young/old division occurs visibly at the retirement age, even if this has little connection with people's genuine capacity to work. Retirement becomes the badge of old age and discriminates between 'productive' and 'unproductive' groups within society. Health care, compared with pensions policy, makes less drastic age distinctions—there will not in general be a separate 'old-age health budget' and, unlike pensions, health care spending is not exclusively devoted to older people. Human ageing is a continuous, variable process that will not yield an obvious, discrete division between homogeneous 'young' and 'old' groups. Attempts to make a division, whether or not they have official backing, will always be somewhat arbitrary.

A step beyond the young/old dichotomy would be to try to construct generational accounts for all government activities. This involves estimating the net public expenditure, in present value terms, received over the life cycle by a typical member of each generation (Kotlikoff 1992; Auerbach et al. 1994). The aim is to make transparent the generational pattern of public spending and thereby permit easier assessment of equity between generations. All public accounts could in theory be disaggregated by age (i.e. generation) as well as on more traditional, functional lines. Despite the superficial allure of intergenerational equity, there are serious difficulties here, including the likelihood of errors and omissions, the sensitivity to the choice of discount rates, and the neglect of private consumption and informal economic activities (Haveman 1994). Also restrictive is the implicit ethical stance, focused on narrow cross-sectional comparisons among adjacent birth cohorts, as against broader life-cycle and many-generation criteria (Daniels 1989). The greater stress on age built into generational accounts might bolster age distinctions and encourage intergenerational conflicts where none existed before. Attempting to monitor intergenerational transfers and promote equity might undermine the implicit intergenerational contract on which pay-as-you-go social policies are based. A real danger with generational accounts is that they be used against the old; it is easier to imagine them being exploited as a pretext for tax cuts than as a case for higher public spending on the elderly.

The foregoing policy questions—the size of the health care budget and the intergenerational allocation of resources—would arise even in societies with steady-state populations and a constant age pattern. When the population is ageing, further issues will arise. Policy involves not just a single allocation decision, but a time path or series of adjustments to accommodate a changing population. Governments are unlikely to be on optimal time paths with preordained adjustments in response to fully accommodated demographic changes—such an optimum would be difficult to establish in stylized theoretical models, let alone in reality. Actual policy will combine policy reforms, motivated by the belief that current policy is suboptimal, with policy adjustments, motivated by the desire to accommodate population ageing. Policy reforms might in some cases coincide with adjustments to accommodate population ageing. An example would be the application of QALY-based output measures in health care: if they concluded that current spending on the elderly is too generous, then this would accord with policies to curtail medical expenditure in an ageing population. If, on the other hand, policy reform was expansive and advocated enhanced services with higher expenditures, then it would be at odds with the policy retrenchments normally envisaged in response to population ageing. Generally speaking, one would not expect policy reforms (often formulated in static, steady-state models) to mesh smoothly with demographic adjustments, and some compromise will be needed.

In health care, as elsewhere, the main policy adjustments recommended in response to population ageing are likely to be retrenchments. Maintaining existing health care services for larger numbers of old people will require greater public spending and higher tax rates. Alternatively, taxes could be held roughly constant and expenditures reduced. Cutbacks in health care spending can take many forms, including efficiency savings, reduced availability, reduced quality, and delays in access. Governments also have the option of protecting health care, at the expense of other areas of public spending. Often there will be no clearly identifiable health budget, nor will there be taxes uniquely linked to health care activities. Although it is straightforward to depict budgetary problems in simplified economic models, the problems are less obvious in practice, where no tax revenue is earmarked for health care, public spending is highly varied, and other influences on public budgets will dilute the effects of population ageing. The slowness and predictability of demographic change will moderate its role compared with more sudden, less predictable events. Any unpleasant retrenchment supposedly enforced by population ageing is subject to a good deal of leeway and can readily be overstated.

Disquiet over population ageing is provoked in part by neoclassical presuppositions about full employment and balanced budgets. Neoclassical modelling of demographic change usually assumes that the economy will converge on full employment in the long run. Under this assumption, there is no demographic slack in the economy, and the rising needs of an ageing population will force cutbacks to be made somewhere, with labour being diverted from existing activities. A non-neoclassical view, following Keynesian, Kalekian and Marxian arguments, would reject the full employment assumption and maintain that capitalist economies operate with chronic unemployment and excess capacity. Since there is no aggregate shortage of workers, a rising dependency ratio (fewer people of working age relative to the retired) can have only a muted effect on the economy and will not immediately compel cutbacks or stir up intergenerational conflicts (Jackson 1992). Unemployment is a problem in its own right, of course, but it does insulate labour markets from demographic shifts in the labour force.

The pursuit of balanced budgets—a touchstone of neoclassical economics—will also accentuate the budgetary impact of demographic change. As with full employment assumptions, a budget-balancing objective will portray the aggregate economy as if it had a single, binding resource constraint being disturbed each period by exogenous demographic changes. Again this will exaggerate the significance of population ageing. Non-neoclassical economics, by contrast, is more tolerant about unbalanced budgets. Keynesians would see the expansionary effect of budget deficits as a welcome boost to economic activity during times of recession; budgetary balance will not always and everywhere be the right approach, as a balanced budget or budget surplus could have deflationary consequences that damage capital accumulation and threaten economic prosperity (Wray 1991; Palley 1998). Where economic debate is less dominated by balanced budget targets, the potential expansionary effects of budget deficits can encourage a more optimistic picture.

The argument that population ageing will lead to a crisis in health care and public services is open to abuse: proponents of cuts in welfare spending can exploit demographic change as a reason for diminished public services (Jackson 1994; 1998: ch. 4). If ageing appears to dictate cuts in social policy, there is no need to justify the cuts on more controversial social, political or economic grounds. Often the proposed cuts take the form of privatization, where people are encouraged or compelled to make their own private arrangements for health care and pensions instead of relying on public provision (World Bank 1994). The ideological content of these ideas is clear enough—an adjustment to changing age patterns is being merged with political reforms towards laissez-faire. Particular economic and social policies are thus being put forward as the unavoidable response to external events, without detailed consideration of whether the response is strictly necessary or whether alternative approaches could be adopted. There is an irony here, because the 'natural' and 'inevitable' effects of demographic change are in large part socially constructed around statutory retirement ages and centralized policy rules. Even biological ageing is thoroughly intertwined with its social context. Both the policy 'problems' caused by ageing and their proposed 'solutions' must always be socially specific and susceptible to prevailing ideological and political currents. One should be wary of those who deny or ignore this and depict demographic change as giving policy makers no alternative.

Conclusion

The age–medical expenditure relation is a long way from being simple, mechanical and biologically predetermined. Ageing has roots in human biology, but it is a complex, variable process contingent on many social and ethical factors. Public policies do not merely respond to an exogenous, biologically driven ageing process; in many cases public policy will mould the social perception of old people and, in this sense, act as a causal influence on ageing. The complex causality makes it hard to identify and disentangle the various factors behind ageing and its social implications. Any academic treatment of ageing should, nevertheless, try to come to terms with its complexity.

The social dimensions of ageing raise doubts about the policy relevance of age. Should policies take for granted the social construction of old age and, in doing so, confirm and reinforce it? Or should they seek to socially deconstruct old age and reduce the impact of arbitrary age boundaries? Health care policy faces a special difficulty on this point, as current ideas of output measurement and economic appraisal, if implemented strictly, would accentuate the role of age in rationing health care. Health care allocation by age-related formulae would strengthen the social construction of old age, not weaken it. Any efficiency gains in maximizing health output would be acquired at the cost of confirming the lower social status of the elderly. Different social values, founded on social solidarity, might suggest alternative health care policies, more generous to the elderly and less dependent on age.

Economists all too often see ageing as a non-economic topic to be handled by academics in other disciplines, such as biology or social policy. When age does impinge on economics, as in health care policy, it enters from outside the core theoretical modelling and appears only as an external, empirical characteristic of the person or population under discussion. The analysis scarcely if ever gets beyond theory-free empirical correlations between age and public expenditures. This can shed little light on the social and economic consequences of ageing and how they might develop.

A better approach would be to work towards an interdisciplinary understanding of both ageing and economic policy. To penetrate beneath the surface correlations between age and medical spending, one has to consider biological and social factors. Ageing also calls forth daunting ethical problems concerned with life, death and health. The many facets of ageing can only be adequately perceived by crossing disciplinary boundaries. Neoclassical economists are notoriously reluctant to embrace pluralism and learn from other disciplines; they differ markedly from social gerontologists, who are among the most pluralistic of academics. Similar pluralism is rare in economics, though it does enter the minority, heterodox approaches, such as institutionalism, Post-Keynesianism and the Marxian tradition. A more interdisciplinary, less neoclassical outlook would be useful in analysing the age–medical expenditure relation and, more generally, in fostering a richer, broader health economics.

References

Auerbach, A.J., Gokhale, J., and Kotlikoff, L.J. (1994) Generational accounting: a meaningful way to evaluate fiscal policy, *Journal of Economic Perspectives* 8: 73–94.

Bebbington, A.C. (1988) The expectation of life without disability in England and Wales, *Social Science and Medicine* 27: 321–326.

Binstock, R.H. and George, L.K. (eds) (1996) *Handbook of Aging and the Social Sciences*, 4th edn, San Diego CA: Academic Press.

Bond, J., Briggs, R., and Coleman, P. (1993a) The study of ageing, in J. Bond, P. Coleman, and S.M. Peace (eds).

Bond, J., Coleman, P., and Peace, S.M. (eds) (1993b) *Ageing in Society: An Introduction to Social Gerontology*, 2nd edn, London: Sage.

Brody, J.A. (1985) Prospects for an ageing population, *Nature* 315: 463–466.

Broome, J. (1992) The value of living, *Recherches Economiques de Louvain* 58: 125–142.

Cumming, E. and Henry, W. (1961) *Growing Old: The Process of Disengagement*, New York: Basic Books.

Daniels, N. (1985) *Just Health Care*, Cambridge: Cambridge University Press.

—— (1989) Justice and transfers between generations, in P. Johnson, C. Conrad, and D. Thomson (eds) *Workers Versus Pensioners*, Manchester: Manchester University Press.

Donaldson, L. (1991) *Fertility Transition: The Social Dynamics of Population Change*, Oxford: Blackwell.

Dugger, W.M. (1999) Old age is an institution, *Review of Social Economy* 57: 84–98.

Easterlin, R.A., Pollak, R.A., and Wachter, M.L. (1980) Toward a more general economic model of fertility determination: endogenous preferences and natural fertility, in R.A. Easterlin (ed.) *Population and Economic Change in Developing Countries*, Chicago: University of Chicago Press.

Estes, C.L., Swan, J.H., and Gerard, L.E. (1982) Dominant and competing paradigms in gerontology: towards a political economy of old age, *Ageing and Society* 2: 151–164.

Finch, C.E. (1990) *Longevity, Senescence and the Genome*, Chicago: University of Chicago Press.

Fries, J.F. (1980) Ageing, natural death and the compression of morbidity, *New England Journal of Medicine* 303: 130–135.
—— (1989) The compression of morbidity: near or far? *Milbank Memorial Fund Quarterly* 67: 208–232.
Fries, J.F. and Crapo, L.M. (1981) *Vitality and Aging: Implications of the Rectangular Curve*, San Francisco: W.H. Freeman.
Fries, J.F. and the Health Project Consortium (1993) Reducing health care costs by reducing the need and demand for medical services, *New England Journal of Medicine* 329: 321–325.
Gruenberg, E.M. (1977) The failures of success, *Milbank Memorial Fund Quarterly* 55: 3–24.
Hall, M.R.P. (1988) Geriatric medicine today, in N.E.J. Wells and C.B. Freer (eds) *The Ageing Population: Burden or Challenge?* London: Macmillan.
Harris, J. (1985) *The Value of Life*, London: Routledge.
Haveman, R. (1994) Should generational accounts replace public budgets and deficits? *Journal of Economic Perspectives* 8: 95–111.
Hendricks, J. and Hendricks, C.D. (1977) *Aging in Mass Society: Myths and Realities*, Cambridge MA: Winthrop.
Jackson, W.A. (1992) Population ageing and intergenerational conflict: a post-Keynesian view, *Journal of Economic Studies* 19: 26–37.
—— (1994) The economics of ageing and the political economy of old age, *International Review of Applied Economics* 8: 31–45.
—— (1998) *The Political Economy of Population Ageing*, Cheltenham: Edward Elgar.
Kotlikoff, L.J. (1992) *Generational Accounting: Knowing Who Pays, and When, for What We Spend*, New York: Free Press.
Le Grand, J. (1982) *The Strategy of Equality*, London: George Allen and Unwin.
Livi-Bacci, M. (1983) The nutrition-mortality link in past times: a comment, *Journal of Interdisciplinary History* 14: 293–298.
Manton, K.G. (1982) Changing concepts of morbidity and mortality in the elderly population, *Milbank Memorial Fund Quarterly* 60: 183–244.
Marmot, M.G. and McDowall, M.E. (1986) Mortality decline and widening social inequalities, *Lancet* 2: 274–276.
McKeown, T. and Record, R.G. (1962) Reasons for the decline of mortality in England and Wales during the nineteenth century, *Population Studies* 16: 94–122.
McKeown, T., Record, R.G., and Turner, R.D. (1975) An interpretation of the decline of mortality in England and Wales during the twentieth century, *Population Studies* 29: 391–422.
McPherson, B.D. (1983) *Aging as a Social Process: An Introduction to Individual and Population Aging*, Toronto: Butterworth.
Means, R. and Smith, R. (1994) *Community Care: Policy and Practice*, London: Macmillan.
Mooney, G.A. (1978) Planning for balance of care of the elderly, *Scottish Journal of Political Economy* 25: 149–164.
Omran, A.R. (1971) The epidemiological transition: a theory of the epidemiology of population change, *Milbank Memorial Fund Quarterly* 49: 509–538.
Palley, T.I. (1998) The economics of social security: an old Keynesian perspective, *Journal of Post Keynesian Economics* 21: 93–110.

Phillipson, C. (1982) *Capitalism and the Construction of Old Age*, London: Macmillan.

Schneider, E.L. and Brody, J.A. (1983) Ageing, natural death and the compression of morbidity: another view, *New England Journal of Medicine* 309: 854–856.

Smith, K. and Wright, K.G. (1994) Informal care and economic appraisal: a discussion of possible methodological approaches, *Health Economics* 3: 137–148.

Townsend, P. (1981) The structured dependency of the elderly: a creation of social policy in the twentieth century, *Ageing and Society* 1: 5–28.

Verbrugge, L.M. (1984) Longer life but worsening health? Trends in health and mortality of middle-aged and older persons, *Milbank Memorial Fund Quarterly* 62: 473–519.

Walker, A. (1980) The social creation of poverty and dependency in old age, *Journal of Social Policy* 9: 49–75.

Wilkinson, R.G. (ed.) (1986) *Class and Health: Research and Longitudinal Data*, London: Tavistock.

—— (1992) Income distribution and life expectancy, *British Medical Journal* 304: 165–168.

Williams, A.H. (1985) Public policy aspects of the economics of ageing, in D. Greenaway and G.K. Shaw (eds) *Public Choice, Public Finance and Public Policy*, Oxford: Blackwell.

Willis, R.J. (1973) A new approach to the economic theory of fertility behavior, *Journal of Political Economy* 81 (supplement): 14–64.

World Bank (1994) *Averting the Old Age Crisis: Policies to Protect the Old and Promote Growth*, Washington DC: Oxford University Press.

Wray, L.R. (1991) Can the Social Security Trust Fund Contribute to Savings? *Journal of Post Keynesian Economics* 13: 155–170.

Wright, K.G., Cairns, J.A., and Snell, M.C. (1981) *Costing Care: The Costs of Alternative Patterns of Care for the Elderly*, Sheffield: Sheffield University Joint Unit for Social Services Research.

9

THE SOCIETAL COSTS AND IMPLICATIONS OF USING HIGH COST CRITICAL CARE RESOURCES FOR THE ELDERLY

Diane M. Dewar

The patient census in the critical care unit and, in particular, the expanded use of mechanical ventilation, can be used to explain some of the growth in health care costs in the United States relative to other countries. It has been estimated that critical care in the US accounts for 20 to 34 percent of all hospital costs, and 7 to 8 percent of total health care expenditures in the economy (Jacobs and Noseworthy 1990; SCCM 1992). Patients requiring prolonged mechanical ventilation in the critical care unit consume as much as 50 percent of critical care resources despite the fact that this population may represent fewer than 10 percent of all critical care unit patients (Wagner 1989; Booth and Cohen 1994; Cohen and Booth 1994). Given the intensity and dominance of mechanical ventilation in the critical care unit, these services will be used to illustrate the economic evaluation of critical care resource utilization among the seriously ill elderly.

Even though mechanical ventilation has been determined to be an effective treatment for acute and chronic respiratory failure (Criner et al. 1995), a ventilator-dependent critical care patient has an estimated cost that is eight times that of a hospitalized general medical-surgical floor patient (Davis et al. 1980). Despite the costs, in-hospital use of mechanical ventilation has risen over the last decade (Swinburne et al. 1993).

A number of factors such as inadequate reimbursement for inpatient ventilator dependency (Gracey et al. 1987; Rosen and Bone 1990; Nava et al. 1997) have resulted in the rapid development of extended care, and home care ventilator facilities (Adams et al. 1993; Cohen and Chalfin 1994). Crude estimates put the nationwide cost of mechanical ventilation for 1995 in the range of $30 billion exclusive of physician costs and the costs associated with long-term post-ventilator care (Cohen and Chalfin 1994).

The striking growth in the prevalence of ventilator dependency is, in part, attributable to the increasing use of mechanical ventilation in elderly patients with chronic disease (Swinburne et al. 1988). However, though many elderly patients clearly benefit from critical care services such as mechanical ventilation (O'Donnell and Bohner 1991; Chelluri et al. 1992; Pessau et al. 1992; Cohen et al. 1993), researchers have shown that preferential allocation of hospital services to younger patients in general is increasingly occurring. This differential does not appear to be due to severity of illness or general preferences for extended care (Hamel et al. 1996). One rationale for the limited use of critical care resources among the elderly could be drawn from the growing number of studies that have found that factors such as prolonged mechanical ventilation, co-existence of chronic diseases and extreme old age impact negatively on hospital survival and long-term survival rates for this subpopulation (Swinburne et al. 1988; Elpern et al. 1989; Knauss 1989; Cohen et al. 1993; Swinburne et al. 1993; Dewar et al. 1999).

Pressures to reduce costs and increase provider accountability are coming from both private and public sectors. Recent studies have shown that managed care patients in general receive less hospital resources than those with traditional fee-for-service insurance (Rapaport et al. 1992; Angus et al. 1996). However, the results are mixed regarding whether the reduction is due to economic incentives of the managed care organization or due to differences in severity of illness that can lead to variations in clinical decisions.

If we view the economics of mechanical ventilation as an example of high-cost, high-intensity critical care services, it is reasonable to ask: 'Are the benefits worth the costs?' We may explicitly consider whether a line should be drawn—based on benefits and costs—beyond which further expenditures are deemed irrational for particular cases or subpopulations. This line might be viewed as placing a dollar value on human life. However, a different perspective would be to view it as an objective way to limit expenditures in cases where the additional health care could lead to a painful prolonging of the patient's life and additional anguish to the patient and family.

This study examines the economic implications of using critical care resources for the frail patients under a managed care organization (MCO) and for those covered by non-MCO payers (i.e. fee-for-service reimbursement or uninsured), through an analysis of hospital survival and costs for patients who underwent mechanical ventilation with tracheostomy and were discharged under Diagnosis Related Group (DRG) 483 in New York State during the 1992–1996 period. The resources utilized under this DRG incur the highest inpatient costs and are being increasingly used as the population ages. The economic evaluation of mechanical ventilation services among the MCO and non-MCO subpopulations is performed for three purposes:

1 to determine if critical care resources such as mechanical ventilation with tracheostomy are differentially allocated among MCO and non-MCO patients;

2 to determine if economically based criteria can be applied to the allocation of higher cost health care resources commonly utilized by an elderly population; and
3 to argue that in-hospital mortality among severely ill patients undergoing critical care treatment is not a 'bad outcome,' but an outcome in which the patient, family, and provider participate in end-of-life decisions.

Managed care and critical care service utilization

Managed care explicitly links clinical decisions with economic incentives through the formal integration of service delivery and financing. Under this arrangement, health service delivery is driven by cost control, access control and quality management, the ultimate goal being the efficient allocation of scarce and expensive health care resources. However, as managed care matures and as the proportion of older and more costly MCO subscribers increases, the initial cost reductions reaped by MCOs are fading, and MCO health care costs are increasing in a similar manner to that under the fee-for-service reimbursement system.

In order for managed care to move forward in efficiency goals, given that health care utilization and diffusion of high-cost technology is increasing, it is hypothesized that this delivery system will limit access to critical care services and control costs of these services rendered relative to the care delivered under the fee-for-service system (Chalfin and Fein 1994). Under managed care, limited access to critical care services can occur in the reduction of hospital admissions through pre-admission review by the MCO. However, it is also assumed that once the patient is in the hospital and critical care services are deemed to be necessary, the demand for these intense services will be relatively inelastic regardless of payer source. Thus, it would be expected that economic incentives would not be influential in the allocation of critical care resources for these patients.

At some point, acute care service utilization can go beyond society's resource availability, and harsh allocation decisions have to be made. Critical care services, in particular, include expensive and risky technological resources. In this setting, explicit social choices have to be made about the types and intensity of health care consumed, in order to achieve ethical efficiency and/or equity goals in society. Methods must be used to provide information and guidelines for rationally allocating high-intensity resources and to raise the fiscal consciousness of critical care providers.

Economic evaluations in critical care medicine

The use of economic evaluation methods such as cost-benefit or cost-effectiveness analysis is one approach to ethically guide critical care resource allocation decisions in an era of cost-control in MCO and non-MCO settings. Here, the joint assessment of clinical outcomes and resource consumption can be used as a criterion to allocate scarce resources to their optimal use (e.g. the biggest bang for the buck) in an objective manner. This efficiency determination is blinded to social or political pressures concerning the health care services, but can be used with social justice goals to improve the opportunity for access to medical technology for those financially, culturally or socially disenfranchised from the health care system. If cost-reduction alone is used to allocate resources, this could lead to a reduction in benefits or the measured health outcome associated with the services received due to inappropriate modifications in staffing, technology, etc., that impact the process and quality of care. An economic evaluation, on the other hand, can be used to help clinicians, administrators, and policymakers set priorities and reach informed decisions based on the combined clinical and financial outcomes of the treatment alternatives under consideration.

Economic evaluation example using DRG 483

An economic evaluation of the more prevalent and costly resources used in critical care concerns the use of mechanical ventilation with tracheostomy under DRG 483. This example will determine whether economically based criteria may be used to objectively compare different clinical or service delivery environments, and/or different forms of medical therapy, in order to make informed, fiscally conscious medical decisions in the critical care setting.

Here, the evaluation of resources used under DRG 483 for MCO and non-MCO patients is performed using hospital discharge abstract data during the period of regulated hospital reimbursements under the New York State Prospective Hospital Reimbursement Methodology.[1] During this period, the main delivery system impact for these patients is in service utilization costs and outcomes under MCO or non-MCO participation. Although the critical care resources account for the majority of costs for these patients, the entire bundle of hospital resources consumed under this DRG for each patient is evaluated, since the critical care unit stay is one component of the entire hospital episode on which the patient's outcome depends.

Data sources

The primary database used in this study is the New York Statewide Planning and Research Cooperative System (SPARCS) database for 1992–1996. This data set reflects the population of inpatients from all New York State general hospitals. Data concerning demographic, clinical, and reimbursement information are obtained for all patients aged 19 to 95 years in DRG 483, which is defined as 'tracheostomy except for mouth, larynx and pharynx disorder.' DRG 483 is a reimbursement classification based on a procedure, mechanical ventilation with tracheostomy, rather than a particular diagnosis. These are heterogeneous medical and surgical patients but they are included in this DRG in order to reflect their intense resource utilization and hospital costs. Overall, these patients are seriously ill, are highly expensive, and have extremely high mortality rates (Kurek et al. 1997). The total population considered is 39,697 patients: 4,005 in MCOs and 35,692 in other insurance plans or without insurance.

A secondary source of data is retrospectively obtained public information concerning the total reimbursement rates for DRG 483 to hospitals in New York State during 1992–1996 (Bureau of Health Economics, New York State Department of Health, personal communication 1997). Given New York's all-payer payment system for the inpatient setting during this period, the average Medicaid payment per year can be used to approximate the statewide average payment per discharge for all ages under a given DRG regardless of third-party payer source, since the distribution of patients across regions and types of hospitals is roughly similar for each payer. Payments are used in this study to capture resource cost. As an alternative to payments, costs could be used. Costs are not available in the SPARCS database, and charges reflect neither the resources utilized nor expenditures incurred. Although payments may be criticized for using an imperfect measure of costs and not reflective of opportunity costs, they reflect the reality from a public or private third-party payer's perspective.

In health care delivery, the functioning of private markets for health risk is impeded by the existence of third party payments. In the US, for example, over two-thirds of all health care expenses are paid by third parties, including commercial and public health insurance. It is well known that third party insurance payments do not allow consumers of health care to reflect through the market their preferences for avoidance of morbidity and mortality risk (Kenkel 1994). For example, if consumers believed that some critical care health benefits were not worth the costs, they would buy reduced critical care in a system of universal self-payment for health care. Alternatively, there would be a market demand for health plans that offered reduced critical care at lower premiums. Since such a market does not exist, collective decisions on health care resource utilization must be made by other mechanisms. Very often, whether desirable or not, these decisions are in practice made on the basis of considerations such as global budget restrictions, threat of litigation, and pressures to reduce costs and increase revenues. In this example, an objective approach to resource allocation decisions is applied that integrates clinical and financial outcomes.

Evaluation method

In order to perform an evaluation from a societal perspective, the age-specific payment per survivor (i.e. the societal cost of allocating resources) under this

DRG is compared to the economic value of life saved (i.e. the societal benefit of utilizing resources) for both the MCO and non-MCO patient sub-populations. A brief summary of the procedure follows, with a more detailed discussion of the estimations in the appendix.

Multiple regression analysis is used to model the relationship between age-specific survival rate (SR_x) with respect to age, payment source, demographics, higher-risk diagnoses, admission type, and yearly general systematic changes in utilization of this DRG. The MCO variable will provide a general measure of any systematic difference in practice/treatment patterns relative to non-MCO payment systems. These expected survival rates are then used to estimate the expected age-specific payment per survivor (PS_x) where:

$$\hat{P}S_{x,y} = (average - payment - per - discharge)/S\hat{R}_{x,y}$$

where: x = ages 19 to 95; y = MCO, non-MCO participation

There is a great deal of variation concerning the appropriate valuation of life. Gillette and Hopkins (1988) found that in most instances federal agencies 'draw the line' in the range from one to two million dollars per life saved. Other agencies do not explicitly estimate the value of life, but instead compare the costs of the regulations to estimates of the number of lives saved. Although no value is explicitly placed on life, decisions regarding the regulations essentially perform the same function. Most estimates of the value of a statistical life come from the analysis of compensating differentials (Olson 1981; Marin and Psacharopoulos 1982; Arnould and Nichols 1983; Dillingham 1985; Fisher et al. 1988; Moore and Viscusi 1988; Tolley et al. 1994; Sloan 1995).

There is agreement that the relevant concept is that of valuing the extension of statistical life (Fisher et al. 1988; Moore and Viscusi 1988; Tolley et al. 1994; Sloan 1995). Lives are not saved, but extended for a period of time depending upon individual life expectancy. Therefore, it is more relevant to look at the value of a statistical year of life rather that the value of a statistical life. In this study, an illustrative value of $120,000 per year of statistical life will be used in accordance with a recent collection of studies (Tolley et al. 1994). A life expectancy table is used to obtain the number of years of life remaining at each age (US Bureau of the Census 1993).

The fact that the value of remaining life is not valued proportionately to the number of years of life has been recognized in contingent valuation studies and suggests that determining benefits by weighing the value of a year of life by life expectancy can be further refined. Recent research found that the median respondent determined that saving the life of one 20-year-old is equivalent to saving the life of seven 60-year-olds, despite the fact that the former saves 56.3 years of life on average compared to a total of 143.5

years of life in the latter case (Cropper et al. 1994). Therefore, the benefits received from the resources utilized are discounted by age-adjustment weights as an illustration of how the public discounts life-saving programs.

In addition to age adjustments, an adjustment for the quality of life differences should be incorporated into the benefits (La Puma and Lawlor 1990; Tvesat et al. 1998). For example, the benefit of saving one year of life for an individual confined to a nursing home bed for a year will not be viewed as equivalent to a year of normal life. Most individuals would place a downward adjustment to the value of life in that scenario to reflect the quality of the year of life. Since direct utility assessment techniques are grounded in decision-analytic theory, they are conceptually complex and impractical for use in clinical trial settings. Therefore, global rating scales with health state classifications are the common alternatives (Weeks 1996) in creating discount weights. Ideally, data on each individual's circumstances would be available in addition to how a large sample of individuals would value each of these circumstances relative to a year of normal life. This is not possible in administrative data such as SPARCS since patients are not followed post-discharge, and quality of life indicators are not recorded.

However, recent studies have analyzed elderly patients' time-tradeoff utility, or their willingness to exchange time in their current health status for a shorter amount of time with excellent health (Tvesat et al. 1995; Tvesat et al. 1998). Time-tradeoff utility measures for quality of life is a preferred method since it is easier to administer these surveys than the standard gamble approach; and these measures avoid the additional confounding inherent in the standard gamble approach resulting from the patient's willingness to take risks (Tvesat et al. 1990).

Studies have also been performed to determine values of extending life for patients with varieties of chronic illness. In this study, estimates of average, lower- and upper-bound estimates of the value of extending life are used from the literature measuring the quality of life of patients with chronic bronchitis (Tolley et al. 1994), in order to show the range in quality of life adjusted benefits received among patients who may have continued complications after the inpatient episode. This sensitivity analysis is used since there is uncertainty inherent in the values attached to different health states reported (O'Brien and Rushby 1990), due to such things as daily or seasonal variations in health status. Measures from those with chronic bronchitis are used, since this condition is associated with moderate levels of disability and may represent a quality of life, for those with respiratory conditions, for typical cases that are weaned from mechanical ventilation prior to discharge.[2] Although it is unlikely that a single instrument for obtaining health-state utilities will become a gold standard for assessing quality of life, the valuation used here is a reasonable and conservative reflection of these patients' health-state preferences.

Evaluation findings

Figure 9.1 shows the unadjusted and adjusted economic benefit to extending life, as well as the cost of extending life,[3] graphed against age for the MCO and non-MCO groups when using the unadjusted value of a year of life equal to $120,000. The value of life extension can be compared to the payment per survivor for the subsamples to determine whether benefits (i.e. the value of life extended) exceed costs (i.e. payment per survivor) at every age. For the MCO group, the unadjusted benefits of applying DRG 483 exceed the costs at all ages up to 93. For non-MCO patients, the unadjusted benefits of applying DRG 483 exceed the costs at all ages up to 91. This implies that, based on these benefit functions, the utilization of resources under DRG 483 at age 93 or older is not economically feasible for those under managed care. Also, these resources are not efficiently utilized at age 91 or older for those with other payer sources. These findings are similar to the results based on the upper-bound estimates of benefits received for the chronically ill patients. The lowest age for which benefits exceed costs is 83 for the lower-bound estimates of benefits for the chronically ill. Even with these estimated benefits, resources are allocated efficiently at ages greater than standard life expectancy.

Table 9.1 shows a summary of the discounted benefits at various ages adjusted for age, quality of life and both age and quality of life, as well as the upper and lower bounds of the quality of life adjusted benefits for the MCO patient group. The age, quality of life, and combination age and quality of life adjustments all theoretically reduce the age at which benefits equal costs. However, even with these discounts, the benefits outweigh the costs of the resources utilized for patients to at least age 80 for unadjusted, age adjusted and quality of life adjusted benefits. For quality and age adjusted benefits to reflect older, more fragile patients, benefits outweigh the costs of the utilized resources up to the age range of 70–80.

Table 9.2 shows a similar summary of the unadjusted and adjusted benefits and costs for non-MCO patients. Based on these value of life and payment assumptions, there is no great difference between MCO and non-MCO patient groups in terms of the ages where resources are efficiently allocated under DRG 483. This similarity could be partly due to the fact that there is no overall statistically significant difference between the patient groups in terms of their clinical risk factors. However, regardless of payer source, a closer consideration of the utilization of these intense resources under this DRG should occur for older more severely ill patients starting in the age range of 70–80.

Discussion

Regardless of MCO participation, the results show that for nearly all age and quality of life adjusted benefits at nearly all ages, the utilization of resources

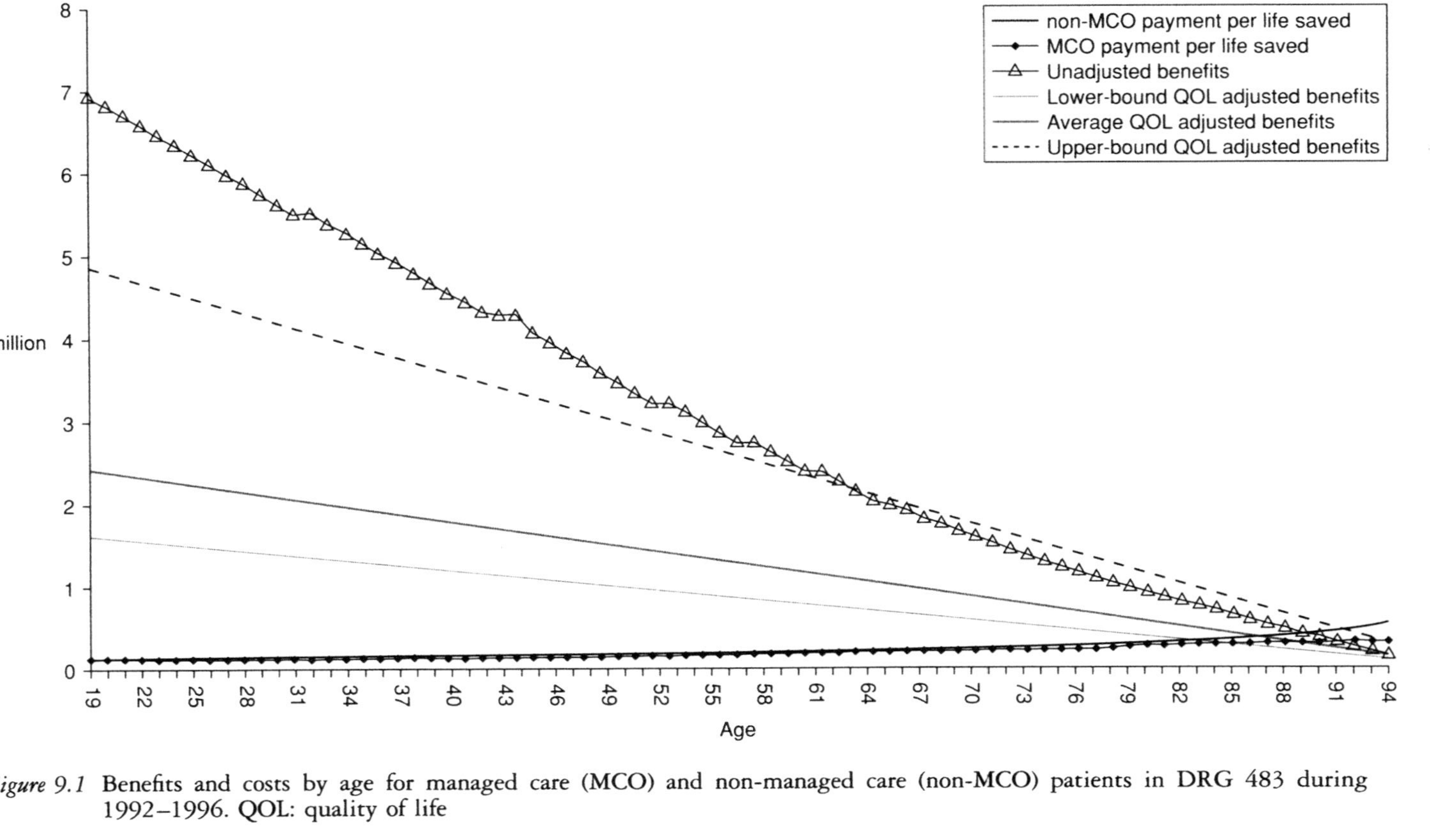

Figure 9.1 Benefits and costs by age for managed care (MCO) and non-managed care (non-MCO) patients in DRG 483 during 1992–1996. QOL: quality of life

Table 9.1 Benefits and costs for managed care patients in DRG 483 in New York State during the period 1992–1996 (thousands of dollars)

Age	*Unadjusted benefits*	*Lower bound quality of life adjusted benefits**	*Average quality of life adjusted benefits*	*Upper bound quality of life adjusted benefits*	*Age adjusted benefits*†	*Lower bound quality and age adjusted benefits*	*Average quality and age adjusted benefits*	*Upper bound quality and age adjusted benefits*	*Cost ($)*
20	$6,840	$1,600	$2,400	$4,800	$6,840 (1.0)	$1,600	$2,400	$4,800	$128.63
40	4,560	1,200	1,800	3,600	3,707 (0.813)	967	1,463	2,927	133.20
60	2,520	800	1,200	2,400	1,419 (0.563)	450	676	1,914	178.87
70	1,680	600	900	1,800	736 (0.438)	263	394	788	209.78
80	996	400	600	1,200	312 (0.313)	125	188	376	266.58
90	444	200	300	600	124	56	84	167	314.31

Notes

* Quality of life adjustment is based on estimates in Tolley et al., concerning patients with chronic bronchitis.

† Figures in parentheses are adjustment weights used for all age adjusted benefits.

Table 9.2 Benefits and costs for non-managed care patients in DRG 483 in New York State during the period 1992-1996 (thousands of dollars)

Age	*Unadjusted benefits*	*Lower bound quality of life adjusted benefits**	*Average quality of life adjusted benefits*	*Upper bound quality of life adjusted benefits*	*Age adjusted benefits*†	*Lower bound quality and age adjusted benefits*	*Average quality and age adjusted benefits*	*Upper bound quality and age adjusted benefits*	*Cost ($)*
20	$6,840	$1,600	$2,400	$4,800	$6,840 (1.0)	$1,600	$2,400	$4,800	$136.95
40	4,560	1,200	1,800	3,600	3,707 (0.813)	967	1,463	2,927	163.21
60	2,520	800	1,200	2,400	1,419 (0.563)	450	676	1,914	199.11
70	1,680	600	900	1,800	736 (0.438)	263	394	788	230.04
80	996	400	600	1,200	312 (0.313)	125	188	376	284.80
90	444	200	300	600	124	56	84	167	408.27

Notes

* Quality of life adjustment is based on estimates in Tolley et al., concerning patients with chronic bronchitis.

† Figures in parentheses are adjustment weights used for all age adjusted benefits.

under DRG 483 is feasible and efficient. This may be partly due to the moderate economic valuation of life estimates and generous quality of life weights that allow for benefits to be somewhat artificially high for the frail elderly who disproportionately use these resources. This rather surprising result leads to the question whether the resources utilized under this DRG can indeed be efficient at most ages. This leads to the further speculation that reimbursement payments under this DRG may be artificially low, thus creating a false sense of economy.

Alternatively, the results based on adjusted benefits imply that at extremely old ages or for those with chronic illness, the costs of this DRG outweigh the benefits received. However, even though this resource allocation is shown to be inefficient for the oldest old or the more chronically ill over age 70, this evaluation should not be used to propose that these health services should be rationed based on age alone. Instead, from the perspective of society, the family, or the patient, there may be circumstances when continuing treatment may not be feasible at younger ages, or when treatment is feasible at older ages. As seen in the variation of ages where efficient resource allocations are attained through sensitivity analysis of the benefits received, even if broad resource allocation guidelines are in place based on efficiency analysis, it would be better to evaluate resource utilization on a case-by-case basis that incorporates both economic and overall patient well-being considerations.

Due to the lack of information in SPARCS concerning the patient's psychosocial functioning, other impairments, social supports, and the chronology of care received, the results of economic evaluations of hospital services based solely on administrative data cannot be the only guide in the establishment of fiscally conscious resource allocations in the critical care setting—especially for the frail elderly population. Indeed, based on the assumptions in this example, nearly all critical care patients requiring services under DRG 483 would receive this level of intense care, which would result in larger shares of resources going to high-cost technologically driven health services at the expense of more broad-based health care or other services that could benefit more members of society. Further, those in the oldest old-age classes would be denied care, which could result in the premature termination of otherwise healthy and productive individuals. Therefore, even if the results of economic evaluations are accepted by society, resource utilization control must be implemented with both clinical excellence and fiscal consciousness.

Cost control with clinical excellence in critical care

Although it can be agreed that the current trend in health care resource utilization cannot be sustained without sacrifices across other sectors of the economy, limiting resources based on chronological age is not justified in the absence of societal consensus or public policy directives. Especially concerning intense critical care services, better prognostic indicators are needed in addition to age; also needed are routine discussions with patients concerning expected quality of life if treatment is initiated or continued, so that informed decisions about care can be made by the patient or the patient's health care proxy. This is especially appropriate when providing high-risk care to frail and/or elderly patients who may have great physical limitations but also have the support of community and/or family care.

In using economic evaluations in the determination of optimal critical care service allocation such as those under DRG 483, patients' psychological characteristics and overall well-being must come into play in both the inpatient and post-acute-care settings. Researchers have found that emphasis must also be placed on holism, quality of life, and respect for life as vital segments of technology assessment and efficacy (Almond 1988; Goodman 1993; Engelking 1994; Ferrel 1994). Further, the psychosocial aspects of high technology care must be considered in order to design treatment protocols that minimize the dehumanizing aspects of technological dependency. Based on this paradigm, it may be reasonable, humane and cost-effective to continue treatment for patients over 80 years while terminating treatment for someone younger than that age.

As seen in the DRG 483 evaluation, quality of life measures such as time-tradeoff utility can provide physicians with information on patient preferences and combine prognostic information with utilities for decision analysis concerning treatment alternatives. These measures are needed in economic evaluations of critical care services as well as process-oriented evaluations of the chronology of care received in order to answer questions about whether the additional cost of the more expensive therapy is justified by the benefit it produces in both the length and quality of the life extended by the technology.

In this era of managed competition and mature managed care, the triage, census and acuity of patients in the critical care unit will continue to change. Recent legislative reforms throughout the nation have decreased the number of intensivists being trained, which can have a negative impact on the quality of care in this setting (Chalfin and Fein 1994). Ethical and efficiency implications also exist, since health outcomes can also become poorer if the number of critical care beds and patients' access to the hospital and critical care unit are decreasing. Therefore, specific triage policies based primarily on clinical excellence, not economic incentives, must be developed and implemented.

End-of-life health care policies

Strategies for optimal resource allocation must be considered to limit marginally beneficial health care so that more general health care will be available at reasonable costs to society. Policies that combine clinical excellence with fiscal consciousness (that may be guided by the results of economic evaluations) include futile-care policies, guidelines for writing Do-Not-Resuscitate (DNR) orders, and team management of clinically complex cases. These protocols allow severely ill patients requiring critical care resources to utilize more appropriate end-of-life or palliative care rather than invasive, intensive life-extending care, which allows for the latter services to be allocated to more clinically and economically appropriate cases. These policies take the view that the patient prefers mortality to enduring some extremely poor health state. Here, health care is coordinated by the patient, the patient's health care proxy, the family, and the provider to facilitate the attainment of the quality-adjusted cost-effective outcome.

Futile-care policies encompass the ethical withdrawal of life support if the acceptable clinical outcome is not achieved. However, intervention studies that have been conducted to improve communication between patients and providers to facilitate futile-care or other end-of-life directives have failed to improve the quality of end-of-life care offered (Bock et al. 1997). Further, few, if any, studies have assessed the economic imperative of implementing this policy in the critical care setting (Cohen and Chalfin 1994). The economics of medical futility needs to be seriously addressed, since intensivists will be called upon more often to justify their medical decisions for continuing life support for severely or terminally ill patients. This is especially true as critical care units have not been expanding and limited facilities for patients on life-support exist in the acute or less costly post-acute settings. However, providers will need to be encouraged to explore cost-effective medical decisions since these protocols may be in conflict with their compliance to the Hippocratic oath, as well as with potential threats of litigation in the event that the aggressive treatment has a remote chance of improving the health status of the patient, or at least do no harm.

The timing of DNR orders has been associated with reductions in length of stay and critical care unit services provided. Early DNR orders (i.e. the first 24 hours of the acute care stay) can decrease the length of stay in the critical care unit and the total number of hospital days by two and seven days, respectively. Patients who have been admitted to the critical care unit with early DNR orders had a more clearly defined set of treatment goals, which allowed for more timely discharges, and the withholding of aggressive and minimally beneficial interventions (Bock et al. 1997). These findings imply that early DNR status may be a mechanism to cap prolonged aggressive critical care unit utilization, which ultimately impacts the end-of-life economies.

Team management of patients can also reduce length of stay in the critical care unit. Researchers have shown that, by implementing a multidisciplinary team that manages hopelessly ill critical care unit patients, critical care unit length of stay and costs can be decreased up to 50 percent (Carlson et al. 1988). Further, those patients in a state of relative clinical stability could benefit from removal from the critical care unit to an environment that is less intensive and invasive while being monitored by a multidisciplinary rehabilitation team that crafts an individualized treatment protocol for each patient (Cohen and Chalfin 1994). This approach can address the discharge planning problem often seen with frail or elderly patients. A major problem in discharge planning is the coordination of post-acute services in home or in other less costly long-term care facilities. While home health services and long-term care facility costs are one-tenth and one-third of critical care unit costs, respectively, placement issues cause prolonged stays in the acute care setting, causing up to 33 percent of in-hospital mortality for critical care patients (O'Donohue 1992). Some of the costly longer-term acute care stays for patients waiting for discharge to extended care facilities can be alleviated by coordinating discharge planning to home care, DRG-exempt rehabilitation facilities, or chronic care facilities. Care teams can also successfully coordinate care in chronic mechanical ventilation step-down units in the acute care setting for patients who do not have the option physically or geographically to go to other less intense facilities. These arrangements have had success (Cohen and Chalfin 1994), since focused rehabilitation can take place in such a dedicated care unit rather than in a busy general critical care unit.

Conclusions

Efficient, ethical health care delivery for the growing elderly population is of great importance in an era of cost controls and high technology. Focusing on critical care resource utilization, a greater emphasis needs to be placed on the use of quality-adjusted economic evaluations in order for health care planners and providers to correctly identify cost-conscious and clinically sound medical alternatives for individual patients as well as among the competing needs of a heterogeneous patient population. Particularly for the chronically ill and those at the end-of-life stage, information is needed that takes into consideration the total wellness of the patient in order to facilitate productive dialogues between providers, patients, and families concerning the best utilization of health care after a certain threshold has been reached in the degradation of the patient's health status.

Some have contended that the opportunity to save resources at the end of life is limited (Emanual and Emanual 1994), while others have disagreed (Esserman et al. 1995). In such populations, spending decisions should be based on health effectiveness (Lamm 1991), as well as the utility of the treatment rather than simply cost control regardless of payer. Objective measures of efficacy and quality of life will yield better estimates of the benefits attributed to the technology, thus allowing providers and planners to determine true clinical patient need rather than simply patient wants for particular services (Dewar 1997). This is essential when considering care alternatives for those in the later years of life or with chronic disability.

References

Adams, A.B., Whitman, J., and Mercy, T. (1993) Surveys of long-term ventilatory support in Minnesota: 1986 and 1992, *Chest* 103: 1463.

Almond, B. (1988) Philosophy, medicine and its technologies, *J Med Ethics* 14(4): 173.

Angus, D.C., Linde-Zwirble, W.T., Sirio, C.A., Rotondi, A.J., Cheluri, L., Newbold, R.C., Lave, J.R., and Pinsky, M.R. (1996) The effect of managed care on ICU length of stay, *JAMA* 276(13): 1075.

Arnould, R.J. and Nichols, L.M. (1983) Wage-risk premiums and workers' compensation: a refinement of estimates of compensating wage differentials, *J Polit Econ* 91(3): 332.

Bock, K.R., Teres, D., and Rapaport, J. (1997) Economic implications of the timing of Do-Not-Resuscitate orders for ICU patients, *New Horizons* 5(1): 51.

Booth, F.V.M. and Cohen, I.L. (1994) Resource utilization in a busy cardiac surgical ICU—the disproportionate impact of the high risk minority, *Am J Respir Crit Care Med.*

Carlson, R.W., Devich, L., and Frank, R.R. (1988) Development of a comprehensive support team for the hopelessly ill on a university hospital medical service, *JAMA* 259: 378–383.

Chalfin, D.B. and Fein, A.M. (1994) Critical care medicine in managed competition and a managed care environment, *New Horizons* 2(3): 275.

Chelluri, L., Pinsky, M., and Grenvik, A. (1992) Outcome of intensive care in the 'oldest' old critically ill patients, *Crit Care Med* 20: 757.

Cohen, I.L., Lambrinos, J., and Fein, I.A. (1993) Mechanical ventilation for the elderly patient in intensive care. Incremental charges and benefits, *JAMA* 269: 1025.

Cohen, I.L. and Booth, F.V.M. (1994) Cost containment and mechanical ventilation in the United States, *New Horizons* 2: 283.

Cohen, I.L. and Chalfin, D.B. (1994) Economics of mechanical ventilation: surviving the '90s, *Clin Pulm Med* 1: 100.

Criner, G.J., Kreimer, D.T., Tomaselli, M. et al. (1995) Financial implications of noninvasive positive pressure ventilation (NPPV), *Chest* 108(2): 475.

Cropper, M.L., Added, S.K., and Portney, P.R. (1994) Preferences for life saving programs: how the public discounts time and age, *J Risk Uncert* 9(3): 243–265.

Davis, H., II, Lefrack, S.S., Miller, D., and Malt, S. (1980) Prolonged mechanically assisted ventilation. An analysis of outcome and charges, *JAMA* 243: 43–45.

Dewar, D.M. (1997) Medical technology in the United States and Canada: where are we going? *Rev Soc Econ* LV(3): 359.

Dewar, D.M., Kurek, C., Lambrinos, J., Cohen, I., and Zhong, Y. (1999) Patterns in costs and outcomes for patients with prolonged mechanical ventilation undergoing tracheostomy: an analysis of discharges under diagnosis-related group 483 in New York State during 1992–1996, *Crit Care Med* 27(12): 2640–2647.

Dillingham, A.E. (1985) The influence of risk variable definition on value-of-life estimates, *Econ Inq* XXIII: 277.

Elpern, E.H., Larson, R., Douglass, P., Rosen, R.L., and Bone, R.C. (1989) Long term outcomes for elderly survivors of prolonged ventilator assistance, *Chest* 96: 1120.

Emanual, E.J. and Emanual, L.L. (1994) The economics of dying: the illusion of cost savings at the end of life, *N Engl J Med* 540.

Engelking, C. (1994) New approaches: innovations in cancer prevention, diagnosis, treatment, and support, *Oncol Nurs Forum* 21(1): 62.

Esserman, L., Belkoiz, J., and Lenert, L. (1995) Potentially ineffective care: a new outcome to assess the limits of critical care, *JAMA* 274(19): 1544–1551.

Ferrel, B.R. (1994) Ethical and professional issues in pain technology: a challenge to supportive care, *Sup Care Cancer* 2(1): 21.

Fisher, A., Chestnut, L.G., and Violette, D.M. (1988) The value of reducing risks of death: a note on new evidence, *J Policy Anal Manag* 8(1): 88.

Gillette, C.P. and Hopkins, T.R. (1988) *Federal Agency Valuations of Human Life: A Report to the Administrative Conference of the United States*, July 7.

Goodman, C.S. (1993) Technology assessment in healthcare: a means for pursuing the goals of biomedical engineering, *Med & Bio Engin Comp* 31(1): HTA3.

Gracey, D.R., Sillespie, D., Nobrega, F., Naessens, J.M., and Krishman, I. (1987) Financial implications of ventilatory care of Medicare patients under the prospective payment system, *Chest* 91: 4124.

Hamel, M.B., Philips, R.S., Teno, J.M., Lynn, J., Galanos, A.N., Davis, R.B., Connors, A.F., Oye, R.K., Desbiens, N., Reding, D.J., and Goldman, L. (1996) Seriously ill hospitalized adults: do we spend less on older patients? *JAGS* 44: 1043.

Jacobs, P. and Noseworthy, T.W. (1990) National estimates of intensive care utilization and costs: Canada and the United States, *Crit Care Med* 18: 1282.

Kenkel, D. (1994) Cost of illness approach, in G. Tolley, D. Kenkel, and R. Fabian (eds).

Knauss, W.A. (1989) Prognosis with mechanical ventilation: the influence of disease, severity of disease, age, and chronic health status on survival from acute illness, *Am Rev Respir Dis* 140: S8.

Kurek, C.J., Cohen, I.L., Lambrinos, J., Minatoya, K., Booth, F.V., and Chalfin, D.B. (1997) Clinical and economic outcomes of patients undergoing tracheostomy in New York State during 1993: analysis of 6353 cases under DRG 483, *Crit Care Med.*

Lamm, R.D. (1991) The brave new world of health care, *Ann Thorac Surg* 52(2): 369.

La Puma, J. and Lawlor, E.F. (1990) Quality-adjusted life-years: ethical implications for physicians and policymakers, *JAMA* 263(21): 2917–2921.

Marin, A. and Psacharopoulos, B. (1982) The reward for risk in the labor market: evidence from the United Kingdom and a reconciliation with other studies, *J Polit Econ* 90(4): 827.

Moore, M.J. and Viscusi, W.K. (1988) Doubling the estimated value of life: results using new occupational fatality data, *J Policy Anal Manag* 7(3): 476.

Nava, S., Evangelisti, I., Rampulla, C., Compagnoni, M.L., Fracchia, C., and Rubini, F. (1997) Human and financial costs of noninvasive mechanical ventilation in patients affected by COPD and acute respiratory failure, *Chest* 111(6): 1631–1638.

O'Brien, B. and Rushby, J. (1990) Outcome assessment in cardiovascular cost-benefit studies, *Am Heart J* 119: 740–748.

O'Donnell, A. and Bohner, B. (1991) The outcome in patients requiring prolonged mechanical ventilation, *Chest* 100: 29S.

O'Donohue Jr, W.J. (1992) Chronic ventilator-dependent units in hospitals: attacking the front end of a long-term problem (editorial), *Mayo Clinic Proceedings* 67: 198–200.

Olson, C. (1981) An analysis of wage differentials received by workers in dangerous jobs, *J Human Res* XVI(2): 167.

Pessau, B., Flager, S., Berger, E., Weimann, S., Schuster, E., Leithner, C., and Frass, M. (1992) Influence of age on outcome of mechanically ventilated patients in an intensive care unit, *Crit Care Med* 20: 489.

Rapaport, J., Gehlbach, S., Lemeshow, S., and Teres, D. (1992) Resource utilization among intensive care patients, *Arch Intern Med* 152: 2207.

Rosen, R.L. and Bone, R.C. (1990) Financial implications of ventilator care, *Crit Care Clin* 6: 797.

Schmidt, C.D., Elliott, C.G., Carmellu, D., et al. (1983) Prolonged mechanical ventilation for respiratory failure: a cost-benefit analysis, *Crit Care Med* 11: 407.

Sloan, F.A. (1995) *Valuing Health Care*, Cambridge: Cambridge University Press.

SCCM (Society of Critical Care Medicine) (1992) *Critical Care in the United States*. Anaheim CA.

Swinburne, A.J., Fedullo, A.J., and Shayne, D.S. (1988) Mechanical ventilation: analysis of increasing use and patient survival, *J Int Crit Care Med* 3: 315.

Swinburne, A.J., Fedullo, A.J., Bixby, K., Lee, D., and Wahl, D.W. (1993) Respiratory failure in the elderly. Analysis of outcomes after treatment with mechanical ventilation, *Arch Intern Med* 153: 1657.

Tolley, G., Kenkel, D., and Fabian, R. (1994) *Valuing Health for Policy: An Economic Approach*, Chicago: University of Chicago Press.

Tvesat, J., Dawson, N.V., and Matchar, D.B. (1990) Assessing quality of life and preferences in the seriously ill using utility theory, *J Clin Epidemiol* 43 (supplement): 73S–77S.

Tvesat, J., Cook, E.F., Green, M.L., Matchar, D.S., Dawson, N.V., Broste, S.K., Wu, A.W., Phillips, R.S., Oye, R.K., and Goldman, L. (1995) Health values of the seriously ill, *Ann Intern Med* 122(7): 514–520.

Tvesat, J., Dawson, N.V., Wu, A.W., Lynn, J., Soukup, J.R., Cook, E.F., Visaillet, H., and Phillips, R.S. (1998) Health values of hospitalized patients 80 years or older, *JAMA* 279(5): 371–375.

US Bureau of the Census (1993) *Statistical Abstract of the United States: 1993*, 113th edn, Washington DC.

Wagner, P. (1989) Economics of prolonged mechanical ventilation, *Am Rev Respir Dis* 140: 514.

Weeks, J. (1996) Taking quality of life into account in health economic analyses, *J Natl Cancer Inst Monog* 20: 23–27.

Appendix

Technical notes for economic evaluation of resources utilized under DRG 483

Multiple regression analysis is used to model the relationship between the age-specific survival rate (SR) for MCO and non-MCO patients with respect to age (in linear, quadratic, and cubic functional forms), payment source, demographics (gender and race), higher-risk diagnoses,[4] and admission type. Dummy variables for years 1993 through 1996 are also included to account for general systematic changes in utilization of this DRG and the associated mortality rates over time. The MCO variable will provide a general measure of any systematic difference in practice/treatment patterns relative to non-MCO payment systems. Interactions between the MCO indicator and age variables are explored to account for any self-selection into managed care that could affect the impact of managed care on survival rate for this DRG. The MCO indicator is a general indicator for any managed care delivery of services under public or private insurance plans. Stepwise regression with a split-half sample validation technique is used in selecting a model based on how well the model fits.[5] These expected survival rates are then used to estimate the expected payment per survivor at each age for MCO and non-MCO patients where:

$$(1)\quad \hat{PS}_{x,y} = (average - payment - per - discharge)/\hat{SR}_{x,y}$$

where: x = ages 19–95; y = MCO, non-MCO participation

A value of $120,000 per year of statistical life is used, and a life expectancy table is used to obtain the number of years of life remaining at each age. Since life expectancy is reported every five years beginning at age 65 until the age of 85, the specific life expectancies between 65 and 85 are obtained by interpolating linearly.

For the baseline value of life estimates, the number of years remaining for each patient is multiplied by this value of life estimate of $120,000. This is averaged by age for the MCO and non-MCO subpopulations, and yields an age-specific value of remaining life—the benefits of utilizing resources under DRG 483. Benefits received are then discounted by age adjustment weights, quality of life adjustment weights, and the combination of age and quality of life weights. Sensitivity analysis using average, lower- and upper-bound estimates of the value of extending life shows the range in quality of life adjusted benefits received among patients who may have continued complications after the inpatient episode. This demonstrates the robustness of the efficiency determinations (i.e. where the payments for resources utilized equal the benefits received).

The model below is chosen as the best predictive form for age-specific survival rate by age for the pooled data.[6]

$$(2)\quad \begin{aligned} SR_x = -2.0.78 &- \underset{(p<0.09)}{0.0378\ AGE} - \underset{(p<0.0001)}{0.0003\ AGE^2} + \underset{(p<0.0436)}{0.0429\ FEMALE} \\ &+ \underset{(p<0.0038)}{0.0236\ WHITE} - \underset{(p<0.0001)}{0.2424\ AFAMER} - \underset{(p<0.0001)}{0.3011\ EMERGADM} \end{aligned}$$

$$+ 0.0446\ TEACH - 0.0417\ MEDICARE + 0.5226\ SELFPAY$$
$$(p < 0.0924) \quad (p < 0.2620) \quad (p < 0.0001)$$
$$- 0.2046\ BCBS + 0.2474\ MEDCRE/OTHER + 0.3937\ MCO$$
$$(p < 0.0125) \quad (p < 0.0051) \quad (p < 0.045)$$
$$- 0.1374\ ELECTROL - 0.0283\ BACPNEUM$$
$$(p < 0.0001) \quad (p < 0.0008)$$
$$- 0.1091\ UNSPNEUM - 0.0980\ PLEURISY + 0.1098\ Y95$$
$$(p < 0.0015) \quad (p < 0.0001) \quad (p < 0.0001)$$
$$+ 0.2930\ Y96$$
$$(p < 0.0005)$$

Adj $R^2 = 0.77$

Age, as well as the dummy variables reflecting yearly systemic changes, payer source and higher-risk diagnoses—i.e. disorders of fluid, electrolyte, and acid-based balance (ELECTROL); other bacterial pneumonia (BACPNEUM); pneumonia, organism unspecified (UNSPNEUM), and pleurisy (PLEURISY) —account for most of the variation in survival rate. The impacts of MEDICARE and AGE are not independent given that age is a determinant of whether a person can participate in the Medicare program. Both are included for completeness of the model, with the focus on the MCO variable.

The age-specific predicted payment per survivor for the period is obtained by dividing the overall average payment per discharge during 1992–1996 by the predicted age-specific survival rate from equation (2).

$$(3)\quad PS_x = \$112{,}352/(- 2.078 - 0.0378\ AGE - 0.0003\ AGE^2$$
$$+ 0.0429\ FEMALE + 0.0236\ WHITE - 0.2424\ AFAMER$$
$$- 0.3011\ EMERGADM + 0.0446\ TEACH$$
$$- 0.0417\ MEDICARE + 0.5226\ SELFPAY - 0.2046\ BCBS$$
$$+ 0.2474\ MEDCRE/OTHER + 0.3937\ MCO$$
$$- 0.1374\ ELECTROL - 0.0283\ BACPNEUM$$
$$+ 0.1091\ UNSPNEUM - 0.0980\ PLEURISY + 0.1098\ Y95 +$$
$$0.2930\ Y96)$$

Notes

1 In 1997, the competitive hospital reimbursement methodology was implemented under the New York State Health Care Reform Act of 1996.

2 Other studies (Knauss 1989; O'Donohue 1992) have shown that only 16 to 25 percent of those on mechanical ventilation are on a ventilator after one week.

3 It should be noted that, for both groups, a fairly large percentage of patients were transferred to long-term care facilities or home health services, where additional costs are incurred that are not captured in the SPARCS data. Therefore, the measured payments for hospital-based acute care are likely to be a lower-bound estimate of the total payments associated with mechanical ventilator-based resource utilization during the study period.

4 The diagnoses were chosen in the following manner: over 5 percent of the discharges had this particular diagnosis category in any of the 14 diagnosis fields on their discharge abstracts; and the diagnosis category had at least a mortality rate that was 1.5 times the population mortality rate for the DRG. These diagnoses were both complications and comorbidities for the patients in this DRG, but all had the common feature that they greatly increased the risk of death.

5 The regressions are estimated on the population aged 80 and younger due to the low volume of patients aged 80 and over in the managed care group. The results of the regression estimation are then used to interpolate the expected benefits of utilizing resources under DRG 483 to age 95 for both the managed care and other payer source groups.

6 Interactive effects between age and MCO, as well as the variables for the years 1993 and 1994, upstate residence region and hospital teaching status, were also included but were not statistically significant predictors.

10

MEDICARE HMOs

The promise and the reality

Rose M. Rubin and Shelley White-Means

Introduction

Medicare is now bigger than General Motors and is the country's largest business-type organization, with spending equal to $212 billion in 1999 (US Department of Health and Human Services 2000). Spending $5,462 per beneficiary, Medicare accounts for about 3 percent of total US Gross Domestic Product (GDP). If its structure remains unchanged, Medicare is projected to account for 5.4 percent of GDP by 2025 (Kellison and Moon 1999). Medicare is growing at more than double the rate of increase of private health spending and over three times the rate of inflation. Yet, despite its size and rate of growth, Medicare spends less than one-half of 1 percent of its budget on research or systems to lower costs or improve quality (Nash 1996). It remains primarily a medical bill payer and, despite Diagnosis Related Groups (DRGs), has done little to flex its considerable financial muscle in health care markets.

One of the most successful and broadly supported US social programs, Medicare has succeeded in attaining its objective of providing access to health care for the elderly, but only at great cost in terms of resources and federal budget share. Due to its rapid growth, Medicare was for years the driving force of annual federal budget deficits; it also diverts resources from alternative uses and will become unaffordable within a decade. The program requires reform, and that can only be achieved by a limited number of strategies. These potential reform strategies include reducing provider payments, increasing beneficiary costs, significantly reducing inefficient or unnecessary delivery of care, or fundamental restructuring (Cutler 1997). The focus of this chapter is one of the critical restructuring approaches, the use of substantial managed care by enrollment of beneficiaries in Health Maintenance Organizations (HMOs). This alternative approach to financing and delivering Medicare includes shifting at least a substantial portion of the financial risk for Medicare beneficiaries to providers and payers.

Although private health care payers have used economic incentives and negotiating power to shift rapidly into managed care in recent years, Medicare has remained largely a bulwark of free choice and open-ended utilization. However, national patience with Medicare's voracious appetite for health care resources is wearing thin, as recognition of its rapidly increasing size and share of total federal spending has expanded. One of the most widely recognized actions for breaking the continuing Medicare cost spiral is more widespread utilization of managed care.

This chapter provides an overview of Medicare managed care with emphasis on differentiating the promise of expected benefits from the reality of declining participation. The next section provides a background perspective on the substantial changes occurring as increasing numbers of beneficiaries participate in HMOs. Sections three and four provide discussions of enrollment patterns and the financing of Medicare HMOs. The findings of recent studies of access and outcomes are presented in the fifth section, and the pros and cons of HMOs for Medicare enrollees are distilled in the sixth. The final section outlines some policy implications of the growth and disbursement of Medicare HMO enrollment.

Background

Since its inception in 1965, Medicare has encompassed managed care options. In 1970, the Nixon administration became alarmed by unanticipated cost increases and introduced a further step toward Medicare participation in HMOs. The 'health maintenance strategy' was developed to provide a choice for enrollees, which was followed by the employee-oriented 1973 HMO Act (Ellwood and Lundberg 1996). However, little progress occurred, as the HMO delivery systems were not prepared to incorporate the older, potentially sicker Medicare population and the elderly were not inclined to shift away from free choice, low cost coverage. In addition, HMOs were oriented to marketing their services to employer groups, but rarely to individuals. Thus, even though the federal government has supported the enrollment of Medicare beneficiaries in HMOs since the 1970s, participation was quite limited prior to implementation of the Tax Equity and Fiscal Responsibility Act of 1982 (TEFRA) under Pres-ident Reagan.

Beginning in 1985, a full-risk HMO option for Medicare beneficiaries was implemented under TEFRA. This risk-contracting program encouraged prospective capitation payment for Medicare with the objective of promoting HMO enrollment. The goal was reversal of the fee-for-service (FFS) incentives toward the provision of more services and cost containment by shifting the risk to the HMO provider (Clement et al. 1994). By the late 1990s, more plans became risk contractors; Medicare enrollees joined risk-based plans in record numbers; and managed care organizations recognized their particular ability to facilitate outcomes accountability to refine their caregiving (Ellwood and Lundberg 1996). Although Medicare beneficiaries agree to being 'locked in' to HMOs for some enrollment period, some HMOs now permit access to non-network providers by offering 'point of service' (POS) options (Zarabozo et al. 1996).

The Balanced Budget Act of 1997 (BBA) legislated Medicare+Choice, a replacement for the risk-contracting program, effective from 1999. Medicare+Choice establishes new rules for beneficiary and plan participation, as well as a new payment method (MedPAC 1998). The expanded choices include broader managed care options. The traditional coverage under Medicare HMOs is continued, but with the additional choices of HMOs with point of service options, Medicare preferred provider organizations (PPOs), and provider sponsored organizations (PSOs). Medicare beneficiaries can choose to remain in fee-for-service arrangements, and a limited number (390,000) may elect to participate in restricted Medical Savings Accounts (MSAs). In addition, some may select private fee-for-service plans (private insurance plans that accept Medicare beneficiaries) or insurance plans offered by religious fraternal benefit societies (HCFA 1999).

Enrollment

Medicare enrollment in full-risk HMOs and other competitive medical plans (CMPs) increased steadily for a decade following the 1982 implementation of TEFRA. The growth of Medicare risk contract enrollment has exceeded the increase in non-Medicare private sector HMO enrollment since 1989 (Henry J. Kaiser Family Foundation 1995). By 1994, the rate of growth was double that for HMO enrollment of those under age 65. The trend of growth acceleration in the 1990s is expected to continue (Meyer et al. 1996; Lamphere et al. 1997). Figure 10.1 shows the actual and projected growth of risk plan enrollment from 1987 to 2007, indicating that enrollment is projected approximately to triple within the next decade.

By 1997, about 14 percent of Medicare beneficiaries had chosen enrollment in HMOs (Riley et al. 1997), which approached the amount projected for 1998. Almost four million Medicare participants were enrolled in about 250 managed care plans, an increase from just over 150 plans in 1988 (Gornick et al. 1996). For many years, enrollment in HMOs was open for new enrollees or switchers only once a year, so enrollees were tied to their HMO enrollment decision for at least a year. This regulation has been changed, giving enrollees much more flexibility. Beneficiaries may now switch from risk-based plans to FFS upon written notification at any time (Meyer et al. 1996). Generally, HMO enrollees are locked in to utilization of plan providers, but some Medicare HMOs have begun offering expanded service delivery options to enrollees since 1996. These systems allow point of service (POS) options that permit the use of non-network providers (Zarabozo et al. 1996).

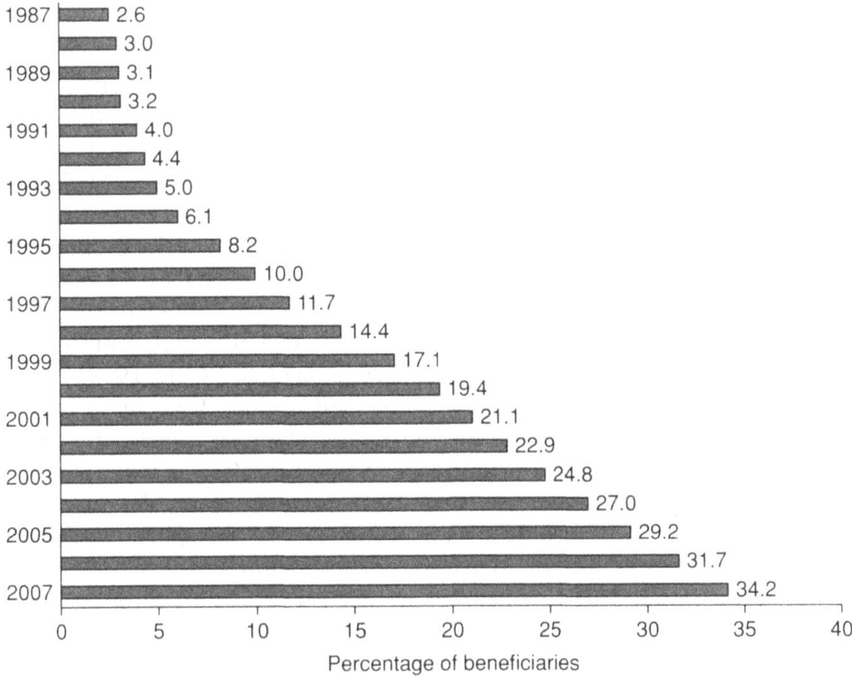

Figure 10.1 Medicare risk plan enrollment as a percentage of total beneficiaries: 1987–1996 actual and 1997–2007 projected (source: Jo Ann Lamphere, Patricia Neuman, Kathryn Langwell, and Daniel Sherman, 1997, The surge in Medicare managed care: an update, *Health Affairs* 16(3): 127–133)

Prior to the BBA, HMO enrollment remained geographically concentrated with 25 percent of subscribers in just five counties (Zarabozo et al. 1996). Six states—California, Florida, Pennsylvania, New York, Arizona and Texas—encompassed 70 percent of Medicare risk enrollment (Lamphere et al. 1997). Three-quarters of beneficiaries lived in areas served by a Medicare managed care plan, and the majority of these had at least two plan choices available (Zarabozo et al. 1996). The thirteen states without Medicare risk-based enrollment shared the characteristics of being rural with low population density, having low average Medicare payments, and underserved populations (Lamphere et al. 1997).

Following implementation of the BBA, Medicare enrollment in managed care increased substantially. In the first nine months of 1998, 70,000 beneficiaries per month enrolled in managed care. By September 1998, 6.5 million beneficiaries (17.2 percent of the Medicare population) were enrolled; but by May 1999, only six million or 16.4 percent of beneficiaries were enrolled (Coalition for Medicare Choices 1999). This decline occurred as numerous managed care organizations withdrew from the program due to inadequate Medicare reimbursements.

The high degree of beneficiary managed care concentration shifted notably following enactment of the BBA, as the potential of this market became more fully recognized (MedPAC 1998). A noticeable increase occurred in rural areas that were adjacent to urban areas. Between 1997 and 1998, enrollment rates increased from 1 to 3 percent. There were 307 Medicare risk contracts in 1997 and 346 by 1998. MedPAC (1998) also noted that between 1996 and 1998 the proportion of Medicare beneficiaries with at least one managed care organization available rose from 65 to 72 percent. However, from 1998 to 1999 the number of Medicare+Choice contracts declined by over 10 percent to 310 contracts. The projected number of Medicare risk contracts for 2000 was 269 (Kronfield and Gold 1999).

From an enrollee perspective, managed care options have increasingly been recognized as a viable insurance option by Medicare beneficiaries, because these options provide a broad range of benefits, often at lower out-of-pocket cost than traditional care. One 1997 estimate places the potential out-of-pocket savings to beneficiaries in the range of $700–$900 (Coalition for Medicare Choices 1999). Managed care providers are more likely to provide prescription drug benefits that are not covered by traditional plans. This potentially expensive benefit is of particular value to the elderly or disabled. In addition, managed care providers may offer early detection of life-threatening medical conditions through emphasis on preventive care. Some routine coverages not offered under traditional providers, such as dental, hearing, or eye care, may be included by managed care providers.

> From a provider perspective, Medicare beneficiaries are increasingly recognized as a viable market segment for HMOs, as three of the five largest HMOs in the country are among the five largest Medicare risk contractors. In the earlier years of Medicare risk contracting there was rapid turnover among contractors, but this has changed with the role of the larger, more stable HMOs increasing. From 1990 to 1996, the number of risk contracts doubled, increasing by 24 percent in 1995. By 1996, there were only nine states without Medicare risk HMOs (two of which were served by neighboring state HMOs).
>
> (Zarabozo et al. 1996)

Medicare beneficiaries who select HMO options appear to be a somewhat defined group, compared with those who opt for FFS. Medicare HMO enrollees generally self-define to be in better health than non-HMO enrollees, with 50 percent of HMO enrollees rating their health as excellent or very good, compared to 39 percent of FFS enrollees. Enrollees are less likely to be limited in their activities of daily living (ADLs) than the FFS Medicare elderly (Eppig and Poisal 1996). Enrollees at the highest income levels tend to select FFS. Those at the lowest income levels are unlikely to choose HMOs, and dually eligible beneficiaries (i.e. those with both Medicare and Medicaid eligibility) are significantly less likely to enroll in HMOs than Medicare beneficiaries in general. The share of institutionalized beneficiaries under managed care is only about 1 percent, compared with 5 to 6 percent of the general Medicare population.

Riley et al. (1997) analyzed HMO disenrollment of beneficiaries. Using the Medicare Enrollment Data Base, they found a disenrollment rate of slightly over 14 percent in 1994. However, only 38 percent of disenrollees shifted to FFS, with the remainder switching to another HMO. Those who disenrolled to FFS were likely to be age 80+, black, dual-eligible (i.e. Medicaid eligible), and recent enrollees. Over one-quarter of those shifting had been enrolled for only three months and disenrollment was highly concentrated geographically. A Families USA study found a 1996 disenrollment rate of 13 percent, and HMOs with the lowest rates tended to be large non-profit plans with long business histories and stable membership patterns. The study discovered wide variations in dropout rates and suggestions of deceptive advertising as motivating disenrollment rates (Elderly find . . . 1997).

Financing

Before implementation of the BBA, the Health Care Financing Administration (HCFA) funded three types of contracts for Medicare HMO coverage: risk contracts, cost contracts, and health care prepayment plans. HMOs were permitted to charge a monthly premium not greater than the actuarial value of the deductibles and coinsurance that would be paid under FFS. However, only one-third charged extra premiums, with those not charging a monthly premium providing a cost advantage for enrollees. The average monthly premium in 1997 was $13.52, a decline from $32.00 in a two-year period (Henry J. Kaiser Family Foundation 1997; Lamphere et al. 1997).

HMOs must provide all services covered by Medicare and may offer additional benefits. Most Medicare HMOs do offer extra benefits, with the most important being inclusion of coverage of outpatient prescription drugs, which are not covered under standard Medicare (Gornick et al. 1996), and other coverages such as prescription eyewear. The percentages of risk plans that offer additional benefits vary with the type of benefit: 96 percent offer annual physicals, 91 percent offer eye exams, 86 percent offer immunizations, 74 percent offer ear exams, 69 percent offer outpatient prescription drugs, 39 percent offer dental care, and 31 percent offer foot care (Henry J. Kaiser Family Foundation 1997). Another financial advantage of HMOs is the elimination of enrollees' need for supplemental Medigap coverage.

Initially, prepaid Medicare plans participated only in Part B, covering physician and supplier services on a cost basis. The Social Security Act

(1972) amendments expanded HMO coverage to both Parts A and B, allowing either a cost basis or a risk-sharing basis. Enrollees in risk HMOs must be enrolled in both Medicare Part A and Part B. The TEFRA provisions, implemented in 1985, established the pre-BBA HMO payment methodology. Under TEFRA, risk contracts provided a prospective payment capitated rate of 95 percent of the average adjusted per capita cost (AAPCC) for a Medicare beneficiary.

The AAPCC was based on estimates of what Medicare would have expended for HMO enrollees under FFS coverage. It was set prospectively and adjusted by geographic area, age, sex, Medicaid and institutional status of the beneficiary. Because the AAPCC was based on a county-by-county estimate of Medicare cost per enrollee in the FFS sector, payments varied widely. For example, the AAPCC ranged from $350 monthly in Portland, Oregon, to $615 in Dade County, Florida (Henry J. Kaiser Family Foundation 1995). AAPCC payments encompassed 54 percent of Medicare HMOs and covered 7 percent of Medicare beneficiaries.

Mills (1996) concluded that the AAPCC 'easily covers the medical cost for well managed seniors leaving an opportunity for profit' (278). This conclusion was supported by the data on enrollment and payment growth. Annual Medicare payments per risk contract enrollee increased from $2,497 in 1988 to $4,213 in 1995, at a 5.5 percent annual compound growth rate. During this period, the total number of Medicare enrollees increased from 1.1 to 2.9 million, while total payments increased from $2.6 billion to $12.2 billion, an annual growth rate of almost 24 percent (Gornick et al. 1996).

As a development incentive, risk contract managed care providers, including Medicare HMOs, were not required to support graduate medical education (GME), which provided a substantial cost competitive advantage. In 1982, the law was revised to permit risk-contract HMOs to retain profits up to the level earned on non-Medicare subscribers. Profits exceeding this level had to be returned to enrollees either as payment reductions (i.e. reduced cost-sharing) or as enhanced benefits.

The second type of HMO coverage, cost contracts, paid the HMO for actual service and administrative costs. These cover 13 percent of HMO contractors. Enrollees under cost contracts were permitted to seek care outside of the HMO at Medicare's expense. Health Care Prepayment Plans, the third form of risk contract, paid HMOs on a cost basis only for physician and other outpatient services and cover 33 percent of contractors. Some 2 percent of Medicare beneficiaries were covered under cost contracts and prepayment plans (Meyer et al. 1996).

In December 1995, Medicare paid risk HMOs $1.3 billion, which was 9 percent of total Medicare outlays. The average monthly payment was $440 per enrollee. Based on their revenue and expected coverage expenditures, most HMOs provided more generous benefits and reduced out-of-pocket expenses to Medicare enrollees than traditional providers. Thus, HMO enrollees have generally had reduced out-of-pocket expenditures for covered services and often receive services not otherwise covered, including prescription drugs in 60 percent of plans.

All Medicare beneficiaries paid the monthly Part B premium, and those with Medigap policies paid additional premiums, averaging $1,200 in 1996 (Armbrister 1996). Those in risk contract plans sometimes also paid a monthly premium, ranging from $0 to $111 per month, but the average premium of $22 was lower than that for a typical Medigap policy (Henry J. Kaiser Family Foundation 1995). Almost two-thirds of risk plans provided a basic package with zero premiums (Zarabozo et al. 1996).

A payment transition period, 1998–2002, was created under the BBA, Section 1853(c), in order to shift from the area-specific AAPCC rates to a blend of regional and national rates with a floor (Dacso and Dacso 1999). In the initial transition period the payment rate is equal to the greatest of three options: a blended capitation rate, a minimum monthly payment amount (floor), or the 1997 AAPCC adjusted by an annual 2 percent growth rate. In 1998, 60 percent of the counties operated under option three and the rest received the minimum monthly payment amount.

Since passage of the BBA, the adjusted AAPCC Medicare plan rates have been determined by a complex formula, based on the county of residence and primarily reflecting the past distribution of Medicare spending. In 1998, the minimum monthly per capita county payment rate was $367. Medicare payments are risk-adjusted to reflect differential patterns of health care utilization among beneficiaries. Risk factors include age, sex, institutional status, employment status, and Medicaid eligibility. The risk-adjusted payment rate is determined by multiplying the unadjusted county payment rate by the beneficiary risk adjustment factor (MedPAC 1998).

Access and outcomes

The results of several empirical studies demonstrate the differences and similarities between treatments and outcomes of Medicare patients in HMO and traditional FFS systems. Recently developed national health care databases and the ability of HMOs to provide data for outcomes accountability, as well as growing policy interest in the ability of managed care to control Medicare costs, have facilitated comparative research studies.

The Physician Payment Review Commission surveyed 3,080 Medicare beneficiaries enrolled in a risk plan in 1996, finding that 15 percent reported that they were in fair or poor health. Three-quarters of the enrollees indicated that they would recommend their plan to a family member or friend with serious or chronic health problems (Henry J. Kaiser Family Foundation 1997). HMO enrollees have been shown to receive more preventive services than those under FFS. For example, substantially more had flu shots, mammograms, and pap smears under HMOs than FFS (Eppig and Poisal 1996).

Clement et al. (1994) compared access and outcomes of a national random sample of Medicare patients enrolled in HMOs and FFS plans. They reported several differences: HMO enrollees were less likely to see a specialist, less likely to report recommendation of follow-up care or subsequent monitoring. While the differences observed indicated less intensive HMO care, outcomes for both groups were similar for three of the four measures analyzed.

Several studies have analyzed the outcomes of managed care enrollees, compared to outcomes for fee-for-service beneficiaries. Ware et al. (1996) compared both physical and mental health outcomes of the chronically ill under HMOs and FFS systems. They found that for Medicare patients, the elderly in HMOs were nearly twice as likely to decline in physical health during the four-year study period as those in FFS plans, regardless of their initial health. However, the results for mental health favored HMOs over FFS; the elderly in an HMO were twice as likely to improve. Overall, they concluded that elderly (and also poor) chronically ill patients had worse outcomes under HMOs than under FFS.

Access to managed care benefits by low-income and elderly enrollees has also been evaluated. Kilborn (1998) notes the presence of a selection process among HMOs that results in withdrawals of HMOs from service provision in areas with large concentrations of either poor or elderly persons. As a result, these groups suffer loss of choice of service providers. However, Lille-Blanton and Lyons (1998) report that low-income populations (whether covered by managed care or FFS) do not differ in their access to a usual source of care, a regular provider, or emergency rooms. They found that managed care enrollees who were in fair or poor health were more likely to put off needed care, compared to those in fee-for-service. These managed care enrollees were also more likely to report problems in obtaining medications or specialty care. Similarly, Davis et al. (1999) concluded that managed care providers may skimp on care for patients who are chronically ill.

Access differentials for low-income populations have also been looked at from the perspectives of race and ethnicity. Leigh et al. (1996) found that neither African-American nor Hispanic managed care beneficiaries differed from their FFS counterparts in access to a usual source of care or a regular provider. However, African-Americans did differ in terms of receiving needed care, as those under managed care contract were less likely to obtain the needed care. Conversely, low-income whites under managed care were found to have greater access to care than low-income whites under FFS.

The HMO experience of non-elderly disabled Medicare beneficiaries was studied by Gold et al. (1997) from a special telephone survey of this group. Compared to disabled FFS beneficiaries, disabled Medicare HMO enrollees tend to be considerably older and less likely to be institutionalized or to be covered under a Medicaid buy-in. Compared to elderly HMO enrollees, non-elderly disabled HMO enrollees are more likely to be male, to be African-American, to be in low income households, and to be new enrollees. Further, they are more likely to report fair or poor health. These factors indicate that the relative costs and benefits of HMOs have particular appeal to the non-elderly disabled as motivating factors to overcome their access problems and financial barriers to care in FFS settings.

There are numerous issues still to be resolved by empirical studies as the numbers of Medicare enrollees grow to a sufficient mass for more comprehensive analysis. The empirical studies to date demonstrate the importance of longer term studies, especially for the chronically ill, and the importance of over-sampling the elderly and poor in comparative outcomes studies (Ware et al. 1996).

The reality of Medicare HMOs

The shift from rapid growth of Medicare participation in risk HMOs to recent declines was driven by the transition from relatively high Medicare payment rates to rates that did keep pace with inflation. As the growth of managed care enrollment of the employed population peaked, managed care providers first perceived the Medicare population to be an avenue for expansion. However, the legislative changes in the BBA have reduced the profitability of serving Medicare managed care participants. While numerous questions remain regarding the future impacts of risk-based health care for the elderly, the advantages and disadvantages of their growth can be weighed.

Pros

There are both societal and private (individual and business) advantages and disadvantages of Medicare HMOs. At the societal level, managed care systems have the capacity to provide data tracking and analysis of population groups, as well as of potential groups for controlled medical studies. They have the ability to provide preventive care and monitoring. They can institute health promotion programs and provide enrollee health education or develop outcomes measures and clinical protocols. They can also accomplish rational resource management, for example by providing home care more widely as an alternative to hospitalization, or by providing prescription drugs on an outpatient basis rather than only on an inpatient basis, as is done by standard Medicare. Such approaches may reduce hospitalizations and create more appropriate health care resource allocation patterns, without reductions in health or patient satisfaction.

One important potential use of HMO data systems is the ability to track underserved enrollees and to identify persons who need specific care, but are not receiving it. Many such services are oriented to prevention and their extension can result in measurable cost savings. An example of such a procedure is notification, or sending reminders to a covered HMO population to take advantage of Medicare coverage of flu shots at the appropriate time. Another example is the use of HMO service data to track diabetics' regular retinal and foot examinations (Fox 1997).

Because about 15 percent of Medicare beneficiaries are 'dual-eligible' with their premiums and other health costs paid by Medicaid, structural changes in Medicare will affect Medicaid costs. If increased numbers of Medicare participants elect or are directed toward HMOs with little or no cost sharing, the cost burden on Medicaid may be reduced. Further, if the use of HMOs succeeds in improving preventive care and maintaining ADLs, institutionalization to nursing homes may be reduced. This could provide cost-effective rationalization of health care resources and major savings to Medicaid, which bears almost half of all nursing home costs. However, governmental and paperwork institutional barriers remain significant for dual eligible participation in HMOs, which appear to discourage their enrollment. Dual-eligible beneficiaries are two-thirds less likely to enroll in HMOs than Medicare beneficiaries as a group (Zarabozo et al. 1996).

HMOs also provide potential advantages to individual participants. Enrollees in HMOs generally receive more preventive services (e.g. flu shots, mammograms, Pap smears) than those in Medicare FFS (Eppig and Poisal 1996). Since HMOs provide built-in Medigap coverage, they are generally less expensive, requiring moderate or no out-of-pocket premiums, and may include otherwise uncovered items, most notably outpatient prescription drugs. They also minimize the paperwork required of enrollees, in contrast to the often onerous amount of paperwork and forms required for standard Medicare reimbursement. Managed care also provides the setting for coordination of both medical care and medical records, which may not occur under traditional multi-point delivery systems. This can be of particular importance to the elderly, who are likely to see multiple providers and to take numerous prescriptions initiated from different sources. In addition, there are advantages in Medicare HMOs for employers that provide retiree health care coverage. Firms can reduce their liability under Financial Accounting Statement (FAS) 106 by being able to calculate their retiree health costs in advance. Such reductions have been calculated at 50 to 100 percent for each retiree who enrolls in a Medicare HMO (HCFA urges employers . . . 1993).

Cons

The move of Medicaid and Medicare to managed care may have the unintended effect of shifting resources away from the traditional health care systems that have had responsibility for providing public health and indigent care. The growth and profitability (for for-profits) of numerous managed care entities are based on the existing, often not-for-profit and taxpayer supported health care infrastructure (Showstack et al. 1996). Evidence is mounting that the continued growth of managed care has negative impacts on the public safety net, as profit or surplus margins are reduced and the potential for cost shifting declines.

An area of potential concern for elderly HMO participants is the limited experience of HMOs in dealing with frail and chronically ill patients. Thus, special concerns exist with the ability of managed care to meet the needs of the most vulnerable Medicare population.

For individuals, one of the earlier problems encountered with HMOs was often the lack of relevant information or the inability to perceive and ask relevant questions at enrollment. For example, an individual may have been successfully using a specific prescription medication for some time, only to discover that it was not included in the formulary of his/her HMO. It is not unusual for switching medications or even brands to have unanticipated effects on the health of elderly patients (Jeffrey 1997). Further, there may be substantial differences and limitations in prescription coverage among HMOs. Following passage of the BBA, this information issue has been ameliorated, as education and counseling services about coverage options are mandated.

An additional issue of Medicare managed care for low income beneficiaries is the greater likelihood that managed care organizations will withdraw service provision from areas where they reside. This may result in a relatively greater concentration of low income beneficiaries in the FFS system, generating a two-tier system.

Policy implications

In the face of previously uncontrolled cost escalation, Medicare is in the process of testing new formats that may lead to broader structural change. This process is part of Medicare's evolution from almost exclusively traditional and fee-for-service providers to a broader array of beneficiary choices. The outcomes of this evolution are expected to be a more organized set of providers with more appropriate services provided and with greater selection opportunities for participants.

One of the most important benefits of expanded Medicare managed care is the further development of databases and empirical analyses of the efficacy of procedures or protocols. Large HMOs have both the capital and the incentive to develop and utilize management information systems for efficiency and improved delivery. These potentialities are just beginning to be realized and provide the basis for further development of scientific studies of protocols, of procedure or medicine efficacy, of delivery efficiency, and of quality and accountability measures. Evaluating health care services, measuring outcomes, and developing systems for accountability can generate both cost containment and quality improvement.

Medicare risk contract HMOs accomplished a provider objective that was widely predicted—they succeeded in enrolling relatively healthy beneficiaries.

Consequently, the payments to these HMOs were higher than they would have been if these beneficiaries had been under the traditional Medicare program. While this increased the attractiveness of Medicare patients to providers, anticipated Medicare savings were not realized. This problem was tackled by reimbursement changes instituted under the BBA. However, this approach had the unintended consequence of reducing the number of Medicare managed care organizations to 1996 levels.

Managed care enrollment may not solve the financial solvency issues for Medicare. In the light of recent declines in Medicare managed care enrollment, additional funding options will have to be identified to promote the attractiveness of Medicare enrollees as clients. The Medicare problem for the long term may lie not in efficiency or cost-containment, but in generating adequate revenues (Feder and Moon 1998). Even though costs per patient are contained by managed care organizations, the sheer numbers of future beneficiaries in relation to the number of tax-paying supporters may overwhelm the ability of the system even to fund efficient needed care. As the ratio of working supporters to beneficiaries declines, continued growth in the number of eligible beneficiaries threatens the viability of the equation.

Much of the promise of Medicare managed care has yet to be realized, but the foundations for cost containment, and beneficiary and provider acceptance are well under way. The critical issue is implementation of managed care reimbursement rates that will assure the provision of quality preventive and acute health care. For the long term, Medicare reimbursement will need to promote wide-scale provider acceptance with payments that adapt to the demographic and health characteristics of an aging and long-lived group.

References

Armbrister, Trevor (1996) An answer to the Medicare mess, *Reader's Digest* 149(12): 129–133.

Clement, Dolores G., Retchin, Sheldon M., Brown, Randal S., and Stegall, Meri-Beth H. (1994) Access and outcomes of elderly patients enrolled in managed care, *Journal of the American Medical Association* 271(19): 1487–1492.

Coalition for Medicare Choices (1999) Keeping your out-of-pocket costs low. Available at http://www.medicarechoices.org/outofpock.htm.

Cutler, David M. (1997) Restructuring Medicare for the future, in Robert D. Reischauer (ed.) *Setting National Priorities*, Washington DC: The Brookings Institution.

Dacso, Sheryl and Dacso, Clifford (1999) *Managed Care Answer Book*, 3rd edn, New York: Aspen Publishers.

Davis, Karen, Collins, Karen, and Hall, Allyson (1999) *Community Health Centers in a Changing U.S. Health Care System*, Policy Brief, The Commonwealth Fund. Available at http://www.cmwf.org/programs/minority davis_ushealthcenters_ 300.asp.

Elderly find some Medicare HMOs fall short, study shows (1997) *Pensacola News Journal*, December 5: 12A.

Ellwood Jr, P.M. and Lundberg, G.D. (1996) Managed care—a work in progress, *Journal of the American Medical Association*, 276(13) (October 2): 1083–1086.

Eppig, F.J. and Poisal, J.A. (1996) MCBS highlights—Medicare FFS populations versus HMO populations: 1993, *Health Care Financing Review*, 17(3) (Spring): 263–267.

Feder, Judith and Moon, Marilyn (1998) Managed care for the elderly: a threat or a promise? *Generations* (Summer). Available at http://www.asaging.org/generations/gen-22-2/gen-22-2-toc.html.

Fox, Peter D. (1997) Applying managed care techniques in traditional Medicare, *Health Affairs* 16(5): 44–57.

Gold, Marsha, Nelson, Lyle, Brown, Randall, Ciemnecki, Anne, Aizer, Anna, and Docteur, Elizabeth (1997) Disabled Medicare beneficiaries in HMOs, *Health Affairs* 16(5): 149–162.

Gornick, Marian E., Warren, Joan L., Eggers, Paul W., Lubitz, James D., De Lew, Nancy, Davis, Margaret H., and Cooper, Barbara S. (1996) Thirty years of Medicare: impact on the covered population, *Health Care Financing Review*, 18(2) (Winter): 179–237.

HCFA (Health Care Financing Administration) (1999) *Medicare & You 2000*, Washington DC: HCFA.

HCFA urges employers to direct retirees to Medicare HMOs (1993) *Employee Benefit Plan Review* 47(7): 52–53.

Henry J. Kaiser Family Foundation (1995) *Medicare & Managed Care* (May), Menlo Park, CA.

—— (1997) *Medicare Chart Book* (June), The Kaiser Medicare Policy Project, Menlo Park, CA.

Jeffrey, Nancy Ann (1997) Seniors in Medicare HMOs should know the drugs that prescription plans cover, *Wall Street Journal* (May 16): C1.

Kellison, Stephen and Moon, Marilyn (1999) Status of the social security and Medicare programs: a summary of the 1999 annual reports, social security and Medicare boards of trustees, Washington DC: HCFA. Available at http://www.ssa.gov/OACT/TRSUM/trsummary.html.

Kilborn, Peter T. (1998) Largest HMO's cutting the poor and the elderly: a managed-care retreat, *New York Times* (July 5). Available at http://www.globalaging.org/elderrtslkilborn.htm.

Kronfield, Thomas and Gold, Marsha (1999) Is there more or less choice? *Monitoring Medicare+Choice Fast Facts*, Washington DC: Mathematica Policy Research, Inc. Available at http://www.Mathematica-mpr.com/med+choicehot.htm.

Lamphere, Jo Ann, Neuman, Patricia, Langwell, Kathryn, and Sherman, Daniel (1997) The surge in Medicare managed care: an update, *Health Affairs* 16(3): 127–133.

Leigh, Wilhelmilna A., Lille-Blanton, Marsha, Martinez, Rose Marie, and Collins, Karen Scott (1996) Managed care in three states: experiences of low-income African Americans and Hispanics, *Inquiry* 36: 318–331.

Lillie-Blanton, Marsha and Lyons, Barbara (1998) Managed care and low-income populations: recent state experiences, *Health Affairs* 17 (May–June): 238–247.

MedPAC (Medicare Payment Advisory Commission) (1998) Health care spending and the Medicare program: a data book, July, Washington DC: MedPAC.

Meyer, Jack A., Silow-Carroll, Sharon, and Regenstein, Marsha (1996) *Managed Care and Medicare*, Washington DC: Public Policy Institute, American Association of Retired Persons (August) 9614.

Mills, Patrick J. (1996) Arbitrage opportunity: Medicare HMOs are on the rise, *Missouri Medicine* 93(6): 278–280.

Nash, David B. (1996) *Reforming Medicare: Strategies for Higher Quality, Lower Cost Care*. Washington DC: Public Policy Institute, American Association of Retired Persons (December) 9621.

Riley, Gerald, Ingber, Melvin, and Tudor, Cynthia (1997) Disenrollment of Medicare beneficiaries from HMOs, *Health Affairs* 16(5): 117–124.

Showstack, Jonathan, Lurie, Nicole, Leatherman, Shelia, Fisher, Elliott, and Inui, Thomas (1996) Health of the public—the private-sector challenge, *Journal of the American Medical Association* 276(13): 1071–1074.

US Department of Health and Human Services (2000) *1999 HCFA Statistics*, Washington DC: Health Care Financing Administration, Office of Financial Management. Available at http://www.hcfa.gov/stats.

Ware Jr, John E., Bayliss, Martha S., Rogers, William H., Kosinski, Mark, and Tarlov, Alvin R. (1996) Differences in 4-year health outcomes for elderly and poor, chronically ill patients treated in HMO and FFS systems—results from the medical outcomes study, *Journal of the American Medical Association* 276(13): 1039–1047.

Zarabozo, Carlos, Taylor, Charles, and Hicks, Janet (1996) Medicare managed care: numbers and trends, *Health Care Financing Review* 17(3) (Spring): 243–261.

Part IV

THE CHALLENGE OF TECHNOLOGY

11

SAFEGUARDING GENETIC INFORMATION

Privacy, confidentiality, and security?

Robert F. Rizzo

Introduction

In an age of computer networks, the United States faces the challenge of protecting the privacy, confidentiality and security of genetic information. It is part of a larger challenge of safeguarding personal information from prying eyes. Will the nation have the wisdom and the fortitude to meet it? Concern over these issues has prompted much discussion and written commentaries. Although 'privacy' and 'confidentiality' often have the same meaning in common parlance, they do have specific meanings (Cushman 1996). The right to privacy means the right to be free from unjustified governmental restrictions of one's basic rights (see *Griswold vs. Connecticut* 1965). The right of privacy applies directly to personal zones that involve the exercise of fundamental rights. Confidentiality refers to the duties that individuals and institutions assume under an implicit or explicit contractual relationship to individuals when they possess information received in their professional capacity. Confidentiality, therefore, embodies obligations to protect the information relating to those personal zones, which the right of privacy embraces. 'Security' covers the various ways used to preserve personal data from unauthorized inspection and use.

Current threats to privacy

Despite the discussion and a collection of federal and state laws, the movement to more comprehensive statutes and regulations has been frustratingly slow in view of what is now occurring. So extensive is the intrusion that financial, medical, consumer, familial, and workplace privacy is in jeopardy (see Dowd 1997). No one would claim that efforts to make electronic files more secure are not worthwhile. But it will take the best technology, personnel, and a great deal of money to establish a foolproof system that will store and manage computerized data, while at the same time monitoring its use over networks. In any area where the prospect of profit looms large, there will be not only the temptation but also attempts to break the system, utilizing sophisticated and costly methods. Anyone who doubts the power of profit as a motive ignores the lessons of history. The economic cost-benefit analysis will tilt in favor of committing intrusion and running the risk of being caught if the financial rewards are perceived to be promising.

An historical perspective

In view of the development of a health care 'system' in the United States since the turn of the twentieth century, there is the real possibility that the profit motive may induce some to circumvent laws and regulations to gain access to personal medical data. This is not unexpected in view of the fact that profit has become an important consideration in health care (see Rizzo 1993, 1999). Since the reform of medicine and medical schools in the early part of the twentieth century, the health care products and treatments created by medical and other scientific research are regarded as commodities to be sold and purchased. Since 1945, physicians have become increasingly less dependent on direct payments from patients and private foundations and more reliant on external funding from philanthropies, government, investors, commercial banks and insurance companies to support technological and scientific medicine. Consequently they are more subject to pressure from these sources for a profitable living. In addition, they are more dependent on pharmaceutical companies for the application of research through drug therapy, becoming the bridge for the marketing of the industry's products, with both parties reaping the financial benefits. As a result, economics and politics emerged as two powerful factors in shaping the health care system (Brown 1979). A century-long development has led to the commercialization of health care. As one analyst (Emanuel 1997) states, there is the need to reassess whether commercialization promotes or undermines efficiency, quality and social values in some areas of health care. The need becomes more relevant in examining the implications of genetic testing and therapy.

With advances in biotechnology, the system faces challenges that threaten its capacity to deliver care and protect the interests of patients and their families. In a special symposium, *Oncology and Genetics in the Community*, Henry T. Lynch, MD, a leading researcher in establishing the genetic basis of specific colorectal, breast, and ovarian cancers, emphasized the increasing complexity of cancer genetics in terms of clinical, molecular, socioeconomic, and ethical dimensions (Jewler and Egan 1997). Lynch posed troubling questions that must be kept in focus to appreciate the challenges to health care, a system now struggling with problems of delivery, malpractice, negligence, and commercial interests. These are specific issues relating to strategies for monitoring the progress of patients who have tested positive for hereditary cancers and the effectiveness of preventive measures. Physicians face the issue of advising their patients concerning the relevance of genetic data for health care decisions and their legal responsibilities to incorporate genetic information into their medical history. They also confront the legal responsibilities of ordering genetic tests, providing counseling, surveillance, effective management, and safeguarding confidentiality. Beyond the clinical issues are the broader questions concerning the reliability of scientific understanding concerning the interaction of genetic and environmental factors, the prospects of gene therapy, the incorporation of genetic information into the delivery of health care, and the training of counselors.

The significance of these issues will become more apparent in the examination of the various aspects of genetic testing: the commercial interests, the uniqueness of genetic tests, voluntary informed consent, privacy, confidentiality, and legal regulations for the protection of privacy and confidentiality. An historical perspective on the development of health care as a commodity is very relevant to understanding why the system confronts serious difficulties in protecting privacy, confidentiality, and security of genetic information.

Corporate interests

Corporate interests focus on five objectives: discovery and sequencing of tens of thousands of genes formed by segments of double-stranded DNA (deoxyribonucleic acid). The expression in terms of individual characteristics (the person's phenotype), however, is the result of the interaction of genetic factors with other factors from the environment. The proximate objectives of research are as follows: deciphering the sequences related to major diseases, identifying the biochemical pathways, determining the function and activity of proteins, and providing the genetic testing and development of therapies (Myriad Genetics, Inc. 1999). Over the past twenty years, diagnosis of genetic diseases has rapidly expanded to encompass testing of chromosomal, dominant, and recessive defects through prenatal and postnatal screening (see, e.g., Genetics and IVF Institute 1999: Directory of Laboratory Services).

Companies involved in gene discovery are interested in mapping and cloning genes that cause a disease in order to understand their function. This is an important step in discovery because without knowledge of the function, the investigator cannot readily meet the legal standard of utility to justify patent rights (Beardsley 1996). To reap the financial rewards, companies engaged in primary research will have to hold patent rights to diagnostic and therapeutic use of the genes and be able to join forces with pharmaceutical companies to apply the discoveries to drug therapy. Opinion is divided on whether the corporate investors envision diagnostic testing or drug therapy as offering greater earning potential (Benowitz 1996). Drug therapy could be favored to counter the effects of genes for such conditions as Alzheimer's, diabetes, cancer, and cardiovascular disease by affecting either their protein products, or cellular and molecular pathways. However, the large investment of companies in isolating genes could signal their immediate interest in the enormous market potential of diagnostic testing of individuals without symptoms.

Moreover, the development of 'pharmacogenomics' could well be a major area of interest for pharmaceutical companies because it could lead to the identification both of specific diseases by genetic testing and their varied responses to drug therapies (Münker 1999). The determination of the various reactions that patients have to new drugs based on their genetic differences has the potential of avoiding the risks of harmful side effects as well as saving time and money in drug development and clinical application. Advances in molecular diagnosis could make genetic screening routine for the purpose of prescribing the best drug (Münker 1999). Such a development would make genetic testing part of clinical practice, but it would also raise the issues of genetic privacy and confidentiality across the broad spectrum of personalized medical care.

Since the 1980s, biotechnology has promoted the collaboration between commercial interests and research centers, including university centers (Benowitz 1996; Nelkin 1996). However, the commercial enterprise raises serious questions in regard to the marketing at this stage of scientific knowledge, regulations, and surveillance. Without support systems in place, genetic testing for various diseases such as breast, ovarian, colon cancers, Alzheimer's, and mental disorders would jeopardize individuals and their families on an economic, social, and psychological level. The uniqueness of genetic tests, particularly predictive ones, reveals the significance of such concern.

Genetic tests: unique diagnostic tests

Predictive genetic tests are different from other diagnostic tests for several reasons (Codori 1997). The non-genetic tests relate to current health condition, thereby leading to therapy if there is a present problem; genetic tests that are predicting a predisposition to a condition (presymptomatic) may or may not lead to therapy or preventive measures. It depends on the reliability of the tests and the availability of therapy. The information from genetic tests also affects the family members as well as the patient. There are personal ramifications since they too may have the same mutation and have to decide whether to be tested.

Moreover, because of the probability of risk associated with discovery of specific mutations (e.g. mutations in genes related to hereditary nonpolyposis colorectal cancer and in BRCA1 and BRCA2 related to hereditary breast cancer), there is more scope for personal interpretation of the information. Personal decision making must evaluate what kind of behavior is justified in the light of the probable risks of having the disease later in life. At this stage of genetic diagnosis, for example, there are various estimations of the risks facing women with a gene mutation in BRCA1 of developing breast cancer and ovarian cancer later in life (see Kahn 1996; Couch et al. 1997). The variations result from two sources (Pike and Wood 1998). The first is the measure of frequency (expressed as a percentage of the total cases observed) that the mutated gene will show its effects (i.e. penetrance) in distinct high-risk families under study. The second is the possible inaccuracy of present genetic analysis in discovering the extent, for example, of BRCA mutation.

As genetic testing moves from the context of research to clinical application, skilled genetic counselors will be in ever greater demand for several important reasons. The first is to ensure voluntary informed consent. A second reason may be the preference of the subjects for a genetic counselor over a medical specialist for reasons of support (Alexandre 1997). As one study (Audrain et al. 1998) of women tested for breast-ovarian cancer indicated, those who wished to discuss psychosocial issues were more likely to prefer a genetic counselor. A third is the reality that primary care physicians may not have the skill, time and confidence to provide the pretest education and counseling (Green and Fost 1997). The personal and familial impact of genetic information highlights the importance of skilled counselors. However, there is a shortage of trained genetic counselors and interpreters of genetic information among physicians who will carry the burden of informing until more specialists are trained (Dutton 1996).

The difference between genetic testing and other diagnostic testing reveals why society needs to take a closer look at the benefits and costs. The question is whether, in a health care system under the strong influence of market forces, genetic advances can be reconciled with the best interests of the patients and their families. There is much analysis of the demands of implementing genetic testing and therapy. However, there seems to be little recognition that, if these demands are to be met on all levels of decision making and care, they will clash with the underlying structure of the US health care system. Its economic reality poses challenges to counseling and the implementation of laws protecting privacy, confidentiality and accessibility to affordable health, disability, and life insurance.

Insurance industry's interests

Before genetic testing, the health insurance system was able to defray costs by having the healthy and the sick share costs and risks, for example by increasing the pool of the insured through group policies. From the perspective of the commercial insurance industry, which bases standard premiums on anticipated results for large numbers of individuals with similar risks, the concern is that restrictions on the use of genetic information in setting premiums will jeopardize profit and the survival of the industry.

In the industry's view, underwriting policies setting terms and conditions for insurance are essential to protecting their financial interests and making insurance affordable to healthy individuals. The fear is that instead of sharing the costs of insurance, individuals may decide to purchase coverage only after a genetic test reveals their susceptibility to a disease (Hudson et al. 1995). Since health and disability insurance usually exclude coverage for 'preexisting conditions,' companies are eager to use genetic information to set conditions and terms. Genetic predisposition does not fit the standard understanding of a preexisting condition, defined as a condition previously diagnosed or treated. Nevertheless, companies see such information as the only way to prevent adverse selection. This would occur if individuals with knowledge of higher risks unknown to the company purchase more insurance at the same rate, as do those with lower risks (American Society of Human Genetics Ad Hoc Committee 1995).

That insurance companies are interested in using reliable diagnostic tests for genetic disorders is obvious for a number of reasons (Brom 1991). They have been in the practice of reviewing family histories and using biochemical tests for HIV and drugs. They have not been reluctant to express their desire to see the results of testing for the dominant gene for Huntington's disease, which emerges in middle age. Moreover, they have investments in research for testing. As the tests become simpler and more reliable, physicians will use them not only to improve diagnosis and therapy but also to protect themselves against malpractice. Even if the explicit results are not recorded, other clinical observations correlated with the genetic data will provide strong hints of the results. If laws severely limit access to DNA data, insurers may opt to leave the business of health coverage in anticipation of the implementation of the laws leading to adverse selection. If they stay the course and thereby suffer losses from adverse selection, then they may go bankrupt and leave the funding to the government. Unless state and federal governments are willing to create a publicly funded system with strong cost containment, they will be under intense pressure to succumb to insurance lobbying and permit some use of genetic information in the assessment of rates.

Counseling: crucial for privacy and confidentiality

The challenge of genetic testing

A critical component in protecting the privacy and confidentiality of genetic data is counseling. The expertise, personnel, time, and money required for genetic counseling are critical factors in the cost-benefit assessment confronting health care. From the positive side, the counselor must help the individual understand the full implications of the information and ways of safeguarding it. From the negative side, the records of the counselor could become vulnerable to unauthorized inspection. Therefore, security measures must be in place to protect the wealth of data stored in the counselor's files. From the perspective of those who assist in coping with the practical and emotional implications of genetic disclosure, skilled comprehensive counseling should receive as much attention as laws protecting against discrimination (Oktay 1998).

A comprehensive approach covers three phases: pre-test education, counseling with the focus on voluntary informed consent, and post-test education and counseling (see Acton 1997; Council on Scientific Affairs 1999). This puts limits on the number of patients counseled by one counselor. If counseling is to fulfill the conditions of voluntary informed consent, it will consume much time, energy, and money, both for the sessions and the training of counselors. In the long run, genetic testing and therapy may reduce costs by prevention and even by offering a cure of chronic as well as acute illnesses. However, in the transition, the nation confronts the economic commitment to counseling, costs of new tests and security measures.

Counseling must address the possible effects not only on familial and social relationships but also on the ability to procure employment as well as health, disability, and life insurance. There is already the perception among some facing the prospects of a genetic disorder that they must also deal with discrimination. A study of 332 members of genetic support groups with one or more of 101 different disorders in the family (Lapham et al. 1996) illustrates this concern. Results indicated the belief that revelation of genetic data had resulted in the refusal of either life insurance (25 percent) or health insurance (22 percent), or in the denial or loss of a job (13 percent). There are reports of genetically tested individuals facing discrimination in regard to pricing of premiums or direct refusal of insurance (Gostin 1991; Hudson et al. 1995). For example, companies have refused insurance upon the discovery of data that the individual, whether healthy or not, has a gene expressing itself in a later illness, Huntington's disease, or upon the discovery of a family history of a genetic disorder even without testing. The risk of refusal may discourage many from testing even if there are some health benefits from early medical intervention. In the process, the ranks of the millions of uninsured are bound to grow without strictly enforced regulations that prohibit use of genetic data for discrimination.

Counseling and voluntary informed consent

In the light of ethical and legal standards developed in the twentieth century, the counselor must be attentive to the principles that were established in the 1947 Nuremberg Code to prevent abuses in experimental medicine (Nuremberg Tribunal 1946–1949). The standards have undergone refinement in the World Medical Association's declarations (e.g. The Declaration of Helsinki in 1975) and in national codes to protect against abuses of the autonomy, freedom, and well-being of each individual, not only in experimental medicine but also in standard therapy (see Veatch 1997). The US Department of Health and Human Services (henceforth HHS) promulgated regulations covering a wide range of research under federal support (HHS 1981–1983). Moreover, precedent-setting rulings (*Canterbury vs. Spence* 1972; *Cobbs vs. Grant* 1972) established that what is required for proper consent is the information a prudent person would need to make a mature decision.

The strict requirements of consent illustrate the formidable task facing genetic counselors (see Wertz et al. 1994; Parker and Majeske 1996). Applied to experimental and therapeutic procedures, the principles require that the individual be fully informed of the procedure in terms of method, duration, and scope. In addition, instructions should cover the reasons for the procedure, the benefits and risks, alternatives, if any, and the right to withdraw at any time in the light of an ongoing assessment of the results, and the right to counsel. After full disclosure, the individual must be free to give consent. This demands that the person be competent to give consent and free from any physical or psychological coercion or manipulation. Only by strict adherence to these principles can society uphold the values of autonomy, confidentiality, privacy and equity (Committee on Assessing Genetic Risks, Institute of Medicine 1994, henceforth Committee).

Genetic counselors face the challenge of conveying very specific information. They should inform patients about the risk of false positives and false negatives and the rating of laboratories for accuracy. Furthermore, they must disclose the different implications of an actual disease and presymptomatic risk, and the chances of passing on a genetic defect as a carrier of a defective recessive gene such as cystic fibrosis or a defective dominant gene such as Huntington's disease (National Institutes of Health Consensus Development Conference Statement 1997; Committee 1994). Counseling becomes even more difficult when dealing with disorders for which genetic information is very specific and not always certain. In regard to renal disorders, for example, the counselor must contend with information as varied as the diseases and help the patient, family, and physician to confront the medical, psychological, social, and economic benefits and risks of genetic testing (Marsick et al. 1999).

The very nature of genetic data raises both a moral and legal question: Can genetic information remain a private affair in view of the serious implications for other members of the family and those intimately related? (See Sommerville and English 1999, for their analysis from a British perspective.) One might argue that there are limits to genetic privacy when the genetic data are relevant to the welfare of others closely related to the individual receiving the information. However, the dilemma is whether a moral responsibility to disclose should be enforced in particular circumstances. The dilemma becomes more intense in a system of health care that does not provide guaranteed universal coverage and exposes individuals and their families to financial burdens resulting from high premiums, loss of access, and discrimination. One can more readily speculate on the limits of genetic privacy and confidentiality in a system that provides national health insurance than in one that is market oriented.

Statutes protecting against invasion of privacy and discrimination

By the early 1990s, there were already laws and judicial rulings protecting against invasion of the right of privacy and against discrimination (see Nobles 1992). Titles VI and VII of the Civil Rights Act of 1964 protect against discrimination in education and employment, respectively. The Americans with Disabilities Act of 1990 prohibits discrimination against a qualified individual with a disability in regard to hiring, advancement or discharge, compensation, training, or other terms and privileges. An analysis of 'disability' and the legislative history of the Act (e.g. The House Report 101–485 II) indicates that genetic defects would fit the definition of disability intended by the law, which forbids discrimination based on fears and perceptions (Zeitz 1991; cf. Saunders and Mortell 1995). In 1995, the Equal Employment Opportunity Commission (EEOC) established a guideline that confirmed this interpretation. The practical effectiveness of such a guideline in the legal arena is open to question because of the hurdles confronting the plaintiff in proving that there was discriminatory action and that it was based on the employer's perception of a genetic defect (Colby 1998).

Special legislation is needed to cover the use of genetic information in law enforcement, adoption, employment, life and disability insurance, as well as in health insurance. The reason is that, once health insurers resort more routinely to genetic testing of clients, other corporations will follow their example to monitor and screen for the health of employees in the workplace (US Congress, Office of Technology Assessment 1991), as well as for other purposes. Effective laws, however, depend on the clarity and scope of concepts. What should be the operative definition of genetic information? Should genetic information be defined in terms of its use? One position would define it as information used for the purpose of genetic counseling (College of American Pathologists 1996). Such specific data would then become the main focus of laws and policies protecting privacy, confidentiality, and security. However, there are other data resulting from research that can be used to discriminate against classes based on genetic data relating to sex, race, or age (Clayton 1995). This is an obvious danger in regard to the insurance rating of premiums for individuals in various groups. Such data, therefore, warrant special protection.

An examination of earlier federal laws (Cushman 1996) notes that protection against disclosure is related to information in the records of federal agencies. The Privacy Act of 1974 (5 USC, Sec. 552a) and the Computer

Matching and Privacy Protection Act of 1988 (amendment to the Privacy Act) protect the privacy of files under federal auspices or under federal contract. They allow the use of their data only if they are relevant to the reasons for their collection or to public policy established by statute. The latter law also establishes an agency, the Data Integrity Board, to monitor usage. However, its effectiveness has been limited because of a less than aggressive supervision of the agency and use of 'routine practice' exemptions. Ironically, another law, the Video Privacy Protection Act of 1988, provides more protection against the disclosure of rental data of individuals than federal laws relating to medical data. Even with the addition of the Social Security Act (Sec. 1106)'s inclusion of all records held by HHS, the laws do not cover the large number of databanks not under federal auspices or contract.

The Health Insurance Portability and Accountability Act of 1996 (henceforth HIPAA), which amended the Employee Retirement Income Security Act of 1974 (henceforth ERISA), restricts the ability of insurance companies to exclude individuals. Its provisions supersede those of state laws, while allowing the states some discretion in the application of key provisions.

Key provisions of HIPAA (29 USC, Secs. 1181 *et seq.*) prohibit insurers of small (two to fifty employees) and large (fifty-one or more) groups from establishing rules for eligibility (including continued eligibility) of any individual based on 'health-status-related factors,' among which is genetic information. The law addresses the issue of 'preexisting condition exclusion,' which involves either a limitation or exclusion of benefits. The period for such exclusion is for a time of not more than twelve months (or eighteen for a late enrollee) after date of enrollment if the physical or mental condition, regardless of cause, existed within the six-month period ending on the enrollment date. The statute specifically states that a preexisting condition exclusion may be imposed only if 'medical advice, diagnosis, care, or treatment was recommended or received within the 6-month period ending on the enrollment date.' It states that genetic information alone does not constitute such a condition when there is no diagnosis of the condition related to such information. Therefore, insurance companies cannot use genetic information without a diagnosis of a condition caused by a genetic defect.

HIPAA may provide protection of the eligibility of individuals relying on group plans for health insurance. However, there is still the problem of affordability because genetic testing and therapy will be expensive. There are many conditions caused by genetic defects that are chronic and that can be diagnosed long before the condition becomes severely debilitating or terminal (e.g. Huntington's disease, familial hypercholesterolemia, or familial polyposis of the colon). If a significant number in a sector of the population have some preexisting genetic condition diagnosed at an early stage, companies could raise premiums for all the groups, thus affecting the individuals participating in the group plans.

Moreover, HIPAA is deficient on several other fronts because as an amendment it did not correct the omissions of ERISA. In July 1997, HHS critiqued 'serious gaps' (HHS 1997; see also Colby 1998, citing Congressional testimony). It leaves individuals who buy their own insurance vulnerable to denial or excessive premiums. Though only a small percentage buy health insurance outside the group health insurance market, the number is likely to grow with age. With increasing knowledge of personal genetic information gleaned from various sources, the concern is that if one has to buy in the individual insurance market, one may later be haunted by that information. Thus, those not covered by group plans are as vulnerable as ever to preexisting condition exclusion. The result will be that individuals under individual plans will be unable to afford them and have to resort to some publicly financed plan.

HIPAA does not address adequately premiums of group plans. Although it prohibits insurers from singling out individuals within the group for different treatment, all participants in the group may be exposed to increases flowing from information about individual members. A further omission is the failure to prohibit or limit an insurer from requiring access to genetic information in medical records or family history, or demanding genetic tests for applicants. This omission is even more troubling in view of the fact that HIPAA exempts self-insured plans of employers and HMOs from state regulations. Another insightful critique (Engelhard 1996) of the law's impact is that it fails to address the issues of cost of new coverage and benefit levels and does not require the provision of health insurance on the part of all employers.

The complexity of the law and its wording have led to different interpretations in regard to what extent states must regulate the insurance market in terms of individual and group coverage (Meier 1997). A conservative interpretation foresees a limited number of new regulations and restrictions, whose effects will probably be to discourage competition, increase costs of compliance, and reduce the number covered by private insurance. These effects will be even more dramatic if states follow the more liberal interpretation of the National Association of Insurance Commissioners, namely, that HIPAA requires states to compel insurers to offer all small group policies at an affordable rate, 'guaranteed issue.'

From a conservative perspective (Meier 1997), price controls may result in insurers leaving 'hostile' markets, resulting in a loss of competition with an increase of insurance costs. Employers too may choose to leave the group plans. If they are compelled either to purchase insurance or pay a payroll tax to support a social insurance, many may opt for the latter with the consequence that publicly funded programs will have higher costs because of an increasing number of high-risk individuals and greater demand for new treatments.

Though a conservative opinion paints a grim picture of an overly regulated market, it seems incapable of recognizing that, whether health insurance is moderately regulated or stringently regulated, the system will be severely stressed by genetic testing and therapy in view of the costs of tests, drugs, and counseling. There is a penchant for overlooking what others (e.g. Lippman 1991; Committee 1994; Cushman 1996) have recognized, namely, that low-income and high-risk individuals without adequate health insurance would likely be excluded from genetic testing and counseling.

A healthy realization of the impact of genetic information on health care and insurance has dawned at the state level. Throughout the 1990s there have been proposals for state laws, a number of which have become law. The objectives are to ensure voluntary informed consent, preserve confidentiality and prevent discrimination in health insurance and employment. A fifty-state survey of privacy statutes (Health Privacy Project 1999) noted that, although virtually every state has some law protecting the confidentiality of patient information, only three (Hawaii, Rhode Island, and Wisconsin) 'have anything approaching comprehensive health privacy laws.' The analysis of state laws is made more difficult by the fact that many of the specific statutes protecting confidentiality are included in broader laws dealing with other matters such as licensing (Health Privacy Project 1999).

Well over half of the states have passed some form of laws prohibiting genetic discrimination relating to health insurance. Many have passed laws to place restrictions on insurers by prohibiting the requirement of genetic tests as a condition of coverage and the use of information from genetic tests to determine rates. As in other areas of legislation dealing with medical and biological advances, the narrow wording of the laws undermines their effectiveness. The statutes that specifically refer to 'genetic testing' or 'genetic tests' open the door to the use of genetic information that can be derived from other sources, such as protein analysis, family history, medical exams and records, and only protect individuals without symptoms (Bornstein 1996; Andrews 1997; Colby 1998; Rothstein 1998). Prior to the manifestation of the disease to which the individual has a diagnosed genetic predisposition, there is protection from higher rates or denial. But once the individual becomes ill, he or she is left to the mercy of the insurer under the provisions of each state's insurance code.

Moreover, state laws are severely limited in their scope of protection. They do not protect the employees in the self-insured plans of employers and HMOs because such plans are exempted by ERISA from state insurance codes. One recommendation (Rothstein 1998) for more comprehensive protection of employees or prospective employees would be a law like Minnesota's, which strictly limits use of medical examination and information to the specific needs of employment and business (see also Andrews and Jaeger 1991). It makes more sense to avoid such terms as 'genetic tests or genetic information' and use instead a term such as 'medical information' that covers a wider range of data for protecting the applicant's privacy.

As more families exhaust their assets in providing care and come to rely more on Medicaid for assistance, the costs of long-term care will be an increasing challenge to families, and state and federal governments (Lisko 1998). If the federal government reduces Medicaid and Medicare funding, the burden of financial support would shift increasingly to the states and long-term care insurance. In this event, the states, in particular, will have to face the policy issue of whether such insurance is to be regarded as health or life or disability insurance in order to determine the scope of the insurer's access to genetic information of applicants (Rothstein 1998). Because the majority of states have yet to prohibit insurers from either use of or testing for genetic data to determine coverage or rates, the future of long-term care insurance remains uncertain in view of an aging population with genetic predisposition to diseases such as Alzheimer's (Lisko 1998). Moreover, genetic screening by 'continuing care retirement communities' would raise ethical and economic dilemmas (Thomas et al. 1998). They revolve around the question of whether priority should be given to the protection of the privacy and nondiscrimination of applicants or the economic well-being of community members ultimately sharing the responsibility for care of those with late-onset illnesses such as Alzheimer's. The state approach to the policy issue could very well have an impact on both the affordability and accessibility of long-term care insurance and the viability of the insurance business.

However, the approach that relies on states to take the initiative is myopic for three reasons. First, in matters of health care, state legislatures have had difficulty in dealing with the issues and forging some uniformity of legislation as recommended by the National Conference of Commissioners on Uniform State Laws in 1988. A comparison of state laws relating to health care issues reveals that statutes have not always been notable for their clarity, comprehensiveness, and uniformity. No better example of the arduous process has been the legislating on the living will and health care proxy (see Rizzo 1989). Second, the transmission of computer data spans state and national boundaries through a network of telecommunication services. Protection of such data is a national problem, not just a state-by-state concern. Third, unlike Europe and Canada, the United States has been moving at a snail's pace in passing a comprehensive law. European governments have established national privacy laws and commissions, and in 1995 the European Union adopted a directive on the protection of personal data (Cushman 1996). This leaves the United States in the awkward position of having to conform to these standards if it intends to integrate its information system with that of the European Union.

It is probably unrealistic to expect that the courts can substitute for comprehensive federal legislation. In *Norman-Bloodsaw vs. Lawrence Berkeley Laboratory* (135 F.3d 1260, 1998), the US Court of Appeals for the Ninth Circuit revealed the complexity of the privacy issues the courts face in the area of medical testing. The significant conclusion of the ruling is that employees have grounds for claims based on Title VII and federal and state constitutional privacy interests when employers perform unauthorized tests.

Such interests embrace the storage as well as the collection of the data. The fact that individuals consent to medical examinations for the sake of employment (in this instance, employment entrance and follow-up examinations) does not grant employers permission to conduct 'separate and more invasive' tests without the knowledge or informed consent of the former. At issue were blood and urine tests for syphilis, sickle cell trait, and pregnancy. The court remanded the case for further judicial judgment on the issues of material fact and a reconsideration of the validity of Title VII and privacy claims. The *reasonable person* test is to be applied to the question of fact: whether reasonable persons finding themselves in the same position 'would have had reason to know' the specific tests to be performed. The answer to this question bears directly on the validity of the claims. This ruling puts employers, particularly private and semi-private, on notice that privacy interests relating to medical information are at stake in unauthorized testing as well as in disclosure to third parties (Risse 1998).

Proposals for protection of genetic privacy and confidentiality

The 1990s saw mounting concern over protection of privacy and confidentiality of genetic information in particular and medical records in general. The lack of protection may have an adverse affect on the delivery and quality of health care. As the Health Privacy Project (2000) describes the dilemma, individuals may withhold information from their physicians or not consult because of fear that exposure of personal information will have dire consequences for careers, social status, and insurability. The institute's hope is that safeguarding privacy and improving quality of health care need not be in conflict. However, its overview seems to have missed the insight that the structure, financing, and interests of the present system are incompatible with a comprehensive law. In this context, with linked databases, it may be impossible to impose readily 'enforceable limits' on the uses of medical data to protect privacy and confidentiality. Without doubt, beneficial results can flow from use of data in an integrated system. Among them are better diagnosis, care, research, detection of fraud and abusive practices, and marketing of services and smoother administrative and financial operations. The issue is whether the flow and dissemination of medical data can achieve these benefits without severely compromising privacy and confidentiality in a system gripped by the market economy.

Prominent groups during the 1990s proposed rules in the hope of guiding the passage of protective legislation (see, e.g., Committee 1994; Hunter 1994; Annas et al. 1995; College of American Pathologists 1996). They uphold the autonomy, privacy, confidentiality, and freedom of the person who is the source of the DNA to remedy the present vulnerability to genetic discrimination in health insurance and employment. Heavy emphasis is on the requirements of voluntary informed consent on the part of the source of DNA, covering collection, access, storage, and distribution of genetic information, and on the need for strong security. The source or legal representative should have control over all phases, with the responsible custodians and transmitters providing security measures to protect the data throughout the process. The proposals seek to establish regulations sufficiently comprehensive to reduce as far as possible the potential harm to liberty and privacy, while at the same time allowing for beneficial use on behalf of individuals, their families, and society's interests in such areas as public health, research and law enforcement.

Building on previous work, the NIH-DOE Working Group on Ethical, Legal, and Social Implications of Human Genome Research (ELSI Working Group) and the National Action Plan on Breast Cancer (NAPBC) collaborated on recommendations relating to health insurance (1995) and employment (1996) for state and federal legislation and policy (NIH-DOE 1995 and 1996). They broadened the definition of genetic information to cover genes, gene products, or inherited characteristics derived from the individual or family members. Insurers should be prohibited from using or requesting genetic tests or information for the purpose of denying or limiting 'any coverage' or establishing 'eligibility, continuation, enrollment or contribution requirements.' The recommendations for employment are equally as strict, covering hiring, terms, conditions, privileges, benefits, termination, collection, disclosure, and prior authorization. An examination of congressional legislation reveals points of agreement and the influence of the NIH-DOE Joint Working Group (ELSI) and NAPBC proposals.

The last three sessions of Congress (104th, 105th, 106th) have seen a number of legislative proposals whose main purpose is to protect genetic privacy and prohibit genetic discrimination (see Colby 1998 for comparisons of bills of the 104th and 105th sessions). Their complexity and length have grown with the years. They illustrate the difficulty of legislating on genetic issues.

In the 105th session, the bill that received the approval of President Clinton and had wide support in Congress was the Genetic Information Nondiscrimination in Health Insurance Act of 1997 (1997a, b) (H.R. 306, S. 89) introduced by Representative Slaughter and Senator Snowe. This bipartisan proposal followed closely the joint recommendations of the NIH-DOE (ELSI Working Group) and NAPBC. The legislation remedied the shortcomings of HIPAA, by prohibiting rate increases in the group health insurance market based on genetic information and the use of genetic information obtained in the individual health insurance market, and by restricting the collection and disclosure of genetic information by insurers. Despite the broad base of bipartisan support, the bill did not pass.

The 106th Congress saw additional bills. Receiving the strong recommendation of President Clinton was the Genetic Nondiscrimination in Health

Insurance and Employment Act of 1999 (1999a, b), introduced by Representative Slaughter (H.R. 2457) and by Senator Daschle (S. 1322). This is more comprehensive in its coverage of the issues and received broad support. It enacts protection of genetic privacy and prohibition of discrimination on the basis of 'predictive genetic information' to group and individual health insurance, to Medicap under Title XVIII of the Social Security Act, and to employment embracing employer, employment agency, training programs, and labor organizations. Predictive genetic information covers data obtained from genetic tests of the individual or family members or from the occurrence of a disease or disorder in the family (Sec. 101). Predictive genetic information does not include information about sex or age, chemical, blood or urine analyses (unless they are genetic tests), or information about physical exams and current health status.

As in other proposals, collection and disclosure of genetic information come under the strict provisions of privacy and confidentiality that protect against invasion by agents or agencies involved in the insurance business. Enforcement has the backing of provisions that permit civil action for equitable relief and governmental action for monetary penalties by the Secretary of HHS enforcing the specific provisions. The insurance providers may request that an individual authorize the disclosure of predictive genetic information or genetic services directly related and necessary for payment of a claim. Though health care providers may request genetic testing, they may not require it from an individual or family members. However, allowance is made for disclosure of predictive genetic information from one health care provider to another for the purpose of treatment of that individual under strict confidentiality. The medical records of employees are also to be safeguarded. The bill permits the request, requirement, collection, or purchase of predictive genetic information, provided several important conditions are fulfilled (Sec. 202). The employees must give voluntary informed consent and be sub-sequently apprised of the genetic monitoring results undertaken to research the biological effects of toxic substances in the workplace. The employer receives the results in aggregate terms that do not identify specific employees. In addition, the results of genetic services are disclosed to the individual or family member that authorized them. In recognition of the complexity of the issues and difficulty of providing certain protection in regard to health insurance and employment in all cases, the bill specifically yields to other federal or state statutes that would provide better protection in various circumstances (Sec. 208).

Because Congress failed to pass comprehensive standards by the August 21, 1999 deadline set by HIPAA, Secretary Donna E. Shalala was required under its simplification provisions to issue final regulations by February 21, 2000. However, because of an extension given to public comments, the promulgation of the rule was delayed. On November 3, the proposed rule appeared in the *Federal Register* (HHS 1999). Its principles are based on those submitted by Shalala on September 11, 1997, before the Senate Committee on Labor and Human Resources, concerning recommendations for national health privacy legislation (Shalala 1997).

To control the confidentiality of electronic transaction systems, the rule proposed by the Secretary of HHS provides standards that govern the interchange of electronic data for a number of administrative, insurance transactions in health care. They also require unique health identifiers for health care professionals, plans, employers, and individuals, and standards for data security. The goals are to allow the free flow of health information essential to high quality care and at the same time protect the privacy of the information (59927). The rule attempts to balance important commercial, professional, and personal interests in the context of the marketplace. In recognition that health care is a business, the Secretary does not intend to interfere with business relationships in the health care industry. The rule requires that the 'covered entity' (the party responsible under the rule) establish privacy policies in light of an assessment of its own business needs, information practices, and requirements. The covered entity should also ensure by contract that business partners not disclose or use information in ways that it does not permit, and that they follow certain security, inspection, and reporting requirements (59925). For purposes other than treatment, payment, or health care operations, the covered entity is required to receive the individual's voluntary authorization that is verifiable and enforceable. The prevailing principle is 'minimum necessary' disclosure or use, which would mean that the amount of protected information allowed to be disclosed or used should not exceed the minimum amount required to achieve specifically intended purposes (59924).

Even amended in the light of public comments (see, e.g., Health Privacy Project 2000), the rule is limited in the scope of protection it provides and in the flexibility allowed the covered entities in establishing privacy policies with its business partners. As the Secretary recommends, there is need for comprehensive federal law to provide more complete protection. The concession to commercial necessities and the attempt to achieve a delicate balance between business needs and privacy are in the long run the weakest points in the proposal. In view of the difficulty of monitoring the whole process, and the pressures of the health care industry on Congress and state legislatures, protection of privacy will not be an easy matter, as long as health care is treated as a commodity and profit is a major motive. Because on the federal level Congress can preempt the regulations by law, the rule would be tentative at best.

There are other more specific limitations that demonstrate how federal legislation is already limiting the scope of protection (see both regulations and comments of the Health Privacy Project). Under HIPAA, the standards proposed by the Secretary can only cover health plans (HMOs, health insurers, group health plans including many ERISA plans), health care clearinghouses involved in the processing of information from health care provider to a payer, and health care providers who maintain or transmit information electronically. The limited coverage leaves out other entities collecting and maintaining health records, such as life insurers, researchers, and health officials. Identifiable health information in paper records is not protected unless later transmitted electronically by the covered entities. Moreover, such information is not protected if compiled by other entities not acting in the capacity of health providers or plans, such as other insurers (for worker's compensation) or employers (schools). The proposed rule does not adequately restrict use or disclosure of medical information by researchers, life insurance insurers, marketing firms, or administrative, legal and accounting services.

Although individuals would have a right to review, copy, and request correction of their health information, their authorization is not required for the use and disclosure of protected information by the covered entities or their business partners for treatment, payment, and health care operations pertinent to treatment and payment. Nor is personal authorization required for the disclosure by covered entities to oversight agencies whose operations deal with audits, inspections, matters, or activities essential to the monitoring and running of the health care system and governmental programs. One exception is the requirement of a separate voluntary authorization for the use and disclosure of psychotherapy notes because of their sensitive and subjective nature.

Under HIPAA, the proposed rule would neither preempt state laws that provide more privacy protection nor prevent states passing stronger laws. At present, this is a good limitation because some state laws are more specific in their protection of data relating to genetic, mental, and communicable disease. But this is not a convincing reason why in the near future a comprehensive federal law enforced by a central oversight agency would not be preferable to a mix of federal and state regulations and laws. In view of the financial interests in the health care industry, an individual state will be under increasing pressure to limit and even reduce the scope of protection, and be subject to threats of higher health care costs if it pursues an aggressive policy. A legal quagmire will also emerge with heavy costs in litigation not only over which specific law was violated but also which law should prevail, federal or state, in a given case. Problems can only intensify with the introduction of genetic testing and profiling. This will be the case not only in health care insurance but also in employment, life, disability, and long-term care insurance.

On February 8, 2000, President Clinton signed an executive order, 'To Prohibit Discrimination in Federal Employment Based on Genetic Information' (Clinton 2000). Its provisions reflect those of the aforementioned bill of Rep. Slaughter and Sen. Daschle (H.R. 2457 and S. 1322) that he strongly supported for the private sector. The order protects federal employees from discrimination based on genetic information derived from genetic tests of the individual and family members or from the occurrence of a disease or condition or disorder in the family member. However, like the bill, it does not exclude information of an individual's current health and data relating to sex, age, physical exams, chemical, blood, or urine analysis, unless these fall under the exclusion of genetic information. One can envision growing debate on whether specific data derived from such analyses provide relevant genetic information. This will occur even more so in regard to diagnosing predisposition to specific diseases and disorders. Nevertheless, the executive order prohibits the use of explicit genetic information or requests for genetic services to discriminate.

With good reason, the time has come for streamlining of protective laws as well as health insurance. As urged by the Clinton Administration, a strong comprehensive national law is needed to guarantee full protection in the face of the formidable task of security and the potential for abuse and misuse of personal health information for profit. However, the Health Privacy Project (1999) expressed doubts that, at present, any broad federal law could substitute for state laws that are more specific. The reasons are that state laws can be more responsive to the unique needs of their citizens with strong and detailed regulations in regard to such areas as mental illness, communicable disease, cancer, and genetic testing, and more tailored to the information requirements of particular entities. On the one hand, the institute recognizes that most state laws allow limited right of patient access to medical records and restrict the ability to prevent disclosure and recourse for damages. On the other, it speculates that at this time a comprehensive preemptive federal law could do more harm than good. Although such a law could provide a substantial benefit 'by establishing a baseline of consumer protections,' a preemptive law could unravel the legal and regulatory systems of the states and thus remove some of the protections already in place for the consumers over a broad range of issues.

Legislation vs. reality

Perhaps the answer to the dilemma is the abandonment of the concept of health care as a commodity and the patient as the consumer. Whether one speaks of a comprehensive federal or state law, one still confronts the problem of trying to pass and enforce such a law in confrontation with the forces and needs of the marketplace. Stringent laws and regulations with a high probability of successful implementation are facing formidable opposition from business interests with their army of lobbyists and treasury for campaign funding. The same can be said for the prospect of comprehensive state laws because individual states are as vulnerable to economic pressures.

The probability of protection is even more problematic if longitudinal health records of individual patients covering the personal history of a lifetime are stored and electronically disseminated for medical care, social and public health policy, and action. The data linked and stored in electronic files can then be subjected to analysis through computer programs developed precisely for this purpose. The inclusion of genetic information from testing and other sources and the linking of data by automated information systems raise serious concerns about preserving the privacy of medical information (see Gostin 1995). However, proposals that attempt to balance the commercial and societal need for genetic information and the privacy of individuals and families are likely to fare poorly under the intense pressure of lobbies seeking to protect their economic interests. With wide access to personal histories through linked computer systems, individuals would find themselves vulnerable to subtle, if not overt, discrimination. In view of legal costs and the length of judicial deliberations, many would not have the resources or time to pursue grievances against powerful interests.

A huge chasm looms between the reality of protection and the reality of health care in the marketplace. Commentators are aware of the economic incentives built into the system to keep the regulations at a minimum and to allow for the use of personal information in health care, insurance, and employment (see, e.g., Bornstein 1996; Cushman 1996; Rothstein 1998). Resolving the issues of privacy and confidentiality demands more than laws dealing with procedural safeguards. The need is to confront the issues of right and accessibility to health care and the countervailing demands of resource allocation and economic survival of those heavily involved in the health care industry. As genetic testing becomes more accurate in revealing predisposition to specific diseases, the viability of the insurance system based on medical underwriting becomes more questionable, and the need to protect the privacy of genetic information becomes more critical.

However, generally lacking in the analyses is an historical perspective on the development of the forces and factors shaping the health care system. Moreover, there is a general failure to state explicitly that these very features undermine the capacity to meet the economic, ethical, and legal challenges of genetic testing and therapy. The belief is that the nation can tinker with health care reform and still cope with the issues raised by genetic testing and privacy. On the one hand, there is the growing consensus that genetic data must be zealously guarded and specific regulations under law must be in place to ensure protection of privacy and confidentiality. On the other, there seems to be little or no consensus in regard to overhauling the whole system in order to remove the economic incentives to spy on, discriminate against, and defraud. To protect against discrimination for financial reasons, security measures must be in place to cover all personal medical information, and not just genetic data. But even the best security measures may be incapable of preventing estimations of underlying genetic problems from personal data drawn from a number of sources. Economic decisions could then be made on the basis of the degree of probability that an individual has an underlying genetic disorder or predisposition to a serious condition.

Security measures and their effectiveness

Security must cover a broad range of procedures to screen and monitor access, use, transmission, and storage (see Electronic Privacy Information Center 1999, henceforth EPIC). All medical data, regardless of their purpose, fall under the blanket of security because of the possibilities of gleaning from them conclusions about predisposition to illness. Laws should protect the right of individuals to full access to personal identifiable data and require their notification on the part of those keeping the records, thus allowing them to make needed corrections and deletions. Any card-encrypted system must allow them access to all personal data on the card.

Monitoring is extremely important for the enforcement of any federal medical privacy law. Without proper supervision by an independent agency whose sole function is to review procedures and investigate cases, enforcement may be only on paper. Oversight of public agencies should be the responsibility of an independent commission. An experienced and skilled staff is essential for monitoring practices, protocols, and procedures relating to privacy, security, collection, informed consent, information, and disclosure (Gostin et al. 1997). This should apply not only to the acquisition and use of protected health information by public agencies for legitimate public health reasons but also to the same activities of other entities (see Hunter 1994). Only compelling state interests should warrant third party access and then only to the extent strictly required in each case.

Technical methods should be employed to safeguard the data in storage and transmission (see EPIC 1999; Goldman and Mulligan 1996). Controls should be in place to restrict access to specific data, based on the consent of the individual and the particular official need of the one requiring the information (e.g. physician, claims processor, or administrator). Encryption of data in storage and in transit is crucial in the face of the dangers of electronic intrusions into databanks. Cryptography can utilize a mathematical technique to scramble information, making it available to designated parties. A necessary accompaniment are measures to track access (audit trails), covering system activity, user's identity, date, time location, data accessed, and function in terms of reading, copying, editing, and deleting.

The abandonment of the Social Security Number for medical use is an extremely important step. Anyone who has received a report on credit history or has had the experience of being victimized by theft of financial identity knows the many activities associated with the number and the dangers of its fraudulent use. Related data are difficult to keep private. Any encrypted health card should have only the purpose of providing information relevant to health care. One proposal is to employ an optical memory card, the size and shape of a credit card, that can be encoded at production with a serial number, which would secure the data to that one card and thereby prevent counterfeiting (Haddock 1994). Whatever the measures taken for security, everyone involved in health care either as patient or provider will have to contend with massive accumulation of personal data and the pressures to have access not only for service but also for profit. At this time, health care delivery encourages and promotes access without commensurate sensitivity to the needs of privacy and the dangers of discrimination (Goldman and Mulligan 1996).

Conclusion

Options merely addressing the economic concerns of insurance affordability, and the profit margins of insurers and employers fall far short of the implications of genetic testing and therapy if they are to be integrated into health care. An analysis of the issues must encompass the dilemmas the nation will face in trying to balance the protection of privacy, confidentiality, security, and voluntary informed consent with the demands of health care in the marketplace. When the examination broadens to explore the wider range of issues, it discloses the severe stresses confronting the health care system as it rapidly evolves from its origin in the early twentieth century. Following the patterns of its early development, health care continues to rely heavily on commercial interests and enterprise with the profit motive having a dominant role. On the part of the public as consumer, there is a growing dissatisfaction and anxiety over the cost of health care, commercial interests, discrimination, and lack of access. The emergence of genetic testing and therapy can only heighten those concerns.

A realistic appraisal of the demands on health care should make clear that the transition from the model of health care as a commodity and patients as consumers would not be an easy one. To ensure affordable access and protect fundamental rights and principles, the evolving system will have to commit many resources in terms of money, personnel, and protective laws and procedures. The public will have to look even more to the federal and state governments to protect its interests. Without vigorously enforced governmental regulations and procedures, commercial interests will likely not take the initiative to ensure privacy, confidentiality, and security, if their profits are threatened.

After much discussion of privacy, confidentiality, and security, the main issues revolve around the uses of genetic data. Genetic information may be gleaned not only from genetic tests and therapy but also from other medical tests and history. Computer analyses that could predict with varying degrees of probability a genetic predisposition or presence of a genetic disease would make it virtually impossible to keep the data private. The chief focus should be on regulations that prohibit the use of personal data derived from health care and other sources to discriminate for insurance, employment, or other social activities. Only when there is a compelling state interest should there be permission to disclose the information specifically relevant to achieve legitimate governmental objectives.

A major obstacle to comprehensive laws and regulations would be the corporate and professional entities finding themselves threatened by restrictions on their ability to gain access to the data. Herein lies the problem. Can individuals and their families be adequately protected in the marketplace of health care? Will they make their voices heard in legislative halls and executive chambers to ensure the security of their privacy and economic interests? To realize what is at stake, one need only look at the vigorous lobbying and advertising by insurers, corporate managers, and providers in the health industry concerning health care reform.

There is likely to be tension between government and parties with financial interests in access to personal health information. State and federal governments could succumb to the pressures of commercial interests to water down the restrictions on access and use of DNA data and genetic information gleaned from various sources. The unwillingness to commit resources could very well lead to a quagmire of inadequate state and federal protections. If the profit motive remains a strong motivator, even the best of statutes will not ensure security without effective monitoring to detect and thwart incursion. The regulatory system would then probably be weak under the pressure of corporate interests that have been playing a larger role in health care since 1945. Such would be the probable outcome if the marketplace approach prevails in health care.

However, there is another possible outcome of the tension between the government acting in the interests of the people and the corporate interests seeking to maximize profit. Diminished access to health care and insurance could lead to greater governmental intervention through funds, personnel, and technology to maintain standards of care and monitor storage and use of genetic data. If there is the will to impose strict controls on the commercial use of genetic information, insurance companies may happily abandon the business of insuring to invest their assets in more lucrative ventures, thereby requiring government to take on a greater financial role. Moreover, if there are tight controls over rising health costs, resulting from genetic testing and therapy, the government will have to subsidize research and development with the inevitable control over delivery.

The US health care system appears to be in dire need of change. Already under stress from the economic pressures generated by biotechnology and other medical advances, it must confront the additional strains created by the threats to privacy, insurability, and employment. Its precarious condition calls for a thorough reform (for specifics, see Rizzo 1993 and 1999). Such a reform will have to break the iron grip of the marketplace that treats health care as a commodity and patients as consumers. Removing profit as a major motive for delivery of care and providing universal health coverage should be national priorities.

An irony of history may be that genetic testing and therapy will bring about the demise of the health care system rooted in the marketplace. Their effects on insurability and employment and the intensified demand for increasing governmental intervention to protect individuals and their families, promote access, and hold down costs will combine to make the present system unsustainable. The system spawned by research and biotechnology of the twentieth century will have to undergo a dramatic transformation in the twenty-first to meet the economic, social, ethical, and legal challenges of genetic testing and therapy as well as other medical advances.

References

Acton, R.T. (1997) Molecular genetic testing for adult-onset disorders: the evolving laboratory, physician, patient interface, *Journal of Clinical Laboratory Analysis* 21(1): 23–27.

Alexandre, L.M. (1997) Genetic testing for cancer susceptibility: what your institution needs to know, *Oncology Issues* 12(2): 18–20. Available at http://www.medscape.com (accessed October 23, 1999).

American Society of Human Genetics Ad Hoc Committee (1995) Genetic testing and insurance, *American Journal of Human Genetics* 56: 327–331.

Andrews, L. (1997) Body science, *ABA Journal* 83: 44–49.

Andrews, L.B. and Jaeger, A.S. (1991) Confidentiality of genetic information in the workplace, *American Journal of Law & Medicine* 17(1/2): 75–108.

Annas, G.J., Glantz, L.H., and Roche, P.A. (1995) Guidelines for protecting privacy of information stored in genetic data banks, in *The Genetic Privacy Act and Commentary*, Health Law Department, Boston University School of Public Health.

Audrain, J., Rimer, B., Cella, D., Garber, J., Peshkin, B.N., Ellis, J., Schildkraut, J., Stefanek, M., Vogel, V., and Lerman, C. (1998) Genetic counseling and testing for breast-ovarian cancer susceptibility: what do women want? *Journal of Clinical Oncology* 16(1): 133–138.

Beardsley, T. (1996) Vital data, *Scientific American*, March, 100–105.

Benowitz, S. (1996) Researchers view genetic testing with high hopes, but caution, *The Scientist* 10(6): 1, 6–7.

Bornstein, R.A. (1996) Genetic discrimination, insurability and legislation: a closing of the legal loopholes, *Journal of Law and Policy* 4: 551. Available at http://web.lexis-nexis.com/universe/docum/ (accessed April 26, 2000).

Brom, M.E. (1991) Insurers and genetic testing: shopping for that perfect pair of genes, *Drake Law Review* 40: 121–148.

Brown, E.R. (1979) *Rockefeller Medicine Men*, Berkeley CA: University of California Press.

Canterbury vs. Spence (1972) 464 F.2d 772 (DC Cir.), *cert. denied*, 409 US 1064.

Clayton, E.W. (1995) Panel comment: why the use of anonymous samples for research matters, *Journal of Law and Medical Ethics* 23: 378–77.

Clinton, W.J. (2000) 'To Prohibit Discrimination in Federal Employment Based on Genetic Information.' Available at http://www.pub.whitehouse.gov/ (accessed October 2, 2000), *Federal Register* (10 February 2000), 65(28): 6875–6880.

Cobbs vs. Grant (1972) 8 Cal. 3d 229, 502 P.2d 1, 104 Cal. Rptr. 505.

Codori, A.M. (1997) Psychological opportunities and hazards in predictive genetic testing for cancer risk, *Gastroenterology Clinics of North America* 26(1): 19–39.

Colby, J.A. (1998) An analysis of genetic legislation proposed by the 105th Congress, *American Journal of Law & Medicine* 24(4): 443–480.

College of American Pathologists (1996) Statement to the National Bioethics Advisory Commission, *BioLaw* II(12) (December): S237–S254. Available at http://www.columbia-hca.com/overview/index.html (accessed April 28, 2000).

Committee on Assessing Genetic Risks, Institute of Medicine (1994) *Assessing Genetic Risks*, L.B. Andrews, J.E. Fullarton, N.A. Holtzman, and A.G. Motulsky (eds), Washington DC: National Academy Press.

Couch, F.J., DeShano, B.S., Blackwood, M.A., Calzone, K., Stopfer, J., Campeau, L., Ganguly, A., Rebbeck, T., and Weber, B.L. (1997) *BRCA1* mutations in women attending clinics that evaluate the risk of breast cancer, *New England Journal of Medicine* 336(20): 1409–1415.

Council on Scientific Affairs (1999) Report 5: review of guidelines for pre-test and post-test education and genetic counseling of the National Society of Genetic Counselors and other organizations. Available at http://www.ama-assn.org/meetings/public/annual99 (accessed April 29, 2000).

Cushman, R. (1996) Privacy, confidentiality, and security issues for electronic health care information, *BioLaw* II(2/3): S: 1–25.

Dowd, A.R. (1997) How to protect your privacy, *Money* 26(8) (August): 104–115.

Dutton, G. (1996) Genetic testing: should you pay? *Business & Health* 14(4) 41–46.

Electronic Privacy Information Center (EPIC) (1999) *Medical Record Privacy* (March 1). Available at http://www.epic.org/privacy/medical/ (accessed May 4, 2000).

Emanuel, E. (1997) Is health care a commodity? *The Lancet* 350: 1713–1714.

Engelhard, C.L. (1996) Kassebaum-Kennedy health insurance reform bill: who will it help? *BioLaw* II(11): S211–S217.

Genetics and IVF Institute (1999) Available at http://www.givf.com/givfhome.html (accessed April 30, 2000).

Genetic Information Nondiscrimination in Health Insurance Act of 1997 (1997a) See US Congress, 105th, 1st sess., H.R. 306. Available at http://thomas.gov (accessed August 25, 1999).

Genetic Information Nondiscrimination in Health Insurance Act of 1997 (1997b) See US Congress, 105th, 1st sess., S. 89. Available at http://thomas.gov (accessed August 25, 1999).

Genetic Nondiscrimination in Health Insurance and Employment Act of 1999 (1999a) See US Congress, 106th, 1st sess., H.R. 2457. Available at http://thomas.gov (accessed August 25, 1999).

Genetic Nondiscrimination in Health Insurance and Employment Act of 1999 (1999b) See US Congress, 106th, 1st sess., S. 1322. Available at http://thomas.gov (accessed August 25, 1999).

Goldman, J. and Mulligan, D. (1996) Ensuring patient confidentiality in the electronic age, *Drug Benefit Trends* 8(11): 10–12, 15-16. Available at http://www.medscape.com/ (accessed March 5, 1998).

Gostin, L.O. (1991) Genetic discrimination: the use of genetically based diagnostic and prognostic tests by employers and insurers, *American Journal of Law & Medicine* 17(1/2): 109–144.

—— (1995) Genetic privacy, *Journal of Law, Medicine & Ethics* 23(4): 320–330.

Gostin, L.O., Lazzarini, Z., and Flaherty, K.M. (1997) Legislative survey of state confidentiality laws, with specific emphasis on HIV and immunization, *Electronic Privacy Information Center.* Available at http://www.epic.org/privacy/medical/cdc_survey.html (accessed May 4, 2000).

Green, M.J. and Fost, N. (1997) An interactive computer program for educating and counseling patients about genetic susceptibility to breast cancer, *Journal of Cancer Education* 12(4): 204–208.

Griswold vs. Connecticut (1965) 381 US 479.

Haddock, R. (1994) Prepared statement on behalf of the Laser Card Systems Corporation Subsidiary of Drexler Technology Corporation, US Senate, Subcommittee on Technology and the Law, Committee on the Judiciary, *BioLaw* 1996 (January 14): 19–25, microfiche.

Health Insurance Portability and Accountability Act (1996) *Public Law 104–191*, 29 USC, Secs. 1181 *et seq.*

Health Privacy Project (1999) (Institute for Health Care Research and Policy, Georgetown University), *The State of Health Privacy: An Uneven Terrain.* Available at http://www.healthprivacy.org/resources/statereports/exsum.html (accessed March 24, 2000).

—— (2000) *Comments on Proposed Federal Standards for Privacy of Individually Identifiable Health Information* (February 17). Available at http://www.healthprivacy.org/latest/comments.shtml (accessed February 22, 2000).

HHS (US Department of Health and Human Services) (1981–1983) HHS policy for protection of human research subjects, *Federal Register* 46 (26 January 1981), and 48 (4 March 1983).

—— (1997) Health insurance in the age of genetics (July). Available at http://www.nhgri.nih.gov/News/Insurance/ (accessed 1999, September 8).

—— (1999) Standards for privacy of individually identifiable health (November 3), *Federal Register* 64(212): 59917–60016. Available at http://www.access.gpo.gov/nara (accessed March 22, 2000).

Hudson, K.L., Rothenberg, K.H., Andrews, L.B., Kahn, M.J., and Collins, F.S. (1995) Genetic discrimination and health insurance: an urgent need for reform, *Science* 270 (October 20): 391–393.

Hunter, N.D. (1994) Prepared statement on behalf of the Department of Health and Human Services, US Senate, Subcommittee on Technology and the Law, Committee on the Judiciary, *BioLaw* 1996 (May 2): 78–81, microfiche.

Jewler, D. and Egan, C. (1997) Managing continuous change, *Oncology Issues* 11(6): 28–32, 34, 35.

Kahn, P. (1996) Coming to grips with genes and risk, *Science* 174: 496–498.

Lapham, E.V., Kozma, C., and Weiss, J. (1996) Genetic discrimination: perspectives of consumers, *Science* 274 (October 25): 621–623.

Lippman, A. (1991) Prenatal genetic testing and screening: constructing needs and reinforcing inequities, *American Journal of Law & Medicine* 17(1/2) 15–48.

Lisko, E.A. (1998) Genetic information and long-term care insurance, *Health News* in *Health Law and Policy Institute* (September), University of Houston Law Center.

Available at http://www.law.uh.edu/LawCenter/Programs/Health/ (accessed August 20, 1999).

Marsick, R., Limwongse, C., and Kodish, E. (1999) Genetic testing for renal diseases: medical and ethical considerations, *American Journal of Kidney Diseases* (the official journal of National Kidney Foundation). Available at http://www. ajkdjournal.org/ abs32_6/v32n6p934.html (accessed August 30, 1999).

Meier, C.F. (1997) How to implement Kassebaum-Kennedy (March 25). Available at http://www.heartland.org/studies/k-k.htm (accessed 2000, April 29).

Münker, T. (1999) Pharmacogenomics: personalized drugs and personalized medicine, *IPTS Report 38*. Available at http://www.jrc/es/pages/f-search.html (accessed December 6, 1999).

Myriad Genetics, Inc. (1999) Gene and drug discovery. Available at http:// www.myriad.com/index.html (accessed April 30, 2000).

National Institutes of Health Consensus Development Conference Statement (1997) Genetic testing for cystic fibrosis 15(4) (April 14–16): 1–37. Available at http:// www.medscape.com/govmt/NIH/1999/guidelines/NIH-cystic/toc-nih.cystic.html (accessed October 23, 1999).

Nelkin, D. (1996) Social dynamics of genetic testing: the case of Fragile-X, *Medical Anthropology Quarterly* 10(4): 537–550.

NIH-DOE (1995 and 1996) Joint Working Group on Ethical, Legal, and Social Implications of Human Genome Research (ELSI Working Group) and the National Action Plan on Breast Cancer (NAPBC), *Insurance Discrimination* and *Employment Discrimination*. Available at http://wwwnhgri.nih.gov/Policy_and_public_affairs/ Legislation/legelsi.html (accessed August 26, 1999).

Nobles, K. (1992) Birthright or life sentence: controlling the threat of genetic testing, *Southern California Law Review* 65: 2081–2114.

Norman-Bloodsaw vs. Lawrence Berkeley Laboratory (9th Cir. 1998), 135 F.3d 1260.

Nuremberg Tribunal (1946–1949) Nuremberg code, *Trials of War Criminals* II(10).

Oktay, J.S. (1998) Genetics cultural lag: what can social workers do to help? *Health & Social Work* 23(4): 310–315.

Parker, L.S. and Majeske, R.A. (1996) Standards of care and ethical concerns in genetic testing and screening, *Clinical Obstetrics and Gynecology* 39(4): 873–883.

Pike, M. and Wood, W. (1998) Inherited breast cancer susceptibility—transforming scientific data into clinical practice, *Online Coverage from American Society of Clinical Oncology*, May 16–19, reported by Harold J. Burstein and reviewed by Eric K. Rowinsky for Medscape, Inc. Available at http://www.medscape.com/ Medscape/CNO/1998/ (accessed October 23, 1999).

Risse, B. (1998) Privacy: nonconsensual testing of employees for medical and genetic information—*Norman-Bloodsaw vs. Lawrence Berkeley Laboratory*, *American Journal of Law and Medicine* 24(1): 131–133.

Rizzo, R.F. (1989) The living will: does it protect the rights of the terminally ill? *New York State Journal of Medicine* 89(2): 72–79.

—— (1993) Health care reform in the light of history, *International Journal of Social Economics* 20(11): 40–56.

—— (1999) Genetic testing and therapy: a pathway to progress and/or profit? *International Journal of Social Economics* 26(1/2/3): 109–133.

Rothstein, M.A. (1998) Genetic privacy and confidentiality: why they are so hard to protect, *Journal of Law, Medicine & Ethics* 26(3): 198–204.

Saunders Jr, A.G., and Mortell, B.B. (1995) Genetic testing—genetic discrimination: state and federal statutes provide possible remedies, *New Hampshire Bar Journal* 36: 23–33.

Shalala, D.E. (1997) Health insurance portability and accountability (September 11), *Testimony of the Secretary of Health and Human Services before Senate Committee on Labor & Human Resources*. Available at http://www.os.dhhs.gov (accessed November 25, 1999).

Sommerville, A. and English, V. (1999) Genetic privacy: orthodoxy or oxymoron, *Journal of Medical Ethics* 25(2) 144–150.

Thomas, A.M., Cohen, G., Cook-Deegan, R.M., O'Sullivan, J., Post, S., Roses, A.D., Schaffner, K.F., and Green, R.M. (1998) Alzheimer testing at silver years, *Cambridge Quarterly of Healthcare Issues* 7(3): 294–307.

US Congress, Office of Technology Assessment (1991) *Medical Monitoring and Screening in the Workplace: Results of a Survey—Background Paper* (October), OTA-BP-BA-67, Washington DC: US Government Printing Office.

—— (1994) *Defensive Medicine and Medical Malpractice* (July), OTA-H-602, Washington DC: US Government Printing Office.

Veatch, R.M. (ed.) (1997) *Medical Ethics*, 2nd edn, Sudbury, MA: Jones and Bartlett Publishers.

Wertz, D.C., Fanos, J.H., and Reilly, P.R. (1994) Genetic testing for children and adolescents, *Journal of the American Medical Association* 272: 875–881.

Zeitz, K. (1991) Employer genetic testing: a legitimate screening device or another method of discrimination? *Labor Law Journal* 42: 230–238.

INDEX

For Product Safety Concerns and Information please contact our EU representative GPSR@taylorandfrancis.com Taylor & Francis Verlag GmbH, Kaufingerstraße 24, 80331 München, Germany